T0300254

Hoshin Kanri

Hoshin Kanri

The Strategic Approach to Continuous Improvement

DAVID HUTCHINS

Routledge
Taylor & Francis Group

LONDON AND NEW YORK

First published 2008 by Gower Publishing

Published 2016 by Routledge
2 Park Square, Milton Park, Abingdon, Oxon OX14 4RN
711 Third Avenue, New York, NY 10017, USA

Routledge is an imprint of the Taylor & Francis Group, an informa business

British Library Cataloguing in Publication Data
Hutchins, David C.
  Hoshin Kanri : the strategic approach to continuous
  improvement
  1. Total quality management
  I. Title
  658.4'013

  ISBN 9780566087400 (hbk)

Library of Congress Cataloging-in-Publication Data
Hutchins, David C.
  Hoshin Kanri : the strategic approach to continuous improvement / by David Hutchins.
      p. cm.
  Includes index.
  ISBN 978-0-566-08740-0
  1. Total quality management. I. Title.
  HD62.13.H883 2008
  658.4'013--dc22

                                                                    2007051242

Contents

List of Figures

Preface

SOME HISTORY, SOME PHILOSOPHY AND A SHORT AUTOBIOGRAPHY

Throughout my life I have had the blessing of good health and I believe a great deal of energy. At the time of writing this book, I am 71 years of age and can see no sign whatsoever of wanting to give up my work and take the easy life. I think that this is because I can never remember a time when I have been unhappy with what I have been doing. I regard that also to have been a blessing for which I am eternally grateful. I think one of the contributing factors is that for whatever reason, I have had a passion for what I have tried to achieve. I have met many people in the Quality profession who feel the same way and I have often wondered what it is about this field of management science that can conduce such emotion. Of course there are people in all areas of science who are passionate about their work; that is a fact, but possibly the one thing that separates Quality from other disciplines is the breadth and depth of its scope. It contains the full spectrum of statistical and analytical tools, it embraces systems, procedures, organisational modelling, corporate change and, as will be seen in this book, combines them all into a people-based strategy that can positively impact on the lives of us all.

Perhaps another important feature is the fact that, unusually in the affairs of human beings, I have never met anyone who is against quality! We all want quality, we all think that we do a quality job and most people have a passion for making things just a little bit better than they were before. We may well interpret differently one from the other what the word 'better' means but, wittingly or not, either formally or informally, Quality methods will be used to achieve whatever the goal may be.

It is not a religion and is practiced by people of all faith groups and political persuasions. Quality knows no boundaries and does not need a passport or visa. The work being done at the City Montessori School in Lucknow, India bears witness to the fact that the Quality disciplines are not something that can only be applied in a work situation. Under the leadership of Dr Vineeta Kamran, the Head of the school, and fully supported by the Principle Dr Jagdish Gandhi, children as young as 8 years old are trained to use the tools of the Quality sciences in their work, with dramatic impact. Most of them are members of Quality Circle and to see a formal presentation made by a group of 10-year-olds using statistical tools to diagnose problems and achieve valid solutions will bring tears to the eyes of most normal people. These children will grow up with the principles of Quality embedded in their minds and it is the hope of Dr Gandhi that at least one of them will, as a consequence, change the world for the better. This is a lofty dream but imagine how much better the world would be if all children were brought up this way? The self-assurance and mutual respect that these children have for each other, for their teachers and their parents is stunning and a model for us all to copy.

I firmly believe that if this work is spread throughout the world, there might one day be an end to violence, hatred and war. Maybe we will never get there but it is better to die in the trying than to give up. It is also a lofty dream but one which I share and a principle reason why I will never give up this work. It is also the reason why I have always been passionate about Quality Circles and why the chapter on this topic is the largest in the book.

I have seen the most remarkable transformations in workplace relationships through the application of this concept. For a variety of reasons many in the West are resistant to the use of Quality Circles because of bad experiences after it was introduced into Western society in the late 1970s/early 1980s. However, all of those who think this way would do well to re-examine their premises because the reason for the failure was not the fault of the concept but the chronically bad way in which most people attempted to use it. The subject was appallingly badly researched by most, advice was sought from so-called 'experts' who probably knew less that those they were being paid to advise and of course it failed. Tragically this has cost 20 years of leadership in Quality whilst industry went down one blind alley after another. It seems that one day we may get it right – after we have tried everything else first! Hopefully my logic is right in the concepts that are included in this book and I hope that in its small way it will help to take us just a little bit further down the road to a better society.

I do not claim credit for any or all of the ideas or material contained in the chapters. It is the result of an accumulation of knowledge and observations made throughout my lifetime and a relatively unusual but by no means unique career path.

I was born just before World War II and lived in London with my mother and two sisters until the bombing got too hot for comfort during the first part of the Blitz. We were split up for a while and suffered some quite dramatic upheavals which did nothing for the development of my academic career. Whilst things calmed down when we left London, the primary school that I went to was not particularly inspiring. I focused on interests outside of school, failed the very controversial 11 plus examination and as a consequence left at the age of 15 with no qualifications of any kind. For the next 2 years I largely continued spending my time on hobbies and sport. The suffocatingly boring job that I had as tea boy in a radio and television laboratory did not in any way capture my imagination and my long-suffering mother had definitely given up any ideas that she may have had of my ever achieving anything.

Then there was a small break in the clouds. A close relative owned a local iron foundry. He realised that I was wasting my life and offered me an apprenticeship. This took me to the age of 22 when I was called up for 2 years National Service in the army. Life in the foundry was tough, very tough, very hot and quite dangerous but I enjoyed it and I began to learn the work ethic. I tried going to night classes but the heavy work during the day was too much and I fell asleep at the back of the class on several occasions. The examination results spoke for themselves and I gave up.

Then came National Service. I was a rifleman in the infantry. At that point there would have been no reason to believe that I might not just go back into the foundry or something like it when I was demobilised but fate took over. I learned that the military were very keen to allow National Servicemen to continue with their self-development in order to minimise the disruption to their lives. As a consequence it was possible to sign up for courses at local colleges to study for O levels. I saw this as an opportunity to get an afternoon off duties. I had no expectation that I would pass the examination because it had been engrained in me that the only people who could pass O levels were students from grammar schools. I made the least number of attendances that I could reasonably get away with in order not to be thrown out and also did the minimum number of work assignments.

Then I suffered the shock that changed my life for ever. I passed the examination! In fact I did rather well. Instead of being happy I was about as angry as it was possible to be. For the first time in my life I realised that I had academic ability but I was now 24 years old and about to be demobilised. In those last few weeks of military life I could think of nothing other than how I could put this newfound ability to the test. I had no time to lose. I determined that I would find a job that was not as strenuous as the foundry and took a job in a design office. I started on an extremely low salary because I did not have much to offer as I saw it. I then began the tortuous process of getting myself qualified in my own time by attending night classes for 8 years, three evenings per week for the first six of them increasing to 4 evenings for the last 2 years in order to achieve a Bachelor's degree equivalent for both Mechanical and Production Engineering. Having wasted so many years I had no intention of wasting any more. Failure was not an option! I studied this way for 8 years. In the examinations at the end of year 1 my lowest mark was 87 and I missed 100 per cent in mathematics by inadvertently putting a minus in one answer instead of a plus. I was awarded distinctions in more than 50 per cent of the examinations and obtained a degree equivalent in both Production Engineering and Mechanical Engineering.

One might imagine that I would have been pleased with myself but the reverse was true. Every year that I passed I became more angry because of the time that I considered that I had wasted in my youth and that for whatever reason I had allowed myself to believe that I was an underachiever. As a consequence I had been denied the opportunity to go to university and receive a classic education. I had felt unjustifiably inferior when in the company of friends and acquaintances who had achieved a classic education and I resented that badly.

It was not until several years later when I had left industry and taken a position in higher education that I was offered the opportunity to take a 1-year sabbatical and study for a Master's degree at Birmingham University and I realised that I had not been disadvantaged at all. Now that I had the opportunity to go to university it occurred to me that I actually had an advantage over those who had a classic education because, unlike them, I had seen and lived in two worlds and I can say, two *very* different worlds! Also, during the time of my studies I had left the design office and took a position as a Work Study Engineer in an automotive component manufacturing company. I progressed during that time through Production Engineer to Works Superintendent. This involved a considerable amount of negotiation with a fairly tough and hard-bargaining Shop Convener at a time when industrial relations in the UK were at a very low ebb (the time of the famous Peter Sellers and Ian Carmichael 'I'm all right Jack' film).

During that time I had unwittingly taken my first steps into the world of Quality. We had a 50 per cent immigrant labour force who mostly came from agricultural backgrounds in India, the Caribbean and so on. I found myself spending a considerable amount of my time showing them how to use micrometers and other tools in the factory. I observed that they were enormously grateful for the time that I spent with them. Of course, looking back on it, I was helping them with their self-development and every small thing that they learned improved their self-esteem and sense of security. Towards the end of that time in the late 1960s the impact of the increasing number of Japanese cars and motor cycles became a worry to us. Whilst most of our sales were to original equipment manufacturers, we did nevertheless have quite a share of the spare parts market.

I also set up a factory-wide gauge control system and implemented Statistical Process Control. I did not realise it but I might well have been pioneering in this respect because it was not until the Six Sigma revolution in the late 1990s that this concept began to become popular. I also set up a Standards Room with traceability of measurement through to National Standards using the gauges I had calibrated using the Standards Laboratory at the local college. It was this involvement with the college that later began my teaching career.

At that time the Japanese automotive companies not only manufactured all of their cars in Japan but they also brought their own spare parts. The shock came for me when one day, we managed to obtain some Japanese piston castings similar to some of our own production. We etched them and studied them in our laboratory and were stunned to see that the grain structure of the alloy was better than anything that we could do. Furthermore, it was better even than the photographs in the relevant British Standard for that alloy. The question for me was, 'How do they do that?'

I then in 1969 began what has since proved to be a 'rest of my life' study of Japanese manufacturing and business management methods. Unfortunately at that time, there were very few if any Westerners interested in Japanese management. Most people were aware that they supposedly sang the company song every day before work, did exercises every hour, ate little raw fishes and they had read sensational articles which suggested that workers punched effigies of their bosses at tea breaks to ease the tension. It never occurred to anyone that we could possibly learn anything useful from them. However, I had a stroke of luck. Having just left industry for an appointment in higher education with responsibility for Quality Courses, I joined the Institute of Engineering Inspection (now the Chartered Quality Institute thanks to sterling work by its recently retired Director General Frank Steer) and soon found myself on its Education Committee and became Secretary of one of its branches.

It so happened that one leading Japanese Professor, Dr Kano, who is today one of, if not the most respected Japanese Quality Gurus, was coming to the UK to give lectures on Quality. I had the task of creating the posters for the event.

Later I met another Japanese Professor, Dr Sasaki, who is now retired but was an eminent economist with an interest in the human sciences. He so happened to be an acquaintance of the now late Professor Kaoru Ishikawa (he died in 1989 and I wrote his obituary for both the *Daily Telegraph* and *The Observer*), who was regarded, alongside Dr Feigenbaum, Dr Juran, Dr Shewhart and Dr Deming, as being a leading pioneer of what is today the science of Quality.

About one month after our meeting I received a package from Professor Ishikawa containing some materials which explained in great detail the philosophy behind their approach to Quality Management. Fortunately it was written in English!

It spoke of their approach to Quality being one of total participation through Quality Circles. Whilst I had been aware of Quality Circles for some time and indeed had written an examination question in 1970 asking students to describe them I had not realised that the philosophy was transferable.

More importantly, for the first time I could see that the concept of Quality Circles brought together all of my key lifetime experiences in one blinding flash.

After I had successfully completed my Master's degree it occurred to me that I had been incredibly lucky. Had I not signed up for the mathematics class during my National Service I had no idea where I might have ended up. How many other people were there out there I wondered who might not have been as lucky as me but who, for the wheel of fortune, were destined to a lifetime of slavery strapped to the buttons and handles of machines? They have little in the way of self-esteem, have low self-confidence, they may be subservient and resigned to a lifetime of repetitive work where no one asks them anything, no one involves them in anything, they get a sick feeling every Sunday night (or Friday night in some parts of the world): 'Hell it is Monday again tomorrow and I have to go through all of that again to pick up a wage cheque.'

I remembered the Sikh Indian gentleman who worked in the piston ring factory, who was so grateful that I had shown him how to operate a piece of equipment that he began sending me Christmas cards. I remembered the others in that factory who might call out, 'Mr David San,' or some such thing, 'Can you please show me how to do this?'

Then there was Dr Feigenbaum's book *Total Quality Control* which I had read and used for teaching at the college. In the chapter on Quality Responsibility he said, and I heavily summarise, 'Quality is the responsibility of all of the functions' (he goes into quite some detail on this) 'but if Quality is everyone's job then it might become nobody's job.' He spends a lot of time in the relevant chapter explaining the possible ways in which this responsibility might be organised.

It was the combination of this together with the texts by Professor Ishikawa that made me realise that business performance can only be optimised by using the brainpower and job knowledge of all of the people to make our business the best that there is. This, it turned out later but was not known to me at the time, was the essence of Hoshin Kanri.

I am very grateful for the fact that later on, through being fortunate enough to make Dr Feigenbaum's acquaintance at EOQ Conferences, I have been able to communicate to him my gratitude for having influenced my thinking through the chapters of his book.

It occurred to me that Quality Circles and their supporting organisation were an excellent way not only of managing the Quality responsibility of the workers but, through the opportunity to train them initially in problem solving and then progressively developing their knowledge of other management tools, the closed loop control system (Plan, Do, Check, Act), they had all the means to progressively develop themselves as I had managed to do for myself all those years earlier.

I saw that this was an opportunity not only for the individuals themselves but if it were possible to unlock all that latent talent in others possibly like me, then the potential for the improvement of our society was beyond calculation.

It seemed to me to be right at the time to introduce something like this when our industrial relations were at their lowest ebb and I could see that Quality Circles might also be a way to break the mould as in fact it had when it was first introduced in post-war Japan in the early 1960s. Prior to that Japanese industrial relations bordered on a red revolution.

I began running short courses on all of this at the college and in fact the first short course that I conducted with the title *Total Quality Control* was in 1973, but the college was not appreciative. Some years later when my work was becoming popular, my boss called me in and told me that the college was not a pioneering institute and was there to meet the certificated requirements of the various professional bodies. I decided that it was time that I took my future into my own hands and left. This was a decision fraught with risk. I had two young children and a relatively large mortgage. Nevertheless, I was so fired up with all of this that I self-funded and put on a conference at the Institute of Directors (I used them as a venue for which I paid, they were not involved) and invited Professor Ishikawa and Dr Sasaki to share with me the chairmanship and delivery of a 3-day conference. Fortunately we made the centre spread in the *Financial Times* and filled the venue. Had that not been the case I probably would have sunk without a trace! We also attracted the interest of World Service Radio and for me there was now no turning back.

For about 4 to 5 years much of my work and that of some others who had joined me mostly involved setting up Quality Circles programmes and they were extraordinarily successful. However, there were dark clouds in the sky and for a variety of reasons, some mentioned earlier, Quality Circles began to acquire a bad name. During that period, two other significant developments took place in my life that moved things towards where I see them today.

I had conducted a 1-day event at the BAFTA Centre in Piccadilly London, during which a number of British and Japanese Quality Circles made alternate presentations of projects. It was an interesting experience because it became very apparent that whilst the British teams made the more entertaining presentations, there was no question that the projects presented by the Japanese teams clearly had significantly more impact on their companies' business performance. I puzzled over this because the training was the same, the tools and techniques were the same and the support structure quite similar. However, I subsequently took an industrial study tour to Japan as I had been doing before. We visited, amongst others, one of the Komatsu plants. It was there that for the first time I made the acquaintance of Hoshin Kanri. The penny then dropped that this was the principle reason why the Japanese teams were more successful. It was because of the Hoshin Kanri goals deployment process. The challenge then was 'how to inspire a British audience that this was the correct approach'. It proved very difficult. The main reason for the difficulty was that industry generally had become infatuated with ISO 9000 and they simply were not listening. Fortunately I had a further stroke of luck. I was contacted by the late Quality management Guru Dr Juran who died in early 2008 at the age of 103. He was survived by his wife who had also achieved the same age and they had been married for 81 years with the world record being 84! Right up to his last year he was still writing books. He had produced a set of 16 video tapes which showed middle- and upper-management how they could participate in Project by Project activities and was interested in giving us at my company the opportunity to sell and support them in the UK.

This was a breakthrough not only for us but also for the Juran Institute because through our experience in project by project involving the workforce it was easy for us to adapt our approach to include management. Whilst this was not Hoshin Kanri as such, it took us a long way towards it. Over the next few years we even outsold the Juran Institute at times and were able to counter the severe competition of the Government-backed ISO 9000 approach.

The 1990s proved a bad time all round for the Quality Movement. The steam had gone out of the ISO 9000 revolution and with it the withdrawal of Government backing. Industry was confused and could not make up its mind between ISO 9000, the newly emerging Business Excellence Awards, the Governmental Charter Mark introduced by John Major's Government or perhaps the newer stars coming over the horizon from the USA in the form of Six Sigma and Lean Manufacturing. Today the mists are beginning to clear a little and I see the beginnings of a fusion between all of these different approaches but there is a long way to go yet, there are too many vested interests in the various alternatives. Maybe there always will be.

Being somewhat numbed by such a succession of so-called panaceas, the market went flat and extreme caution set in. The tragedy is that none of this has stopped either the Japanese companies or indeed those from China, India and around the Pacific Basin. They have continued to march on regardless of the ups and downs of their national economies. As a consequence Toyota, as is well known, has this year replaced General Motors as the world's largest automotive producer after more than 70 years of market domination.

Now that Toyota is in the front it is set to create an ever widening gap which no one will be able to breach unless they adopt the right means to do so. On their own, neither Lean Manufacturing or Six Sigma are the answer. They are both good and very powerful but they are only part of the answer. It is only under the umbrella of a Hoshin Kanri programme which involves all of these concepts plus many more and with powerful Quality Circles programmes will it be possible to stop the gap widening and an even greater effort if it is to be closed.

Returning to the autobiographical part of this preface, even now it seems strange to me that I might have gone from being a totally unqualified foundry worker to having had the wonderful experiences around the world that I have in the past two decades.

In my opinion it is living proof that there are no limits on what people can achieve when they have the self-belief and the persistence to do it. This is true both for individuals as it is for organisations. We are only limited by the limits that we set for ourselves. We are not victims of our situation whether we passed the eleven plus or not. Always there is a way and Hoshin Kanri with its emphasis on making the vision a reality is how it is done. Walt Disney said, 'If you can dream it you can make it happen.'

A NOTE ON THE USE OF THE TERM 'CONTINUOUS IMPROVEMENT'

'Continuous Improvement' which we have used in the title of the book is a smooth curve whereas 'Continual Improvement' may be a series of unrelated, individual incremental activities. Continuous Improvement therefore can be regarded as the summation of a multitude of these individual achievements (rather like the 'integration' process in calculus).

Some practitioners in the field are sensitive about this difference in the terms and I would not wish to add to the confusion. For example, ISO 9000 refers exclusively to Continual Improvement.

If it is understood by the reader that 'continual' means incremental individual improvements and that 'continuous' means the summation of a large number of these, then for the purposes of simplicity, the term Continuous Improvement is used throughout as it can be considered, especially in an active Hoshin Kanri-practising organisation, to embrace the other.

With this being what I believe will be my last but most important book, I would just finally like to express my gratitude to:

Dr Noriaki Kano for his friendship and contribution to my knowledge which has been so freely given especially for his powerful technique the Kano Model which can be found in the text.

The late My Jonji Naguchi who for many years up to the early 1990s was the Managing Director of the Japanese Union of Scientists and Engineers (JUSE). When I first went to Japan to deliver a lecture on Products Liability in 1979 he began to assist me and support my work. It was difficult for him because at that time many foreigners were trying to gain the favour of JUSE and many of them had not been as honest as they might have been with copyright theft and so on. I will always be grateful for his trust in me and I am still very sad that he is no longer here.

Dr Armand Feigenbaum of course as explained earlier in this text.

Professor Sasaki who, apart from having introduced me to Professor Ishikawa, saved me a lot of potential embarrassments in my early visits to Japan by explaining the important cultural differences which are sometimes quite subtle.

The late Professor Kaoru Ishikawa for being so helpful to me and being so encouraging in my development and for his involvement in those early days of the Quality revolution. In fact the visit that he made at my invitation was the only time he came to Europe in his lifetime. I was privileged to have been invited by both Dr Kano and Professor Ishikawa's widow to write a chapter in the book to commemorate his life and this rests on the shrine to his memory.

Dr Juran for his help and guidance to both me and to my colleagues over many years. I would also like to thank him for inviting me to write the chapter on the history of Quality in the UK which is included in his important work *The History of Managing for Quality*.

The late Dr Bill Thoday who regrettably is one of the unsung heroes of the heady days of the Quality Revolution in the 1970s and 1980s. Bill was Quality Manager at one of the Rank Xerox Plants in the UK and was President of the European Organisation for Quality at the time of the World Quality Congress in Brighton, England in 1984. There are many people in the UK Quality profession who owe a great debt of gratitude to Bill for his unstinting support and advice at any time no matter how busy he may have been. It was Bill who first introduced me to the concept of the Cost of Poor Quality.

The late Roy Knowles who was Secretary General of the IQA (now CQI) for many years. Roy was always ready to help anyone and it was he who built the IQA into a nationally recognised institution. Roy could be guaranteed to be supportive and reassuring no matter how risky an idea might have been.

Recently retired Frank Steer who achieved the Herculean task of organising the 2002 World Quality Congress in Harrogate and more recently took the Institute one giant step further and managed it through to becoming a Chartered Institute. This was no mean achievement and deserves considerable recognition. It is unfortunate that this had not happened some 20 years earlier but had it not been for Frank it possibly would not have happened for another 20 years, if ever. I thank you Frank for that and also for your support for me during your years as Director General.

In terms of direct support and being there to discuss everything and to bounce ideas off each other and to work with on courses and behind the scenes organisation, I must include my two close colleagues Dr Norman Towe and John Dansey.

I would also like to include my two brothers-in-law, one of whom, Jim Wagstaff, was the foundry owner who managed to get me to work! And the other, Tony Shaw, a Business Management Specialist, who gave me enormous encouragement and advice during those tortuous years of studying.

Finally and most important of all my long-suffering wife Margaret and children Caroline and Michael who have had to live with my extensive travelling, lecturing and of course the writing. An absent husband and father but we seemed to survive for all of that!

I could fill the book with the names of others who have made a big impact on my working life but I hope that they know who they are, some have been thanked in earlier books and collectively thank you to all of you.

Enjoy the book.

1 *Hoshin Kanri – An Overview*

In the 1950s the American Management Guru, Peter Drucker, suggested that in order to be successful in business it is necessary to be better than all of your competitors for at least something that will be important to the customer. There must be some specific reason why they would choose to buy from you rather than buy from a competitor, even if on average the competitor can outperform you.

If for example your organisation scores more points in total for Quality, Price and Delivery, but a competitor can out score you on one of them, say Quality, then that supplier will win when the customer is mostly concerned with that issue. If another has a reputation for being better on price then he will win in a price competitive market irrespective of your abilities on the other two criteria.

It is not only important to actually be the best, it is even more important to be 'perceived' as being the best. Perceptions and reality are often very different. Many organisations fail because they do not understand this important fact. They may know what they are good and bad at doing but the customer may well see things very differently. Even if the customer is mistaken it will still be their prerogative to choose.

In a fiercely competitive global market, the pressure is on to attempt to be the best across the broadest possible spectrum of customer-sensitive features. This raises several questions. What, for example, does 'best' mean? Again it is the customer's perception of what is meant by by 'best' that is important, not the vendor's. Their perception of our performance may be very different from our own and this difference might well cost us our business in a competitive market. For example, a large Middle Eastern steel company was perceived by its local customer, a large automobile company, to produce rolls of steel strip to a lower quality of surface finish than that achieved by foreign competitors. When this perception became known to the steel producer an investigation showed that there was no discernible difference. However, because they were local and because both they and the customer were located in a dry arid desert, there was no need to protect the steel reels during transportation. On the other hand, the steel produced by the competitor was wrapped in oiled paper to protect it from the corrosive salt air during a long sea journey. The oiled paper gave the impression of superior quality when, in fact, there was no difference. Had the study not been carried out, the producer might well have engaged in an expensive improvement process which might not have changed the perception unless this had also included wrapping the steel in oiled paper, which was the root of the false impression.

When demand exceeds supply and the vendor can sell everything they can make, it is possibly difficult to convince them of the importance of this philosophy. The customer will have to buy their product regardless of the quality of the service, the price, delivery or after-sales support. This will usually be the case in monopolistic situations where the customer has no choice. There is therefore no pressure on the supplier to achieve anything because they know that they are secure.

Alternatively, when supply exceeds demand, the rules change completely. Suddenly the customer becomes king and collectively has the power of life or death over the hapless vendor.

Since in this situation, every competing vendor wants to be amongst the survivors, the pressure is on to be amongst those who are favoured by the customers and in the end it will only be the best who will survive.

Hoshin Kanri is the only proven means by which this can be achieved when competition is at its most severe. It is a systematic approach that can be ruthlessly applied to grind down even the most severe competition.

Toyota have persistently applied Hoshin Kanri-style management for several decades. They have never wavered in this. In the 1950s, they were well behind most of the world's leading automotive producers but, year by year, one by one, they moved through the pack passing one competitor after the other until in the end, in 2007, they outstripped the giant General Motors to become the world's leading automobile producer. For years both Ford and GM attempted to stop their advance but they were unable to do so for no other reason than they did not fully understand Hoshin Kanri, Japanese Total Quality Management (TQM), (they did attempt the American version) and now they are fighting for survival with huge losses reported on the Internet.

Japanese Total Quality Management (TQM) is founded on the principles that each individual in an organisation is recognised as being the expert in their own job, that humans seek recognition and want to be involved and are motivated by a desire to be recognised as a contributor to the success of the community to which they belong. The overall objective of this form of TQM is to attempt to create an organisation (which includes the entire supply chain) in which the collective thinking power and job knowledge of all of these individuals is galvanised into a programme in which everyone is working both individually and collectively to work towards making their organisation the best in its field, both in fact and in the eyes of its customers, and all other interested parties.

It involves both voluntary and mandated team-based activities systematically carried out on a project-by-project basis at all levels of organisation to continually improve business performance in all of its aspects both on an inter- and intra-functional basis.

There are many Western interpretations of this but they are mostly focused on the creation of 'systems' and not the human aspects. As a result they often become policing style regimes parallel to the production processes rather than an integral part of them.

Organisations that have applied Hoshin Kanri have in some cases come from being also rans in their field to becoming performance record breakers in only a matter of 3 to 4 years. Hoshin Kanri is not a difficult concept to understand or to apply. Most organisations will have some of its elements in place and in some cases a large percentage. However, Hoshin Kanri does require meticulous planning, targeted benchmarking and the effective and systematic use of the tools for continuous improvement at all levels of the workforce. In short it is a means of managing a business.

Hoshin Kanri is a Japanese management term which has no direct equivalent in the English language. The term roughly embraces four key elements of business management namely: Vision, Policy Development, Policy Deployment and Policy Control. It is also directly linked to a fifth, which is TQM, which is the means by which the Goals, which have been determined in the Hoshin Kanri process, are achieved.

Figure 1.1 gives an outline of the elements of Hoshin Kanri.

1. The Goals, aims and future scope of the organisation are derived from the Vision.
2. It requires the development of Strategy, Policy, Benchmarking and Targets.
3. The deployment of the Targets must be to all levels through a cascade process and the creation of policy at each level of management.
4. There must be a feedback loop of results to complete the Plan-Do-Check-Act (PDCA) Cycle which is the Shewhart Cycle (which some nowadays refer to as the Deming Wheel).

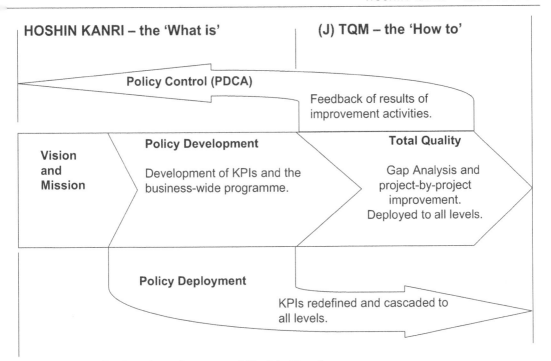

Figure 1.1   The four key elements of Hoshin Kanri

5.   It has no value unless it also includes TQM (the Japanese version not the suspect version that fluttered for a while in the West in the late 1980s) which is not part of Hoshin Kanri but represents the Do part of the PDCA Cycle.

Hoshin Kanri and Japanese-style TQM are intrinsically related to each other. In fact, the Japanese would say that Hoshin Kanri represents the 'what it is that we want to achieve' and TQM (often referred to as Total Quality Control or TQC) is the means by which to close the gap between Current Performance and target performance. Japanese TQC/M includes everything that is to be found in Six Sigma, Lean Manufacturing, Total Productive Maintenance (TPM), Quality Function Deployment (QFD) and Quality Circles and all other quality-related sciences and disciplines. It would be nice to be able to include an in-depth treatment of all of these in this book but unfortunately it would then extend to several volumes. The intention has been to provide a solid base on all the key concepts and to encourage organisations to acquire ever greater expertise in each of the disciplines. As Professor Ishikawa said on many occasions, 'Quality begins and ends with education.'

The term Hoshin Kanri has four components:

1.   Ho – means Direction.
2.   Shin – refers to Focus.
3.   Kan – refers to Alignment.
4.   Ri – means Reason.

It can be likened to 'a leading star' or the way that one point of a compass always points towards the North Pole.

Perhaps more appropriate is the way that iron filings go into alignment on a piece of paper if the pole of a magnet is placed underneath. Each small iron filing could be considered to be just one employee with everyone focused towards the Vision and Aims of the organisation.

The concept is based on the principle that the most powerful organisation is the one which has managed to harness the creative-thinking power of all of its employees in order to make the organisation the best in its business. It requires that each person in an organisation be regarded as the expert at their own job and their contribution recognised. All the members of an organisation must have a clear understanding of the organisation's Vision and Goals. With all members in perfect alignment and clearly understanding their own role in the achievement of those Goals as they are trained and encouraged to work together to achieve them, then the productive power of the organisation would be optimal.

THE CHALLENGE! – THE NEGATIVES THAT HOSHIN SEEKS TO ELIMINATE

Unfortunately most organisations are a very long way from the Hoshin ideal. In many cases, they exhibit a blame culture with recriminations and punishment when things go wrong and very little in the way of praise when they go well. Direct employees are treated as robots, nobody asks them anything or involves them in anything. They are only given the minimum training and in some cases no training at all. They are not given much information as to how the company is doing in its marketplace or even the purpose of their own jobs. Only the directly relevant negative financial Goals and financial constraints are clear. All other organisational Goals are either stated in vague or very subjective general terms and are often open to wide interpretation.

In an organisation which does not practice Hoshin Kanri or something similar, then in the absence of clearly-defined quantitative Goals, managers are somehow mysteriously expected to 'know' them. Usually they struggle to do so but their perceptions as to their meaning will often vary widely from person to person and across the organisation. The resulting confusion will generally lead to serious underachievement against the potential capabilities of the organisation when everything is in alignment.

Since all departmental managers will be managing in line with their own interpretations of the business Goals and Targets, there will be considerable conflict and sub-optimisation. Departmental Goals which may seem clear to the managers will be considered to be more important than organisational Goals which appear vague and indistinct. Goals for Quantity which will derive from the financial Goals and constraints will often appear to be very clear whereas Goals for Qualitative requirements will usually be stated in euphemistic terms, if at all: for example, 'we must have better performance' or 'increase customer satisfaction'. On the face of it, these seem like laudable Goals but in reality they mean nothing because they are too vague. This vagueness cannot compete with the clarity of the financial Goals; as a consequence the qualitative Goals will always be the poor relation even though their sustained non-achievement could result in dramatic financial impact or even threaten the future of the operation.

This lack of clarity also leads to rivalry and conflict between departments. Managers have their own ambitions and these may not always be compatible with the Goals of the organisation as a whole or the local Goals of other departments. For example, the IT manager might have the Goal of perfect information flow. In order to achieve it, they might propose the use of some complex documentation by other departments. In order to satisfy their needs, the relevant managers might be required to spend their precious time filling in the forms required by IT when they would prefer to use it for their own needs. The consequence is that there is now a conflict between the demands of one department and the local needs of the others.

A further common problem is the lack of process ownership. For most of the 20th Century, the so-called Scientific Management System prevailed in the West and also throughout the Soviet system. In such organisations, each department was almost an independent fiefdom. In some cases, it literally bought and sold its products and services from or to the other departments within the organisation. Each of these 'fiefdoms' were fiercely hierarchical. Promotion, hiring and firing only occurred within the department, with the consequence that each was a self-contained unit. Whilst the organisation may have had business-wide advisory and service departments such as maintenance, training, HR, industrial engineering, and so on, they were often regarded as intruders by the managers and treated with hostility and suspicion.

As a consequence, these organisations had very strong vertical fibres of organisation but were very poor horizontally. As can be seen in Figure 1.2, processes run horizontally across departments which meant in effect that no one owned the process.

In the worst case scenario, each department performs its activities and then in effect 'throws the output over the wall' to the next department. There would be very little communication in either direction between the two and virtually no understanding of each other's needs. When things inevitably and frequently went wrong, the practice for each would be to blame the other. Some managers would be more expert at the blame game than others, consequently they would appear to be the most competent and therefore the ones most likely to be promoted. Since this was how everyone was promoted, they then found themselves confronted with a better class of enemy!

The nearer they got to the top of the organisation, the tougher and more sophisticated became the competition.

At the highest levels intimidation was the main weapon. The most successful managers would eat in a separate and more luxurious restaurant, they would have large offices, deep-pile carpets, oak panelled walls, named car park locations, dress differently and never speak directly to the workforce. Such distinctions are regarded as 'perks' but in fact are really a form of intimidation. This method of management could be regarded as the modern equivalent of the Native American's war paint! Companies which pride themselves in more participative styles of management scorn these distinctions and make great efforts to avoid them. Whilst the worst extremes of the autocratic approach have thankfully largely become less obvious in recent years, it is nevertheless more often than not still lurking beneath the surface and few managers are either trained or encouraged to use participative management techniques. We are therefore still faced with the worst in macho-based autocratic management, and no wonder so many executives and managers have stress disorders and heart attacks in their late 30s and 40s!

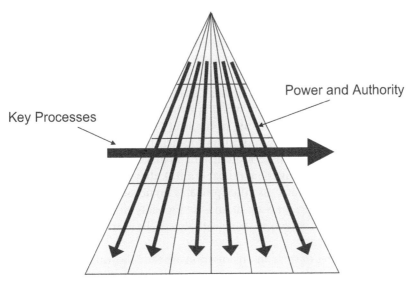

Figure 1.2   **Process ownership**

Whilst autocratic management methods may appear to have receded in recent years and are regarded as being 'politically incorrect', they are nevertheless proving to be self-sustaining and very resilient. The executives and managers who reach the top in such organisations do so because they are good at this style of management. They know how to make the method work in their favour and are not interested in experimenting with any alternative that might make their position less secure. Their belief is also strengthened by their observations of the behaviour of those beneath them. They have created a work environment ruled by fear. People work in such conditions not because they choose to but because they may have little choice. It is a way to earn a crust and nothing more. As a consequence, they will do the least they can get away with in order to satisfy their basic needs and to keep out of trouble, but no more. Their loyalty is minimal because they resent the way they are treated. Managers who have created or are sustaining such an environment believe from their own observations that their workforce are lazy, slothful and indolent and the only way they can get results is through Threats, fear and 'carrot and stick' methods. They are convinced that this is the only way to manage and will not accept that it is their behaviour and not that of the workforce that created the problem in the first place. They will not listen to any alternative, no matter how convincing it might appear.

In great contrast, as will be explained in considerable detail later in this book and especially in the chapter on Quality Circles, Hoshin Kanri demands a very different approach. The Hoshin organisation is seen as a community which has common Objectives and in which each participant has a contribution to make. It is also founded on some fundamental beliefs about the nature of work. At the core of these beliefs is an understanding that each individual is the expert in their own job and that people want to be listened to, perceived to be respected and developed to improve their achievements. Therefore there are two key defining elements to Hoshin Kanri. On the one hand it involves a very clear and well-defined structure of roles, responsibilities and metrics. On the other, it must concentrate on the development of its people with the aim to galvanise the creativity and job knowledge of its entire people to make it the best in its field for the pride and satisfaction of them all.

It is clear that introducing change of this nature is not going to be easy. The challenge therefore is how to persuade what might be an intrinsically autocratic organisation to move towards such a strongly participative style. Some autocratic managers are so entrenched in their beliefs that they are probably incapable of change. Experience indicates that they would rather threaten the very survival of the organisation than change their habits. The business graveyard is positively filled with such companies.

So far we have deliberately set out the contrasting extreme states. Very few organisations will be anywhere near either extreme, they will be somewhere between the two, but where? Undoubtedly, most readers will be able to identify with some elements of both.

Figure 1.3 dramatises the worst case. The large arrows show the distribution of the energies of each of the departments when they are not working well together. Ideally they should all be aligned and pointing towards the top (as in the case of the iron filings and a magnet). However, they are not, they are pointing in all directions, indicating conflicts between departmental Goals and those of other departments and the organisation itself. The managers are probably not even aware that they are behaving in a negative way, they probably think they are doing the best they can in the circumstances in which they operate. Also they probably do not see anything wrong with it because that is the way of the world they grew up in and are probably unaware that things could be very different. The more ambitious amongst them will already be learning how to make it work for them!

The most striking features of such an organisation are the following:

No clear Vision. Whatever the intentions are of the chief executive, they are not known possibly either to themself in any coherent way or to their subordinates. They are managing by hunch and

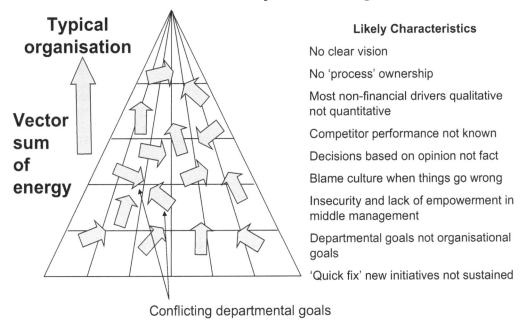

Non-Hoshin-style management

Typical organisation

Vector sum of energy

Conflicting departmental goals

Likely Characteristics

No clear vision

No 'process' ownership

Most non-financial drivers qualitative not quantitative

Competitor performance not known

Decisions based on opinion not fact

Blame culture when things go wrong

Insecurity and lack of empowerment in middle management

Departmental goals not organisational goals

'Quick fix' new initiatives not sustained

Figure 1.3   Non-Hoshin-style management – the worst case scenario

instinct. This applies also to each of the senior executives, who are probably totally preoccupied in defending their own fiefdoms against the attacks of those who should be regarded as their own colleagues and will also be managing by hunch and instinct.

No process ownership. Each function does what it believes to be its job then throws the product 'over the wall' to the next department. There will be very little feed forward or feedback on requirements because people are 'supposed to know'!

Most non-financial Drivers of the business will be qualitative rather than quantitative and will come in the form of vague slogans. There will be few if any tangible measures for anything other than those related to volume of work and those related to time constraints.

Not only will competitor performance not be known, in many cases people will not even know who the competitors are. This ignorance will often lead to crass complacency at all levels even when the Threats should appear very obvious.

A high proportion of decisions will be based on opinion data rather than factual. This will invariably lead to considerable sub-optimisation.

A blame culture will almost certainly prevail. As soon as anything goes wrong, which will be frequently, the question will always be, whose fault was it? A better approach would be to find out the circumstances that prevailed that caused someone who wanted to do a good job to do something that neither they nor anyone else wanted. In other words the approach should be to attack problems instead of people. This is difficult in a macho-style environment.

The likelihood of insecurity at all levels of organisation is obvious. Such organisations usually suffer high levels of staff turnover, sickness and absenteeism.

Departmental Goals are often clearer than organisational Goals largely due to the vagueness of the latter.

Quick fix solutions are frequently not sustained when crisis management prevails.

Figure 1.4 below compares this with the ideal state which is the Goal of Hoshin Kanri and is shown on the right-hand side. This represents the essence of Hoshin Kanri-style management.

Hoshin policy for the organisation

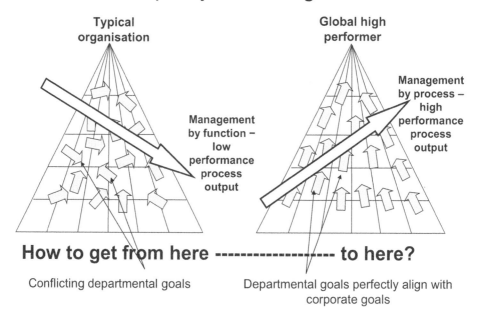

How to get from here ------------------- **to here?**

Conflicting departmental goals   Departmental goals perfectly align with corporate goals

Figure 1.4   Comparison between extremes of management style

Note that instead of the thick arrows being randomly orientated, the arrows in the diagram on the right are pointing towards the top. Notice the effect that this has on the arrow showing performance output. The sum of the energy from all of the departments in the diagram on the right is significantly greater than for the diagram on the left. The challenge of Hoshin Kanri is to be able to move the organisation as far towards the diagram on the right as possible.

Before commencing Hoshin Kanri, people will want to know, 'Where in this spectrum is our organisation right now?' Not only do we need to have at least an idea about this, more important is how far to the right we are in comparison with our competitors and who is moving fastest in that direction. It is this comparative rate of improvement that is critical because even if we are ahead of them now, if they are moving faster than we are then it follows that we will soon be overtaken.

This point is well illustrated in Figure 1.5. The diagram shows two businesses in competition. Initially Business A was far superior to Business B and it is possible that this had been the case for many years. As a consequence both Business A and the market in general will have grown used to it being the market leader. Unfortunately for Business A, this may have led to both complacency and arrogance. Because it has become accustomed to everyone else looking towards it as the market leader, it stops checking on its competitors. Business B then starts to move. It introduces a more dynamic form of management with the intention of closing the gap. Year after year the gap narrows until it closes. Still Business A does not react because it is unaware of what is going on. Its arrogance and conceit are now bigger problems than the performance of the competitor. Now the competitor moves ahead but still it is not noticed by Business A until the gap is quite large. Eventually, the difference becomes such that it cannot fail to draw attention, Business A suffers a slump in profits whilst Business B declares stunning growth and financial performance.

A period of panic now sets in at Business A. At first there is denial and disbelief but eventually action must be taken. Typically this could involve sacking the chief executive, or even the whole Board, closing down some of the least profitable parts of the organisation in order to consolidate. These are short-term measures but, sooner or later, the facts must be faced that the old Strategy no longer works. The new market leader is not going to be easily dislodged. They knew what they were

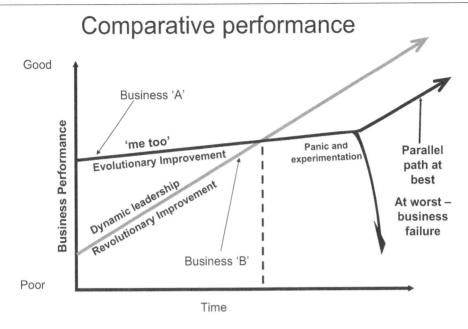

Figure 1.5   Comparative business performance

doing when they moved ahead and they will be watching every move made by Business A. The likelihood is that Business A can never regain its position. At best it can move up a parallel track to Business B. If it wanted to regain its original position it would be forced to move ahead at an even greater rate than Business B and this might not be possible.

The lesson is that whoever we are, we must never let a rival get past us if it can be prevented. We must continually benchmark the competition and try to go up the steepest curve it possibly can irrespective of the policies of competitors because we can never be totally sure what they are doing. Only through Hoshin Kanri-style management can this be achieved and the Goal must be to become and remain the leader in our field or Risk being second to those that are. The consequence of this will be tight margins, tough markets and the ever present threat of being wiped out.

THE HOSHIN MODEL

Enough of the negatives. The remainder of the book will concentrate on how to install the positives and to drive your organisation to the pole position. The Hoshin Kanri model shown in Figure 1.6 has been developed by David Hutchins and is based on many years of practical experience in the implementation of Hoshin Kanri in industry.

It is being used here as a road map for the rest of the book and we will work progressively through each of the boxes in the diagram. Readers will be referred back to this page constantly as we progress through the book.

At first sight the diagram probably appears complicated but it will be quickly appreciated that it starts with the Vision on the left-hand side and then progresses through a series of logical steps through to the point where the full programme has been fully established. To do this properly in a medium to large organisation it could be several years before the process was fully bedded-in and is representative of the overall culture. This should not be surprising because for most it represents a very big change and that will always take time, however high the levels of enthusiasm of the pioneers.

One attraction of Hoshin Kanri is the fact that the programme that you develop will be unique and will reflect the personality of your organisation almost from the start. What is included in this book describes a method of development and implementation. The result of that work will be entirely yours. By its nature you could not go to any other organisation and find a Hoshin Kanri programme identical to yours, you could not buy it off-the-shelf. This book will help you to create your own unique programme. If you want outside assistance, make sure that you vet very carefully the track record of those offering their services no matter how well known they may be.

Each box on the model shown in Figure 1.6 is covered by a chapter in this book. The largest chapter is Chapter 16 which covers Quality Circles (or Kaizen) in some detail.

The reason is that this topic is fundamental to the success of not only Hoshin Kanri but, in fact, all Japanese-originated concepts. This also includes Lean Manufacturing in particular and whilst Six Sigma was a US-developed derivative of the work of Dr Juran, there is no question that Six Sigma programmes would also benefit from the addition of Quality Circles.

Despite a huge quantity of literature most Western organisations simply cannot, or more likely choose not to, understand either the potential that Quality Circles offers or face up to the fact that they must address this issue if they hope to maximise the potential of their organisations.

Hopefully the material included in the relevant chapter will help to address this issue. As a matter of interest, I have taken and updated most of that material from my earlier book published in the early 1980s, *The Quality Circles Handbook*. It is long since out of print but second-hand copies are changing hands on the Internet at well over US$120 per copy. Sadly I do not benefit from that but since the copyright is exclusively mine the readers of this book can benefit from that material simply by reading the Quality Circles chapter!

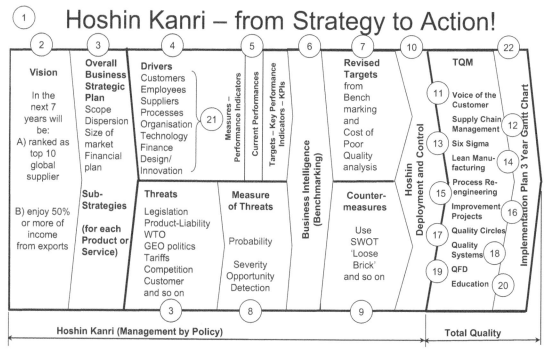

Figure 1.6   The Hoshin Kanri model with chapter numbers

USE OF THE BOOK AND A WORD OF WARNING!

t will be appreciated that Hoshin Kanri is a vast subject embracing every discipline in the organisation and possibly the creation of some new ones. This might indicate the need to use expensive management consultants. This would be absolutely the wrong approach and the temptation to put your fate in their hands should be vigorously resisted however attractive it might appear. Hoshin Kanri can only work if it is the product of the people in the organisation itself. Every step along the way, in the sequence of the chapters in the book, should be the work of the directors and management team in the organisation and no one else.

It is always an attractive idea to delegate responsibility for change programmes to consultants but you will end up with their programme not yours and it will not produce the results that you want. The process of managing your organisation is simply not delegable.

Use an expert Facilitator by all means and it is possible that they may come from outside your organisation. However, remember at all times that the verb 'to facilitate' means 'to make easy' or 'to make possible'. Their job will be to bring everyone together, to guide the discussions, to ensure the relevant facilities and resources are available, to produce reports and to offer advice where requested or when it is deemed necessary. They must never take over the project or create any of the materials at any level. This must be done within the organisation itself. I have facilitated many such programmes for very large and very small organisations. I have always ensured that ownership of every piece of work at every level stays firmly in the organisation itself. The pay off is that the sense of achievement when the results begin to appear is enormous and the organisation concerned can be justly proud of their efforts. In contrast, when the work is done by consultants, there is no sense of ownership, no pride in achievement and the results will be mediocre at best.

I have tried to put everything that is essential for success in this book but it is possible that something that is important to you is missing. I commit through the publishers to address any such issues if they arise, either by correspondence or email.

I very much hope though that this book proves a valuable resource for the future improvement in the performance of your organisation, improvement in its competitiveness and improvement in the quality of life of all your people, their families and society in general. This is a tall order but from what I have seen elsewhere it is achievable, but only if you make the effort. You do not have to be the chief executive to make a difference.

I have seen shop floor people and direct supervisors use the relevant methods at their level, sell them upwards to their managers through the results they have achieved and then on upwards to the top. Nobody is entirely a victim of their fate; everyone can make a difference if they work at it. It is never easy and there are some huge frustrations but sheer dogged determination will get you there in the end. If one thing that you try does not work then do not give up, try something else and again and again. There is always a way if only you can find it, so good luck and I hope that through these chapters you too can make the difference.

2   *Creating the Vision*

Hoshin Kanri – from Strategy to Action!

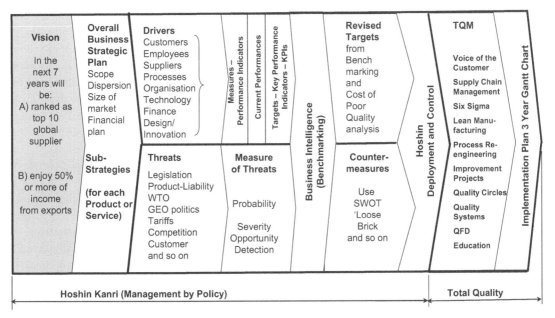

Figure 2.1   Creating the Vision

Vision will be personal and unique. No organisation can copy or modify a Vision created by another and expect it to generate the passion necessary to enable it to be achieved. Ideally it should be brief but some are not, there are no hard and fast rules. Most important is that it must be easily understood and clear in its intent. It must come from the heart of the chief executive and be shared by all directors of the business without any reservation. To create it requires an iterative process that will result in a statement that is shared by the top management team collectively and accepted and understood right through the organisation at all levels.

We may not always realise it but almost all our achievements in life require a Vision of some sort. Often we are hardly conscious of this but it is a fact. The ex-Prime Minister of the UK Margaret Thatcher often said that she had wanted to be Prime Minister from when she was a child. The likelihood is that she would not have shared that thought with anyone until she had actually achieved it because at the time that it had occurred to her, the probability would have seemed preposterous to everyone except herself. Good Vision Statements are often like that. They may seem ludicrous to those other than the person who have them. This will be true for Olympic gold medal winners, those who have excelled in their academic careers and indeed anyone who has been successful in any walk of life. Sometimes the Vision might require a stepwise approach.

The thought of getting 10/10 for some homework as a child may have been the Vision that inspired the effort. On its achievement, the satisfaction gained may have been sufficient to make us want to achieve it again and then again and so on. It is unlikely that as a small child we would have been inspired by some grand Vision of one day obtaining a first-class Honours degree at a prestigious university. This would be too remote and the route towards its achievement far too vague from the viewpoint of a child. They probably would not even have known what a first-class Honours degree was at that point.

A 14-year-old may well have the Vision of getting a high-grade Ph.D. However, it is more likely that they were probably initially inspired by the wish to achieve some good GCSEs which happened to be the first step along the way. After that they may let it be known that they plan to achieve some A grade 'A' levels and so on. Only when the real end is in sight may they share their real objective which is now much more believable to others.

The same can be true for organisations. If someone reading this book is the proprietor of a small corner store retail company, they would wisely be reluctant to let it be known that they have a Vision of having hundreds of stores throughout the world. More likely they would initially appear to be happy having won an award from their local Chamber of Trade for their local performance. However, all of the large organisations that we know today began in some small way and grew through the persistence and continued development of the Vision of the owners. It is hard to imagine that Marks and Spencer's was originally a street barrow in Leeds or that HJ Heinz began his business as a child, waking before dawn each morning, selling produce from his garden in the local market before going to school. Each of these entrepreneurs had a Vision and a passion and they made it work.

Vision is defined in the dictionary of the English Language as: 1. The act, faculty, or manner of perceiving with the eye; 2. The ability or an instance of greater perception, esp. of future developments: *a man of Vision*; 3. A vivid mental image produced by the imagination: *he had visions of becoming famous*.

It follows from definition 3 that Vision may sometimes be dreamy and imprecise but it can readily be converted to a Goal if it has the relevant metrics to determine the parameters for achievement. In the context of this book on Hoshin Kanri, it is assumed that any organisation that takes the trouble to articulate its Vision has every intention of attempting to achieve it. Therefore it will appear that the two words Vision and Goal are to some extent being used interchangeably in the sense that having created the Vision, it is transformed into a Goal or perhaps a collection of related Goals.

Vision is a word that is often greeted with some scepticism and often for good reason. Many Vision Statements are vague and platitudinous to the point of being virtually meaningless and unquantifiable. Also, they frequently make little impact because there may be no apparent mechanism or real enthusiasm to move in the direction indicated. However, even taking all of this into account, Vision is fundamentally important to progress. It follows therefore that the better the articulation of the Vision, the more likely it is that it will be achieved.

Vision does not just apply to companies and organisations. There is no reason why a forklift truck driver in the warehouse should not have the Vision of being an excellent forklift truck driver and eventually a warehouse manager and ultimately the owner of the company. It would by no means be unique, it has been done many times before. If there are clear performance criteria on which the individual and their colleagues can be judged and if the reward for achievement is relevant, then they can aspire to it if they so desire. Not only will this benefit the individual but it will also benefit the whole organisation if the right criteria are set. The same principle can be applied to everyone at all levels right through to the top. Imagine the organisational power if such a system were well designed. It would be a fearsome competitor in the marketplace!

Let us now consider the organisation as a whole. An organisation is a collection of people led by one at the top whose task is to inspire and lead the organisation. In some cases they do and do it well. Some, like Richard Branson, appear to have a gift for this. In other cases it would appear not. They may have a Vision but it might be badly articulated or in many cases not shared at all. This will always result in sub-optimisation with everyone pulling in different directions.

The success of organisations which have managed to share a commonly-held Vision with all of their employees was well articulated in William's book *Theory Z Management*, published in the early 1980s but now out of print. One of the common factors was a very clear Vision for the direction of the company. This Vision was clearly described and in some cases written into the form of a charter. One example used in the book was Hewlett Packard (HP), which it must be acknowledged, is one of the world's most successful office machine manufacturers and which has confronted and survived against fierce competition from Japan.

Ouchi claimed that not only did Hewlett Packard have a clear charter, he also claimed that everyone in the company could almost state it chapter and verse. He was talking about HP in the USA. The author of this book had the opportunity to find out if this was also true for HP employees in the UK and it turned out to be the same.

Some time later, the author also had the good fortune to hear the CEO of HP making a speech at a large conference in the USA when he explained the means by which the company obtained global leadership. His speech was subtitled, 'In the Yukon they have an expression "only the lead dog gets a change of view" – we want always to be that lead dog!'.

THE CORPORATE VISION

An example of a simple Vision Statement might be:

'Our aim is be the unchallenged world leader in avionics by 2012.'

Of course, this is also a Goal but there is no problem with it for the purposes of Hoshin Kanri. Obviously this will need to be updated as 2012 approaches.

As a Vision Statement it is fine and will serve its purpose. Later on in the process we will discuss how it can be clarified. For example, it is perfectly acceptable here to say 'unchallenged leader' but later on, what is meant by this will need considerable further clarification. What do we mean by 'leader'? In whose opinion? What are the criteria by which we and they will judge? Presumably both competitors and the market will be the judges but who are they? For us to be able to take the steps to achieve the Goal, who are our rivals and how good are they on the appropriate criteria in the eyes of those who judge? Clearly we have to know in order to determine the size of our challenge so we must 'Benchmark'. Do we know the opinion of the market and how?

It is no good trying to guess the opinions of others. There is no alternative to asking the customer. This is not always easy and there are many methods for doing this. Also, the right questions need to be asked. To simply say, 'Did you enjoy that?' or 'Do you like our products?' is insufficient. We may get an affirmative to both and yet the customer goes elsewhere, why? The most likely reason is that they like someone else's product better. Therefore the questions need to be comparative. For example, can you rank us in comparison with our competitors on Quality, Price and Delivery? Which of us would you choose and why? The answer might be none of these but they just like dealing with a particular organisation because they like them better. We need to know the answers to these important points but rarely do we make the time.

CREATING THE VISION STATEMENT

The chief executive must have a powerful say in the creation of the Vision but it is most important to have a complete 'buy-in' from their whole team and this must be made very clear at the point of publication.

One excellent way to do this is to use a variation of the Affinity Diagram method. This is a brainstorming-based technique which makes use of the collective thinking power of a group of people to come up with ideas that they might not have come up with when working on their own.

Brainstorming by itself typically involves the listing of ideas on a flip chart. These ideas are randomly generated by a group of people who usually, but not always, are given the opportunity to suggest their ideas by taking turns. At the end of the session, which is usually around 20 minutes to half an hour, this disassociated list of ideas must be clustered in some way into coherent groups where possible.

USE AN 'IMAGINEERING' TECHNIQUE

This is a term first believed to have been coined by Disney. In order to get people thinking about 'where we want to be' at some defined point in the future, one way is to ask them to close their eyes and then think about the following: imagine that in X years time (say 5 years) a journalist from a top media source such as *Time Magazine* or the *Financial Times* was making a visit. An article then appeared as a centrespread 1 week later.

Think about what you would like to read in the column inches. Think about the banner headline across the page. If the team doing this exercise is the top team covering all functions, they will all have a bias towards the outputs of their respective functions but so will everyone else. This is healthy because it makes sure that all aspects of the organisation are represented. The team should then cluster the ideas into groups.

The Affinity Diagram method can achieve this but instead of writing the ideas on a flip chart, each person writes their ideas on 'post-it'-type stickers. One idea is written on one sticker and the idea is written more in the form of a short sentence than the typical bullet that would be more normal in brainstorming. Each person tries to identify around four to seven specific ideas, but there is no restriction on this. The stickers are then stuck to a plain piece of wall (or on brown paper attached to the wall, often referred to as a 'brown paper job') with each idea clustered in groups which have some affinity with each other. There will be more detail on this in a later chapter.

At this stage we are only interested in using the outputs of the thought process to create the banner headline which will form the basis of the creation of the overall organisational Vision Statement.

Often the Vision Statement at this level may have previously been created personally by the chief executive if it has been articulated. However, the work just completed provides an excellent means to adapt this and to obtain a 100 per cent buy-in from the rest of the top team. If it contains a little of each of their aspirations and they have then bought into the resultant output then there will be a sense of total ownership by the group. In some organisations, this statement is then signed by each of the participants and copies are displayed prominently throughout the organisation.

If an old Vision Statement currently exists, it is not advisable to scrap it. Quite often I have worked with companies that have a Vision that was created several years earlier for some reason. The words sound reasonable but nobody is passionate about them. To begin with it is advisable to keep this document out of sight and use the Affinity Diagram method to create the basis of a new one. Then when the ideas have been discussed, compare the original and construct a new one which includes all the accepted good points on the old version but also the ideas generated in this session. The result will be a complete buy-in from everybody and a new refreshed Vision Statement.

Paradoxically, whilst the Vision Statement must be positive in the sense that it points the direction of the organisation, it is often useful to use one or more powerful negatives to help create it.

For example, prior to meeting the chief executive of one large engineering company, the author asked one of his senior managers, 'What is the business problem that worried him the most?' – or what is his biggest headache?

The response was 'competitive tendering'. Apparently, the company had only fairly recently lost out in tendering for a very large contract to someone they had thought to be an inferior competitor. The lost potential work would result in making 500 people redundant every 6 months or so for the next several years. Worse still, the impact on the local community was such that even those who were not going to lose their jobs were unable to get credit or mortgages due to the insecurity of the company in the perception of local traders.

Later on when the Vision Statement had been completed and the Goals established, a project team was formed specifically to look into the possible causes of rejected tender bids. This team comprised key personnel who had previous experience of competitive tendering on earlier successful and failed bids. The team studied many of these and carried out autopsies on the failures. Many useful ideas were generated and recommendations made.

One finding was that all earlier tender document production teams were formed on an ad hoc basis. The teams each comprised up to 70 persons in some cases and the individuals were selected on the relevance of their expertise in the topic area, not on their skill in the preparation of tender documents. As a consequence, because each successive team comprised different personnel, there was no collective learning experience. The improvement team therefore checked to see how many of the skills required in tendering were common to most bids and identified a number of core competences. They then recommended that a core bid team be formed and that resources were allocated. There were many useful such recommendations.

All of these recommendations were accepted. Later, the company had the opportunity to put its new organisation to the test when they were invited to tender for a huge project. The expected winner of this tendering was a competitor supported by a powerful consortium of some of the largest engineering companies in the country. Also, that competitor had more previous experience in that particular type of work. To the surprise of everyone including the media, our organisation won the contract. The result was devastating for the competitor who was subsequently forced into receivership.

Later, two of the senior executives of that competitor were head-hunted by our company. Over dinner one evening, they said that until they joined this company they had no idea how it had won the contract, but since joining them they had never seen a company in the industry with such a professional approach to the tendering process.

Other Vision Statements include:

- 'To be and remain the worlds unchallenged leading XXXXXX company.'
- 'XXXXX to be ranked amongst the top 10 global XXXXX suppliers during the next X years and X per cent of its revenue will be gained from export.'

Note that the main difference between these last two Vision Statements is that one has a time horizon and the other does not. This does not matter because the most important feature of this level of Vison Statement is to give everyone a sense of the direction the Leaders want the business to go in and to give everyone a banner to march behind.

MAKING THE VISION A REALITY

At this point, the Vision Statement is a nice sounding dream. On its own it has no real value and if it is not taken further can even be harmful. In the next few chapters it will be seen how this intangible statement is converted first of all into a list of eight Drivers each with their own policy statements and from there into specific tangible performance indicators (and there can be many of these). This is followed by work on identifying the means of measuring each, then establishing the actual performance before setting Goals and Targets for each. If this process has resulted in a list too long to manage, which is almost always the case, it will need prioritising in order to find the 'key' performance indicators.

SUMMARY

If we have a big ambition, the continual success in achieving small realistic ambitions step by step makes a higher-level Vision become possible. Eventually, there is the prospect of being top of class. When this Goal is achieved, the challenge will be to remain there because now your organisation will be the target of other people's dreams!

No one can create a Vision Statement for anyone else. A Vision is what it is, it comes from the heart or the stomach but it must be the articulation of a strongly-felt emotional feeling. What has been said so far in this chapter will help in the lead up to its creation but in the end it is the head of the operation who must articulate what is in their mind, faced with all of the above evidence.

Once articulated, others can then make a contribution and make suggestions on how to broaden its scope and to include their passions. It can be given more polish if necessary but this is additional and must not subtract from the original and nothing must be done that will dampen the passion of the initial originator. It may also need to be rephrased in terms that make it measurable and to make the intangible become tangible ('If you cannot measure it you cannot manage it' – Lord Kelvin) then it becomes a Goal or collection of Goals. For example, it is OK to say that 'we will be the unchallenged leader in our field' as a Vision but it is not much use if we have not also identified the measurable criteria that will determine how far we are from that point and when it has been achieved.

It is the final version of this Vision that will be the sign of the commitment of the chief executive. This statement will be the single most important statement in the whole organisation. It will be its 'reason to be'. Everything that happens subsequently will be prioritised according to its relative impact on the Vision. It is therefore the banner behind which the whole organisation must march.

However, this is the beginning of the process not the end. Now that we have identified where we want to be, we now have to work out how we plan to get there.

3 *Strategy and Tactics*

Hoshin Kanri – from Strategy to Action!

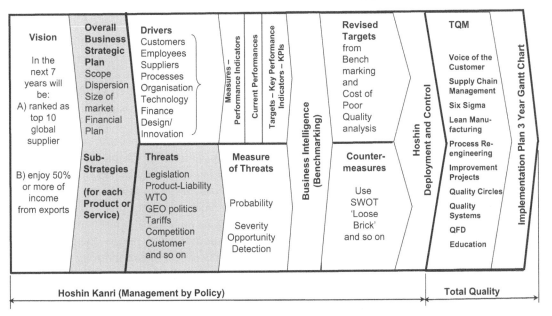

Figure 3.1 **Strategy development**

Any attempt to grow a business in an established market will pose a threat to its competitors and they are certain to react. Competitors are just one negative factor and there will be many others. For example:

- new legislation – especially European Community dictates;
- product liability and consumer protection lawsuits;
- World Trade Organisation – regulations regarding tariff barriers and other constraints on globalisation of trade and trends in geopolitics;
- terrorism;
- UN embargoes;
- trade union resistance;
- inclement weather and the long-term effects of global warming;

- concerns regarding 'carbon footprints', dealing with waste and other environmental issues;
- health and safety issues – society is becoming increasingly intolerant towards these issues no matter how rare;
- increasingly litigious society;
- dealing with potential product recalls.

Attempting to counter these and other Threats just by improving business performance is not the answer. These Threats must be identified and the Risks of their impact on our Vision carefully evaluated. We must also be continually vigilant to ensure that new Threats do not appear unexpectedly and when it is too late to react. If we are not then we will be living in a fool's paradise which might come to an abrupt end if one or more of the worst Risks materialises. There is also the fact that the nearer we get to the realisation of our Vision, the more the negative forces will conspire and sometimes even collaborate to prevent us reaching it and we must foresee and be prepared for that.

If we are a small organisation competing at the bottom end of the market, the competition may be easy to deal with and the big players will not even notice. Later when we are attracting the attention of the serious players and affecting their market, then we can expect a very different level of reaction. These sophisticated operators will be very different to deal with from the small operators. This will progressively become more difficult the closer the business gets to the top. Once there, other problems will also emerge. In addition to the external factors, a sustained period at the top will eventually result in other problems often generated from within. There will be a tendency to develop increasingly stifling bureaucracy; the keenness of the competitive edge will dull followed by increasing arrogance, conceit and contempt for the competition. Eventually the business is in danger of becoming so smug and self-opinionated that it ignores the competition completely and assumes that it cannot be displaced. This will become its Loose Brick (see Chapter 9) and it will be vulnerable to attack by others. The business graveyard is full of such organisations.

At the other extreme, there are many organisations that sit in the middle of the market going nowhere. There is no compulsion to grow, but it is still recommended that they remain cautious; survival still requires the same business methods if not the same intensity. But most are there for no other reason other than that they have no self-belief. They do not compete with the global giants for no other reason than they do not think that they can and therefore do not try or do not want to. In the latter case, there is nothing wrong with that. This is especially true for some large operators in emerging countries. They are mesmerised by the American, Japanese or other global giants and do not even attempt to challenge their position. When they decide to challenge this assumption they may well be surprised to find that it is not as difficult as they thought. In fact, hopefully it can be done simply by following the advice in this book! You will not need to throw millions of hard-earned profits at expensive management consultants!

TO BE THE BEST, DO NOT OVERLOOK THE NEGATIVES!

In the early 1990s an American company won the US National Quality Award but went out of business in the same year.

How could this be? There are three possibilities:

1. the assessment of the company by the award assessors and judges may have been flawed;
2. the award criteria may have been inadequate;
3. a combination of both.

Unfortunately it was not possible for us to conduct a post-mortem on the assessment itself but it was possible to study the award criteria. What we found was that both the US National Quality Award (named the Baldridge Award in recognition of one of its architects who had been killed in a rodeo accident) and also its European equivalent, which was similar in content but different in structure, and which had subsequently been created by the European Foundation for Quality Management (EFQM), had no evaluation features to judge how the organisation either responded to outside potential and real Threats or how it threatened its competition, either strategically or tactically. Consequently, the organisation might well have been extremely vulnerable in its marketplace and yet on the assessment appeared to be doing everything right. Descriptions of both the content and structure of these awards and also the Japanese Deming Prize, on which both are loosely based, can be found on the Internet.

In the next chapter, 'The Loose Brick', we can see how companies have been forced out of business by aggressive competitors who have located and exploited an inherent weakness in its target company. A company or a whole series of companies may be wiped out by such a Strategy often without knowing how they were being attacked. Clearly, survival and growth are not just a question of continuous improvement or quality systems.

If we are up against an aggressive competitor or, worse still, against a whole nation's combined competitors as happened to Western organisations in the 1960s and 1970s in the motor and TV industries, then the right choice of Strategy combined with a linked performance-improvement programme is the only way that survival can be assured.

The boxes highlighted in Figure 3.1 indicate the issues that must be addressed.

In the first box, the top team must agree on the scope, dispersion and the size of market to be achieved, as well as the financial structure and resources required for supporting it.

These considerations must be thought through for each product or service that it intends to sell in the market as the criteria for one may be quite different for others and, in some cases, they may even be in conflict with each other. For example, a cigarette manufacturer may also produce devices to assist stopping smoking in order to hedge its bets.

When the requirements of the first box are achieved, it is necessary to consider 'the means to achieve' and what additional measures might be necessary when our share of the market begins to increase.

In many cases the most dangerous competition to watch for comes from completely different technology from an organisation in a completely different industry. In this case the threat applies to all competitors. This was the case with the incandescent lamp which replaced the oil lamp, the automobile that replaced the horse and cart, the railway that replaced the canal, and in more recent times, the electronic pocket calculator which destroyed the slide rule business and the data projector which has replaced the old overhead projector. These are just a few dramatic examples where the competition came from totally different technology and totally different skills. We must always be on guard to ensure that something like this will not happen to us, however unlikely that might seem. In some cases the new technology is developed within the industry itself, as was the case with the digital camera and the digital watch, but some competitors in those markets had a very hard time adjusting to the new situation. The camera manufacturers did manage to adjust but it still meant closing their roll film manufacturing business and Switzerland lost its unrivalled place in the wrist watch business.

In most cases where a product is superseded by one from a different technology, the switch to the new technology was both rapid and irresistible. Even if the manufacturers of the outdated products had predicted the change, there was virtually nothing they could do about it. Perhaps they could have switched over to produce their replacements but it is doubtful that any but the largest companies could switch to such different technologies and be able to compete with the experts in those fields.

The lesson is that all organisations must be ever vigilant and awake to the possibility that this could at some time also be their fate. A possible solution might be to always be looking for alternative uses for core competencies and these possibilities must be defined.

The slide rule manufacturer may have made the mistake of thinking that they were in the rapid and accurate calculations business and of course they were, but in reality they were really a manufacturer of very accurately-produced high-volume wooden products. It is likely that this is a highly-skilled process with considerable know-how that has been acquired over many years. If necessary, could that core competency be transferred to other products for a different use which has nothing to do with slide rules or calculations?

One of the most important articles on this topic to be published since World War II, and which is still available on the web, was written by Theodor Levitt (http://harvardbusinessonline.hbsp. harvard.edu/b02/en/common/item_detail.jhtml?id=R0407L):

At some point in its development, every industry can be considered a growth industry, based on the apparent superiority of its product. But in case after case, industries have fallen under the shadow of mismanagement. What usually gets emphasized is selling, not marketing. This is a mistake, because selling focuses on the needs of the seller, whereas marketing concentrates on the needs of the buyer. In this widely quoted and anthologized article, first published in 1960, Theodore Levitt argues that 'the history of every dead and dying "growth" industry shows a self-deceiving cycle of bountiful expansion and undetected decay.' But, as he illustrates, memories are short. The railroads serve as an example of an industry whose failure to grow is due to a limited market view. Those behind the railroads are in trouble not because the need for passenger transportation has declined or even because cars, airplanes, and other modes of transport have filled that need. Rather, the industry is failing because those behind it assumed they were in the railroad business rather than the transportation business. They were railroad oriented instead of transportation oriented, product oriented instead of customer oriented. For companies to ensure continued evolution, they must define their industries broadly to take advantage of growth opportunities. They must ascertain and act on their customers' needs and desires, not bank on the presumed longevity of their products. In short, the best way for a firm to be lucky is to make its own luck. An organization must learn to think of itself not as producing goods or services but as doing the things that will make people want to do business with it. And in every case, the chief executive is responsible for creating an environment that reflects this mission.

Published with permission of Harvard Business Review

In addition to all of this, the right highlighted box in Figure 3.1 indicates that there is a large number of external factors to consider as well. Quite apart from the volatility of the market itself, there is a multitude of external factors, many of which are totally outside the control of the organisation. In this case they are potential victims if they do not have the means to respond to these pressures.

Fortunately, however, these external factors not only pose a threat but also provide an opportunity. These Threats are likely to apply to our competitors as well, for example, new regulations. The organisation that responds to this first might well create a situation where it can exploit the market before its rivals have even thought about it.

Not only does Hoshin Kanri provide a means to respond rapidly to all of these outside factors, it also enables the organisation to influence events both for its own protection and to increase the vulnerability of its competitors.

The achievement of the Vision will always be time related because the Vision represents some future Goal which may be many years hence. From the current time to the time of the desired achievement, the world and the markets will be constantly changing and some of these changes may be dramatic. Some of them may have a positive impact on our Vision and others may be negative or even disastrous. Some of these factors, even some of enormous impact, may be impossible to predict, for example, Dr Henry Kissinger said at a conference in Paris just 1 year before the collapse of the Berlin Wall and after the Tiananmen Square massacre (and I paraphrase), 'China will continue to progress towards becoming a Western-style democracy, but the Soviet Union? We do not predict a change in this century.' Less than 1 year later, the Wall had gone and the Soviet Union was history. This was virtually unpredictable less than 1 year before it actually happened.

The fact is that we must be eternally vigilant about these matters and wherever possible turn them to our advantage. We must also attempt to predict the impact of our actions on the strategies of our competitors. This can readily be seen from the following diagram.

Figure 3.2 indicates a situation at the present time where a company is well behind its competitors but is planning to introduce an aggressive Strategy not only to catch up but to take the lead in 5 years. There would be no point in just trying to get to where they are now because in that time many of them will have progressed further, some may not and others might possibly have failed altogether but we need to predict where the best will be in that time and aim for that.

This was the situation facing a large international steel producer in 1997. They then created a Vision, as a consequence of which it was their intention to become a leading producer in just 5 years. They had much work to do! They also realised that should they begin to be successful they would be confronted by considerable hostility in the international markets. Steel production is almost as politically sensitive as oil and any change in the status quo was bound to cause a strong negative reaction.

First of all, if they managed to cut the cost of production and pass this improvement on to the consumer, they would be accused of dumping. At the commencement of the project, this was hard to believe but in less than 3 years, this was the case. During that time they had taken a massive US$125M out of the total cost of production. Not only that but in one of the key parameters of operational efficiency, a statistic known in the industry as 'tap to tap time', they had reduced

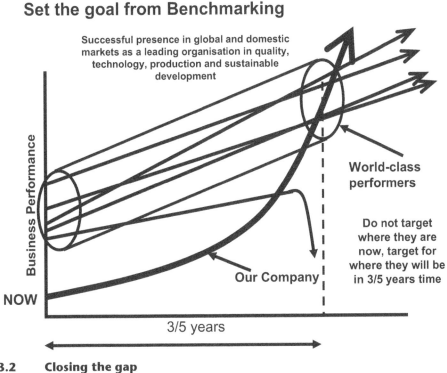

Figure 3.2   Closing the gap

this from 220 minutes to less than 165 minutes which was the theoretical limit for their type of operation. Tap to tap time is the time it takes to convert a quantity of molten iron into steel. Apart from its impact on production time, the energy savings were huge.

A second, somewhat dubious, sign of success might be the sudden apparently friendly interest shown by some competitors. These would include proposals for mutual exchanges, cross training, and so on. The real motive would be espionage. This also happened.

Making sure that the creation of a Vision will not lead us into a potential trap requires some very careful thought. Many board directors are quite cynical about the importance of defining a well-considered Vision and treat the topic quite flippantly. For example, on one occasion, the managing director of quite a large company, whilst attending a business conference, was due to make a presentation of his company's quality Strategy during one of the afternoon sessions. To support him he brought two or three of his colleagues with him.

During the morning session a speaker from a rival company exhibited a slide which included his company's Vision which he spoke about at some length. Clearly he regarded it as a very important part of his company's strategic approach.

Our managing director disappeared for much of the lunch period and no one knew where he was. However, when he made his presentation he put up a hand-made acetate slide on which he had written a Vision statement and about which he spoke at length. His colleagues were astonished as none of them had seen it before. They learned afterwards that this what he had been doing when absent at lunch. Later, it appeared in the reception area in large letters on the wall.

I have been in organisations where the Vision Statement is printed in large letters and hung on the wall in the reception area. I have asked the receptionist if they might explain it to me and invariably I get the retort, 'I don't know love. I have only been here 6 months, it was there when I came.'

Such Statements are not worth the paper they are written on and are valueless. In fact they can do much harm because when the employees see that they are nothing more than empty words they become quite cynical.

At the other extreme there are companies which have spent many weeks or even months deciding on the wording and have gone to the trouble of explaining it very carefully to the entire workforce because they have considered it to be of such importance. Nissan in the UK printed theirs on a small laminated card and put a copy in every employee's monthly salary envelope.

Prior to the creation of a Vision statement it is important to attempt to identify all the Threats and opportunities that impact the organisation, and to know the current situation of the company with regard to its market share and general health compared with its competitors. Toyota post articles from magazines on their noticeboards to see what others are saying about the products and the company.

Important considerations will include:

- Who our competitors are and who they might be in the future.
- What we know and what we do *not* but *should* know about our competitors – all of them, even the small ones, because they sometimes have a nasty habit of growing!
- What global changes are there that might impact on our business, for example, World Trade Organisation tariff policies?
- Impending Government legislation.
- The fact that people are getting ever more sensitive about safety-related deficiencies no matter how rare. The same applies to environmental issues. Will any of these pose a threat in any way?
- Are our products ever likely to be regarded as being risky or environmentally unfriendly even though they may be acceptable now?

- How are we perceived by our suppliers, how do they rank us compared with their other customers?
- How are we perceived by our customers both individually and en bloc? Do we believe their perception to be fair? Why do they think what they do when we think otherwise? This is an issue that needs to be addressed.
- From this and from our own analysis, do we know what our perceived strengths and weaknesses are compared specifically with each of our competitors?

All of this requires some work but it essential if the Vision is to be a serious statement followed by an action plan to achieve it.

The following Figures 3.3 through to 3.6 show how a form of Force Field analysis can be used at this stage. In the example shown in Figure 3.3 a number of interviews had been conducted by a consultant in both the client company (which we will refer to as 'OURCO') and a selected number of its suppliers (referred to collectively as 'YOURCO'). The client company was an automotive parts distributor and the suppliers were the head manufacturers of those parts.

The information obtained in these interviews is vital not only to ensure that the wording of the Vision is realistic but also to add to a database of issues that will assist in the identification of the critical Key Performance Indicators.

Figures 3.3 and 3.4 are only slightly modified examples from a real-life situation. Interestingly, when the results of the interviews at YOURCO were presented to the representatives of OURCO they said that they were quite unaware of these opinions which were something of a surprise.

Figure 3.5 shows the challenges facing OURCO. By combining the results of the interviews with input from research of the global situation in the market for OURCO's products, the key issues confronting OURCO could be defined and illustrated graphically as shown.

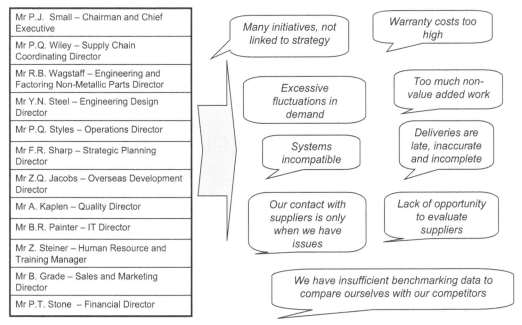

Summary findings – OURCO

Mr P.J. Small – Chairman and Chief Executive
Mr P.Q. Wiley – Supply Chain Coordinating Director
Mr R.B. Wagstaff – Engineering and Factoring Non-Metallic Parts Director
Mr Y.N. Steel – Engineering Design Director
Mr P.Q. Styles – Operations Director
Mr F.R. Sharp – Strategic Planning Director
Mr Z.Q. Jacobs – Overseas Development Director
Mr A. Kaplen – Quality Director
Mr B.R. Painter – IT Director
Mr Z. Steiner – Human Resource and Training Manager
Mr B. Grade – Sales and Marketing Director
Mr P.T. Stone – Financial Director

Many initiatives, not linked to strategy

Warranty costs too high

Excessive fluctuations in demand

Too much non-value added work

Systems incompatible

Deliveries are late, inaccurate and incomplete

Our contact with suppliers is only when we have issues

Lack of opportunity to evaluate suppliers

We have insufficient benchmarking data to compare ourselves with our competitors

Figure 3.3   Headline results of internal interviews at OURCO

Summary findings – YOURCO and suppliers

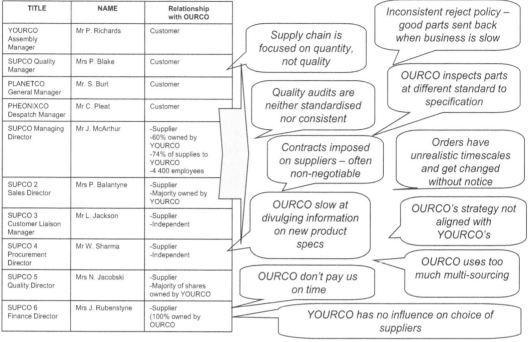

TITLE	NAME	Relationship with OURCO
YOURCO Assembly Manager	Mr P. Richards	Customer
SUPCO Quality Manager	Mrs P. Blake	Customer
PLANETCO General Manager	Mr. S. Burt	Customer
PHEONIXCO Despatch Manager	Mr C. Pleat	Customer
SUPCO Managing Director	Mr J. McArthur	-Supplier -60% owned by YOURCO -74% of supplies to YOURCO -4 400 employees
SUPCO 2 Sales Director	Mrs P. Balantyne	-Supplier -Majority owned by YOURCO
SUPCO 3 Customer Liaison Manager	Mr L. Jackson	-Supplier -Independent
SUPCO 4 Procurement Director	Mr W. Sharma	-Supplier -Independent
SUPCO 5 Quality Director	Mrs N. Jacobski	-Supplier -Majority of shares owned by YOURCO
SUPCO 6 Finance Director	Mrs J. Rubenstyne	-Supplier (100% owned by OURCO

Supply chain is focused on quantity, not quality

Inconsistent reject policy – good parts sent back when business is slow

Quality audits are neither standardised nor consistent

OURCO inspects parts at different standard to specification

Contracts imposed on suppliers – often non-negotiable

Orders have unrealistic timescales and get changed without notice

OURCO slow at divulging information on new product specs

OURCO's strategy not aligned with YOURCO's

OURCO uses too much multi-sourcing

OURCO don't pay us on time

YOURCO has no influence on choice of suppliers

Figure 3.4. **Headline results if supplier interviews at YOURCO**

Summary: Challenges

Figure 3.5 **Summary Force Field analysis**

Interestingly, this analysis was being carried out at the same time that the Rover Group in the UK was being put into liquidation. This fact had a significant impact on the importance that OURCO attached to the findings of the study.

The issues identified in Figure 3.5 are quite negative and can be depressing. However, they can be presented in a positive light. First of all, OURCO is still in business and has some market share. Having now identified the key issues that it must tackle, it is well placed to be able to resolve these issues and strengthen its business. By presenting the findings in a positive sense, it can be extremely motivational and show strength of leadership. Figure 3.6 therefore can be regarded as the flip side of Figure 3.5.

Success therefore requires both Strategy and Tactics. Strategy is the means by which the long-term Goals are to be achieved, and Tactics are the short-term responses to hostile activities and also help to achieve the minor Goals along the way. Tactics therefore require the means of rapid response to unexpected change. This requires a very clear picture of the current deployment of the operating forces, an evaluation of the current priorities of the Key Performance Indicators and resource availabilities. The development of a Hoshin Kanri-based Management System is the most effective way in which this can be achieved. As will be explained and illustrated later, Hoshin Kanri enables the continuous re-evaluation of all levels of business activity in a highly-visual structure to ensure that the most effective use of resources is being used at all times.

Without Hoshin Kanri, it is quite common for organisations to feel that their future is determined largely by fate and that their ability to influence market forces is minimal. This can be a catastrophic mistake and a self-fulfilling belief. It is only true in the case of sudden and totally unexpected natural disasters or international conflagration, but in most other cases organisations can have considerable influence, not only on their own futures, but also in many cases on those of their competitors. Rarely is the failure of an organisation an act of fate.

Figure 3.6   **Summary Force Field analysis of the opportunities for OURCO**

Henry Ford put it perfectly when he said:

Good business, which in turn means general prosperity and employment, is not something which comes about by chance. It is a result of the skill with which business in general is managed – and business in general is only the sum of the activities of the business units (Hoshin Kanri!). Through all the years that I have been in business I have never yet found our business bad as a result of any outside force. It has always been due to some defect in our own company, and whenever we located and repaired that defect our business became good again – regardless of what anyone else might be doing. And it will always be found that this country has nationally bad business when business men are drifting, and that business is good when men take hold of their own affairs, put leadership into them, and push forward in spite of obstacles.

This is the essence of Hoshin Kanri and it was published in 1931 in Henry Ford's book *Moving Forward*.

According to Henry Ford, therefore, the situation that we are in is never a fate, but always the consequence of our own management.

In contrast, business leaders are always complaining that 'our problems are due to a range of external factors over which we have no direct control – Government policy, balance of payments, currency values, unfair trade, and so on'. What they choose to ignore is the fact that in many cases, these external factors apply not only to themselves but to their competitors as well. The successful organisation will be the one that best deals with these external factors.

Risk and Strategy are intrinsically interconnected but we will look at Risk Management in a later chapter. In this chapter we are more concerned with Strategy from the point of view of the identification and management of our ever-changing market strengths and weaknesses in order to achieve the Goals of our Vision through building our strengths, the satisfaction of our customers and interested parties, and exploitation of the weaknesses of our competitors.

The Vision tells us where we want to be but to get there we must first establish where we are now in terms of the attractiveness of our products, our customers impressions, Supply Chain Management, the state of the competition, global trade variations both short term and long term and the long-term viability of our product – will it become obsolescent as a consequence of design evolution or from radical change to totally different technologies and skills?

SUMMARY

The eventual achievement of the Vision will impact on the rival Visions of competitors whose own Visions will be intended to prevent the achievement of ours. If they are alive to our Strategy, they will respond with counter strategies.

In fact, even whilst you are reading this chapter, there may well be any number of competing organisations which are actively attempting to steal your customers. As your business becomes more successful, the more vulnerable it becomes and the more likely it is to be attacked. It follows therefore that the greater the attainment, the greater should be the consciousness of competitors' strategies, but paradoxically, instead of becoming more sensitive to market changes, the reverse is often the case.

Success tends to breed arrogance and conceit. These in turn lead to self-indulgence, excessive pride and an unwillingness to accept the possibility that any of what will now be regarded as lesser organisations could possibly pose a threat. The consequence is that the activities of competitors are ignored when in fact they should be studied in even greater detail to avoid unwelcome surprises.

The most important thing is to attempt to be aware of their efforts, to respond accordingly and attempt to make sure that they can never close the gap that we have created.

Toyota has replaced GM at the top after more then 70 years dominance. Toyota began this journey in 1950 and has never wavered. The probability is that it will continue to grow and continue to pose a threat to the specialist auto makers such as Mercedes and BMW through the Lexus models. One day perhaps Toyota might become arrogant and conceited but there is no sign of it yet.

4

Driver Policies: Becoming Fit, Fast, Lean and Hungry!

Hoshin Kanri – from Strategy to Action!

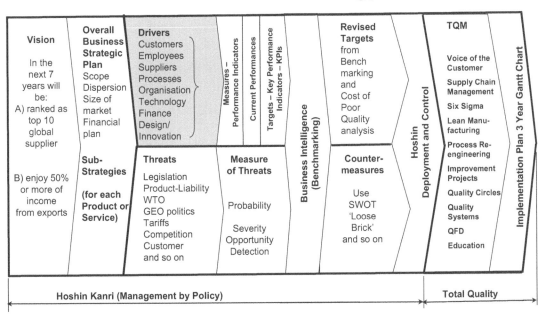

Figure 4.1   Defining the Drivers

The Vision is the dream; the Strategic Plan defines the scope and dispersion of the business, the size of the market we aim to achieve and the dispersion of operational facilities throughout that market.

In this chapter we will consider the means by which all of these Objectives can be achieved. We refer to these 'means' as being the Drivers. If the Objectives are to be achieved, it is the Drivers that make it happen and we need a very carefully-defined policy for each of them. If we get it wrong then we will probably underachieve against our plan.

We have defined eight of these:

1.   customer (internal and external);
2.   employee;
3.   suppliers (internal and external);
4.   processes;

5.   organisation;
6.   technology;
7.   finance;
8.   design and innovation.

Later in the book, each of these eight Drivers will be given a short chapter of its own and it is recommended that when this stage is reached, the content of these chapters is used for reference.

Each of the Drivers can be considered at both operational and departmental level if each department is considered as a unit which buys and sells products and services to the other departments within the organisation.

The relative importance of each Driver will vary from situation to situation and from time to time depending upon market pressures and other changing circumstances but it is unlikely that the total number will be fewer than the eight listed above. It is best to play safe and consider all of them all of the time. Conceivably, there may be more in some situations but in many years of experience with a range of organisations across a spectrum of industries we have not yet found such a case.

We discovered the eight Drivers during our work in the early days by use of the Affinity Diagram method. Today, we use a variant of that method which combines part of the Affinity Diagram and part of the Ishikawa Diagram technique and it works very well.

THE DRIVERS

Customer

The customer is often considered to be the end user. In Hoshin Kanri thinking, everyone downstream from the previous operation in a process is the customer of that activity. This means that there are both internal and external customers. However, if the organisation is to survive and grow, it will need to attract customers away from its competitors whilst at the same time making sure that it retains the hard-won customers that it already has. In a growing market, it will also need to consider how to attract new customers and all of this should be reflected in the statement for the customer Driver. It is also advisable to consider what are often referred to as stakeholders and other interested parties in this element.

Employees

In a service operation, some of the employees are the main contact with the customer and will often determine the customer's opinion of us. It is therefore a paradox that frequently these are our lowest paid, least qualified and least well-trained on the payroll. How much business do we gain or lose as a consequence of our people management skills?

Behind that interface our products and services depend upon the skills and interactions of a complex web of individuals whose output determine the quality, reliability and cost of everything we produce irrespective of the technology involved. When things go wrong, there are usually people involved in the situation, it is rarely due to technology and it is people that choose and maintain the technology!

Success in business depends upon being able to use the collective thinking power and job knowledge of all of our people to become and remain the best in our business. How well are we doing on that Driver? Are the competitors doing better than us? How do we know?

Why is it that both Toyota and Honda have policies for 100 per cent membership of Quality Circles, there are claimed to be more than 20 million of such groups in China and proportionally the same in India and throughout the Far East, and yet they are virtually non-existent in the West. Which part of the world is in the ascendant right now? It might have nothing to do with Quality Circles per se but it is the management system which supports them that is important and that just happens to be Hoshin Kanri. Ignore this if you will but your organisation will be the loser.

Suppliers

In most businesses more than 50 per cent of the goods and services that are used are outsourced. A significant proportion of the quality of our produce is therefore predetermined by the capabilities of our suppliers. How well do we manage them? Suppliers are both internal and external, as are customers.

Do our suppliers fully understand our needs and those of our customers? How did we select them? Are they capable of supplying what we want? In most organisations, Supply Chains are complex interactions. In Chapter 12 we will look at this in some detail but clearly an organisation's Supply Chain policy may be critical to success. Organisations which use Hoshin Kanri will agree that we must view our Supply Chain as an extension of our own. If we abdicate responsibility for the design and manufacture of supplied parts and services we will never have control over our destiny. We need to know as much or more about these matters than any supplier no matter how specialised they may be.

Processes

Everything we do is part of a process. Organisations have three levels of process. The Key Business Processes are those which end with the ultimate user and run back through the Supply Chain to the primary materials. Six Sigma advocates refer to this as SIPOC meaning Supplier, Inputs, Processes, Outputs, Customer.

Then there are Support Processes such as training, maintenance, HR, finance, and so on. Encapsulating all of these is the overall business management process. All processes have inputs and outputs. The end user customer received the end result of the sum total of this complex web of interactions. Many of the problems in organisations result from the poorly managed interfaces between each of the activities along a process and the interface between support and Key Business Processes. Process Management is treated in some detail in Chapters 15, 16 and 21.

Organisation

This can be regarded as a process but under this heading organisation is treated as being the business as a whole, as a macro-organisation or the organisation of each individual department if each of these is regarded as a being a business in its own right as micro-organisations.

Later, in Chapter 10, it will be shown how the Plan-Do-Check-Act (PDCA) cycle can be used to manage the interfaces between these separate components.

Technology

This Driver is more concerned with how technology is used than with its capital value. Research indicates that sometimes, the use of the latest technology might not always be as beneficial as it might at first appear. For example, in the 1980s a large British electronics company which produced electronic equipment for the Government and also a range of high-volume domestic products had invested a vast sum of money in the use of very expensive and sophisticated 'pick and place' robots for the assembly of printed circuit boards. Superficially, this appeared impressive but a closer examination showed that for much of the time very few of the robots were actually producing product. They were either being set up or were idle and waiting for work.

On the other hand, in Japan another company was producing similar products entirely by hand, unaided by any automation, at a far higher rate of output and lower fixed and variable costs. The Japanese managers explained that they had studied the possible use of such technology and found it to be unnecessary. It was more economical to produce by hand provided that the right production methods were used and the people properly managed. There is more information on this in Chapter 14.

Finance

Management accounting and cost control have always been regarded as the most important parameters for business management and it cannot be denied that these are crucial to success. However, if these dominate all other Drivers it is likely that the business will fail no matter how well it is managed financially. The financial considerations must be balanced against the needs of all of the other Drivers. The problem however prior to the development of Hoshin Kanri has been the lack of quantifiable non-financial data.

Financial matters can be stated in the form of asset ratios, return on investment, profit per unit of sale and so on. In contrast, before Hoshin Kanri most of the other measures were usually stated in non-tangible form, for example, 'customer satisfaction', 'happy employees' and so on. These measures are important but they are vague and it is impossible to evaluate whether they have been achieved. The vagueness of the non-financial measures cannot compete with the very clear tangible financial Goals with the result that the business Drivers will not be in balance with each other. As will be seen, the attraction of Hoshin Kanri will be to make these intangible measures tangible.

Design and innovation

This Driver is not only concerned with the design and innovation of the products and services themselves but also with the design and innovation of processes, operational methods and everything that might result in giving us an advantage over the competition. The Goal is to harness the creativity of the organisation in every respect and to encourage creativity amongst all employees in all sections of the business. In Toyota for example, from a payroll of 40 000 people they regularly have more than 26 million improvement suggestions per year, of which many are innovative!

DEFINING THE DRIVERS

We have found that the best way to do this is by using an adaptation of the Ishikawa Diagram and the Affinity Diagram blended together. The whole process can be done with the Affinity Diagram method alone but we have found that there is a danger of leaving out some essential ideas. The main difference between the following approach and the Affinity Diagram method in its pure form is that with the latter, we do not predict the group headings (in this case Drivers) in advance, whereas in our method we do. The reason is that at one time we did but invariably they always resulted in the same eight headings coming up. As a consequence we can skip that part of the process. Then by using our eight Drivers as bones on the Ishikawa Diagram we can brainstorm the specific features for each as shown in Figure 4.2

However, we recommend that the Affinity Diagram method of writing each individual idea on small notelets such as 'Post-it' notes is used in preference to open brainstorming. We can also include all of the 'Post-it' notes' that were used for the creation of the Vision Statement.

There is more treatment of the Affinity Diagram method in Chapter 19 on QFD. Our recommended method for the creation of the policies for the eight Drivers is as follows:

This should involve the whole of the top team in the organisation representing the heads of every key function – finance, operations, sales, research and development and so on.

Scoping the Mission – Policy Process

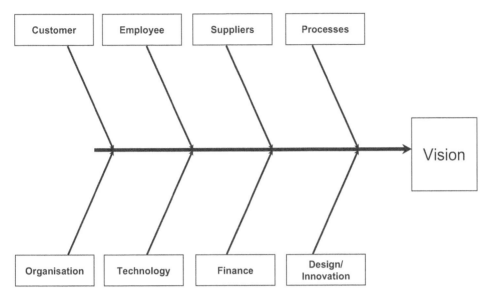

Figure 4.2   Fishbone diagram

Step one – visualisation

Just as with the creation of the Vision Statement, as a group think ahead to the time when you feel that you would realistically like to have achieved the Objectives of the Vision. Something beyond 5 years but less than 10 years would be ideal.

As before, imagine then that a journalist from a world-class business publication was visiting your company (this procedure also works for non-industrial organisations), imagine that they had full security clearance to see everything that they wanted to and to meet everyone they wish. People could say what they wanted to without fear or favour.

Again, imagine the article has been published on the centre spread of the journal. Imagine the headlines, and think about the content of the column inches. Think what you would like to read. Take more than a few moments over this as it is very important.

Step two – identify the species

Now take a few of the 'Post-it'-type stickers and write on each a short sentence describing each of your specific thoughts of what you would like to see written in those column inches. For example – 'high numbers of innovative ideas in design', 'extremely low labour turnover', 'record levels of customer retention', 'voted to be the best company in the city' and so on. Try to come up with approximately 5–10 ideas per person. If there are 10 people present this will mean something like 50–100 ideas, but there will be more later.

Step three – pool the ideas

If the Affinity Diagram was being used in its pure sense, these ideas would then be posted on the wall and clustered into types and reorganised until a clear number of specific groups emerged. We will skip that step by using our predetermined eight headings as shown below:

Figure 4.2 shows the Fishbone Diagram before the 'Post-it' stickers are added.

Each participant will add their suggestions to the appropriate arm. Completion of this step of the diagram will probably look similar to the Figure 4.3. By the time all of the participants have posted their suggestions there will be something like an average of ten stickers per arm. However, do not expect these clusters of stickers to be evenly distributed. Typically there will be some much larger clusters around some and few around others. It may be of course that in some situations, this reflects reality and perhaps some of the Drivers may be more important than others but it may also point to a different reason. Perhaps the participants are not as sensitive about some of the Drivers as they should be.

Interestingly, having facilitated many groups with this work, it is surprising how often there is an almost total lack of sensitivity to the customer Driver as appears in the example above. In fact at the time when we used the pure Affinity Diagram method, there were occasions when none of the stickers were related to this topic. It was then found to be necessary to give the team a lecture on customer needs and customer expectations and also to remind them that the next activity in the processes they were responsible for was in fact their own 'internal customer' before conducting a short brainstorming session just on this one aspect. It was a graphic illustration of the sometimes surprising disregard that some organisations have for this critical issue. It is suggested that should this happen whilst using this book to create their own Hoshin Kanri, then before proceeding further it would be advisable for every participant to read Chapter 11 'Voice of the Customer' before moving onwards and of course brainstorm this again.

Even after we began using the Fishbone Diagram to force the team to think about each Driver, the number of stickers is frequently greater for the functional issues that participants have to deal with on a day-to-day basis. Presumably it reflects the high level of sensitivity that participants have their own functions as opposed to the business as a whole. It is therefore important for the session Facilitator to make sure that this part of the work has been thoroughly completed before moving on. Otherwise there is the Risk that something very important might have been overlooked. It is

Defining the DRIVERS

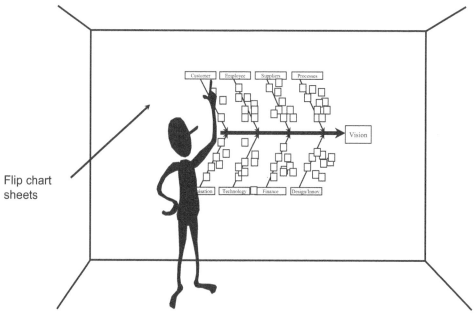

Figure 4.3   Fishbone diagram with 'Post-it' stickers

also recommended that the team review this work at the beginning of their next session which might be the following day. Typically, the mind continues to work over things subconsciously when the conscious mind has moved on. The next day, participants will frequently identify some quite important points that were completely overlooked in the previous session.

Step four – creating the policy for each Driver

Once the stickers have all been placed, the next step will be to try to create a short policy statement for each Driver. An effective way to do this will be to underline the key words on each sticker in a particular cluster.

For example, one sentence on the people Driver may have read, 'To be recognised as a safe company to work for.' The key words here would be 'safe company'. Let us suppose for this example, the other stickers in the people group were:

- high levels of job <u>knowledge</u>;
- maximise the <u>skills</u> of the workforce;
- encourage a high level of <u>creativity</u>;
- be an <u>attractive employer</u> to work for;
- a <u>team-based</u> environment;
- low labour turnover because no one wants to leave;
- be seen as a <u>caring employer</u>.

Notice the words that have been underlined. These will be used to create the policy for that Driver.

After some work and several iterations, the policy statement might read like this:

Our people are the company's most important resource of whom we are proud.

It is our Goal to use a team-based approach to harness the knowledge, creativity and skill of all of our people to make our company the best in our business and be recognised as a caring and attractive employer.

Notice that with the exception of 'low labour turnover' all of the previously underlined words or terms appear in the sentence. The term 'low labour turnover' has been excluded here but it is used later on because it was regarded as a measure of 'caring and attractive employer'. It was thought that if that has been achieved then it would be reflected in 'labour turnover' statistics.

The process of creating policy statements this way would be used for each of the Drivers and so there would be eight in total. However, some organisations split both customer and supplier into 'internal' and 'external' and produce statements for each making ten in total. It is a matter of preference.

There is a lot of hard work in the creation of these statements and they must not be treated lightly. Sometimes, participants can appear to be quite emotional when they have finished this work and think that they have made significant progress. However, this is only the start of the work. Whilst these statements might look impressive, in reality on their own they are quite meaningless. In fact, left at this level they can do considerable damage because they are totally intangible and will mean different things to different people until they are quantified.

The statement printed above sounds wonderful. Frequently we see statements like this in visitor reception areas, on sales brochures and so on. However, when we take a look behind the scenes we may see a quite different story. Reality can be quite different. The statement is just a meaningless set of words to attempt to impress the visitors, mislead quality auditors (which is often regrettably easy) and achieve nothing. In fact it can make the workforce, who know the truth, quite cynical.

A further problem is that even to the team that created the statements, the meaning of the words might be quite different from one individual to the other. It would not be difficult to imagine the following scenario.

Let us suppose that the statement had been created with the assistance of a consultant some 3 or so years earlier. Now he is back for a performance review with the same group that created the statement. It is projected onto the wall and the conversation might well go something like this:

HR Director – 'I think we have done very well. When I think what things were like 3 years ago and how things are now, I think it is marvellous.'

The Operations Director is looking on in amazement – 'You must be joking. I cannot see any improvement at all. Yes, absenteeism has gone down a bit but that could be for several reasons, there is a recession on. No I am very disappointed.'

The Sales Director intervenes looking thoughtful – 'I think that you are being a bit harsh. I believe we have made some progress but I would not go as far as the HR Manager.'

The reason for this discrepancy is simple. Whilst they had all agreed the statement, the picture it created in each of their minds was completely different. So we need to take the process further. There is nothing wrong with the statement. It is good and if it evoked some passion then it did its job. What it lacks is metrics, which is the subject of the next chapter. What for example does 'caring employer' mean? It sounds nice but how will we know if we are or we are not? And what does it mean to us? If we can define some metrics then we can discuss them and hopefully reach a consensus. Then we can measure whether or not we have achieved our collective idea of being a caring employer.

5 Driver Measures to KPIs

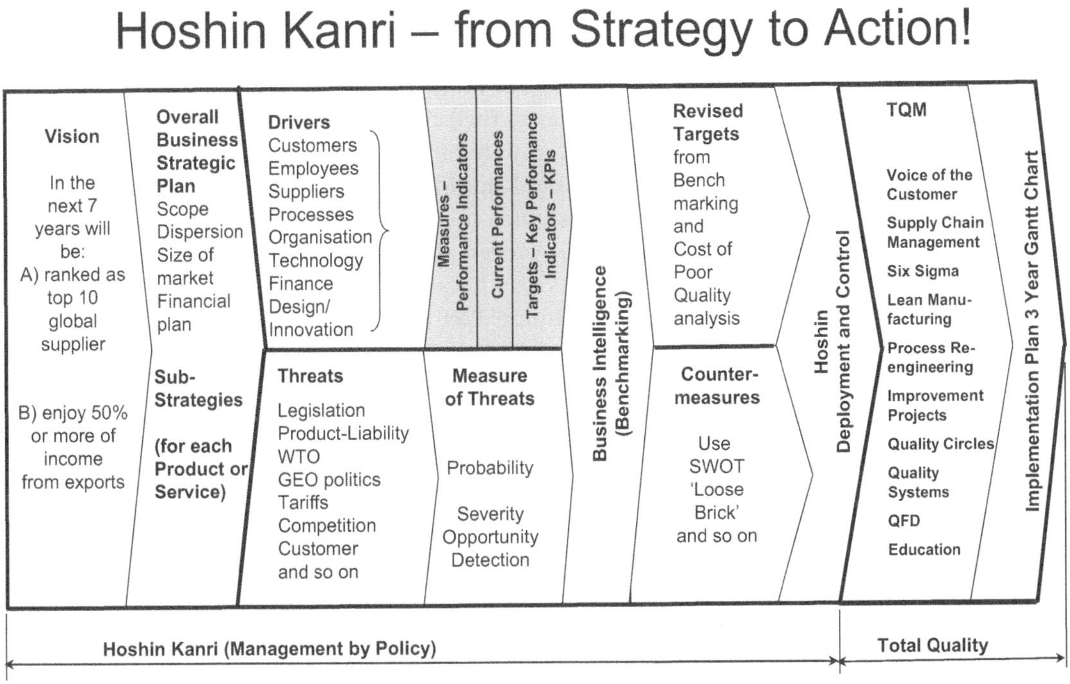

Hoshin Kanri – from Strategy to Action!

Vision	Overall Business Strategic Plan	Drivers	Measures – Performance Indicators	Current Performances	Targets – Key Performance Indicators – KPIs	Business Intelligence (Benchmarking)	Revised Targets	Hoshin Deployment and Control	TQM	Implementation Plan 3 Year Gantt Chart
In the next 7 years will be: A) ranked as top 10 global supplier	Scope Dispersion Size of market Financial plan	Customers Employees Suppliers Processes Organisation Technology Finance Design/ Innovation					from Bench marking and Cost of Poor Quality analysis		Voice of the Customer Supply Chain Management Six Sigma Lean Manu-facturing Process Re-engineering	
B) enjoy 50% or more of income from exports	Sub-Strategies (for each Product or Service)	Threats Legislation Product-Liability WTO GEO politics Tariffs Competition Customer and so on		Measure of Threats Probability Severity Opportunity Detection			Counter-measures Use SWOT 'Loose Brick' and so on		Improvement Projects Quality Circles Quality Systems QFD Education	

Hoshin Kanri (Management by Policy)   Total Quality

Figure 5.1   From Measures to KPIs

In the last chapter we saw how the policy statements for the Drivers could be created. In this chapter we will see how the Key Performance Indicators (KPIs) can be derived from these statements. It is also worth noting at this point that this method of identifying the KPIs ensures that they link directly to the Vision. This is important.

Today, there are many organisations that use KPIs but they do not link to anything. This is particularly true for Governmental organisations such as Health Care Trusts, the Ambulance Service and so on. The consequence is that because they are imposed rather than created from within, there is no sense of ownership and no passion to achieve. For this reason, many will attempt to find ways to fiddle the statistics rather than attempt to improve performance.

One example might be the pressure to reduce hospital waiting times. Faced with an externally-set KPI of this type and not having the means to achieve it, there are stories of some hospitals taking patients off one list and putting them on another to give the impression that they have halved waiting times. Of course, they have improved the apparent statistics but the patient is no better off.

Another example of the hazards of this sort of KPI is the Government-imposed requirement that over 70 per cent of emergency calls require the paramedics to be at the scene of the emergency in less than 9 minutes. We are not criticising the need for rapid response, it is nice to know that if we were the victims of an accident trained help would be there sufficiently quickly. The danger is, though, that in order to achieve the statistics it is possible that an ambulance might travel at unnecessary high speeds and kill a bystander in the process.

Unfortunately, many organisations which have large numbers of externally set KPIs such as those in public service become preoccupied with attempting to achieve or fiddle these rather than create their own. If the organisation is to be successful it should have both externally-set and internally-created KPIs because without the internal ones there is no value in the Vision. There will be no sense of achievement and it can lead to some quite cynical reactions.

In this chapter we will show how specific prioritised KPIs can be derived directly from the Driver policy statements explained in the previous chapter. If there are external KPIs these must be added to the list after this process has been completed. Of course some of them may be replicated but this is not a problem.

Before moving on, we must mention KPIs which have been obtained from websites or from industry-based consultants. Some of them might be of value but there is no way of knowing without going through the process recommended here as to their relative importance to our organisation. However, it can be useful to check such lists but only after the exercise of creating your own in order to ensure that we have not overlooked anything. Later in this book in the chapters which cover each of the Drivers, there are checklists of sorts which might be helpful for this purpose but again, do not look at them until you have worked the process through with your own uncontaminated thoughts.

To identify the possible metrics to determine Performance Measures, we might use the brainstorming technique again, but this time in its freeform approach. Each member of the team, taking turns, can make suggestions as to the possible metrics that determine the specific measures for each of the key words, underlined on page 40, for each Driver. For example, in the previous chapter when the policy statements were created, the statement for the Employee Policy may have included the key words 'caring employer'. The question then arises, what might be the criteria for determining whether or not we are a 'caring employer'? The results of a mini brainstorm on this topic might produce the following ideas:

- low level (we prefer zero of course) of lost-time accidents;
- absenteeism;
- sickness (sometimes people are only sick of coming to work);
- increase in job applicants as the local market learns the reputation of the company;
- number of day release students on courses;
- articles in the local press;
- applications from graduates – the word is reaching universities and enabling us to cream off the best;
- and so on.

The team can then discuss each of these and decide which they consider to be the most important as measures for each Performance Indicator (notice that at this stage we use the term Performance Indicator not KPI, there is more work to be done before we reach that point.

Figure 5.2 shows the steps from Vision through Strategic Planning, creation of the Drivers, to the relevant Measures of Performance.

Figure 5.3 now provides a road map of how to progress from Driver through to the KPIs. Notice that the key words that were underlined to assist in the creation of the policy statement can now be used in Tree Diagram form as Performance Indicators to assist in defining the measures in the

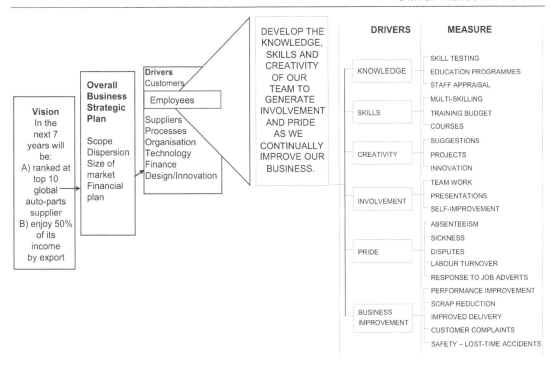

Figure 5.2   A road map of how to progress from the Driver through to the KPIs

Identifying <u>Key</u> Performance Indicators (KPIs)

DRIVERS	Performance Indicator	MEASURE	CURRENT SITUATION	BENCHMARK SOURCE	Gap – Current Benchmark	KPI
DEVELOP THE KNOWLEDGE, SKILLS AND CREATIVITY OF OUR TEAM TO GENERATE INVOLVEMENT AND PRIDE AS WE CONTINUALLY IMPROVE OUR BUSINESS.	KNOWLEDGE	SKILL TESTING		WORLD-CLASS ORGS		
		EDUCATION PROGRAMMES		UNIVERSITIES		
		STAFF APPRAISAL		CHAMB. TRADE		
	SKILLS	MULTI-SKILLING		WORLD-CLASS ORGS		
		TRAINING BUDGET		WORLD-CLASS ORGS		
		COURSES		COLLEGES		
	CREATIVITY	SUGGESTIONS		CHAMB. TRADE		
		PROJECTS		WORLD-CLASS ORGS		
		INNOVATION		PROF. INST.		
	INVOLVEMENT	TEAM WORK		LIBRARY		
		PRESENTATIONS		CONSULTANTS		
		SELF-IMPROVEMENT		INTERNET	PRIORITISE	
	PRIDE	ABSENTEEISM		CHAMB. TRADE		
		SICKNESS		CHAMB. TRADE		
		DISPUTES		LOCAL COMPANIES		
		LABOUR TURNOVER		LOCAL COMPANIES		
		RESPONSE TO JOB ADVERTS		WORLD-CLASS ORGS		
	BUSINESS IMPROVEMENT	PERFORMANCE IMPROVEMENT		WORLD-CLASS ORGS		
		SCRAP REDUCTION		WORLD-CLASS ORGS		
		IMPROVED DELIVERY		WORLD-CLASS ORGS		
		CUSTOMER COMPLAINTS		TRADE ASSOCIATIONS		
		SAFETY – LOST-TIME ACCIDENTS		WORLD-CLASS ORGS AND ROSPA, ETC		

Figure 5.3   Identifying the KPIs

column to the right. These measures do not have any Values at this point. In a sense they are the 'means of measure'. In the next column the Current Situation for that measure is stated where it is known. In a large number of cases it will not be known or it may not have been calculated.

If the data is available it will be a task for one of the team to locate it and bring it to the next meeting. For example, let us suppose that one of the measures is 'mean time between lost-time accidents'. We may have the base data but perhaps not in this form. From the accident record book, the requirement can be calculated from the records. Let us suppose that it is 850 000 man-hours between lost-time accidents. This will be recorded in Current Situation.

At this point we know the current situation but unless we have prior information we do not know whether this level is good or bad. Nor do we know what the top companies are achieving, so we have to find out. This involves the technique of Benchmarking and is covered in Chapter 6. Sometimes Benchmarking is easy and may simply involve picking up the phone and asking. At the other extreme it might involve a great deal of planning and foreign visits. If the planning is poor then the Benchmarking might end up being little more than industrial tourism.

In our example, we may have discovered that the best world-class companies are achieving somewhere in the order of 7 million man-hours between lost-time accidents. Immediately, this makes our 850 000 appear very poor and clearly, if we need to close the gap then considerable work will need to be done. Also, it likely to take some time to reach that level, possibly several years in some cases.

We have just considered one single performance measure, but in our illustration there are 22. For all eight Drivers there are therefore likely to be in the order of 170–200. In fact it is not unusual to find somewhere in the order of 400 measures at this point. If all of these were of the same level of importance and the differences between the current situation and world class were as large as indicated in our accident example, we would have a hopeless lack of resource for dealing with them. Fortunately, they will not all be of equal importance and the gaps will not all be as in our example. In fact in some cases we may already be world class or even world leaders. This will effectively reduce the work but there will still be a long list so it will be necessary to prioritise.

If the 400 measures seems overwhelming, then it may seem surprising that many organisations (frequently but by no means always Governmental) that have been forced to use KPIs have more than 1000. Without the linking and prioritised processes of Hoshin Kanri and without any means of prioritising against a Vision, such a list would be hopelessly beyond the resources of any organisation to achieve. As a consequence some of them may randomly be addressed but most will not.

There are at least two filters that can be used for prioritisation. Firstly, we should rank the indicators in order of importance against their impact on the achievement of the Vision. This ranking is likely to be subjective and a simple technique can be used which we call the Selection Matrix, as shown in the Figure 5.4.

By numbering each of the Performance Indicators this technique enables them to be subjectively ranked in their perceived order of importance. It is a good aid to decision making but of course it is not foolproof, neither is the result to be regarded as a permanent feature. If there are changes in the marketplace then the priorities should be re-evaluated, but at least we now know what the important issues are and it enables us to change direction very rapidly when necessary.

A further way of organising the KPIs is to segregate them according to their relevance to some important criteria. Some organisations use the following approach:

- *Category 1.* Includes those KPIs that clearly directly impact on customer loyalty and if not achieved will have a negative impact on the achievement of our Vision. This can include response to product support needs, warranty costs, competitor analysis and so on.

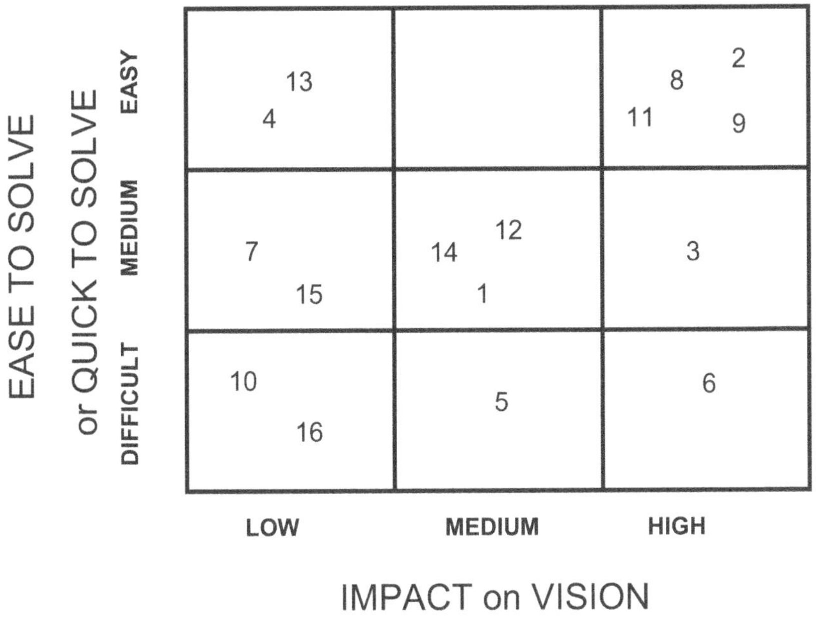

Figure 5.4   Selection Matrix

- *Category 2.* Includes those KPIs where we need to be as good as or better than other businesses in our field, in order to achieve our Vision. For example, a bank would select such features as 'average service time at the counter', 'average number of people waiting to be served', 'APRs', 'bank charges' and so on.
- *Category 3.* Includes those KPIs where we need to be as good as or better than anyone irrespective of industry if we are to achieve our Vision. Such features would be non-industry specific, for example, the time it takes to answer a telephone, missed calls, personnel policy, management accounting, debt recovery, time period of accounts payable and receivable and so on.
- *Category 4.* Includes those KPIs where we need to be the best in our locality if we are to achieve our Vision. These would include issues that are non-industry specific and relevant mainly to businesses in the locality. These might include staff turnover, absenteeism, lateness, the number of job applications, safety record and anything that we could use as a positive discriminator and encourage the best of the local population to seek employment in our company.

SUMMARY

It will be realised by now that there is a great deal of work to be done in the initial stages. Hoshin Kanri cannot be achieved overnight. It is an iterative process which can be continuously developed over many years. Do not attempt to do everything at once. Make a plan for the first year as a pilot programme. Therefore use the Selection Matrix as a means of picking the low hanging fruit – those KPIs which are relatively easy to tackle, do not require huge resources and which will make a difference when solved.

The important thing is to prove that success is achievable. Do not be put off by the fact that there are literally hundreds of issues and that it will take a huge amount of effort to deal with them. Rome was not built in a day and remember, your organisation has survived thus far without Hoshin

Kanri and with all the problems we have just uncovered, so unless it is currently already under severe competitive pressure it will no doubt survive a little longer.

What we are achieving with Hoshin Kanri is to increase the rate of performance improvement and hopefully on a steeper curve than our competitors. The more problems we solve and the more gaps we close between actual performance and target performance, the better our share of market (provided that we select the right issues to tackle) and the lower our costs.

Remember the example of the steel plant in Chapter 3. They were told that if they seriously applied Hoshin Kanri, even though they were at that time quite low in terms of international rankings in their industry, it would not be more than 2 to 3 years before they would be accused of unfair trading and dumping in international markets. They did not believe this at the beginning but it happened. Since then they have consistently won their national Quality Award, which is based on the European Quality Award criteria, several years in a row.

It is our opinion that there is no company and no country in the world that cannot achieve world-class status if it uses the principles of Hoshin Kanri to the full.

6   *Benchmarking*

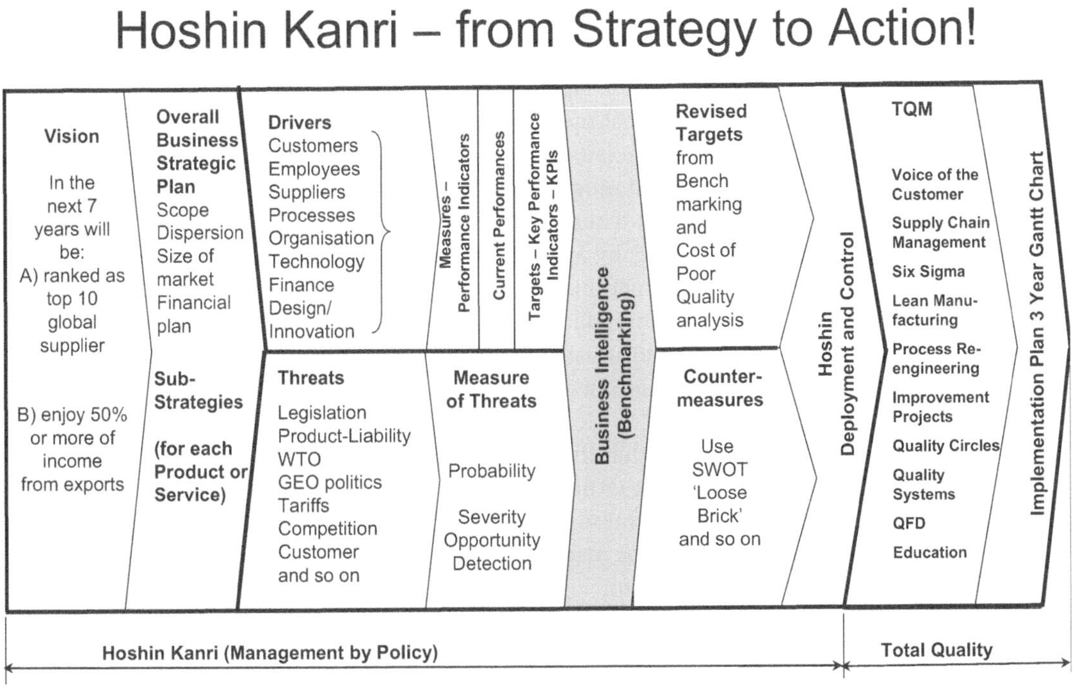

Hoshin Kanri – from Strategy to Action!

Vision	Overall Business Strategic Plan	Drivers	Measures – Performance Indicators	Current Performances	Targets – Key Performance Indicators – KPIs	Business Intelligence (Benchmarking)	Revised Targets	Hoshin Deployment and Control	TQM	Implementation Plan 3 Year Gantt Chart
In the next 7 years will be: A) ranked as top 10 global supplier	Scope Dispersion Size of market Financial plan	Customers Employees Suppliers Processes Organisation Technology Finance Design/ Innovation					from Bench marking and Cost of Poor Quality analysis		Voice of the Customer Supply Chain Management Six Sigma Lean Manu-facturing Process Re-engineering	
B) enjoy 50% or more of income from exports	Sub-Strategies (for each Product or Service)	Threats Legislation Product-Liability WTO GEO politics Tariffs Competition Customer and so on		Measure of Threats Probability Severity Opportunity Detection			Counter-measures Use SWOT 'Loose Brick' and so on		Improvement Projects Quality Circles Quality Systems QFD Education	

←――――――― Hoshin Kanri (Management by Policy) ―――――――→ ←――― Total Quality ―――→

Figure 6.1   Benchmarking

The term Benchmarking originates from ground survey work where the relative heights of land or other features are 'benchmarked' against some reference. In this case the 'benchmark' feature is usually the highest hill or mountain in the vicinity. Strictly speaking Business Intelligence might be a more appropriate term in the sense that it is more like Military Intelligence than surveying and we are looking for many more features than simply highs and lows. Seeing who is on the high ground is just one of the Objectives of Benchmarking. Neither is the term Benchmarking the original term. For example, in the 1950s and 1960s the now Chartered Institute of Management sold a product entitled Interfirm Comparisons. This was essentially a Benchmarking service.

In the 18th Century, innovator Abraham Derby blocked the keyholes in his workshop whilst he was developing the technique for casting wide-bellied pots. Apparently competition was so severe that this was necessary to prevent spying! Benchmarking of sorts clearly existed all that time ago.

Much of what the Japanese learned was gifted to them by the Americans in the immediate years following World War II as part of the Martial Aid Plan. In one reference, senior managers from Toyota admitted that the Ford Motor Company had shown them everything they wanted to see. They commented that what they saw was vastly superior to Toyota's own manufacturing methods but they could see how they could improve even on the Ford methodology. In another reference which was broadcast some years ago in the BBC 2 series 'Nippon', the former head of the Japanese ship-building industry explained that after they had introduced the modular system of construction for the production of large oil tankers, he wanted to study the methods used by the shipbuilders in the UK. He claimed that when he arrived in the UK he was barred from entering the yards. So, to obtain the information he required, he used his camera and pair of binoculars and studied the yards from the outside. He said that from what he saw, the British workers were working well but the methods he saw were outdated and inferior to those currently used in Japan.

At that time the UK had over 50 per cent of the world market in commercial ship production but it was his opinion that by the 1960s Japan would be the world's leading producer. Interestingly, the development of the modular construction system for shipbuilding which the Japanese developed came as a result of a now popular Benchmarking concept of studying parallel industries. In this case, following World War II, the head of Japanese aircraft construction was appointed head of shipbuilding. In those days, the traditional method of building ships was to lay the keel and then build the ship from the bottom up. Aircraft construction was different; in this case, a modular construction method was used. Large but movable sections were constructed individually and then welded or bolted together. This method required greater accuracy in the manufacture of the units but overall it reduced construction times by a factor of ten. The same improvement resulted when the method was applied to ship construction. As a consequence, in less than 10 years Japan had replaced the UK as the world's leading shipbuilder, a situation from which the British industry never recovered, even when it began to adopt the same methods many years later. This is a classic case of Benchmarking one industry to benefit another.

Effective Benchmarking is essential to Hoshin Kanri and the principles should be thoroughly understood in order both to make sure that the Strategy remains sound and that the KPIs are valid. In the commercial or industrial world the term is used to describe activities which are aimed to make comparisons against 'best' or 'better' business practices, not just in your own industry but across all industries where valid comparisons can be made.

Benchmarking is essential to be able to:

- develop a good Strategy;
- prioritise PIs to create and prioritise KPIs;
- ensure that the organisation is not vulnerable to a 'Loose Brick' attack;
- enable a Loose Brick attack on competitors;
- keep up to date on the latest practices regardless of industry;
- ensure the use of the best methods;
- watch out for extraneous Threats from legislation, international developments and so on.

It is a widely held but mistaken belief that Benchmarking can be applied only to our competitors. In fact, there is much more useful information that we can obtain from non-competitors for a variety of reasons, the main one being that most Business Processes are not industry specific. For example, the personnel selection process, management and financial accounting, training, quality management and so on are common to most industries. This is useful for two reasons. Firstly, it is much easier to obtain information from a non-competitor than it is from an organisation which is our sworn rival. In this latter case espionage might be the only means but that can lead to big problems, as McLaren discovered in their Formula 1 rivalry with Ferrari. The second and more important reason is that whilst people in the same industry tend to do the same things the same way, it is possible hat people in different industries may do the same things but in very different ways, for example, he case of Japanese shipbuilding methods versus those used to construct aircraft. The reason is that a lot of information circulates in one industry by people moving from one competitor to another, trade magazines pass on information and so on. However there is likely to be far less cross over from one industry to another. There is more discussion of this aspect later in the chapter.

When properly applied, Benchmarking may be conducted in some principal categories. These are known to us as the seven point benchmark plan.

1. customer surveys;
2. competitor analysis;
3. best in class Business Processes;
4. best in class technological processes;
5. best in class task performance;
6. internal cultural surveys;
7. financial performance;
8. 'green' teams.

Customer surveys

The objective here is to determine customer attitudes towards our organisation *relative* to the competitors. It is worth noting here that we might get some surprises. For example, it is possible that we may be concerned that our competitor is better than us on some features of the product or service but we may discover from a customer survey that these features are not perceived to be important to our customer. In this case, we might not waste our scarce resources trying to catch up, the Loose Brick approach would be to let them continue to waste their money.

Another possibility is that there may be other features where we know that we are as good as or even better than our competitor but our customers' 'perception' is otherwise. Such was the case with our Steel Corporation. In this example, the plant is located on a high plain in a desert region of the Middle East. The air is extremely dry for almost all of the year. Their cold-rolled product was sent directly on the back of an open truck to their main customer, an automotive manufacturer. There was no need to wrap the product to protect it against corrosion in such a dry atmosphere. However, it was the customer's perception that the reels of steel were inferior to foreign imports. We investigated this and found that there was no discernible difference so why the perception? Eventually, the reason became clear. The foreign products were transported by ship across oceans. In order to protect them from the salty atmosphere, they were packaged in oily paper. This gave the impression that the foreign producers took more care by wrapping them hence the different perception.

It is always a good thing to check out the validity of perceptions otherwise we might attempt to improve something that is good enough anyway. The challenge will be to try and change the perception.

Key factors therefore include perceptions related to the relative qualities of:

- deliverables – quality, Price, delivery;
- support service;
- attitudes;
- corporate image.

Buyers'/sellers' market

In the decades leading up to the late 1970s there has existed a predominantly sellers' market for most products and services. In this situation, most suppliers could sell everything they could make even if it was shoddily produced. The seller had an advantage over the customer which was mostly exploited in every way. The same applies in countries where products and services are nationalised Because there is only one source of supply there is no pressure on the supplier to respond to customer needs.

Neither is there any pressure on them to produce quality goods and services in their protected market. The consequence is that their approach to customer needs is grossly underdeveloped.

However, they had better watch out because it is more than likely that the customer will be well aware of the difference. As soon as the country attempts to join the World Trade Organisation and it is forced to reduce tariff barriers, the public will buy the foreign products for no other reason than to show their anger at their former treatment even despite the local suppliers having improved their products and Prices.

However, in the Western world, this market situation began to change rapidly in the 1970s. This was mainly due initially to the emergence of high-quality low-cost Japanese products. As their penetration of the markets increased, saturation occurred in many industries and they swung from a sellers' market to a buyers' market. Very few Western competitors were prepared for this and still continued to behave as if they could dictate what the customer could have and what they could not. They failed to realise that in a buyers' market, it is the customer who decides who will survive and who will not. A significant number of them went down without ever realising that they were at fault, not the Japanese or anyone else. They behaved like dinosaurs and paid the Price.

Even today with so much evidence of this, still businesses continue to behave as if they have a right to survive and a right to the local market. Experience indicates that national loyalty to local products is non-existent when the foreign product is better and cheaper, wherever it is manufactured.

With the emergence of both China and India on the world scene it is unlikely that a sellers' market will ever return.

If any reader is surprised that Chinese products are mentioned here, then they would be advised to begin Benchmarking them now. We do not yet see Chinese cars in the UK but it will not be long before we do. It is most probable that they have learned from the Japanese the technique of the Loose Brick – see Chapter 9 on this topic. In 2007 whilst this book was being written, the author was working in Alexandria in Egypt. There are two Chinese cars on sale, a 1.6 ltr and a 2.0 ltr model. They are very stylish and have every electronic feature that can be found on a top of the range Mercedes and their cost is only middle of the range for a family saloon car.

It will not be so long before Chinese cars begin to appear in bulk in all Western countries and when this happens Benchmarking may be too late.

The key questions to ask right now are:

*   What does the market think of us?
*   How can we find out?
*   How does a scientific market study compare with our own perceptions?

The study should include not only our loyal customers but where possible those who go to the competition.

Competitor analysis

Much of this can be obtained from a well-designed customer study and from Customer Focus group activities. However, there are many items related to the competition which cannot be determined from this type of study. In addition we will want to determine competitor strengths and weaknesses in terms of business results and from the remaining five points in the Benchmarking plan.

This is an area where Japanese competitors are particularly thorough and refer to the analysis as 'looking for the loose brick'. Here they are attempting to discover an exploitable weakness through which they may gain a market advantage. Where they discover some strengths they will put plans into action to reduce the importance of the advantage.

Competitor analysis is often referred to as 'industrial espionage' but this usually refers to technical secrets. Of course, this is important but it is likely that more businesses fail due to the adoption of inferior business strategies than to inferior product features.

There are many methods available to Benchmark competitors products. These include purchasing them and stripping them down to attempt to find the production methods, how long they take to assemble and what simplification methods have been used through Value Engineering. Employ ex-employees and read articles about the products in the technical press. Magazines such as *Jane's Fighting Ships* contain a huge quantity of this type of useful information.

Best in class business processes

The CEO of Hewlett Packard, Mr John Young, once said, 'We used to compete in units of product, now we compete in units of time.' Product development times have reduced in the case of automobiles from 5 years to 22 months and even less: the time period is dropping all the time. There are many other examples. These improvements are not made through any form of exhortation cascade but by seriously challenging the ways of the past.

Fortunately, in this aspect of Benchmarking we do not need to use any form of subterfuge to prize secrets from our competitors since most Business Processes are common to competitors and non-competitors alike, for example Just In Time or stockless production principles. To obtain information on these aspects, the same sources as for competitor analysis can be interrogated.

Best in class technological processes

This is probably the easiest form of Benchmarking and is familiar to most people. Here we are generally talking about 'off the shelf' technology and information about this is usually obtained from magazines and advertisements. Of course, there are cases where companies seek to obtain a competitive advantage through development of their own technology but this is relatively rare and becoming more so as the capital required for such forms of research and development becomes more scarce.

Manufacturers of plant and equipment are often useful sources of information about the competition. They will often divulge such information in order to get sales from us. Of course they will do the same in reverse so we need to be careful.

Best in class task performance

Under this heading the organisation must identify specific business activities which may affect overall performance and these will vary from business to business, sometimes even in the same industry.

For example, in a company engaged in the manufacture of plastic containers the process may be such that a particular injection moulding machine may prove to be a bottleneck. In this case, 'set-up' or 'change over' time on the specific machine may have a significant effect on work-in-progress, delivery times and so on.

For such activities, it would be important to discover what is the best achievable. The same may apply to the credit control operation. Perhaps the debtor-creditor ratios may be unsatisfactory due to late invoicing. In this case the financial control department may be Benchmarked.

Internal cultural surveys

No organisation can successfully compete if it suffers bad relationships and low morale internally. The winners will be those who are best able to galvanise the resources of all of their people to work towards making their organisation the best in its field. This cannot be achieved with strategies based upon Threats and fear, secrecy, blame and destructive internal competition, ego projection or macho-style management. Always the winners will be those who recognise the fact that work itself can be intrinsically satisfying and recognition, and the opportunity for continuous development, are major Drivers in human performance.

The key questions are:

- How are we compared to others?
- Who is the best?
- How do they do it?

Again, this is a relatively easy feature to Benchmark because we are not concerned only with our direct competitors. There will almost always be many non-competitor organisations with similarities to our own against which comparisons can be made.

Financial performance

This is probably the best developed area of all which has been conducted by most businesses irrespective of the state of the market. Here the indices can be obtained from such data sources as Dunn & Bradstreet, *Financial Times* and so on.

Green teams

There are many other names for this activity. Basically a Green Team comprises several people who are not employees but who are involved in the business of the company. They may be buyers, users, environmentalists and a range of others depending upon the product and who will have an informed opinion about this company, its competitors and the market generally. Typically they will be invited to visit the company for a few days. They will be well looked after in the best local hotels and they may be escorted on some sightseeing activities during the visit. They are likely to be shown the latest innovations before they are fully developed, they will solicit opinions about these and also attempt to get whatever knowledge they can about their rivals. They will also be looking for trends in the marketplace and any other useful information they can get from the team. In some cases, they may be loaned prototypes of development projects in exchange for feedback information and comparative assessments.

WHAT TO DO NEXT

It can be seen from the above that Benchmarking represents a major business activity which if conducted seriously will produce an overwhelming quantity of data.

Not all of this data will be equally important and it would be impossible to react to everything simultaneously. Analysis, however, will indicate those features which demand immediate action and the Pareto 80/20 principle can be used to aid their identification.

Key features identified in this way may result in project-by-project improvement activities, educational programmes or assignment of specific responsibilities. All of these can be absorbed into a properly designed Total Quality Strategy which operates from the boardroom to the shop floor.

Directors in leading Japanese companies such as Komatsu spend around 6 months of the year in the development and implementation of business strategies based upon this type of information. Unless the West gears itself up to do the same it will never be able to counter this form of competition.

SUMMARY OF THE STEPS FOR SUCCESSFUL BENCHMARKING IN HOSHIN KANRI

Benchmarking is most effective when it is included as an integral part of Hoshin Kanri and involves 12 clearly defined steps.

1. Articulation of the Vision.
    This involves the identification of the desired scope of the organisation, its purpose and general reason to be.
2. Creation of the Mission Statement.
    This is an elaboration of the Vision and also includes a statement of the Values of the organisation.
3. Construction of the Business Strategic Plan.
    This sets out the key market objectives for each product or service offered based on core competencies and includes growth Objectives and the long-range financial plan.
4. Identification of the Drivers.
    These include the identification of the policy with regard to all of the means to achieve the Goals of the Strategic Business Plan.
    For example: employees, customers, suppliers, processes, organisation, technology, finance, design/innovation.
    Clearly-stated policies should be formulated for each of these as to how they are expected to contribute to the achievement of the Plan.
5. Selection of the most appropriate measures by which achievement of the policy with regard to the Drivers is judged.
    For each Driver, specific measures must be determined in order to be able to assess performance against requirement. For example, it may be a stated policy element that employees should be 'highly trained and motivated'. To achieve motivation, a policy of care must be evident. One of the measures for care might be 'number of man-hours between lost-time accidents'. Measures of motivation might include such metrics as: absenteeism, sick leave, stoppages and so on. Another employee policy may be skill. This may be achieved through multi-skilling based on a Training Needs Analysis. Each of these measures is likely to lead almost directly to the need to Benchmark because Targets will require objective data if they are to be both relevant and realistic.
6. Determination of Current Performance.
    For each measure it is necessary to identify Targets but first of all it is necessary to determine what is the Current Performance for the feature in question. For example, supposing in the case of 'lost-time accidents' Current Performance is found to be 120 000 man-hours.
7. Benchmark to determine the Targets.
    The question then arises, 'Is this Current Performance good, bad or indifferent?' It may be that the statistics are not available. The only way in which to find the answer is to Benchmark against others in relevant situations.
    This may include organisations in similar industries, but it will also include parallel industries. It is now recognised by some that whilst organisations in the same industry tend to do the *same* things the *same* way, people in other industries often perform *similar* activities by *different* means. This is because methods that are established in one company very soon appear in others in the same industry because employees move around and take their knowledge and experience with them. Suppliers are often suppliers to competitors and again there is leakage, then there are the trade magazines, salesmen who see things and pass them on and so on.

On the other hand, whilst other industries have similar needs, they may find different methods which become perpetuated in those industries for the same reason. Therefore when cross-industry Benchmarking is carried out, many new ideas may emerge.

8. This is the Benchmarking activity itself.

Many of the Targets may be Benchmarked on the same Benchmarking assignment. On one occasion in a session conducted by the author using this model a participant exploded saying, 'We went to Nissan at Washington, County Durham last week. It was very interesting and a good day out but we did not learn very much. If we had done this type of preparation beforehand there would have been very many more questions we would have asked.'

9. Setting Revised Targets.

Prior to the Benchmarking activity itself, it may be necessary to set some arbitrary Targets for some measures. In such cases these are likely to be reviewed and reset in the light of Benchmarking results.

10. Identifying possible Disablers.

So far we have discussed the route taken to determine what to Benchmark with regard to the Drivers or Enablers. Now we should look at how to deal with potential Disablers. It was possibly the lack of appreciation of this that caused the Wallace Corporation in the USA to fail. The company won the USA National Quality Award and went down only a few months later. The USA Award places great emphasis on the importance of Benchmarking so the question arises, 'How could this have happened?'

In all probability, the company did everything right when it was focused on what to improve. However, it almost certainly had a blind spot when it came to the question of locating and responding to potential Threats to the business. These Threats can come from several sources and are largely probabilistic.

11. Measuring the likelihood of the threat or measures of Threats.

The Threats may include such items as: unexpected competitor Strategy, new competitor with product using completely different technology (for example, the wood and plastic slide rule was eclipsed by the electronic calculator), labour unrest, Government legislation and changes to interest rates and so on. In all cases Benchmarking should be used to track these and others in order to ensure that there are no unwelcome surprises. The Philips example was a case in point. The probability of these Threats being realised is of course probabilistic and may range from a certainty in some cases to very unlikely in others. There is also the question of the severity of the threat with regard to its potential effect should it eventually materialise. There may be some Threats which, whilst of low probability, could, if they materialise, have catastrophic consequences. It may therefore be prudent to determine a counter Strategy just in case.

12. Establishment of Countermeasures.

Not only should an organisation attempt to discover its own potential Threats, it is important to attempt to discover the potential 'Loose Bricks' of its competitors, as in the example of the TV industry, SWOT Analysis (Strengths, Weaknesses, Opportunities and Threats) can be used to identify possible counter-strategies to perceived competitor strengths and of course perceived competitor weaknesses may present opportunities to improve a market position.

DEALING WITH THE RESULTS OF BENCHMARKING – DEPLOYMENT OF THE ACTIONS

Setting up effective organisations for Benchmarking may be a daunting task and by its very nature will occupy the time of some of the most important people in the business. If this is not bad enough, then taking action on the findings certainly will be. Some of the changes believed to be necessary resulting from the findings of some Benchmarking assignments will have major implications for the whole organisation. A Benchmarking visit to such organisations as Bombardier Short Bros. Ltd in Belfast could lead to major changes in many observers' organisations, particularly if the visit included the presence of an open-minded chief executive.

However, a word of caution. Many visitors have witnessed the dramatic improvements made in companies such as Short Bros., Mobarakeh Steel, Wedgwood and so on. Interestingly the experience has often had a negative effect. The improvements that they have seen has made them think that they could never reach this level and instead of being inspired, they give up! There are comments such as, 'Well of course they are in a different industry from us. It might work there but not in our business, it is a different culture.' Alternatively, 'Well they must have been good to start with, our people can never do that.' All of this is nonsense. Every organisation can do it if the will is there. Sometimes one suspects that they do not do it because they are too lazy or too complacent. Dr Juran was once asked at a conference in London, 'Why is it that I have shown our management the Cost of Poor Quality (COPQ) which is something in the order of 30 per cent sales revenue and also what we can do to reduce it. but they will not listen. What do you suggest?' Dr Juran replied, 'Pray that things get worse!'

Short Bros. performance improvement achievements since they began their intensive study of best practices have resulted in some remarkable developments. The man-hours to produce a pair of wings for a major international aircraft was cut in one year from 72 000 to 44 000, in the next year to 24 000 and the following year to 19 000! This resulted from the achievements of some 300 or more project teams.

In other cases, the result may reveal the need to make radical changes to a whole series of major processes in the organisation. Such was the case with Kodak when it discovered that its rival, Fuji, could completely redesign and introduce a product successfully into the marketplace inside 10 weeks when at that time it took Kodak as long as 2 years to achieve the same. Fortunately for Kodak they had the commitment to make the very revolutionary changes that were proved necessary.

In another case a Benchmarking visit to Toyota by a hearing aid manufacturer resulted in the reduction of set-up times from over 8 hours to less than 2 minutes. The effect on work-in-progress and the freeing up of floor space was stunning.

Some of the actions which are deemed necessary in the light of Benchmarking data may be carried out by upper management. However, the vast majority in terms of number, if not value, can only be dealt with effectively through the involvement of the entire payroll. This will probably become evident if the right organisations are Benchmarked anyway. Such a programme will be no mean achievement and the success rate is not encouraging. Therefore, questions to those who are successful in this respect may be more important than any other. It seems logical that there is little point in observing best practices if they cannot be either repeated or preferably surpassed.

7 Prioritising KPIs and Cost of Poor Quality

Hoshin Kanri – from Strategy to Action!

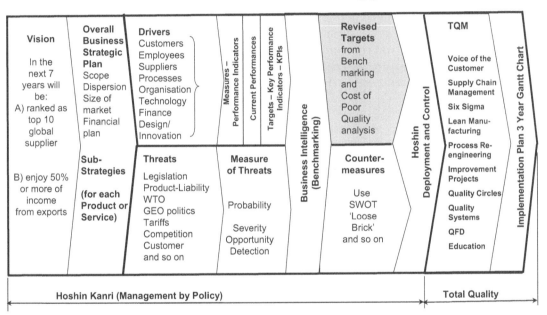

Figure 7.1   Prioritising the KPIs

PRIORITISING KPIs

In Chapter 5, it was shown that the total number of Performance Indicators can be huge and sometimes runs into several hundreds. This can be quite discouraging but the problem is not difficult to deal with. Initially the simple Selection Matrix can be used as a subjective tool to quickly prioritise what are thought to be the most important Performance Indicators. This will enable the development of Hoshin Kanri and get the process working but it is a subjective method and is inferior to the use of factual data. However, once the programme has started and Benchmarking has produced more information it will become possible to refine this important stage and use more objective data to prioritise the Performance Indicators and convert to KPIs.

The most important Performance Indicators which will become KPIs are those that have the biggest impact on the achievement of the Vision. The Benchmarking process should be a continual activity and if it covers the broad spectrum suggested in the last chapter, the importance of some KPIs will be constantly changing as market forces determine.

Obviously this book cannot predict what these will be and it will be the responsibility of those who are driving Hoshin Kanri in the organisation to analyse the data and make the decisions. What is likely to be somewhat more constant are the internal problems that result in poor process performance. In this chapter these problems will be referred to as Quality-Related Costs. In this sense the word Quality is the big 'Q' meaning the quality of business performance and not the small 'q' meaning product quality. The focus will be on those important Performance Indicators resulting from unnecessary Quality-Related Costs. Most people are unaware of the very high cost of this problem. This lack of awareness is due to the fact that most of the important Quality-Related Costs are buried in the processes and thought to be part of the process.

As a consequence, most managers have become used to them and accept them as a fate. However, once we start to attempt to isolate them, they become more obvious and managers are shocked not only by the scale of the problem which is likely to be in the order of 30 per cent sales revenue! If they had appreciated this fact and known how to deal with them, they might have tackled them a long time ago. When they are isolated and listed, they can be many and varied.

Once identified, they can be prioritised using the Pareto Principle. This states that where large numbers of items are to be ranked against some common criteria, for example, cost, approximately 80 per cent of the impact will come from just 20 per cent of the items. The converse is also true. Only 20 per cent of the impact will come from the remaining 80 per cent. Dr Juran refers to this as the important few and useful many. The task therefore will be to identify these costs so to be able to prioritise them.

QUALITY-RELATED COSTS

The COPQ or 'Quality-Related Costs' – whichever term is preferred – includes all costs and activities that do not add value. The cost of lost business is also worth considering but is unfortunately not quantifiable. However, it is usual that when successful attempts are made to reduce COPQ, there is generally a significant increase in business as a consequence. This fact applies as much to service industry as it does to manufacturing organisations, in fact experience indicates that these costs are often much higher in a service industry because they are less visible.

For example, the consequence of many manufacturing problems results in excessive inventory, process downtime, customer returns and warranty costs, and late payments due to disputes over quality, quantity and delivery. These are usually highly visible.

In contrast, the costs in a service operation might include the less visible computer crashes, slow operators, poor software and so on. In the travel industry, the equivalent to a customer repair or return may be booking the wrong hotel room. In many cases, this would be dealt with by the hotel staff and it is possible that neither the hotel nor the customer will inform the travel agent of the error. Nevertheless the reputation of the agency will suffer and consequently its market share will be lost without the agent knowing why. Equally, the agent will not have the equivalent of a returned product appearing in the profit and loss account. In the office environment the equivalent to a scrapped or reworked product may involve redoing a task, but the effect will be far less apparent than an equivalent manufacturing problem since there will be no visible scrapped or reworked product.

In non-manufacturing situations, inspection is frequently an ad hoc activity carried out either by a colleague or by supervision. The time involved is not monitored and if the work being inspected is returned to the originator to be redone or corrected, this may not be recorded either. Because these costs are less visible and therefore unlikely to be controlled, there is a tendency to ignore them and, therefore, these costs slowly increase as inefficiencies creep in.

The daily activities of a secretary, travel courier, nurse, surgeon or salesperson may not be recorded, and the breakdown of time spent on each activity may not be known even to the individual concerned, other than by unreliable, subjective means. Even when timesheets are used to record time spent on various activities, it does not follow that the time was used efficiently. A secretary is unlikely to record that 3 hours were spent looking for a file, if the location of it was the secretary's responsibility.

Also, in service industries, as distinct from manufacturing, the customer is part of the process and affects the quality of the process. A polite customer will often receive a different quality of service from an impolite customer. The customer is present when the service is provided and observes and influences the delivery of the service.

Unnecessary operations in manufacture in many cases will require additional plant and this must be justified financially. A machine operator's tasks are usually precisely defined and leave little scope for variation.

QUALITY-RELATED COST ELEMENTS

Within the scope of Hoshin Kanri, there are two classes of quality-related cost:

1.   costs related to non-conforming products or services;
2.   the costs incurred because the system to produce them is itself less than adequate. This includes the costs which Toyota refer to as 'MUDA' and is dealt with in Chapter 14 on Lean Manufacturing.

In both cases, the consequential costs are frequently far greater than the cost to repair or replace.

Quality-Related Costs can be placed in three categories and are often referred to as FAP: Failure, Appraisal and Prevention:

•   *Failure costs* – (internal and external) including the associated consequential costs.
•   *Appraisal costs* – the cost of monitoring, surveillance and inspection.
•   *Prevention costs* – the cost of the activities designed to prevent failures from occurring.

Failure costs – (internal)

Internal failure costs can be many and varied. They include all costs and losses due to doing again what has already been done, or repairing or modifying the result of an activity, the cost of post mortems and all other consequential costs together with the waste of resources performing the tasks that need to be redone.

The consequential costs will include the effect on the balance sheet of excessive inventory and work-in-progress resulting from quality-related deficiencies. In service situations, the equivalent problems do not show in inventory, but are hidden in direct costs. Most inventory and 'work in progress' (other than work actually being processed) can be regarded as a Quality-Related Cost:

•   Reworking, redoing or repeating activities already performed because of inadequate performance at the first attempt. Costs of modification resulting from previously undetected design or planning weaknesses. These costs include the associated design or planning activity, changes to software and cost of retraining if methods are changed.
•   Retro design of products with a known design fault and all of the associated new jigs, fixtures and tools. Extra space in stores to accommodate replacement parts with different

issue numbers. Revisions to parts lists, instruction manuals and the increased complexity of related service activities.

- Increases to inventory and work-in-progress due to disruptions to the smooth flow of work.
- Storage space.
- Modifications due to poor quality design.

The Ford Motor Company conducted an intensive study of its main Japanese rivals across a wide range of criteria including the cost of design changes after the vehicle had gone into production. It found that whereas Japanese companies invest more at the design and planning phases, their overall costs are substantially lower due to significantly fewer alterations both during and post-production.

Failure costs – external

These costs can be further subdivided into residual and random categories. The residual problems include the underlying costs of warranty calls, servicing, complaints, engineers and so on. Some of the more spectacular costs may be in the random category which, if they do occur, can produce catastrophic results. These will include:

Product recall or product withdrawal: the Perrier Water case, John West Canned Foods, Farley's Baby Foods, bones in fish fingers and many examples from the automotive industry. Companies normally spend fortunes on advertising how good they are, then suddenly they are plunged without warning into huge expenditure telling the public that they have put their lives at Risk. In many cases, this negative publicity is overwhelmed by media attention which puts the very survival of the business at stake.

The costs to Union Carbide from the Bhopal disaster, John West and Farleys with food poisoning, and Perrier with its chemical problem have become historical milestones. Chernobyl already has its place in history and the English nuclear plant Windscale was renamed Sellafield in an attempt to shake off its bad reputation following the radiation leakage disaster. All of these incidents were preventable, as was the Zeebrugge ferry disaster. The Risks associated with all of these would have been greatly reduced had the principles of Hoshin Kanri been employed.

The catalogue of events leading up the series of DC9 failures and the account of security at Birmingham Airport broadcast on Trevor McDonald's Today TV programme have done nothing to increase the confidence of the wary air traveller.

Other external costs which can also be included in the statistics include:

- Failed product launches which are due to deficiencies in the product and identified and exposed by its first customers. These costs are invariably incurred when the producers of a product or service are overzealous in their attempt to obtain prior franchise with an innovative new product and is a common problem. In these cases, the organisation tries to take shortcuts and fails to test and prove the product's performance characteristics prior to sale. This results in the customer unwittingly being the first inspector.
- Failure to meet either the emotional or specified needs of the customer: this is usually caused by poor market research and poor competitor-related information, inadequate and misdirected promotion, wrong launch time, short shelf-life in the case of chemical, food and pharmaceutical products, contamination, poor packaging and consequent adverse publicity.
- Customer complaints and the recording and analysis of customer complaints, and the cost of running a so-called customer service department, a euphemism for customer complaints department.

- Excessive after-delivery, service or maintenance support. Excessive costs including storage, delivery and all related administration, particularly those that infer, conceal from or mislead the public.

Appraisal costs

Appraisal or monitoring activities include those activities that exist for no other reason than the probable presence or expectation of some deficiency that must be detected at the earliest opportunity.

Appraisal costs have two components:

Firstly there are those that must be incurred regardless of the probability of the Risks because the consequences of such an event are severe and potentially life threatening. Such is the case for many of the controls and procedures at nuclear power stations. This form of appraisal cost is not included in this argument because they will always be incurred regardless of the likelihood of an event.

The second type of appraisal cost, and what is included, are those costs related directly to the likelihood of error or failure. In this case, the amount of appraisal costs increases as the likelihood of error increases more or less in direct proportion and vice versa. Activities which are included embrace all the costs of online inspection, testing and monitoring, which are carried out for no other reason than that the related failures occur.

Some of these failure costs can be eliminated by foolproofing or mistake proofing (referred to in Japan as 'Poke Yoke') but this would be classified as a prevention cost.

Prevention costs

These can also be divided into two categories. There are those prevention costs that may be regarded as an essential part of the process, for example: field testing, design proving, failure modes and effects analysis. These are really a cost associated with good business practice, they would be incurred regardless of the failure and appraisal costs and are not included in this argument.

The prevention costs that are included are those that must be incurred if the current cost of failure and appraisal is to be reduced. These represent an investment in the Continuous Improvement process and, if effective, should result in a significant reduction in the overall costs as shown in Figure 7.2. Obviously they are likely to be too small otherwise the failures would not occur and the relevant appraisal cost would not be necessary.

COST OF POOR QUALITY RATIOS

It was claimed earlier that the COPQ as a ratio of sales revenue is likely to be at least 20 per cent of sales revenue and probably much higher. This is because many of these costs are hidden in the accounting process. For a company with sales of £10 million per year, the total COPQ is likely to be at least £2 million! Assume also that annual net profit is 10 per cent of sales at £1 million.

Figure 7.2 shows that by increasing the expenditure on prevention the total cost of the three types combined can be reduced by some 50 per cent in 3 years. This means that total costs can be reduced by £1 million and the saving in this example will double annual profit. The increase in prevention costs is likely to be a maximum of 10 per cent of the saving at £100 000. This implies a very good return on investment and is achievable!

It is for this reason that this chapter on prioritising the KPIs is concentrated on this topic. Many of the KPIs will include some hidden Quality-Related costs and this should be taken into account when prioritising.

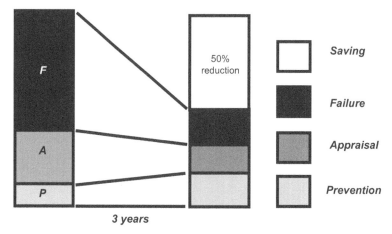

Quality-Related Costs
The FAP relationship

Figure 7.2   The FAP relationship

THE OPTIMUM QUALITY COST FALLACY

There is a serious flaw in the FAP argument which can lead to problems. Many readers will be familiar with the graph shown in Figure 7.3. The theory underlying this set of curves is intended to convey the impression that there is an optimum level of quality cost, which therefore becomes the desirable target. This is a flawed argument.

The curves suggest that if a producer is at position A, then the total costs will be high due to excessive failure and appraisal costs. It is then suggested that costs will fall as more attention is given to prevention costs. This is correct. However, the advocates of this model then suggest that continued and progressive reductions in Quality Costs will eventually lead to a situation where an optimum value is reached, beyond which the cost of further prevention efforts will outweigh the benefits; hence the overall costs will rise.

For example, in Figure 7.3, the company would move from position A, through position B to position C. The flaw in the argument results from the fact that it ignored the fact that the organisation has competitors. At point A the probability is that all of them are fairly tightly bunched at the same place on the graph. The reason being that if any one of the competitors were much better than the others, then at least the worst one would be pushed out of the market. The customer would naturally prefer the better products. This is what happened in the automotive industry in the 1970s. What then happens is illustrated in Figure 7.4.

Figure 7.4 indicates that as the 'best producer' continually reduces their Quality-Related Costs, it will effectively drive the costs of the less capable competitors upwards behind them. The reason being that society will now expect the better product and will recalibrate their expectations accordingly. This will result in a lower level of tolerance for the poorer performers with the result that they will get more complaints and fewer sales.

This implies that the 'best' producer (in the eyes of the customer) will always be at the optimum, irrespective of other considerations, provided that the improvements that they have made result in greater consumer preference. The optimum therefore will appear always to move ahead of them. This is why there are no markets where anyone has ever reached an optimum. Always there are better ways of doing things and for the Hoshin Kanri-led organisation, this is another opportunity to exploit the competition.

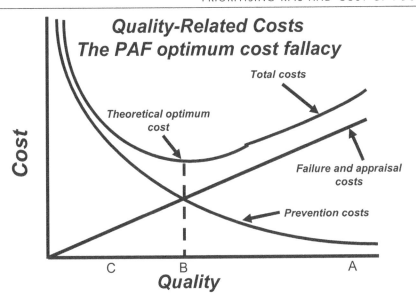

Figure 7.3   The fallacious Minimum Cost curve

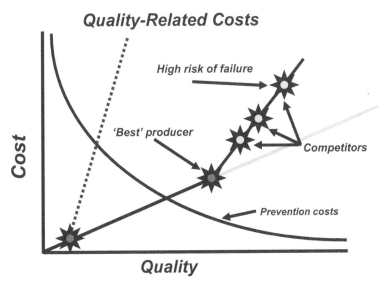

Figure 7.4   The real effect of one competitor aggressively reducing Quality-Related Costs

The customer's perception of their wants are to a large extent driven by the best and most perceptive supplier. By examining the KPIs collectively, all those which can result in both cost reduction and greater customer satisfaction should be given priority.

The only way in which a poor performer can compete with a high performer if they are not able to close the gap is to attempt to sell at a lower price. Of course this is a popular Strategy for many people because there is always someone looking for a bargain. However, as Figure 7.5 indicates, this is of dubious merit because the better performer will have the advantage of lower costs and can also sell at premium prices. The profits of the poor performer on the other hand are squeezed both on selling price and by incurring higher costs to produce. They are also vulnerable if the better performer decides to use price competition and sets a level below the inferior company's cost to produce.

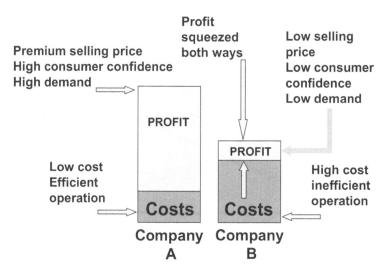

Better Quality costs more or less?

Figure 7.5   **Comparative costs – best and worst**

It is evident, therefore, that *there are no absolutes where quality is concerned*. Quality is a comparative concept, and is and always will be dynamic. That is why no one has *ever* reached the optimum. It does not exist. Always people will want something better if someone finds a way to produce it.

IDENTIFYING QUALITY-RELATED COSTS

Having argued the case for Quality-Related Cost reduction, the interested reader will want to be able to identify Quality-Related Costs in their own organisation but it is already mentioned that many of these are hidden in the accountancy process.

Fortunately there are ways that we can use to pull them out. One way is to use the Hidden Factory concept first described by Dr Feigenbaum in his book *Total Quality Control* first published in the 1950s.

The Hidden Factory concept

In this concept, Figure 7.6 shows that an organisation really consists of two organisations. In one of them only good work is produced. In the other, only rubbish, waste, delays and errors. In this latter organisation how many people does it employ? How much floor space, how many machines or equipment are used just to produce the bad product?

Figure 7.7 shows some of the more likely of these on a department by department basis.

UNNECESSARY PERFECTIONISM

The argument thus far is based on the assumption that improvements in quality are perceived by the customer to be desirable, and that the customer is prepared to pay for them. Quality improvements that cannot be perceived by the customer, or to which the customer is indifferent and which cost more to achieve, or for which the customer is not prepared to pay, must be regarded as unnecessary perfectionism and should be avoided. These improvements should be regarded as quality deficiencies just as much as those that relate to failure to achieve.

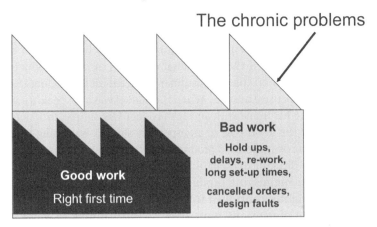

Figure 7.6   The Hidden Factory concept

The Complexities of Identifying Avoidable Quality-Related Costs

Figure 7.7   Some typical Quality-Related Costs

Sometimes unnecessary perfectionism can be one of the most significant Quality-Related Costs.

One example of this was the manufacturer who had a near absolute monopoly of the smoke detector market. At that time, soon after clean-air laws had been introduced, the company was able to sell its products at premium prices because they had no competition. However, the company had also fallen into the trap of unnecessary perfectionism. The directors insisted that the outer cases of the product should be die-cast and vitreous-enameled in order to look nice and to be consistent with the appearance of its other products. These design features were extremely costly to produce and were totally unnecessary from a practical point of view.

Once it was installed in a chimney, the customer would be indifferent as to the product's aesthetics and much more concerned with its reliability, effectiveness and, of course, safety compatibility with related instrumentation. The aesthetic product features were included for no other reason than vanity. Because of the importance of the visual characteristics of other products in its range, the company made the false assumption that its customer expected all its products to look alike.

This turned out to be an expensive mistake. When the market was at its peak, a competitor appeared. The competitor has also done his homework and his product was simple, functional and cheap. The customer naturally preferred the lower-cost item, especially since it was going to be located in a tall chimney and out of sight. The over-specified product was wiped from the market at a single stroke.

The most insidious and difficult to control form of over-specification occurs in the tolerances on dimensional variation in engineering products. Only a relatively small number of dimensions on most products require tightly-controlled tolerances. For most of the remainder, the designer often faces a dilemma. The dimensions must have specified limits to guide manufacture, but there are few guidelines as to what would be acceptable to the user. The designer is most likely to be cautious, because they know that if the tolerances are too loose, the product will be regarded as inferior in some way and the designer will be blamed. However, if they are unnecessarily tight the designer is unlikely to suffer criticism because the dimension will probably not be challenged, provided that the product is manufacturable. In most instances this would be the case – but only at a price! Production engineers, production departments and inspectors will make the assumption that the designer knows best and therefore accept the specified constraints. Any items that subsequently fail to meet these requirements will either be scrapped or reworked, even though in practice they may be perfectly functional. Costs associated with such over-perfectionism must run to untold millions every year and may even threaten the life of the organisation.

ISO 9000:2000 – COST OR VALUE?

Many organisations have become wary of any quality-related initiative as a consequence of bad experiences with ISO 9000. They have often introduced this standard not because they wanted to but because some overbearing customers have virtually forced it on them. In some other cases, they have introduced it in order to take advantage of its marketing value in being able to claim to be a 'quality' organisation. In most cases, their aim has been simply to obtain the certificate with the least amount of effort. Since 'fooling the auditor' is not at all difficult, a significant number of these programmes fall far short of the intentions of those who drafted the standard. As a consequence, most of them incur all of the costs associated with certification and little of the benefit. This is unfortunate because the content of the standard, especially ISO 9004:2000, is excellent and well thought out. If it is implemented for the purpose of improving the business and not as a means just to mount a certificate on the wall of the visitors' reception area then significant benefit can be obtained.

SUPPLY CHAIN QUALITY-RELATED COSTS

Many Quality-Related Costs are built in even before the component goods and services reach our company. This is because unless our Supply Chain in total is also operating a Hoshin Kanri management system, then we will inevitably be paying for and absorbing the cost of all their inefficiencies.

However we cannot force them to do this against their will. If we do then they will simply attempt to fool us with a sham scheme with similar results as discussed in the ISO 9000 argument above.

Toyota and other leading Japanese companies have largely overcome this problem by dispensing with multiple sourcing and changed to the development of long-term relationships with a selected number of suppliers that they have learned to trust and who participate willingly in mutually beneficial improvement activities. In Toyota this is referred to as 'The Toyota Family'.

SUMMARY

1. Quality-Related Costs occur in all industries and in all forms of work.
2. Quality-Related Costs can be categorised into three elements:

    (a) failure
    (b) appraisal
    (c) prevention.

    These collectively account for a minimum of 20 per cent of sales revenue and can be as high as 30 per cent and even more than 40 per cent in some cases, the largest being failure costs, which normally represent 60–80 per cent of the total.
3. By identifying and tackling failure costs, the COPQ can be reduced by over 50 per cent in 3–5 years. These savings represent profit.
4. Quality-Related Costs include the consequential cost of failure. When that is included, Quality-Related Costs become comparable to the 'best' performer. The best performer will always be operating at the optimum value. Inferior competitors' costs will be progressively higher and will increase if the best performer improves, even though their performance remains the same – the Hutchins Hypothesis.
5. Quality-Related Costs due to excessive stocks of raw materials and part-finished products. Finished goods and work-in-progress can only be reduced through first-party assessment in collaboration with suppliers. Reliance on third-party assessment schemes such as ISO 9000:2000 cannot produce Total Quality performance.
6. The concept of multiple sourcing of suppliers is outmoded and must be eliminated. The 'Toyota Family' system is the most promising alternative.

Finally, from all that we have now organised, how will the KPIs be achieved? Generally there will be some important and significant gaps between where we are and where we want to be. The means to close the gaps will depend on the nature of the situation. Sometimes they will require Six Sigma projects, in others Lean Manufacturing and of course Quality Circles. The next few chapters cover the main means to achieve them and collectively they may be regarded as TQM (Total Quality Management). They are not exhaustive and the content is nowhere near definitive. If they were then this book would have to be split into many volumes. Every one of these chapters could be expanded into a book in its own right.

8 Risk Management

Hoshin Kanri – from Strategy to Action!

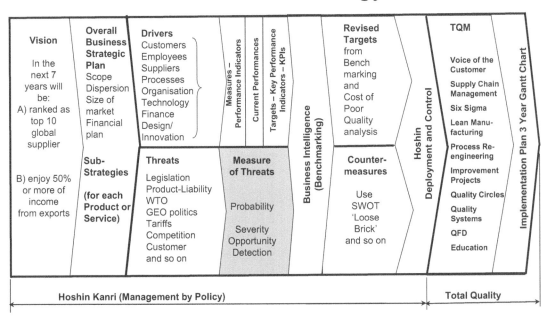

Vision	Overall Business Strategic Plan	Drivers	Measures – Performance Indicators	Current Performances	Targets – Key Performance Indicators – KPIs		Revised Targets			TQM

Figure 8.1   Risk Management

In Figure 8.1, we have progressed from Vision through Strategy, then along the top of the diagram through Drivers, Performance Indicators and Benchmarking to the setting of the KPIs at corporate level and prioritising using the COPQ. Before moving from these to the TQM 'how to' topics, we must retreat back to the Strategy feature and work through the Threats and Countermeasures. This is covered in this chapter and Chapter 9. When this has been completed, then the process of Hoshin Planning is over and these also may require similar treatment using the 'how to' tools and concepts which are the key part of the TQM complementary concept to Hoshin Kanri.

No matter how intensive the business improvement process may be and no matter how rapidly the organisation is advancing in its market, there will always be Risks. Markets can be fickle, up one minute and unexpectedly down the next. In a growing market when you can sell everything that you can make, it is hard to think about Risk, just keep pushing more product out of the door. However, this is precisely the time when Risk should be considered, when you expect it the least. Not so long ago, one company in the OEM mobile phone business was growing so fast that they opened 30 new factories around the world in 12 months. At that time they could not see a cloud in the sky. Just 1 year later they were laying people of by the thousands. Managing growth may be difficult but managing shrinkage can be a far greater problem and it is a negative experience. So the Hoshin Kanri organisation, if it is to be able to cope with the next stages, will need the TQM concepts in order to convert the planning into action and to deploy the whole process down through the successive layers to the workforce.

The process of Risk Management deals with – Threats – Measure of Threats – Benchmarking – Countermeasures – followed by connection through to the various improvement concepts in order that the means are in place to counter any threat including the possibility of some emergency that takes us by surprise no matter how diligent we may have been.

An example of what can happen when Risks have not been properly considered was well illustrated in an earlier chapter by the fate of the Wallace Corporation in the USA. The Wallace Corporation together with TNT won the US National Quality Award in its third or fourth year of existence. Before 1 year had passed from receiving the award, TNT transferred its European operations and the Wallace Corporation went bankrupt.

At the time this was a complete shock. How could a business that presumably did everything so well that it could win a coveted national award then go out of business? The possibilities were:

1. The assessment of the company was flawed and the assessors did not pick up what was going wrong.
2. The Award criteria were flawed and potentially the same thing could happen again and again or possibly, at the time, everything was OK and the crippling events occurred after the assessment.

Whatever was the real reason, the event caused me to study both the detail of the American National Award and the European Models to see if they covered Risk. Unfortunately neither of them did. It seemed to me that this was a major deficiency and reminded me that without containing a counter to the Loose Brick concept, then regardless of the effectiveness of any business performance improvement programme, any organisation would remain vulnerable to attack. The most dramatic example of the use of this technique was the awesome attack on the American Sixth Fleet at Pearl Harbour. There, the American Sixth Fleet was thought to be almost invincible. The USA had done everything possible to make the most impregnable Naval force in modern times on the open waters. However, in characteristic style, the Japanese studied everything to see if they could find a Loose Brick (see Chapter 9). What happened is history but the point is that by following the USA National or the European Models or indeed ISO 9001:2000 or any other Quality Management model, the organisation will still have a soft underbelly vulnerable to Threats if these are not also considered as a part of Hoshin Planning.

It was this situation that resulted in the further development of our Hoshin Kanri model to close the door on this area of vulnerability. Soon after this feature had been introduced to our Hoshin Model we were working with a client who manufactured building products. We had developed Hoshin Kanri along the upper part of the model and we were now considering possible Threats. To identify possible Threats we conducted a brainstorming session. During this activity, one of the Directors said 'U' values. After the session, we asked what he meant. The 'U' value is the coefficient of heat loss through an insulator. If the value is near to 1.0, the heat will almost completely escape. If the value is close to zero, the material will be an almost perfect insulator. At that time, the legal requirement for building blocks for external walls was 0.45. He said that in 3 months from that date, it would be reduced to 0.35. No other Director or senior manager in the room at the time was aware of that. Worse still, none of that particular company's products were capable of meeting the limits of the new regulations and they had just 3 months. Even worse, one of their competitors was already in the marketplace advertising and selling products which did meet the new regulations. Fortunately, as a consequence of our discussions, they did make a crash programme to eliminate the threat and they are still in business but had we not had that session, the cost to the business of finding their products to be perfect but perfectly missing the requirements of the new legislation might have been catastrophic.

The Risks that confront any business are many and varied. Some have a high probability of occurrence but the effect when they do occur may be slight. At the other extreme, the probability might be low to the point of being almost non-existent, but if they do occur the effects could be catastrophic.

The technique of Failure Modes and Effects Analysis (FMEA) provides a systematic approach to dealing with this and managing Risk but unfortunately, in the end, all we can do is to attempt to minimise it. It would be nice to eliminate it altogether but this is not possible. The reduction of Risk usually involves a cost and the more we reduce Risk, the more we have to spend. In the end, there comes a point where we have say that the cost of reducing it further is worse than accepting that level of Risk. This might be easy when dealing with fiscal Risk but is almost impossible when considering the Risks to human life. Over the years society has become increasingly intolerant towards the Risk to human life and for that matter the lives of animals, no matter how rare, and this trend is likely to continue into the future.

Whilst the types of Risks that we face may be many and varied, fortunately the means of managing them are remarkably similar.

In this chapter therefore we will deal with subject generically. However, for each type of Risk it will be necessary to employ the services of an expert in that particular field mainly because Risk Assessment involves the collection and analysis of relevant data in order to determine probabilities. Unfortunately, in many cases, the data either does not exist or it would be either impossible or highly inconvenient to collect it. In this case we must use the services of whoever is the best expert in that field to make an informed subjective judgment. The data will only be as good as the experience of the expert!

The following discussion on Risk Management is based on an article written by the author together with Michael Debenham who is Professional Affairs Manager at the Chartered Quality Institute and published in its magazine *Quality World* in September 2002.

MANAGING RISK

Corporate Risk comes in many guises from the smallest of pitfalls, which at worst might cause an organisation expense or embarrassment, to outright disasters – the result of which can be catastrophic.

> Mike Debenham, IQA Professional Affairs Manager, and David Hutchins, Chairman of David Hutchins International Ltd, explain what measures can be taken to reduce and manage Risk.

When the word Risk is used in an industrial context, it usually refers to the possible but uncertain and undesirable outcomes of business-related activities. The particular Risk concerned may be either predictable and foreseeable or unpredictable and unforeseeable. In the case of the latter, by definition, there is little we can do but hope that it does not occur. However, some seemingly unforeseeable Risks may actually be anticipated if sufficient time, thought and research are applied to the situation.

WHAT'S THE RISK?

Organisations that are confronted with high-likelihood Risks to life invariably have very high-profile forms of Hazard Analysis, involving well-trained experts in the specific Risks involved. Their activities involve Risk identification, Risk analysis and prevention and quick reaction when an incident occurs to limit the effect on life.

To many who are involved in this work, the term Risk Management has a scope that relates to nuclear, chemical, explosive, poison and occupational health and safety type Risks. While we must acknowledge the importance of these, we must not forget that there are other forms of Risk that might not be life threatening but that can be catastrophic in other ways.

The Barings crash

The fate of Baring traders is one example. Who, other than possibly Nick Leeson himself, could have predicted only days before the facts became known that one of the world's most reputable financial institutions would have crashed so dramatically and without any warning?

And there are other types of Risk. For example, industrial action, unwelcome legislation, currency value changes, insurrection, trade barriers, products liability, hostile take-over bids, aggressive competitors, new competitors, new products and the impact of the electronic calculator on the slide rule business – the list is endless. What is important in all of these cases is that action is taken:

- to identify all of the possible Risks confronting the organisation;
- to determine their probability of occurrence and the consequences of such an occurrence;
- to conclude what action should be taken for prevention or Risk reduction.

Underpinning all successful Business Processes is the effective management of Risk. If Risks are identified, categorised and proactive measures are implemented to manage them, there will be evidence on file to support the day-to-day business decisions made on behalf of management or shareholders. If the presence of Risk is simply ignored then management will find itself exposed when Risks, which could have been foreseen and planned for, occur with the associated financial penalties.

The management of Risk can be viewed from two perspectives, first from the level of managing corporate Risk and setting in place the necessary strategies and associated control measures, and second from the perspective of personnel who use the Risk-based procedures for making day-to-day business decisions.

THE CORPORATE RISK

Much has been written about the management of corporate Risk. A number of tools are available to control an organisation's exposure to Risk:

- formal systems management;
- partnering arrangements;
- insurance;
- Risk-tolerant work packages;
- prototype and product testing;
- provision of Risk-reduction resources;
- Risk Assessment and Risk Management.

Formal systems management

The application of the basic principles of formal systems management may also form part of the package of Risk-control measures.

The management of the organisation's exposure to external Risk is addressed through the Gap Analysis between external requirements and the defined system requirements, while internal Risk is addressed through the definition of system requirements, training in those requirements and measurement of evidence that the requirements have been executed.

Partnering arrangements

Where items or materials are purchased on a regular basis, a customer may decide to develop a partnering arrangement to contract out the associated Risks to the supplier. The customer will make a commitment to the supplier and, in return, the supplier will take on some or all of the Risks associated with late or non-compliant delivery. The customer may categorise items of equipment and materials as well as specify limits for financial penalties.

Alternatively, in the case of Product Liability Risks where the customer has large resources, it is common for the customer to underwrite or take over the Risks of its supplier. This is particularly the case in the automotive industry where Product Recall is a high-level Risk with a high rate of occurrence. It also carries with it the threat of potential bankruptcy if products liability lawsuits are successful. The reason for this being that in law, when a Product Liability case arises, it is in the interest of the pursuant to sue everyone in the Supply Chain – initially from the retailer back – and then focus on the one most likely to be able to pay. Many suppliers to the large automotive companies would not trade if they were confronted with this level of Risk. Partnering may also reduce the Risk of unpredicted bankruptcy of a critical supplier.

Insurance

Where the use of partnering arrangements is impractical then the customer may identify those Risks to be insured in-house and on the open market.

Risk-tolerant work packages

To reduce the cost of insurance, either in-house or by a third party, the customer may develop Risk-tolerant work packages. The use of suppliers' standard items that have already been extensively tested in previous use, rather than custom-built untried items of equipment, is an example of this type of package. Boeing for example has a policy that each new design of aircraft must contain at least 70 per cent components in use in earlier models. The adage 'innovate at your peril' is extremely apposite.

Prototype and product testing

To reduce the Risk of recall (covered later in this chapter) and prosecution under the product liability laws, prototype and product testing and validation of service has been used as an effective form of Risk control. There are two aspects to this approach:

1. Risk prediction – this can be done using such tools as FMEA and Fault Tree Analysis. These tools are quite similar to each other and involve such techniques as brainstorming, Affinity Diagrams and Relationship Diagraphs to predict high-likelihood Risks and possible Countermeasures. In the case of management and financial Risk there is an adaptation of FMEA known as a Process Decision Programme Chart. It can be very effectively used for the prediction of management-related problems, identification of Countermeasures,

identification of problems caused by the Countermeasures on an iterative basis until either achievement of the desired outcome can be reasonably assured or the mission abandoned.

2. Risk analysis – this involves life testing, accelerated life testing, environmental testing, Weibull and other forms of failure analysis. From the results of these tests preventive strategies can be developed. For example, it is known from the results of extensive product testing that sodium streetlights run for a fairly predictable 8000 hours. Rather than replace each one individually on failure it is more economic to replace all of the lights in the area whether they have actually failed or not. This is known as a Block Replacement Policy and is extremely economical.

Provision of risk-reduction resources

Risk-reduction resources are generally provided in the form of inspection (see later in this chapter – Managing Risk – the human factor), expediting or auditing services, but may also include Risk Management planning resources. The extent to which inspection and the associated expediting activities are undertaken for any item of procured equipment will depend on the perceived Risks of items being delivered to the site or the receiving warehouse – not in accordance with the specification requirements and programme delivery requirements. It is therefore industry practice to carry out a Risk Assessment that addresses the consequences, in terms of cost, for either of these events occurring, that is, in non-conformance to quality requirements and late delivery.

Depending on the industry sector, this assessment will be carried out for all or only the major categories of procured equipment. A typical Risk Assessment will address the following topics:

*   Criticality of the product based on the consequences of failure. A criticality rating will typically address the following factors:
    - product safety implications;
    - design complexity and maturity;
    - complexity of production process;
    - product characteristics;
    - environment issues;
    - operation issues;
    - direct and indirect economic consequences of failure;
*   cost of rectifying defective items, if any;
*   cost from consequential delay to programme in rectifying defective items;
*   cost from delay to programme for late delivery of items;
*   cost of inspection and expediting as a percentage of purchase price;
*   whether a vendor quality plan is required.

Once these costs have been assessed it is necessary to identify the following:

*   pre-award audit of the supplier's Quality Management System (QMS);
*   pre-inspection meeting;
*   intermediate inspection visits, if needed, how many and for what?;
*   final inspection visit;
*   expediting visits, if needed, how many and for what aim.

Risk Assessment and Risk Management

It is not the intention of this chapter to cover the various tools and techniques currently in use to manage and assess Risk-hazard and operability studies (HAZOP) and FMEA, to mention just two.

These techniques have been covered in great detail in other publications. The only exception is Risk-based decision making which has received less exposure and is included as an example of one of these techniques.

Most of the decisions made in the working environment will benefit from an analysis of the Risks involved. In practice, there is usually too little time, and the actual process of Risk analysis is perceived to be too lengthy, for this course of action to be undertaken with the associated record being placed on file.

There is a clear need for a simplified system of identifying and analysing Risk so the process can be applied on a more regular basis. In particular, those decisions classified as minor, but that can still materially affect the prosperity of a company or the success of a project, will benefit. Paradoxically, however, it can also be argued that without Risk analysis, an organisation remains vulnerable to all levels of Risk and will be the least prepared to deal with them if any materialise. The process of Risk-based decision making is suited to these minor decisions and, under normal circumstances it can be conducted in about 1.5 hours, usually involving two or three people. The result is that for the investment of approximately 3 hours of time spent on analysis, a decision can be taken having considered and budgeted all Risks involved and the related outcomes. Risk-based decision making can also be applied to major decisions such as the selection of joint venture or alliance partners, but the time required to develop the analysis will be even greater. Risk-based decision making is typically used for the following types of decisions:

- review of invitations to tender;
- selection of contract agreement type;
- placing of sub-contracts;
- equipment selection (the design process) and procurement;
- resolution of problems encountered on projects;
- development of plant maintenance philosophies;
- selection and employment of company personnel.

OTHER BUSINESS RISK STRATEGIES

Scenario testing

In order to be prepared for any contingency, however unlikely, some organisations in high-hazard level environments practice a technique known as scenario testing. A high-level catastrophic Risk is imagined to have occurred. Documents are prepared that graphically describe the situation in some detail even to the extent of faking newspaper cuttings and video clips of news broadcasts for maximum dramatic effect. The scenario is then passed to various management teams who are expected to assume a real occurrence, analyse the situation and produce recommendations for a solution – and to plan subsequent limitation and prevention should the scenario happen in reality. The technique can produce an extremely high level of Risk awareness. The best proposal for Countermeasures is then filed away but is ready to be activated if the event occurs.

Risk Management system testing

In this instance, the Risk system is tested during normal operations partly to test effectiveness and also to ensure a high level of sensitivity to the Risk. An example is the system used in airports where officials disguised as normal passengers attempt to pass through the security system with drugs or fake guns and explosives. The staff know this will happen on average twice per day.

Alarm testing

This is something that we are all aware of. It is necessary but suffers from the possibility that people may be desensitised to potential real occurrences if the practices are too frequent and are scheduled into specific time slots. This is also often the case when alarms go off by accident, for example, car and property alarms.

HOW TO DEAL WITH RISK

There are basically five ways an organisation can deal with Risk:

1. Ignore it and hope that it will not happen. If the Risk materialises the plan is to face the consequences even if this proves beyond the resources of the organisation, which may then simply cease to exist. In some states of the USA, insurance premiums are so high that many organisations adopt this Strategy for a range of Risks, particularly Product Liability.
2. Share the Risk with others – particularly suppliers in partnering arrangements.
3. Transfer the Risk to a third party through insurance. Premiums for this approach are related to the insurance companies' assessment of the Risk. Typically the organisation protects itself for a given level of claim that theoretically can occur several times during the period covered.

    For example, in a train crash, it may be that several victims have a valid claim approaching the maximum amount. In the case of Product Liability insurance, however, many insurance companies and brokers will determine the total maximum payable during the insurance period. When this is exhausted, the insured is no longer covered and must negotiate new insurance. In this case the new premium is likely to be prohibitively high and in all likelihood the Risk will be effectively uninsurable.
4. Reduce the Risk by careful management of high-Risk activities. This usually involves Quality Assurance, Hazard Analysis, FMEA and other quality-related tools. The approach is not exclusive and can be used together with other approaches. The advantage is that possible Countermeasures can be identified and deployed if the Risk materialises.
5. Cease the Risk-making activities. In the case of Product Liability this may mean stopping the production of some product where there is high level of known Risk. Drug companies for example may withdraw a particular product line

MANAGING A PRODUCT RECALL

Like heart attacks, cancer, road accidents and muggings, Product Recalls happen to other organisations but could never happen to us! That is what everyone thinks until it does happen.

If it did happen to your organisation, could you cope? Would you know what to do? Could the company survive the cost let alone the bad publicity?

Twenty years ago, when Product Liability legislation was more a discussion point than reality, there was considerable speculation that Product Recall would be one of the most crippling side effects of the European Draft Directive on Product Liability if it ever became law.

Since then, of course, it has become law. The manufacturer of a product can be held liable if a defect in the product or in its design could be determined to have resulted in an injury. The product would be regarded as defective if it caused the injury.

So what has been the impact on the number of Product Recalls since the introduction of this legislation in the late 1980s?

It is difficult to say whether or not there are more than there were 20 years ago because it is doubtful if anyone collated the data. However, judging from the number that appear in the national press and are announced on the radio, it would certainly appear that there are more today.

In February 1998, Vauxhall Motors announced the recall of a large number of one of its brands due to the discovery of a defect in the design of a handbrake. Just prior to that Ford announced something similar. Mercedes narrowly avoided a complete disaster when its new baby car was found to be so unstable that it was capable of rolling over in relatively foreseeable conditions. The problem is not just restricted to the American and European auto manufacturers. Toyota and other Far Eastern manufacturers have all had their share despite their renowned Quality Control capabilities.

But away from the automotive industry other product providers are equally as vulnerable, even those whose very name is associated with quality. For example, a headline in a copy of the *Daily Telegraph* ran, 'Salmonella shuts M & S sandwich factory. Marks and Spencer were forced to withdraw about 80 000 sandwiches due to traces of salmonella being discovered.' In another example, B&Q took advertising space of 17 x 25cm advertisements in national media to say, 'Product Recall – stop use immediately – Landia Halogen Organiser Table Lamp. DO NOT TOUCH THE METAL TELESCOPIC LAMP ARMS – immediately switch off the mains supply at the plug. Return to ....' These were examples of defective products. In this next example, again involving a 17 x 25cm announcement, there was nothing specifically wrong with the product itself but, 'KP regret to announce that the above promotion offering free "milk caps" in packets of KP Skips has caused distress amongst some customers because of a small number of instances of people accidentally putting these "milk caps" into their mouths.' The advertisement went on to say, 'Whilst the product itself is unaffected and completely safe to eat and the "milk caps" conform strictly to European safety legislation, the company regrets any distress amongst its customers.'

There have been numerous others across a wide range of products including the Moulinex juice extractor, Dimplex heaters – a dangerous Risk of fumes and fire, Habitat 'jelly' candleholders – a Risk of catching fire if the candle burns to its base, Mr Sheen aerosols – a Risk of leakage, Mother & Baby Magazine – a recall of free rattles distributed with their November 1995 issue an unspecified defect in the rims of Mavic cycle racing wheels, a Risk of fracture in Shimano mountain bike cranks, 'J' bolt defects in Flying Trapeze Gym sets and other related products, Micromark fans, Berchet rocking horses, Ericsson mobile phone chargers, Kwicksave lightbulbs, Servis Rainwave washer dryers, Great Mills bench grinders, Mascot electronic mobile phone chargers and many, many others.

It is clear that a Product Liability situation can arise at any time and almost always without warning. It can happen to the most quality conscious organisation as well as the careless. No one could ever say with absolute certainty that it could not happen to them if they manufacture or distribute products into the marketplace.

What then can be done to protect ourselves? There are four possibilities:

1. Ignore it and hope it doesn't happen. (If you are lucky, this is the least expensive approach. If you are unlucky, it could wipe out the company).
2. Attempt to insure against it. In other words pass the Risk on to others. But this assumes that insurance is available. In many cases it will not be.
3. Attempt to reduce the Risk through the application of the Quality disciplines. Not only will this reduce the Risk, the right approach will cut cost significantly as well.
4. Minimise the impact through the establishment of a Product Recall procedure.

With the exception of item one, the remainder are each affected by the others. The higher the Risk, the higher the premiums, if indeed insurance can be obtained at all. The Risk can be reduced but not completely eliminated through the application of Quality-related disciplines. A Product Recall procedure can greatly reduce the costs and minimise the effects if the worst happens.

The establishment of a recall procedure is analogous to the purchase of a fire extinguisher: one hopes that it will never be required, but if it is, it could prove to be a life saver.

A Product Recall will always be the result of the discovery of a real or potential hazard which will require the fastest possible location of every item responsible for the Risk and its removal from the market.

One would imagine that if we knew where every such item was, then withdrawal should be easy, but experience indicates otherwise. For example, in order to be prepared for such an event, ITT in the 1960s established a scheme through which every purchaser of its steam irons was logged in a database. Further more, there was an incentive built in to encourage subsequent second-hand users also to record the change of ownership.

Even with this level of information, and only months after the initial distribution of the product and intensive television and other media advertising, the company was only able to recover about 70 per cent of the defective products. The remainder simply disappeared without a trace. Attempting but failing to recover such items does not absolve the distributor of their responsibility so any one of the missing 30 per cent would remain a hazard both to the user and to the company.

Clearly, failure to be able to act quickly, or acting with a disorganised approach, could result in chaos, and the resulting costs will be appreciably higher than if a proper plan is ready. A Product Recall plan, to be effective, must be capable of instant implementation. In the worst case decisions will need to be made on the recall of products from overseas, the tracing of individual purchasers, television and newspaper advertising, the withdrawal or freezing of stock in warehouse and retail outlets, stock replenishment, the issuing of instructions for the safe use of the product or its disposal, the subsequent monitoring of the health of those who may have inhaled or consumed doubtful chemicals, foodstuffs, gasses, radiation and so on, not to mention the internal costs of product modification, replacement and the administration of the plan.

The state-of-the-art

Apart from the pharmaceutical industry, where the Medicines Act imposes certain obligations on licence-holders with regard to withdrawal and recall from sale, British industry at present has little in the way of a formal approach to the problem of Product Recall.

Owing to the relationship between the manufacturer and the eventual consumer which existed before section 6 of the United Kingdom Health and Safety at Work Act (HASAWA) and Product Liability legislation, there was little or no pressure on industry to develop recall strategies. It was rarely possible for the ultimate consumer to bring a successful action against the manufacturer, because it was not usual to buy the product from them directly, and no contract of sale existed between them.

Because the impact of Product Liability legislation to date has been far less dramatic than was pessimistically predicted before its introduction, there has been little pressure on industry to consider Product Recall as a serious Risk. Unfortunately, however, as the above examples demonstrate, Product Recalls are a significant reality.

Furthermore, the insurance companies do not look favourably on the idea of Product Recall insurance. This is due to the fact that the most costly recalls are likely to be initiated as the result of a new design fault. The more limited recalls will most likely be caused by a manufacturing fault, such as a mix-up with labels. The insurance companies generally regard innovation as a development Risk which should be borne by the company. Consequently, for the unfortunate company confronted with the reality, exposure may be unavoidable.

Recall responsibility

Should a recall be required, speed of action is of the essence. This is not the time to have long discussions as to who should be in charge and to direct the plan. This should have been decided long before such an event. Ideally, and in general, this responsibility should fall upon the shoulders of the quality manager because they will be the most familiar with the systems in operation. However, there will be many specific cases where others may be more appropriate – for example, the Risk Management department.

Whoever is selected, they will be responsible for calling together a team of qualified people as soon as a situation demands and should report directly to the chief executive for this purpose. They will also be responsible for leading the resources assigned to deal with the media should the need arise. In the case of urgent or serious Product Recalls, which may be costly, likely to damage the companies reputation, or receive any form of national or local publicity, it should usually be necessary to obtain board approval for any announcements or interviews that may take place.

Recall policy

A recall should always be initiated when it has been ascertained that there is a definite or potential danger to life or health, and when the continued use or circulation of the product is likely to result in legal action. A recall may also be initiated when it is found that a fault in the product, or lack of performance, is likely to affect the reputation of the company and when the lack of performance fails to justify the claims made in advertisements. This would also include drugs, where the dosage advised was found to be at variance with requirements.

Recall data

The first stage in a recall programme will be some form of notification of a hazard. This could come from a number of sources and in many forms, depending upon the product. The most likely sources include:

- the user;
- an independent test house report;
- government sources;
- own reliability test programme or research;
- research institutes and laboratories;
- overseas sources.

Hazard evaluation report

Immediately a hazard is identified from any source, it will be necessary to evaluate the level of danger and the category of recall, if required. Levels may be set as:

- *User level recall* – likely to be extremely expensive, particularly in the case of consumer products. It would be essential in all urgent cases and probably in most serious cases. It entails recall from users, retail outlets and warehouses. Subsequently it would be necessary to reimburse the owners for losses sustained as a result of the withdrawal. The order for such a recall would always be made at board level.
- *Retail level recall* – less serious cases to do with probable law breaking, particularly in cases where an existing product has been in widespread use for some considerable time and now information has revealed a minor hazard.
- *Wholesale level recall* – will entail product recovery from the first stage in the distribution chain and may be applied in the case of non-safety critical situations.
- *Limited recall* – will mean the recall of individual batches and consignments and will probably occur most often when manufacturing faults have been discovered or are suspected in an established product.

This evaluation should be carried out by the manager responsible for the recall programme. In any case, it is recommended that a hazard report be prepared and circulated to all concerned within 2 days of instigation, regardless of the action taken. The report should include a description of the type of hazard, the category and the recall level. Apart from good housekeeping, hazard reporting provides a good source of data for future Risk probability evaluation. As with accidents, near misses are far more numerous than actual events. By recording near miss recalls, the company will soon be able to evaluate the likelihood of an actual event and its consequences.

The report should report a nil return, where applicable, on the following aspects:

- No health and safety hazard, no action required for product improvement or modification. The hazard evaluation report should state, 'No hazard expected,' followed by the date and name of the responsible person(s) making the assessment and brief reasons for the assessment.
- If a hazard is considered possible, all relevant information must be obtained for assessment by the recall team. The evaluation information should state:
  - whether any disease or injuries have already occurred;
  - whether the use of the product in any particular circumstances could lead to a hazard such as in the case of Vacwell Engineering Ltd versus BHH Chemicals Ltd, circa 1971. Vacwell were manufacturers of plant equipment designed to produce transistor devices. The plant and equipment required the use of certain chemicals. BDH were manufacturers and distributors of chemicals, which they had supplied to Vacwell over a period of time. It was known that boron tribromide reacted on contact with water, emitting a toxic vapour, but neither of the parties knew that it reacted violently and exploded on contact with water. Warnings against the explosion hazard were to be found in scientific literature extending from 1897 to 1938, and three of these earlier books containing explicit warnings were in BDH's library, but their research into the relevant literature before placing boron tribromide on the market had been limited to four more recent scientific works, none of which contained any reference to the explosion hazard, and the entry in BDH's catalogue appeared without an appropriate warning. Early in 1966 Vacwell gave BDH an order for 400 glass ampoules of boron tribromide. These were supplied, and a label affixed to each ampoule bore the warning words 'harmful vapour'. In April 1966, while two physicists were engaged in washing the labels off some 40 to 100 ampoules in two adjacent sinks prior to using them in the manufacturing apparatus, an explosion occurred, killing one of the two men and causing extensive damage to Vacwell's premises. The overwhelming probability was that the explosion occurred as a result of the deceased physicist's dropping into the sink one or more of the glass ampoules, which had shattered, so releasing boron tribromide into the water which in turn shattered the remaining ampoules in the sink. Vacwell claimed damages against BDH, alleging that the accident was caused by breaches of contract and of duty at common law. On the trial of the issue of liability: it was held that BDH were liable to Vacwell.
- A full explanation of this case can be found at www.lawteacher.net.
- This should be supported wherever possible by the appropriate supporting evidence or research data. It should also give the following:
  - an assessment of the particular segments of the population at Risk, for example, work people in general, work people in specific occupations, the general public, medical patients, people engaged in leisure pursuits, men, women or children and so on;
  - an assessment of the seriousness of the hazard;
  - an assessment of the probability of occurrence;
  - an assessment of the consequences of occurrence;

–   an assessment of the appropriate remedial action required;
–   estimated total cost of the recall;
–   estimated consequential cost of the hazard;
–   a statement signed by the chief executive authorising the initiation of the recall.

Product Recall initiation

Upon receipt of the agreement by the chief executive or their nominee to initiate the recall programme, a hazard warning notice may be required. This should contain all the information necessary to bring the Risk to the attention of all those likely to be exposed to the hazardous product and the circulation may include:

*   field specialists including service staff;
*   appropriate Government or local authority departments;
*   police and other emergency services;
*   press, local and national where applicable;
*   radio and/or TV, local and national where applicable;
*   retail outlets;
*   customers, where possible;
*   trade journals and trade associations;
*   professional institutions and research establishments;
*   export agencies/licensees, foreign Governments, and so on;
*   relevant test houses.

Depending upon circumstances, the warning notice may include:

*   a statement of the hazard and likely consequences;
*   clear instructions and illustrations to enable the repair, correction, removal, immobilisation or shielding of the product;
*   warning or hazard signs, which may be detached from the notice and attached to the product and its container;
*   instructions appertaining to the return of the product and a recall return card, preferably reply paid. This could take the form of a tear-off portion of the letter.

Recall effectiveness assessment

Once the recall procedure is under way, it will be necessary to assess the effectiveness of the procedures adopted and to consider the possibility of stepping up the campaign. Similarly it will also be necessary to make a decision to terminate the recall when all possible items have been returned.

Post-recall investigation

The initiation of a Product Recall must be regarded as a catastrophic failure of the quality plan. Even in the case of a limited recall, entailing the return of a small number of items from a retailer, there must be a post-mortem. The post-mortem should be conducted by the most senior personnel from the departments implicated, headed by a senior executive and supported by the quality manager. The objective will be to determine where the organisational weaknesses are that allowed the event to occur. Failure to do so means that the same thing could potentially happen again. This should not entail a witch hunt. Except for specific cases where negligence may have been involved, the problem is more likely to reflect on the management system in place than on the actions of any individual. The most effective approach is to examine the management processes to identify where the weaknesses occur.

The cross-functional project-by-project improvement process when correctly applied is the most effective method for resolving such problems. However, typical places to look for causes are:

- lack of relevant training;
- insufficient reliability testing of prototypes, components and pre-production models;
- inadequate research, in the case of products using chemicals;
- insufficient knowledge of existing data (see Vacwell Engineering example on page 78);
- lack of coordination of production feasibility before release for production;
- inadequate specifications for the testing of incoming materials or components;
- lack of coordination between design and other departments, particularly market research, reliability engineering and production, resulting in the production of inadequate specifications;
- too much pressure to rush designs through, with the consequence that short cuts are taken.

MANAGING RISK – THE HUMAN FACTOR

Most text material on the subject of Risk deals exhaustively with the probabilistic mathematics of Risk Assessment but there are very few which deal with the human aspects.

This might be of critical importance because at one extreme there those who are Risk averse and extremely cautious by nature and at the other, Risk takers, who include stunt men, firefighters, those who engage in extreme sports and so on. Therefore the psychological make-up of teams involved in Risk Assessment is an important factor.

This subject is very well covered in the book by Drs Hillson and Murray-Webster,[1] coincidentally by the same publisher as this book. The following is an extract from their introduction and it is a thoroughly recommended addition to the Hoshin Kanri bookshelf:

The most significant Critical Success Factor for effective Risk management is the one most often lacking: an appropriate and mature Risk culture. Research and experience both indicate that the attitude of individuals and organisations has a significant influence on whether Risk management delivers what it promises. Risk management is undertaken by people, acting individually and in various groups. The human element introduces an additional layer of complexity into the Risk process, with a multitude of influences both explicit and covert. These act as sources of bias, creating preferred Risk attitudes which affect every aspect of Risk management. Risk attitudes exist at individual, group, corporate and national levels, and can be assessed and described with some degree of accuracy. This allows sources of bias to be diagnosed, exposing their influence on the Risk process.

But diagnosis is different from cure. Where preferred Risk attitude is not conducive to effective Risk management action is required to modify attitude. Recent advances in the field of Emotional Intelligence provide a means by which attitudinal change can be promoted and managed, for both individuals and organisations.

It is important firstly to understand Risk attitudes and the impact they can have on the Risk management process if their presence and influence are not recognised or managed. It is also important to understand how development of Emotional Intelligence can provide practical and powerful tools for modifying Risk attitudes.

---

1   David Hillson and Ruth Murray-Webster, *Understanding and Managing Risk Attitude*, Gower Publishing.

Conclusion

It is hoped that the prospect of being faced with the consequences of having to implement the procedures described in this chapter will be sufficient to convince everyone of the importance of attempting to 'get things right the first time'. During recent years the number of major Product Recalls seems to have been on the increase, and by now must be a major source of worry to industry. Quite apart from the actual costs of managing such a project, the damage to the reputation of the company can be lasting. Also, there is the question of negative advertising. Most organisations spend enormous sums attempting to convince the world that they are the best. Now they have to spend the same sums of money explaining that their product is actually quite harmful. Even with the most intense application of quality-related concepts the Risk is never zero. The Ford Motor Company for example is probably one of the biggest advocates of FMEA and even they get it wrong sometimes! Maybe Six Sigma or Lean Sigma programmes are the best form of defence?

PRODUCT RECALL SUMMARY

It makes no difference how good a QMS might be, there will always be Risks. Sometimes the Risk may come from legislation. For example the 'U' value case, Product Liability requiring a recall, international terrorism, currency and interest rate fluctuations, weather and global warming which hit the market generally or may be from aggressive competition. For a Hoshin Kanri programme to be successful, all of these Risks must be considered and constantly reviewed.

In some cases, by protecting ourselves against some specific Risk we may be able to put a competitor in a difficult position (the Loose Brick).

9   *The Loose Brick*

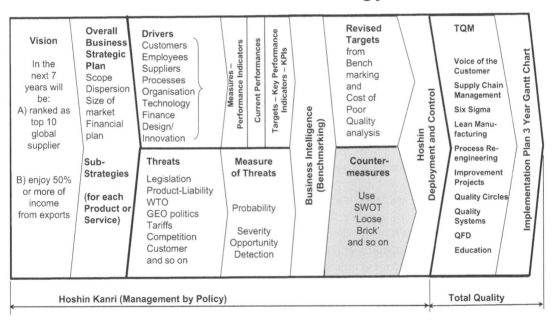

Hoshin Kanri – from Strategy to Action!

Figure 9.1   The Loose Brick

If Chapters 3, 6 and 8 have been followed, a number of high-level Risks are likely to have been identified which require action. Some of these Risks may just apply to your organisation because of internal problems or because you have been targeted by a competitor, whilst others might apply to the industry as a whole.

All of this can be dealt with in the first place by using the Loose Brick concept. It is a weapon that can be used against your competitors or to counter a threat from them and, when used together with the concepts of TQM, will in time enable your organisation to become irresistibly powerful in your market and safe from attack by others.

The Loose Brick concept is not widely known in the West but is consistently used to devastating effect by Japanese international competitors. It is equivalent to the concept of the Achilles Heel which is well known from Greek mythology but rarely, if ever, used as a strategic weapon in industry. The object of the method is to search for an opponent's weak or blind spot and then ruthlessly exploit it. As a management tool intended for the destruction of the competition, it has no equal.

For example, in 1980, Rank Xerox controlled almost 100 per cent of the world market for plain paper copiers. By 1985, that share of market had plunged below 50 per cent and was rapidly headed downward towards 40 per cent. The same happened more or less at the same time to Caterpillar at the hands of Komatsu. It also happened to the British motorcycle industry in the 1960s, and to the British shipbuilding industry just a few years earlier. This example is included in the Benchmarking chapter but as with motorcycles, the UK had more than 50 per cent of the shipbuilding market in the 1950s and this was almost wiped out by the mid 1960s. The process is still repeatedly happening in other industries and there is evidence that the same method has been learned by the Chinese automotive industry.

At the beginning of the 1960s, UK companies had more than 50 per cent of world trade in the manufacture of motorcycles. At that time many business people in the UK still erroneously saw Britain as 'the workshop to the world', a position it had long since relinquished to the USA, but many still clung to the belief regardless of the evidence to the contrary. Only a mere handful of years later, the industry had been virtually wiped out.

In 1973 the UK had about ten major manufacturers of television sets: McMichael, Sobell, Bush, Ultra, Decca, HMV, Redifusion, Pye, Ferguson and the Dutch-owned company, Philips. One year later, only Philips and Ferguson remained, but the latter was a special case. Sony, Hitachi, Toshiba, JVC, Panasonic and several others replaced the local TV brands. Incredible though it may seem today, the general public in the UK had previously never heard of these Japanese names. Prior to that time people were generally mistrustful of the Japanese ability to manufacture electronic goods despite the inroads they were making into the automobile market. They still had the idea that the Japanese could only produce shoddy imitations to their Western counterparts and yet they bought their TVs and in such numbers as to enable them to wipe out almost all of their competitors at a stroke. Why? Or more to the point – how?

In every case, the same phenomenon occurred: with no prior warning there was an overwhelming assault on the fated companies by not just one Japanese competitor but by virtually all of them collectively. Ever since this first happened to the British motorcycle industry at the hands of Honda, Kawasaki and so on, the evidence was all around, yet virtually no one seems to have recognised that these events had a commonality. The consistency with which this Strategy has been used over so many decades promises that it will continue to happen into the future if the targeted victims do not wake up to what is happening and develop corresponding counterstrategies. However, in spite of the attention given to Japanese industrial strategies in general, and also the wide attention given to total Quality-related concepts and the popularity of such books as 'The Toyota Way', there still remains a further element that has eluded the attention of those who are struggling to counter this market-dominating offensive.

The secret is simple. The Loose Brick simply means, 'Looking for and then ruthlessly exploiting the competitor's blind spot.' This is generally a market-sensitive measure of some kind of which, preferably, the competitor is unaware. Once their Benchmarking strategists have identified this measure and before it is exploited, the hopeful aggressors will attempt to improve their own performance with respect to that measure to a level which they believe is beyond the short-term ability of their intended victims to respond. Only then will they enter the market in the near certain knowledge that they will put the victims out of business before they are even aware of the reasons for their failure.

In the case of the motorcycles it was the split crankcase design of the British and other Western cycles that sprayed leaking oil over the legs of the driver. At that time the motorcyclist assumed that this was something they had to accept for the pleasure of riding a bike. Of course, the phenomenon restricted the use of motorcycles to those who were prepared to endure this.

Despite the obvious disadvantages, the UK manufacturers stubbornly and arrogantly claimed that motorcyclists were a special breed of people who liked to be covered in oil and therefore would not see it as a problem! Their Japanese rivals however, saw this erroneous premise as an opportunity. If they could produce motorcycles with solid crankcases that did not spray oil, not only would the enthusiast prefer it but it could open the market to include potential customers who would like a bike but would not accept being covered in oil. In the case of the motorcycle therefore, this was the Loose Brick. Incredibly, even though the British already had designs with solid crankcases, they refused to admit that they were wrong even despite plummeting sales and preferred instead to be forced out of business.

The concept is ever present in the Japanese approach to business. In contrast, in the West, and particularly the UK and the USA, even today after so many examples of its effects, industry appears almost blind to the Loose Brick concept.

PRODUCT OR MARKET ORIENTATION – THE BRITISH MOTOR CORPORATION VERSUS DATSUN CASE

Following their success with both motorcycles and shipping, and before Japanese automobiles entered the Western markets, competition among Western auto manufacturers in Europe and the USA was focused on technical innovation and differentiation by major differences in styling. Unlike today, where many cars of differing makes appear to be very similar, the Morgan, Vauxhall, Jaguar, Austin, Rover, Wolesley and Citroen were all instantly recognisable by their very distinctive appearance.

Prior to the time when Japanese automobiles first appeared in the early to mid 1960s, the industry in the West was locked in competition with its rivals, believing that market share was determined by technological innovation. The then British Motor Corp. was at least equal to its competitors in this respect and following a series of significant technological breakthroughs with the introduction of hydro-elastic suspension and the transverse engine, the company felt confident that it was in a strong position to hold its share of the market in both the UK and abroad. Such innovations were clearly more elegant from an engineering point of view than their predecessors, but they lost out in the marketplace to the simple Datsun almost as soon as it appeared in the marketplace. In contrast to the technological elegance of the Austin/Morris 1100, the Datsun was about as basic technologically as it was possible to get. Western manufacturers even laughed at it and claimed that its technology was based on concepts that were new in the 1930s but had long since been superseded. Despite this, the Datsun immediately began to make steady and significant inroads into the BMC market, why?

In hindsight, the reason was simple. It was another example of the Loose Brick.

The Datsun had a radio as standard and neither the Austin/Morris 1100, nor indeed any other European rival vehicles, did. The Japanese were aware that the average customer was unlikely to either understand or care about the technology of sophisticated suspension systems. To the customer, an auto is an auto, but a radio as a standard item has value added at no extra cost. This was a highly visible differentiator that changed customer's expectations overnight. The roads were not in a bad state at that time and the differences between competing suspension systems were not obvious to most potential customers but the customer did know a radio when they saw one!

This single factor was the beginning of one of the more profound changes in the history of the motor car since the advent of mass production.

In the eyes of the public, this Japanese company had done something no other manufacturer had even attempted to do. The Japanese, in this case Datsun (Nissan) were market orientated and recognised that the customer is king. In contrast, Western manufacturers, however, were still 'heads in the sand' and product oriented. The thinking was, 'We are the experts at designing and making automobiles, so we know what is best for the customer. They are making a mistake buying Japanese cars so we must educate them.' They then had another unpleasant surprise. When demand consistently exceeds supply, which it consistently had until the Japanese intrusion, manufacturers could dictate what the customer could and could not have. As Price was the main competitive differentiator, no Western manufacturer would entertain the idea of providing rust protection as standard. The claim was that it would put the price up and people would not buy the car. This theory was never put to the test. It seems incredible today in an age of environmental awareness but at that time they tried to convince the potential customers that we were moving towards a 'throw away society'. Do not worry if it goes rusty or breaks down, just throw it away and buy another one. If we made them more reliable and extended their life nobody would pay the extra cost. Here was another Loose Brick and one that proved fatal to the industry both in Europe and in the USA. The Japanese began to ship cars that did not rust and were incredibly reliable – they simply did not break down – and no Western manufacturer was able to match this performance.

Unfortunately at that time, Western understanding of the principles of Total Quality were virtually non-existent. As a consequence Western manufacturers were reluctant to introduce any features where they could not see the possibility of an immediate advantage over their rivals.

For the Japanese with their newly developed TQM-based production methods and with the workforce engaged in continuous improvement activities on the shop floor, this presented an opportunity too good to miss. Here was an obvious Loose Brick of monumental proportions. The rest is history.

Western manufacturers did not learn from this experience. Japanese manufacturers continued to attempt to provide what the consumer required and, eventually, as Dr Juran indicated in a number of publications, the Japanese overtook their Western counterparts in the USA in the mid 1970s.

The real Loose Brick in the case of automobiles was the manufacturers 'we-know-best' mentality which presented their Japanese rivals with a multitude of possibilities. Even today with all that has happened in the industry, few Western auto manufacturers appear to have any Countermeasures to recover their lost markets.

It is true that most Western auto manufacturers have developed Total Quality strategies but these do not appear to be as well developed as those of Toyota, Honda and so on despite years of study and intense rivalry. Almost all have attempted to introduce project-by-project improvement, supplier control, Lean Manufacturing, Six Sigma and other Quality-related sciences and disciplines to improve reliability, reduce stocks, shorten lead times, and so on. However, none appears to have recognised the Loose Brick concept and all seem unable to stop the relentless march of their Japanese counterparts.

Until Western manufacturers seriously rediscover Quality Circles and enthusiastically support the concept throughout their organisations, educate and intensively train their managers from the very top right down to line supervision in people skills, and understand that managers do not make anything as such, their job is to get results through people, and that they will be judged and promoted on the visible demonstration of their ability to encourage participation and that this is extended right down through their Supply Chains, they will continue to fail.

Today, the steady march of the Japanese automotive companies is not the only threat. There is now much evidence that the Chinese auto industry is in the process of adopting a similar Loose Brick Strategy to that so effectively exploited by Komatsu in its battle with Caterpillar.

At the time of writing this book, there are very few Chinese cars in the USA and Europe generally. However, the same is not true in Egypt and many other parts of the developing world. In Egypt, Chinese cars are very much in evidence and they are good products with many sophisticated electronic features that are normally only found on much higher-value Western vehicles. If the Loose Brick concept is being exploited by the Chinese, then the possibility is that they are in the process of creating a bridgehead by building a strong market with strong and effective local product support in those countries before attempting to make a significant assault on the market in the developed world. By this time they would not have to support their products from remote parts of China but from their more local bases in their host countries.

TELEVISION MARKET DOMINATION – THE PHILIPS CASE

The case of television was different. The Loose Brick was not the product, its features or the manufacturers' attitudes in response to customers. Instead, the target was the dealer. With a product such as television, it is difficult to introduce features that are not easily copied or which add to the attractiveness of the product without also adding significantly to its cost.

Moreover, research indicated that for such products, because of the lack of distinctive differences in appearance or price, it is somewhat easy for a retailer to influence the end user towards whichever product they prefer to sell. With TV, there were two key possibilities: first, to be able to offer good margins for sales, possibly leading to price wars and accusations of dumping; second, to provide a significantly more reliable product.

The attraction of a differentiator such as reliability was that the difference may be apparent to the retailer because of significantly fewer warranty claims. These differences would be far less visible to the competitor unless they themself purchased large quantities of their competitors' products and tested them exhaustively. The difference was not apparent to the end users either. All that customers knew was that their TV sets kept working but they did not know whether the brand that they had purchased was any better or worse than any other make. They probably assumed that they were all more or less the same.

Early on, Philips conducted a defensive study to learn why the Japanese were taking market share at such a phenomenal rate and why their own European competitors were being forced out of the market altogether. Their research showed that unless they did something dramatic and decisive, they would also be forced out of that business in about 1 year. Philips found few differences in Price or appearance between the Japanese and Western sets. These were the key criteria that had previously influenced consumer choice. However, they did find that where the Western standard for warranty claims on new products was 6 per cent, the Japanese manufacturers had achieved an incredible 0.5 per cent. This statistic was not a differentiator from the end users' point of view because unless they purchased hundreds of sets they would never know. However, the large retail organisations and particularly the TV rental business in those days would quickly get to know which sets came back for repair and which did not. Naturally they preferred to sell the ones that did not come back and so naturally they strongly promoted the Japanese products.

The main problem confronting Philips was the fact that in order to achieve 6 per cent warranty claims it was necessary to ensure that batches of component parts contained defects in the order of 1 per cent of parts per hundred defective and this was known as percentage defective. Suppliers would be selected on their ability to manufacture to this level of quality or better and sophisticated statistical sampling schemes based on American Military Standards (MIL Std 101) were used (in the UK British Standard 6001) to keep control at that level.

However, in order to achieve the 0.5 per cent which the Japanese were able to do required supplier quality levels in the order of parts per million (ppm). At that time the term ppm was unknown in the West and even worse, nobody had any idea how it could be achieved in volume parts production. Philips realised that possible or not, unless they did achieve it within a year, they would not be able to continue in that market. As a consequence they contacted all of their suppliers and demanded that they attempt to achieve ppm. They also said that Philips engineers would be available to help them. If they could or would not do it they would not get preferred supplier status. Fortunately for Philips they did achieve it.

Incredibly, Philips was able to equal Japanese competition in product reliability within 1 year, which was a remarkable achievement. As a result, Philips is one of the few Western electronics giants to remain in competition. The difference in reliability as a major exploitable weakness was a classic case of the Loose Brick Strategy.

FLAWED MARKETING STRATEGY 1 – THE CATERPILLAR CASE

The case of Komatsu against Caterpillar is another example. When Caterpillar joined with Mitsubishi Heavy Industries in 1960, Komatsu, as a smaller operator, recognised the possibility that it could be forced out of business. To prevent this and by using the Loose Brick Strategy, Komatsu created the slogan 'Encircle Caterpillar'. At that time, it appeared almost as achievable as a flea surrounding a herd of elephants, but it was a long-term Strategy.

While looking for the Caterpillar blind spot, Komatsu discovered that though Caterpillar was a giant in the developed world, it had very little presence in underdeveloped counties. Not wishing to alert the competitor too soon, Komatsu began to develop a network of product support and distribution throughout all continents away from the gaze of this giant competitor. By the late 1970s the plan was complete and the economic strength of Komatsu in the early 1980s had become substantial. At this point, Komatsu made a direct assault on Caterpillar's markets. Caterpillar was unprepared for this. It had not been anticipated and Caterpillar was slow to respond. Consequently its market share slumped from 90 to 40 per cent in some 5 years.

The giant was now fighting for its life and to do so was forced to sell some of its overseas operations and retrench. To rub salt in the wounds, Komatsu even bought the Caterpillar site which they had closed in the North East of England.

FLAWED MARKETING STRATEGY 2 – THE PLAIN PAPER COPIER MANUFACTURER CASE

In 1980 Rank Xerox had more than 90 per cent of the world market in plain paper copiers which amounted to virtual total market domination and total dependency of its customers on the conditions of use of the products it supplied. At that time Xerox would not normally sell one of its copiers but only hire them out. The machine remained the property of Xerox. For this reason they could also dictate how it was to be used. Only Xerox copy paper and ink was allowed and the machine could only be serviced by a Xerox employee and on average there was only one such engineer/salesman in each large town or city. If the machine broke down, which was not infrequent, the user was forced to wait until a Xerox engineer was available. The machines were huge by today's standards and filled a fairly large room. Typically they were operated by a member of staff who had been trained by Xerox and only very large companies would have more than one machine. The Xerox operator therefore had considerable power and was someone who needed to be treated with respect!

This was a nice cosy position for Xerox until, in the UK, Canon appeared on the scene in 1980. At first, Canon only concerned themselves with getting into the market in Edinburgh, Scotland. There was only one Xerox representative there at the time. Canon had many. They went to petrol stations and doctors' surgeries, as well as all of the commercial companies. Although they were analogue not digital, the Canon machines were much the same in appearance as they are today; they were considerably smaller than the monster Xerox equivalent.

Apart from the size, there were a number of significant design and marketing innovations included in the Japanese models. They had used the concept of Robust Design to make the paper feed mechanism sufficiently accommodating to be able to take a wide variety of different makes of copy paper so the client could buy what they wanted. The machines could be both purchased or leased from local approved suppliers who had been trained in product support. One could imagine the Xerox representative becoming desperate as a consequence of this intense competition and calling head office. However, they were not getting any similar reports from anywhere else so they probably confidently assumed that the job was getting on top of him.

After having established a foothold in Edinburgh they then selected another city, then another and another. Eventually, with a good network established, they went for a full frontal attack on Xerox. Having achieved a bridgehead into the UK market, they were followed by Ricoh, Panasonic and the other Japanese manufacturers. They began taking full-page advertisements in national newspapers and on television. By 1985, Xerox's share of the market had slumped to around 45 per cent and they were on the ropes.

Their first defensive reaction was to put more than 100 000 employees worldwide through project-by-project continuous improvement training. This enabled them to make the same out-of -date machines more reliable, it reduced production costs and shortened lead times but they were still cumbersome and still the gap continued to grow.

Then they discovered the real reason, they were being outsmarted in the marketplace. Their Japanese rivals had done their jobs well. They had Benchmarked Xerox to such an extent that they could almost predict everything they were likely to do. Fortunately for Xerox, the company had amassed huge resources, as had Philips in the TV scenario. Also they were not simply dependent on their plain paper copier market; they had other products so they still had time to react.

They discovered that whilst it was beneficial to have the continuous improvement teams, the Japanese products were much smaller and cheaper. The customer preferred to own the machine and have a choice of suppliers and product support services and to choose their own paper suppliers. The Japanese products were appearing in places that Xerox had never considered, such as small offices, doctors' surgeries, petrol stations and so on. Also, these early users were beginning to offer services themselves by selling copy services.

Eventually Xerox were able to respond to this and bring out competitive products of their own. They survived but the damage done by their over-confident customer-unfriendly earlier approach was severe. They remained in the market but could never regain their earlier dominance. The lesson is simple. It does not matter how large your share of market or how impenetrable you think your reputation is, history shows that everyone is vulnerable to the Loose Brick Strategy, no matter how strong you think you are.

BENCHMARKING FOR THE LOOSE BRICK

When used as part of an industrial Strategy, Loose Brick Strategy forms an essential part of Hoshin Kanri.

It is necessary to study the relative strengths and weaknesses of the competitor with a view to negating the strengths and exploiting the weaknesses including the blind spots or Loose Bricks. This can be done by Benchmarking, which is the subject of Chapter 6.

Benchmarking at this level must be done by a business strategist who is probably also a company director supported by specialists. In Japan, directors have the time to do this because they have deployed problem solving on a day-to-day basis through the organisation. The Western companies have not yet learned to do this effectively. Consequently, the directors, senior managers and specialists in these companies spend too much of their time solving everyone else's problems.

As an illustration, the directors of Komatsu spend an average of 6 months per year engaged in Benchmarking and Strategic activities – this means they have been able to run rings around Caterpillar and other competitors. Typically, Western directors may spend only 3 days per year on what they often refer to as 'back to the woods' sessions.

Loose Bricks are not always evident and may be difficult to locate. Survival may require that a firm's executives try to begin thinking like their best competitor. Such competitors may be a valuable resource.

What do all of these examples have in common? In every case, the target industry or company had an exploitable blind spot or weakness. The Japanese competitor had identified that weakness, then developed the means to exploit it. There were no quick fixes. Each case was carefully researched, thoroughly thought out, and launched with stunning effectiveness.

The example of Datsun's auto radio may seem thin compared with the other examples, but in fact it represented a profound change in thinking. Japanese knew that Western auto builders would not respond. First the radio came as standard, then wing mirrors, mud flaps, cassette players and so forth. Of course, the industry has eventually responded to this, but how long did it take and how much market share had been lost first? There are indications that we have not yet learned from these experiences. They are still happening.

BENCHMARKING FOR THE LOOSE BRICK

Look for both your potential Loose Bricks and those that you might exploit in your competitors.

First of all study the market that you are in or wish to penetrate.

Identify the performance capabilities of the competitors collectively. Are there any standards that have been accepted by the customers that are less than perfect but which would appear to be unchallenged (in the case of the TVs, the customer was the distribution network and the parameter was warranty claims)? Reference: the Philips case.

Can you find anything comparable in the market you are in that might be exploitable in the same way?

Do you, any or all of the competitors have a flawed marketing Strategy? Reference: the Caterpillar case and Chinese manufactured cars.

Are you or the competition excessively product oriented or market oriented? Reference: British Motor Corporation versus Datsun.

Do you have a tendency to bring under-developed products into the market and then use retro design to get out of trouble at the same time that competition is beginning to appear?

Reference: the case of Clive Sinclair's revolutionary ZX81 computer.

In the mid 1970s a British scientist Clive Sinclair attracted huge publicity for an innovative computer product which is claimed to have brought computing to the homes of families across the UK. At the time there was nothing like it. The machine required the use of a small Ferguson black and white TV (which is the reason why Ferguson survived the Japanese TV onslaught). A simple cassette audio tape served as what today would be a hard drive. It was very simple but extremely effective. The low cost enabled everyone to own one of these machines and there was soon an abundance of software available. It was incredible what became possible on a few kb of memory. Unfortunately, there proved to be a flaw in Sinclair's judgment. In order to ensure prior franchise and to be the first in the market, the product was under-designed in the method used to connect the peripherals which included the tape player and any additional external memory that might have been purchased. These connectors were so bad that the number of customer returns for this reason was astronomic. In fact the author of this book was forced to return five in order to get one that worked at all and it was claimed that Sinclair's company had several warehouses stacked with their returns.

However, having stimulated interest and a market for this type of product, aggressive competitors were on the move. It was not long before Amstrad appeared in the market with a superior machine that had none of the flaws of the Sinclair product. Soon there were others; Commodore was one popular model and then a series of competitors. It was not long before the Sinclair product became a distant memory. The Loose Brick in this case was the flawed design of the connectors.

- Find the Loose Brick by researching the competition, including its distribution process and marketing policies.

- Identify best-in-class competitors and their strengths and weaknesses.
- Find best-in-class processes including their equivalents in parallel industries.

    Sometimes businesses in parallel industries do the same things in different ways, and these are worth studying. (People in the same industries usually do the same things the same way).
- Find the best people policies; these can come from any industry.
- Identify best-in-class technology.
- Identify best-in-class financial performance. These data are probably the easiest to obtain and subjected to Benchmarking by easy access to public company reports.
- Study business strategies across a spectrum of industries with particular focus on those that have produced stunning results in terms of market penetration.
- Study the root causes of failure of some companies that have collapsed. The cases stated here have only been selected to stimulate thought, there are countless others. What are the lessons learned?

Some examples to look at:

- Why did Marks and Spencer suddenly and almost without warning find themselves in dire trouble in the late 1990s?
- Why is the Hoover vacuum cleaner nowadays just one of many when it totally dominated the market in the post-war years? Why do people say they are going to 'hoover the floor' when they have a Dyson?
- How has Hewlett Packard managed to survive and grow in the face of almost impossible competition from competing Japanese computer and computer-peripheral manufacturers?
- How did Tesco manage to leap from being a very unimpressive high street retailer to becoming one of the most successful supermarkets in the world taking all before it?
- What happened to the 'slide rule' back in the mid 1970s? Could the manufacturers have prevented what happened or even have produced the rival product? Is our product vulnerable in this way? Can our product be adapted to do this to some products in other markets?
- What happened to Rolls Royce cars and why? Why is the Rover Group now in Chinese ownership?

When you find the answers to these and others that you can work out for yourself then ask: 'What can we learn from all of this that could be applied to us?' That is the essence of Loose Brick thinking applied to Hoshin Kanri planning.

Finally, from this research, do we need to rethink the priority that we have given to any of the KPIs? Perhaps some of them are more important than we first thought? If so then they may need to be considered as Six Sigma, Lean Manufacturing, Quality Circle or some other TQM project either to counter a threat to us or to exploit a potential Loose Brick in our marketplace to the detriment of our competitors.

10 Policy Deployment and Control

Hoshin Kanri – from Strategy to Action!

Vision	Overall Business Strategic Plan	Drivers	Measures – Performance Indicators	Current Performances	Targets – Key Performance Indicators – KPIs	Business Intelligence (Benchmarking)	Revised Targets	Hoshin Deployment and Control	TQM	Implementation Plan 3 Year Gantt Chart
In the next 7 years will be: A) ranked as top 10 global supplier	Scope Dispersion Size of market Financial plan	Customers Employees Suppliers Processes Organisation Technology Finance Design/ Innovation					from Bench marking and Cost of Poor Quality analysis		Voice of the Customer, Supply Chain Management, Six Sigma, Lean Manu-facturing, Process Re-engineering	
B) enjoy 50% or more of income from exports	Sub-Strategies (for each Product or Service)	Threats: Legislation Product-Liability WTO GEO politics Tariffs Competition Customer and so on		Measure of Threats: Probability Severity Opportunity Detection			Counter-measures: Use SWOT 'Loose Brick' and so on		Improvement Projects, Quality Circles, Quality Systems, QFD, Education	

Hoshin Kanri (Management by Policy) | Total Quality

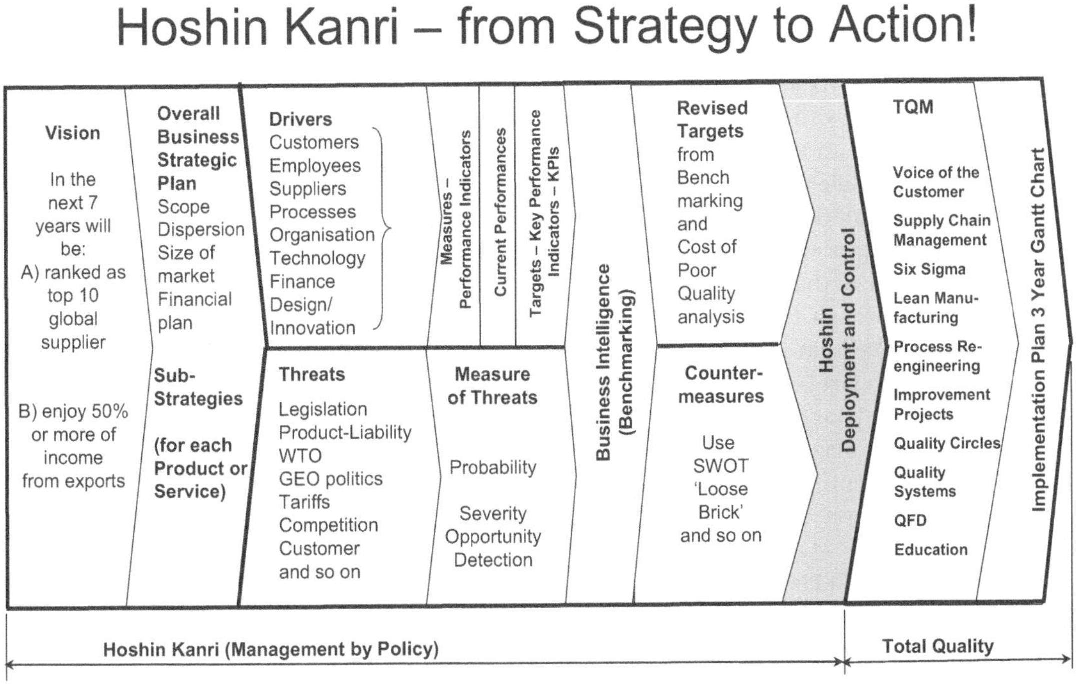

Figure 10.1   Hoshin Deployment and Control

There are three key elements to Hoshin Kanri:

1. Hoshin Planning.
2. Hoshin Deployment.
3. Hoshin Control.

So far this book has dealt with the core of Hoshin Planning. Progressively, this chapter deals with Hoshin Deployment and Hoshin Control. Hoshin Deployment is not dissimilar to a well-designed staff appraisal scheme. In this case, the KPIs created by the top team are discussed with their direct reports. Some of them can only be dealt with at the highest level but a high proportion can be deployed down into the organisation layer by layer. However, as they are taken downwards, they may be broken into sub-KPIs and reworded into the terms used in the respective functions. For example, the word 'yield' may have one meaning to the finance director but a different meaning to the chiefs of design or manufacture. In the latter cases it will need to be more specific and stated in terms of per cent yield from raw material or new products per designer, and so on. This deployment process will continue downwards, layer by layer until it reaches direct supervision and the workforce, and is restated each time that it moves down. By the time that the KPIs reach the bottom layers they will have been broken down into multiple and very specific objectives.

Whilst this is taking place, each layer of management will go through a similar process to the top team to identify Departmental Vision, Drivers and their own KPIs. These will be submitted up to the top team and agreed together with the top-down issues. This is sometimes referred to as a 'catch ball' process. This may seem tedious and a lot of work but it does not actually take up a huge amount of time and the results are often surprising. Not only do people know what is expected of them, they also feel that they have had the opportunity to contribute their ideas and feel part of the organisation as a community.

It also deals with the problem that the KPIs developed at the top are usually in corporate language similar to the terms used in the financial report. This language is generally unfamiliar to middle management and the workforce who are concerned with the day-to-day issues of meeting the specific demands of output and daily management.

Equally, the issues that are thought to be important to middle management are not well appreciated by those at the top. As a consequence, communications as to priorities are often dysfunctional across this interface with the result that top management fails to communicate its priorities to middle management and vice versa. The usual consequence of this is that top management have the impression that middle management are not properly motivated and middle management believe that top management do not understand the issues.

The catch ball process in Hoshin Policy Deployment is an effective way to remove this barrier.

It could be argued that this chapter should have preceded the TQM chapters so that the KPIs are cascaded down through the organisation before the improvement activities are started. However, experience indicates that most organisations are impatient to begin the improvement process as soon as possible. In fact both the development of the TQM activities and the Deployment of Hoshin Kanri can be carried out in parallel if the resources are available.

The following diagram shows how the PDCA Cycle is integral to the Hoshin Planning, Deployment and Control process.

Figure 10.2 shows a typical structure of a Hoshin Kanri-compatible business management system.

Some high-level KPIs may require the acquisition of resources for their achievement. For example, the move from traditional production methods to Lean Manufacturing might require the appointment of a new manager specifically tasked with this objective. They will require facilities and physical and human resources if it is a large organisation.

Some KPIs such as the introduction of Lean Manufacturing will also take several years to achieve. Therefore it will be necessary to set Goals for each year. The next step will be to decide which KPIs must be dealt with at this level and then to share the KPIs with direct reports.

The final major activity involving the top team will be to establish the Goals for the first year. There are two aspects:

1. Identification of those KPIs which must be achieved quickly or which may take more than a year to achieve. For example, it may be known that some competitors are much 'Leaner' than we are and as a consequence are able to undercut costs and shorten lead times. Part of our reaction to this might need to be a dramatic reduction in inventory and finished goods stocks. This might take several years to achieve so short-term goals might be to make interim improvements. The same may apply to man-hours in production. For example, one large aircraft manufacturer set the achieved goals to reduce man-hours for the manufacture of wings for a large civil aircraft from 72 000 hours to 44 000 in the first year, to 24 000 in the second and 19 000 in the third year.

Hoshin Policy Deployment

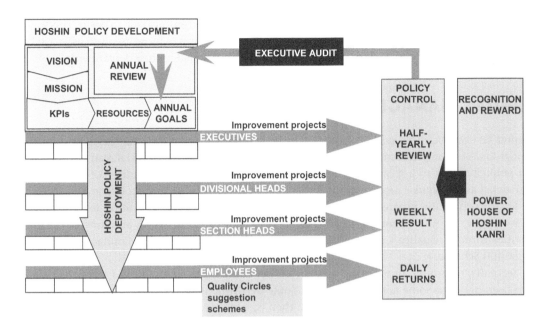

Figure 10.2   The full Hoshin Policy Deployment model

2. The roll-out of Hoshin Kanri into the organisation. In a small company, it might be possible to roll-out the whole programme in 12 months. However, this would be unusual. More typically it might take 3 to 5 years to develop everything and even then there will be some ongoing developments. For example, the involvement of the whole Supply Chain. To give some idea as to the work involved, it is now some 10 years since the new Toyota plant in the UK was opened. In a lecture given by the chief executive officer of the plant when it had been operating for 7 years, he was asked by a visitor if its performance had equalled that of the parent plants in Japan. He said, 'Not yet, we expect it to take another 3 years!' And this was in a company that fully understood the concepts. The lesson is, do not expect too much too soon. However, most companies will make some very early quick wins if they do things in the right sequence and are careful in the prioritisation process. It is the culture change that takes the time, especially in a brown field site. When people have spent many years of their lives working in non-Hoshin-style environments it is a bit like learning to drive on the other side of the road. There is always a tendency to revert back especially when you lose concentration. Perhaps it is not a particularly good analogy because most will still be driving on the other side! This is why many Japanese companies operating in foreign countries prefer to take on school leavers, so that the only work culture that they know is the one at that operation.

START WHERE THE GRASS IS GREENEST!

Since the roll-out will not be across the whole organisation and in all aspects of the business, the task will be to select the most appropriate areas in which to begin. The answers will depend upon where the biggest problems are but there is another alternative. In many cases it is best to start where the grass is greenest. Since this management process will be new to most who read this book, it would make sense to start where it is easiest and where there is the best chance of success. There will almost always be some departments where this is obvious. Select those where the managers already have a good relationship with their workers, where they are most likely to be cooperative and enthusiastic to begin. This way, the process will begin to show positive results quickly and the enthusiasm of those involved will soon begin to affect others. Success comes when others are pressing to get started in their departments.

ANNUAL MANAGEMENT REVIEW

Chapter 18 describes how system audits might be carried out. In addition to this there will be the Annual Audit by the president or chief executive officer. This is not a superficial scan of the activities or a publicity stunt to appear interested, but a serious and penetrating audit. Not perhaps in the same detail as the regular departmental audits but selectively penetrating on two levels.

Firstly, review the progress on a selection of the most important KPIs at all levels through to the workforce, the effectiveness of cross-functional improvement activities and intra-departmental activities through Quality Circles, 5S/C activities (see Chapter 14, Lean Manufacturing) and the Suggestion Scheme.

Secondly, determine how far the process has penetrated the organisation. Progress is bound to have been better in some areas than others. Some departments will be way ahead of expectations and others may be floundering. The question then is, why the difference?

Following the audit, top management should have all the information that it needs to review progress in that year against the original plan and to set new Goals for the following year.

When this work is completed, then, apart from surveillance, the initial work of the top team is finished and the process continues to be developed through the organisation and down the Supply Chain.

By the time the initial KPIs have been synthesised in the manner described, all the way down to the bottom layers of the organisation, they will be very specific and in the language of that department. For example, the word 'yield' which will be very meaningful to managers at the highest level will mean very little to a forklift truck driver in the warehouse. However, by the time it has worked its way through to the forklift truck driver, it will have been broken down to include such specifics as 'broken pallets', 'flat battery', 'picking errors', 'handling damage' and so on.

At each layer, personnel should be trained in the problem-solving process so that they have the means to bring actual performance up to target performance. At the middle management level, this will result in multifunction improvement teams which have been trained to Green Belt Level if Six Sigma is to be part of the programme. However, the same level of training can be given even if Six Sigma itself is not included.

At the base of the pyramid, Quality Circles should be developed both as a means of encouraging 'self-management' and for the large number of workplace improvement possibilities to be achieved (Chapter 17). However, this will also include the opportunity to introduce some of the Lean Manufacturing concepts such as the 5 Ss and Total Productive Maintenance (TPM) as well (Chapter 14).

THE PRINCIPLE OF MANAGEMENT CONTROL

The PDCA Cycle

The PDCA Cycle is fundamental to Hoshin Planning, Deployment and Control. It is often referred to as the Deming Wheel but the term Shewhart Cycle is more accurate since it is then named after its originator, Dr Walter Shewhart. In the 1920s he recognised that the principle of Management Control was similar to the control of an electromechanical servomechanism during his years at the Hawthorne Plant of the Western Electric Corporation in the 1920s and 1930s.

A typical example of this is a full air conditioning system. Such a system is capable of both heating and cooling. It also contains a thermostat. In this case, the thermostat is set to the desired temperature, say 22 degrees Celsius in a given building. (In the language of PDCA this represents the Plan). The device senses the actual temperature and finds it to be low (this represents Check) and switches on the heater (this represents Action by switching on the heater and Doing by the heater when activated). The thermostat continues to Check and eventually the desired temperature is reached. It sends the information to the heater by switching it off. The same cycle of activities would have been taken if the room was too hot in which case the cooler would have been activated. This is referred to as a 'closed loop system' because it is capable of both heating and cooling. Had it not had the cooler, it would have been described as an 'open loop system' because it could be heated up to the target temperature but could not bring it down if it went over. Shewhart recognised that these features are precisely analogous to the process of Management Control.

Of course, in the normal operation of a servomechanism there is additional sophistication to avoid overshooting the target by operating damper systems and to prevent resonance, but the same can also be applied to management systems as well.

The PDCA concept should be applied to all activities and all processes, including the overall management process of the organisation as a whole.

Originally Dr Shewhart used it to describe the activities necessary for the control of physical processes using statistical methods for the checking and diagnostic activities.

This concept was initially introduced to post-war Japan by Homer Sarasohn in his concentrated series of courses for Japanese management. Most people are aware of the contribution later made by Drs Deming and Juran but fewer are aware of the enormous contribution made by Dr Sarasohn. Forgive a short diversion taken from the website http://honoringhomer.net/bio.html to emphasise that contribution:

Mr. Sarasohn was 29 when General Douglas MacArthur summoned him to Tokyo to restore Japan's communications industry following its destruction during World War II.

From 1946 through 1950, as Chief of the Industry Branch of the occupation army's Civil Communications Section (CCS), Mr. Sarasohn took the lead in helping Japan rebuild its capacity to manufacture radio, telephone, and telegraph equipment—and to assure the reliable quality of its industrial production.

Addressing the need to modernize management practices, Mr. Sarasohn instituted the CCS Management Seminars as a training program for senior executives in the communications industry. Collaborating with CCS colleague Charles Protzman, an engineer from Western Electric, Mr. Sarasohn taught strategic planning, principles of organization, management policy formulation, product innovation, and quality assurance. Those attending the seminars represented more than 100 companies, universities, and government agencies.

In teaching management science and quality assurance to those who went on to lead corporations such as Panasonic, Sony, Sharp, and Toshiba, Mr. Sarasohn emphasized the importance of defining organizational Objectives and articulating a statement of purpose. In Fundamentals of Industrial Management *(Maruzen Press, 1949), the book that Mr. Sarasohn co-wrote with Mr. Protzman as a text for the CCS seminars.*

Dr Shewhart was invited to fly over to participate in one of those courses but unfortunately suffered an attack of influenza just prior to the event. Deming took his place and became immediately popular with his presentation of the Shewhart Wheel but the foundations had already been laid by Homer Sarasohn.

Application of the PDCA Cycle

All work includes the 4 elements of the PDCA Cycle. To take a very simple example, suppose that we are tasked with preparing a meal. First of all we would need to Plan what we were going to prepare. For this we might use a cookery book or attempt to be creative. Let us suggest that we plan to roast a chicken. Once we have decided what we are going to do and how, this becomes the Plan. Then comes the Doing part of the cycle where we select, purchase and prepare the ingredients. If this requires cooking then we will have decided in our plan how long this should take and at what temperature. After the prepared chicken has been put into the oven, which we will have set at the Planned temperature, we note the time and get on with something else whilst the cooking takes place. However, suppose that our Plan suggested 2 hours at some specific temperature? It is unlikely, unless we have used this recipe many times before under near identical conditions, that we would simply leave the chicken in the oven for that time without Checking from time to time to see if all is well. Possibly, we might find on one of these Checks that it is cooking faster or slower than we had Planned. In this case we will take Action to put things right and get back on course.

After we have cooked our splendid meal, we will have gained experience from the process. If we are sensible, we will make notes in the recipe book regarding the changes that we made so that should we decide to prepare this dish again in the future we can profit from this experience. In other words, not only have we used the PDCA Cycle to control the process, we have by the action of recording the corrections that we have made, also taken the first step in Continuous Improvement.

Self-management

Every time we go through the PDCA Cycle we can improve on the previous cycle until we begin to approach perfection. This is the essence of Quality Control and when the Japanese use the term this is what they mean. But note that in our example, the whole of the cycle was carried out by one person. In our homes and private lives we can do that. As a consequence our personal pursuits are meaningful to us because if we are 'in control' we decide what to do, what outcomes we want and we have the means of correction if we do not like the result. This is very satisfying because we can feel that we are improving and that is a good feeling. Just look at the faces of people on television when they have won a competition, whether it be athletics, flower arranging, pumpkin growing or whatever. The sense of pride and self-esteem is obvious, as is the admiration of those who have looked on.

Unfortunately this is not always the case with our processes in a work environment.

The PDCA Cycle is still there but it is often not in the control of any one individual. Typically, the Plan is created by 'management'. This is not a problem in itself but all too often it is not communicated to those who will be responsible for the Doing. Often they are very remote from any information that tells them what they are doing and why. For example, a worker might be working a machine for winding steel springs.

They wind perhaps hundreds per day but nobody has taken the trouble to tell them what they are used for. Worse still, they may not inspect the steel springs themself, this is done by an inspector who accepts or rejects their work according to some predetermined limits on a gauge. The inspector does not know what they are used for either, nor do they know the consequences of the springs being too long or too short.

Sometimes, the inspector's gauge may be wrongly set and they reject good work or pass bad. In some instances work that they have rejected is, for some reason not known to them, sold to the customer. What has happened is that the customer is desperate for some more parts and has been told that there are some parts which are outside the specification. On this occasion, the customer is able to make adjustments to be able to use the defective parts on a concession basis. Unfortunately, nobody thinks to feed this information to either the worker or the inspector.

They see the work being transported and conclude that the pass or fail criteria are not really that important so why make trouble and fail parts that will be shipped anyway? Eventually this lapse is discovered and both the worker and the inspector are in trouble. What is their conclusion? We are just being treated as robots, management is inconsistent and does not know what it wants and just makes trouble for us. This is a possibly a worst case scenario but it is not far from reality in many jobs, not just in the manufacturing industry but across the board. It happens in hospitals, hotels, the tourist industry, finance and everywhere.

Notice also in this example that not only is the work (Doing) remote from the Planning, it is also remote from the Checking (inspection) as well. This means that the Action element will be flawed or non-existent because those who would take the Action and ensure Continuous Improvement lack the information because it was not they who collected it. Therefore the process will continue to produce poor-quality products ad infinitum until something is done to connect the elements of the PDCA loop.

This problem first became evident in Japanese industry in the late 1950s. The Japanese business community were passionate about their resolve to re-establish Japan as a great nation. They were set on closing the huge gap between themselves and the USA. The USA had not thought this possible, so in the early post-war years they were prepared to show the Japanese everything that they knew. They did not realise that the Japanese had no interest in simply copying the Americans, they wanted to know what the Americans were doing and then find a better way of doing it.

Consequently, by the late 1950s, when they had copied everything that they thought might be useful they began to study the methods they had absorbed more carefully. One thing that they discovered was that the American System of Management, which was first illustrated by Adam Smith in his book *The Wealth of Nations* – despised by Karl Marx in the mid 19th Century and refined by such pioneers as Fredrick W Taylor, Frank and Lillian Gilbreth and the production lines of Henry Ford – had some fundamental flaws which resulted in severe alienation of the workforce.

The solution to the problem was attributed to Professor Kaoru Ishikawa. He suggested that this method of managing people was alien to Japanese culture. In all probability it is alien to the whole of humanity but unfortunately this belief is not as popular as it might be in most Western societies and this is one of the key reasons why Toyota is first and getting stronger by the day and, by comparison, both GM and Ford are getting weaker, but this is the author's opinion.

Professor Ishikawa suggested that industry could not go back to the Craftsman system where each individual was fully in control of their own work because, as Adam Smith had demonstrated, it could not possible compete with the Division of Labour approach for productivity. However, he said that perhaps it would be possible to obtain the advantages of both if they could bring the concept of Craftsmanship back to work groups rather than to individuals with the supervisor as team leader.

This idea was first published in 1960 in a factory floor magazine entitled *Gemba to QA* which was targeted at the factory foreman. In 1962 the Nippon Wireless and Telegraph Company reported that it had set up six teams according to Professor Ishikawa's suggestion and that they had been extremely successful not only as a means of solving factory-level problems but also from the point of view of motivation. The following diagrams demonstrate: 1) the pure Craftsmanship approach; 2) The American Division of Labour approach and; 3) Professor Ishikawa's Quality Circles approach.

Figure 10.3 illustrates the PDCA Cycle for the work of a craftsman. In this model they plan their own work, perform the operations, check it themselves and take action on anything that does not come up to their standards.

In the model shown in Figure 10.4, management manages and people 'Do'. In the ultimate form of this model, work is broken down into its smallest possible elements (in one form, it is taken to the extreme where even the movements of the joints of the hand and the eyes, trunk and so on are regarded as the fundamental elements which are referred to as 'therbligs' which is 'Gilbreth' backwards after the founder of the method). Notice also the appearance of management 'specialists'.

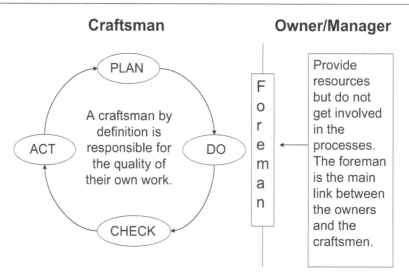

Figure 10.3   The basic PDCA Cycle

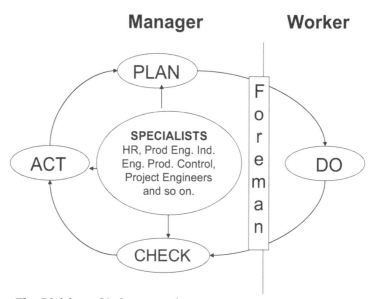

Figure 10.4   The Division of Labour version

They include human relations experts, industrial engineering, production engineering and so on, who act as consultants to line management. They do not act as consultants to supervision because it is their job that they have dissected and expanded. In this model, all problem solving is carried out by management or the management specialists. The workers are treated as robots, nobody asks them anything or involves them in anything and they are often paid directly by the quantity they produce. The same is also true for the foreman or supervisor whose esteem has been significantly diminished in this version of the model.

In the version of the model shown in Figure 10.5 it can be seen that the Plan at the managerial level is 'macro' in the sense that it represents the overall plan for the work to be carried out as a whole. Ideally this plan is shared with the supervisor or foreman who in turn shares it with the workgroup. This may be done on a weekly or even daily basis within the scope of daily management.

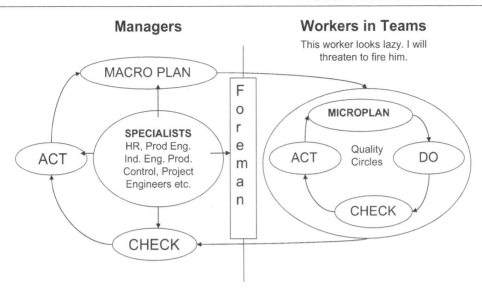

Figure 10.5   Participation in daily management

Notice also that in this version of the model, the specialists also act as consultants to the supervisor and the work groups.

The circle with the participation of the supervisor/foreman will discuss and agree as to how the micro plan will be achieved, what problems they may have to deal with, and so on.

By this means, unlike the previous model where the workers are just given their work instructions and otherwise largely ignored, here they are treated as mature people who are kept informed and actively encouraged to participate in the improvement of the performance in their work area. If, in addition, they are trained in problem-solving tools such as those included in Root Cause Analysis, they will be in a position to complete the PDCA Cycle and this effectively brings Craftsmanship back to the work team. It means that the organisation can get the best of both worlds. It can benefit from the productivity advantages of the Division of Labour approach whilst at the same time bringing the sense of ownership and achievement back to the work groups.

Figure 10.6 shows how the complete management system can be constructed to take advantage of the PDCA concept.

This is the fully-developed form of the model. Here it can be seen that it involves a nested set of PDCA Cycles where at each managerial level the Do is broken down into another PDCA Cycle for the level below until it reaches the workforce level.

Note also that whilst the work teams are developed to be self-managing, the specialists, which first appeared in the American Division of Labour approach, are still included. This is important because whilst some of what they had been doing may now be carried out by the workforce as part of their self-managing activities, in fact it relieves them of much tedious work and they will now be able to do some of the more sophisticated work that makes better use of their education and training. In some Japanese companies for example, regardless of the fact that they have approaching 100 per cent membership of Quality Circles, they will still outnumber their Western equivalents' staff of industrial engineers by an order of magnitude.

Figure 10.7 shows the Hoshin Policy Deployment Process, the project-by-project improvement activities, the feedback loop and the Management Review in more detail with the PDCA Cycle superimposed.

Unless the KPIs are derived directly from a well-thought through Vision statement and the relevant Strategy, Tactics and Drivers, they are at best a 'hit and miss' approach. Some may take the

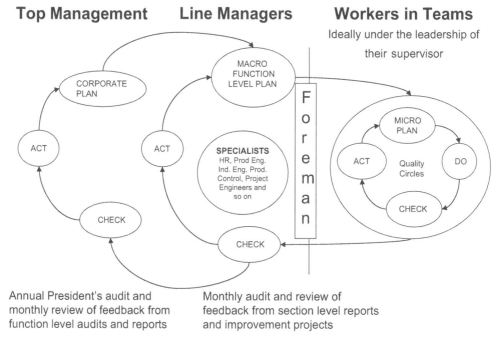

Figure 10.6   The full Management Control PDCA model

Hoshin Policy Deployment

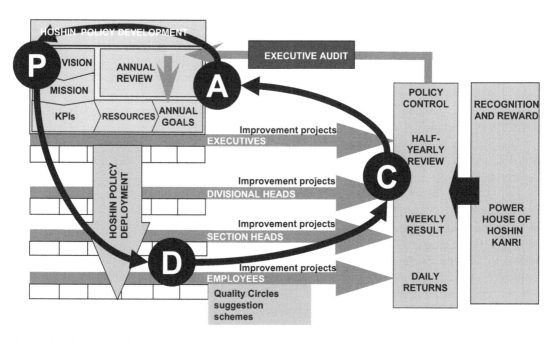

Figure 10.7   Hoshin Control

organisation forward and others could be a waste of time and resources. They must be successively broken down and finally translated into the language of the workplace. Otherwise the 'Quality Objectives' which are constantly referred to in documents such as ISO 9001:2000 will be of doubtful integrity, however well intentioned the organisation might be.

POLICY CONTROL

At the operational level, the feedback and review will be informal and weekly, or even possibly daily for some operations, because daily Targets will be related to Takt Time (see Chapter 14 on Lean Management) and other daily requirements.

As we progress upwards, the period between reviews becomes monthly at the departmental level and half-yearly at middle to higher management levels. Finally, this feeds in to an annual 'Presidents' review, at which the entire programme and its achievements both in terms of meeting the Goals of the KPIs and the extent of development of the Hoshin company-wide programme has progressed is reviewed.

MOTIVATION FOR RESULTS

In Figure 10.8 the box on the right-hand side of the diagram refers to Recognition and Reward as being the Power House of Hoshin Kanri.

Hoshin Kanri is not perpetual motion which, as far as we know, does not exist if entropy is a reality. There are two theoretically possible and contradicting ways to make a Hoshin Kanri system work.

One possible approach might be to attempt to use Threats and fear and 'carrot and stick' methods to force people to work according to the rules. This is referred to by the behavioural scientist Dr Douglas McGregor as the Theory 'X' approach.

Managers who adopt this approach have an almost instinctive belief that people are lazy, slothful and will only respond positively to pressure. Their belief is that when the pressure is removed, they

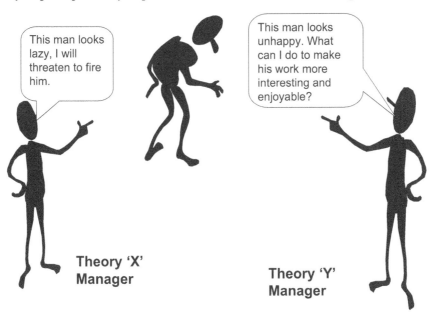

Figure 10.8   Theory 'X' and Theory 'Y' managers

will slow down or stop. Unfortunately, their beliefs are reinforced by their own senses. People resent being treated this way and dislike those who impose such regimes on them. Consequently they will do the least they can get away with and even attempt to cheat the manager given the opportunity but they will work whilst the threat is being applied and whilst they are under surveillance.

In contrast, McGregor's Theory 'Y' manager takes a very different view. They believe that work is as natural as breathing and sleeping. People have an innate desire to be considered a contributing member of the community, to have a sense of belonging and their self-esteem is derived from feeling appreciated. Therefore the Theory 'Y' manager believes that their task is to attempt to make the work interesting, rewarding, satisfying and enjoyable. Recognition for achievement is important in this type of regime. Belief in this approach is also reinforced by one's own senses because it is a fact that people who are treated in this way also respond positively.

This explains why it is so difficult and, in many cases impossible, to convince either the Theory 'X' style manager or the Theory 'Y' manager that the other approach is superior. Their beliefs are reinforced by their observations. Whilst experience of Toyota and others clearly shows that the Theory 'Y' approach is better, the Theory 'X' manager refuses to believe it.

This is one of the main reasons why the West is still struggling with Quality Circles and related management concepts which include Supply Chain Management. The West has been so enveloped in the so-called Scientific Management approach perfected by Fredrick Taylor et al. that even though it has made some progress away from it since the 1970s, it does not realise that it is still a very long way from a true Theory 'Y' style.

PRACTICAL APPLICATION OF HOSHIN POLICY DEPLOYMENT

Figure 10.9 shows a practical method for the deployment of the KPIs.

At each level of organisation, specific KPI Score Cards can be made out for each individual, usually on an annual basis. These give people a clear idea of expectations and also can be used for auditing. It is strongly recommended that these KPIs are agreed between the individual and their report and not simply imposed upon them as this would be a Theory 'X' approach.

Figure 10.10 shows how progress towards the achievement of the KPIs can be tracked and displayed graphically. Komatsu in Japan refer to this as their 'flagship' approach. This derives from the tradition in Japanese fishing fleets to display flags on their masts when coming back into harbour to show the size of their catch.

Note that in this example, the achievements are classified as being 'daily performance' and 'projects'. This is because some improvements may be achieved by improving work-related skills and not through improvement projects. Others must be achieved by formal projects if the cause of the gap between desired and actual performance is unknown at the time. These graphs can be displayed in the work area and are yet another form of recognition. Visitors to the area will be impressed with the work that is being done.

SUMMARY

Hoshin Kanri comprises three key elements:

1. Hoshin Planning.
2. Hoshin Deployment.
3. Hoshin Control.

Policy Deployment – (Achieving KPI targets)

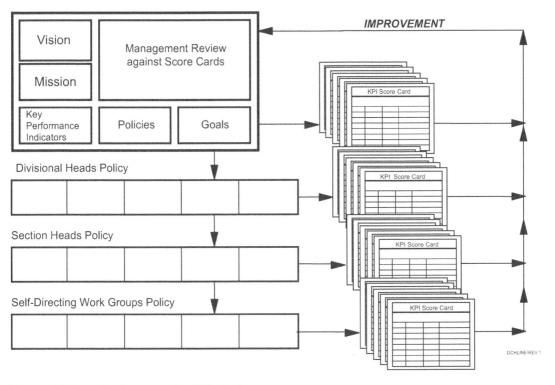

Figure 10.9   Card system for KPI deployment

(Achieving KPI targets)

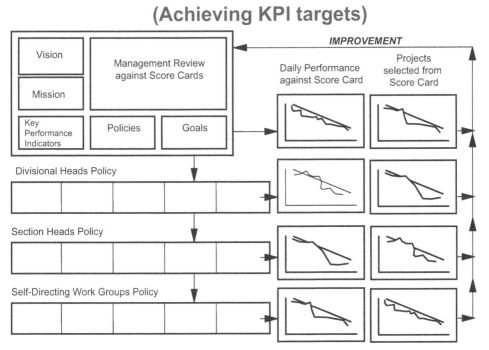

Figure 10.10   The 'flagship' approach to KPI deployment

The concept depends upon the use of the PDCA (Plan-Do-Check-Act) Cycle.

The process depends upon the development of a Theory 'Y' work environment and this must be transmitted down through the Supply Chain.

The three elements of Hoshin Kanri represent 'What it is that we want to do'. TQM provides the means to achieve. Hoshin Kanri without TQM is a wish list. TQM without Hoshin Kanri is a rudderless set of tools and techniques that will only produce results on a hit and miss basis and many of the improvements will be of dubious value. The remaining chapters of the book concentrate on the TQM methods.

11 *The Voice of the Customer*

Hoshin Kanri – from Strategy to Action!

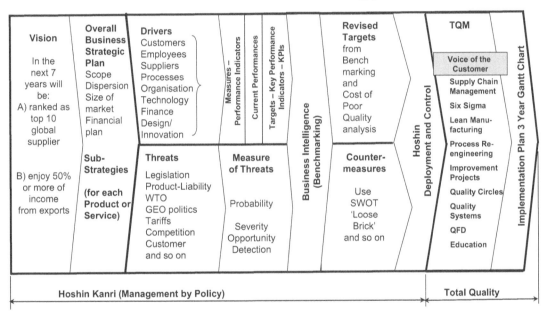

Figure 11.1   The voice of the customer

OBJECTIVES

- Develop a customer-based Vision.
- Enable staff from senior management to direct employees to have a shared understanding of how Business Processes deliver value to customers.
- Establish how to reduce time to market-acceptance for new products.
- Reduce customer turnover by keeping customers.
- Increase market share through increasing current customers' share of income.
- Reduce unit costs through greater efficiency and lower wastage.
- Target investment so that it better aligns with the overall business Vision and Strategy.

THE SITUATION TODAY

- New products are expected to be better, faster than previous models.
- We expect better service and technical support.
- We do not expect products to fail but when they do we expect the supplier/producer to take care of us.
- Our expectations are continually moving upwards.
- Business must continually improve at an equal or greater rate than customer expectations.
- We can drive customer expectations!

Figure 11.2 shows that there are two routes to the achievement of Customer Satisfaction. Route 1 is the process of improving the performance of existing products and typically uses the tools of Six Sigma, Lean Manufacturing and Continous Improvement.

Route 2 is the process for the development of new products and services. This uses the QFD process.

PERCEIVED QUALITY

It is the customer's *perception* of our performance which is important *not our actual performance*. If the customer perceives that we are poor when we are good there is no point in making improvements. We need to change the perception!

For example: reels of steel leave a steel company in Iran unwrapped and are tied to the platform of open-backed trucks with no protection and are delivered to their customer, an automobile company, 150 miles away. This leads to a perception that the steel may be rusty even though the climate was so dry that the steel did not need protection. The reason for this perception was because customers have seen foreign steel – presumably because it travelled by sea – protected from the salty air on board the ship by wrapping it in oily paper.

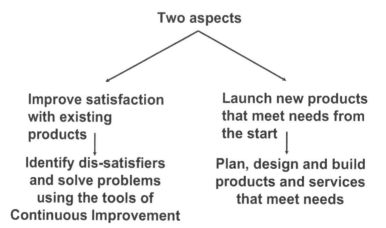

Figure 11.2   The two arms of Customer Focus

We know that the steel is perfectly good, but if that is the perception, then making the steel shinier will not make any difference. We have to change the perception.

Do we know what our customer's perceptions are? We cannot guess other people's perceptions, we have to find a way to ask!

WHAT DO OUR CUSTOMERS WANT?

There may be a difference between the customer's stated needs and their real needs. Do we know what they are? For example, a potential bank customer may state that they want to open a bank account. This is their stated need not the real need. Opening a bank account is only a means to an end. They want to do so in order to be able to transfer money easily or to arrange a loan, buy a car and so on. These are the real needs and it is the ease and ability to satisfy these sometimes unstated needs that they will judge the service of the bank on in comparison with other possible means to satisfy them. If they find a better alternative to doing this other than using a bank account, the bank might lose its business without knowing why. So what are the options available now or possibly in the future?

The bank that gets closest to the real answer will increase market share and customer loyalty. These needs can change from time to time so we must continually review. For example, the cheque book is less important now that we have electronic transfer. What changes does this mean for skills, staffing, logistics and so on? The bank that gets it really wrong may go out of business!

WHO IS THE CUSTOMER?

The customer will be a cast of characters. Take the example of a hospital. This may appear to be one customer but it has many faces. The buyer or purchasing department, laboratories, maintenance and repair, training, doctors, surgeons, nurses, cleaning staff, the patient and so on.

Each will have their own needs and may deal with different departments and have their own impressions of our organisation but often for very different reasons. Do we know what they are? Have we ever tried to find out? How?

WHAT DO THEY WANT?

The buyer

The buyer will be interested in Price, offers, delivery schedules, invoicing and other relevant documentation. They will deal directly with the sales department of our company and it will be their behaviour that colours the view of the organisation.

Supply quality assurance

The customer will deal directly with their quality counterparts at our organisation and their view will be coloured by the quality system as they see it and also the way they are treated. Quality Assurance may be good but if they are badly treated by security, staff arrangements and so on they may form a poor opinion.

THE ROLE OF THE CUSTOMER

It sounds trite to say that if we do not have a customer we do not have a business. This seemingly obvious comment may, on the face of it, seem banal but the fact remains that even in a highly competitive market there is a surprisingly high level of ignorance as to the critical importance of making sure that customer satisfaction is achieved.

The company has customers but so do people at each stage in the operation. The next downstream operation is the customer of the one before it.

The same questions apply:

- Who are *our* customers?
- What are their needs?
- Do we satisfy their needs?
- How do we know?
- Have we ever asked?
- How much of the difference is determined by our suppliers?
- Do they know?

Looking at industry as a whole, the spectrum ranges from high sensitivity towards customer needs through to the point where the customer is made to feel that they are extremely fortunate to have this particular supplier available to them. There are many reasons for this spread of attitude. It is most obvious in those countries which are attempting to emerge from many decades of state ownership. They have become so accustomed to working in an environment where the customer has no choice that they treat them as if they do not exist. This can also be true in a market economy where one operator has a near or total monopoly or where there is a cartel of independent operators who collaborate for no other reason than to have a shared advantage over their customers, as appears to happen in insurance, energy and so on.

In many cases the least well-trained and lowest-paid workers are those that interface with the customer. This applies to high street stores and hotels in particular but is common throughout the travel industry and the retail sector.

During her gap year before going to university, my daughter took a job with a very well-known high-profile high street chain store. She had one familiarisation day at their head office where she was told about the fiscal arrangements, employment contract and so on. The next day she was behind the counter in a store selling with no training whatsoever, no knowledge of the range of products, and nor did any of her colleagues. I guess that most people will have their own versions of that story or have had to deal with hotel reception staff equally poorly prepared. The fact that the organisation is totally dependent upon the abilities of these people is an appalling indictment but it is widespread.

Ask the questions, 'Is that a problem in our company?' and 'If I were a customer how would I be treated?' Telephone the sales department pretending to be a customer and see what treatment you get. How were you treated by the telephone operator? Did you have to wait a long time either before the phone was answered or from there to actually speaking to someone who could help? We have heard of one organisation that conducted research on this question and found to their horror that 7 per cent of all callers hung up before speaking to anyone because they were not prepared to go through a tedious routine of pressing this number followed by another and another before reaching a human being, and then being entertained by some music that they may not have liked anyway. How many of those might have been potential new customers?

The following statistics indicate the scale of the problem. These have been collected from several sources on the Internet and are a synthesis of data provided by some of the large global companies.

WINNING AND KEEPING CUSTOMERS

- It costs six times as much to gain a new customer than to keep an old one, and 12 times more to regain one that has been lost!
- On average one dissatisfied customer will tell 11 others, who on average will tell five others.
- Often an organisation's lowest-paid people are the ones who actually meet the public.
- 96 per cent of customers don't complain when they have a problem, they just don't come back.
- Half of those who say they are 'fairly satisfied' won't come back.
- The average company will turnover 10–30 per cent of its existing customers because of poor service. Most could have been retained.
- Organisations giving quality service grow twice as fast and pick up market share three times quicker than their competitors.
- Companies giving quality service charge up to 9 per cent more for their products or services.

For any Strategy to be effective it is vital to obtain and analyse customer-related statistics. In the context of this book, the word customer includes everyone who has an influence on current and future sales and pricing. This involves the end user, the retailers, stockists, relevant specialists, the media and the means of distribution.

Clearly, sustaining customer satisfaction is vital to success but this is a dynamic and volatile situation that requires constant monitoring and adjustments to the Strategy.

Experience indicates that it is very dangerous to take advantage of the customer in a near monopolistic situation thinking that the customer has no choice. This was the case with state-owned companies and utilities. As soon as the monopolistic situation changed, people switched to their competitors at the first opportunity even when the service might have been inferior just to show their resentment at the treatment they had been forced to accept. This is a serious problem today for those countries that are attempting to liberalise state-owned monopolies.

It is easy to fall into the trap of believing that 'customer dissatisfaction' is the opposite of 'customer satisfaction' but it is not. As it shows in Figure 11.3, these two are at the extreme ends of a spectrum. At one end is 'customer delight' whilst the other is 'customer anger'!

Between these two extremes in varying degrees is 'customer indifference'. Unfortunately we only get data at the extremes. Between these points, unless we take active steps to find out, we will have no idea as to our relative position, either where we are on the scale or where we are relative to our competitors. Because there is no feedback it is easy to assume that the customer is contented but this is a dangerous assumption. In fact the customer's loyalty becomes increasingly vulnerable as they move along the spectrum from satisfaction to dissatisfaction, as shown in the statistics above.

To illustrate the point, imagine a situation where there are a number of competing restaurants in a town. A family decides to eat at Restaurant A having never been there before. Prior to entering the restaurant they check the menu in the window. It looks fine, the prices are OK, the variety is OK and they go inside. There the lighting is OK, the ambience is fine, the tables are clean and the settings are attractive. The waiter is polite, they are shown to a table which is OK, the service is OK, the food tastes OK and the wine is good. After the meal the bill is offered and is OK and the group make to leave. The waiter asks if everything was OK and they are affirmative. The waiter passes this information to the owner and the owner is satisfied. However, the group never returns, why? Because they find somewhere else that they like better! Restaurant B further up the road is always packed, it is necessary to book in advance and the car park is always full. The owner of Restaurant A cannot understand this. No one ever complains and yet the customers rarely, if ever, come back.

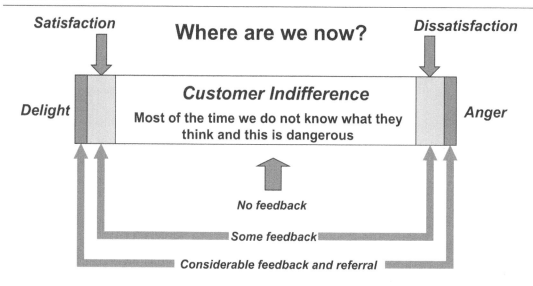

Customer Satisfaction is not the opposite of dissatisfaction, they are opposite ends of a spectrum. You cannot measure one by the presence or absence of the other except in fairly extreme cases.

Figure 11.3   Customer satisfaction

Part of the reason is that the owner asked the wrong question when the visitors were leaving. Had they asked for a comparison between Restaurant A and Restaurant B, the owner might have obtained some more useful information to enable them to be more competitive. Of course, when they put the new Strategy in place, and if the owner of Restaurant B is paying attention, they should expect and allow for a counter-attack of some sort.

The restaurant is a simple but typical example of the importance of obtaining customer information. Generally when it is unsolicited it will be from one of the extremes, but the most important information is that which is not easily forthcoming so competitor comparisons must be obtained by other means. These include: new customer interviews, non-customer interviews (why do you use other service providers?), free samples that require feedback, exit interviews (why are you leaving or why have you left?), shadow customers (use trained outsiders to sample the service and compare with the competition), focus groups, questionnaires, telephone calls and emails. They may be very scientifically designed or they may be casual but anything is better than nothing. Obviously the more scientific the more useful the results but initially simple sampling will be sufficient to be able to make some comparisons. Following this, a plan should be created to continually monitor customer trends in terms of customer retention, satisfaction, competitor comparisons and changes in customer taste.

Markets change and customer expectations change at the same time. Sometimes it is customer pressure that drives change but more usually it is the aggressive strategies of the market leaders that change the expectations of the customer. For example, in the early days of black and white televisions, the sets were unstable, the vertical and horizontal hold features caused the picture to break up or roll but the customers rarely complained. They were only too appreciative of the fact that they could watch world affairs in the comfort of their own homes. Today, nobody would tolerate such performance and manufacturers who were unable to improve at the average rate of improvement in the market or better would be forced out of business. This improvement in performance was not forced by the customer but by the aggressive performance of the competing television manufacturers.

To remain successful it is important to be able to identify what features of the product or service result in the maximum customer sensitivity. These can change unexpectedly and sometimes dramatically without warning. Often they are changed deliberately by a perceptive competitor in order to make their products appear superior. Chapter 9 'The Loose Brick' covers this aspect of competitor/customer strategies in some detail; it also impacts on Chapter 7 in the discussion of Quality-Related Costs. In that chapter it was the competitor who was able to drive down his costs and still maintain or even improve on product quality that was the biggest threat to the competition.

STATED NEEDS AND UNSTATED NEEDS

Customer needs are many and varied. Some of these are stated in specifications which may be given either by the vendor or the purchaser and are therefore quite clear and will have legal status in transactions. However, it is interesting that the needs which are often unstated are frequently more important from the point of view of customer satisfaction than the stated ones. Usually most serious competitors can equal each other's performance with regards to the stated needs but competitive edge is likely to be gained by the one who is best at identifying and reacting positively to the unstated needs. A situation that most of us are familiar with is the local car service and repair organisation. Of course, in many cases we may be almost forced to use the one that has the franchise for our particular brand of vehicle but even then there may be others that can carry out the service and who can legitimately stamp the service record book. The probability is that as far as the work itself is concerned, unless they make a serious mistake, we have no way of knowing which alternative is the most competent. Their pricing may also be very similar. However, there will usually be one that we invariably use. If we ask ourselves why the reasons may be: 'I trust the person that I speak to', 'they are more polite', 'they appear to be more helpful and sometimes make useful suggestions', 'they are keen to show me what they have done', 'they make a better job of cleaning the car which is an extra that I did not request but I am grateful for', 'their reception area and toilets are more attractive and they supply free coffee and newspapers when I have to wait'.

None of these items will be in the contract but they will be influential in customer retention. Whatever the business it is definitely worth making a serious study of this aspect of Customer Satisfaction to see what advantages you can gain over your competitors.

PERCEIVED SATISFACTION

Sometimes Customer Satisfaction is derived from erroneous premises where the customer believes a product either to be superior or inferior due to unfounded rumours or by jumping to the wrong conclusions from some observations. For example, the customer of the steel company in Iran mentioned in earlier chapters strongly believed that foreign steel was corrosion free on delivery whereas the supplier of steel from the local plant was not. This belief had puzzled the steel supplier for years because they were convinced that their steel was at least as good as the competition. Eventually a study pointed to the real reason. The foreign steel came from overseas by ship. In order to protect it from the corrosive effects of the salty air, the rolls of steel were wrapped in oily brown paper.

On the other hand, the steel sold by the local supplier came overland across the extremely dry desert of central Iran. There was therefore no need for the oily brown paper because the steel would not corrode in that environment. The customer had therefore concluded that the foreign steel was superior but there was no tangible evidence to prove it. Once the reason was known, the supplier was able to prove this to the customer. Had this not been the case then the internal supplier might have been forced to purchase expensive machinery and incur the cost of solving a problem that was never there.

CUSTOMER RETENTION

It was claimed above that approximately half of the customers who say that they are fairly satisfied do not come back. Assuming that the statistic that it costs six times as much to get a new customer than it does to keep an old one is correct, it makes sense to focus attention on the needs of existing customers, especially if it costs nearly 12 times as much to get them back once lost. Actually this is a dubious statistic. In practice, depending upon the reasons, it might be impossible to get them back. Also there is the problem that a dissatisfied customer will tell 11 others, who in turn will tell another five.

It was stated earlier that it is estimated that on average it costs six times as much to get a new customer than it does to retain an existing one. Not only is this true, but it can be seen from Figure 11.4 that there are other possible and significant benefits.

Marketing and selling are costly activities but referrals are not only free but potential customers are more likely to take notice of a referral than expensive advertising which they do not trust anyway.

It is a key question for the Performance Indicators. How much of our business comes from existing customers and how much from one time buyers?

Being able to sell at premium prices is another advantage of having a good reputation. Customers want predictability. If they liked what they got before they do not mind paying a bit extra if they can guarantee that it will provide them with satisfaction. Of course there are people who look for bargains but that is also possible. At least one language-teaching audio tape company sells the same product under more than one label. One is the name that is well known; the other is not well known and is sold through weekly news advertisements at bargain prices. They get the best of both worlds.

Of course, the higher the sales volumes, the more keenly can the Price paid for component parts be negotiated and greater power and influence gained over suppliers.

Higher volumes also make economies of scale possible.

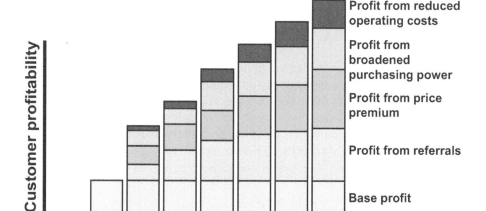

Figure 11.4   How profitability is achieved through customer retention

CUSTOMER SATISFACTION MEASUREMENT

The following are some examples of methods which can be used to find out what customers think of our existing products. See also the Kano Method in Chapter 19 (QFD):

- mailed questionnaires;
- shadow customers (employees or agents acting as if they are customers);
- interviews and interviews using questionnaires;
- non-customers (especially those who use rival sources);
- ex-customers (especially where some form of resignation is involved);
- others in the trade and focus teams made up of technical specialists and users;
- study competitors by Benchmarking.

RULES FOR GOOD CUSTOMER-RELATED DATA COLLECTION AND ANALYSIS

- Fully supported by top management;
- addresses issues that are important to our customers;
- unbiased;
- statistically reliable;
- addresses strengths, weaknesses and competitive advantages;
- determines relative importance of KPIs;
- comparable across business units;
- consistent over time;
- backed up with corrective action.

Running a pilot sample of questionnaires is essential. This will validate the process before distributing it in bulk. Use a small-scale try out on some colleagues first then follow with some friendly customers.

- Is the questionnaire easy to complete?
- Does everyone interpret the questions the same way?
- Is the sampling method valid?
- Does the data make sense?
- Can the data be easily analysed?
- Can the results be replicated?

SUMMARY

The customer is the key to growth. The leading organisations will be those who give the most attention to the achievement of Customer Satisfaction and customer retention.

Statistics show that when 75 per cent of customers say that they are fairly satisfied, 25 per cent or more will try somewhere else. Getting an old customer back may sometimes be close to impossible especially when they have gone to what they regard as being a more customer-focused competitor.

12 *Supply Chain Management*

Hoshin Kanri – from Strategy to Action!

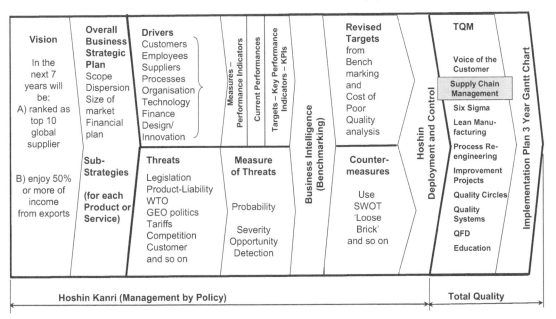

Figure 12.1   Supply Chain Management

See also Chapter 18, Business Management Systems.

The majority of companies today outsource more than 60 per cent of the work content of their products and services and the trend is towards higher and higher levels with the possible consequence of greater supplier dependency. However, it is now becoming widely accepted, at least amongst the pacesetting companies, that the Supply Chain should be regarded as an extension of our own processes and responsibility for their performance is not delegable. Whenever an organisation devolves responsibility to a supplier they are losing control of the process and at some time this will prove painful.

THE CURRENT SITUATION

Prior to the 1990s, many organisations used multiple sourcing and adversarial relationships to obtain their requirements from suppliers. There was widespread use of Vendor Rating Schemes.

In the 1980s and 1990s the majority of companies focused on re-engineering Supply Chain cost structures. This is claimed to have reduced costs by some 33 per cent.

From 2000 onwards, quality no longer provided an advantage, only a qualifying factor. The focus is now on revenue growth through Customer Satisfaction. The costs may be in the Supply Chain!

With the enablement of new technologies such as the Internet, outsourcing and partnering with other enterprises are becoming more commonplace as companies seek to share the burden of demand for more complex products and more responsive services.

The building blocks of successful Supply Chains are numerous and their interactions are complex.

Supply Chain Management has evolved from corporate necessity to enhancing competitive advantage for leading organisations.

This means transforming a company's Supply Chain into an optimally efficient, customer-satisfying process where the effectiveness of the whole Supply Chain is more important than the effectiveness of each individual element.

Positive trends in purchasing and procurement include:

- reduced number of suppliers;
- long-term relationships with suppliers;
- suppliers located close to customers for improved access;
- integrated information infrastructure: EDI (the transfer of structured data, by agreed message standards, from one computer system to another without human intervention), electronic catalogues;
- suppliers considered to be an essential part of the business;
- suppliers involved in future product development programmes.

If Quality Costs are, as is claimed in other chapters, some 20 per cent or more of our sales revenue, the probability is that this is equally true of our suppliers. This cost will be passed on to us. If we are competing with others who are not only aware of this but who treat their suppliers as extensions of their own processes then they will be reducing these costs significantly year on year.

Leading international companies such as Toyota who recognise this consider their suppliers as being part of the family – they are known as the 'Toyota Family'. These suppliers are expected to use the same managerial approach as Toyota itself or, if not, then to demonstrate that they have found something better.

Toyota also recognises that some of its newer suppliers do not have the knowledge or expertise to manage in this way. Consequently they offer to assist them if they are serious about joining the team. The pay off for the supplier is that they can expect long-term business because Toyota will only retain a narrow base of selected suppliers that they can trust. This means that Toyota deal only with a select number of companies for each product part. If they sometimes fail to comply but have tried, Toyota will not penalise them. Instead they will offer to assist them to improve whatever the process was that resulted in the failure.

In contrast, the concept of multi-sourcing is still very prevalent in Western society with its attendant adversarial relationships where the penalty for non-conformance is likely to include non-renewal of contracts. There will be no assistance forthcoming and the likelihood is that the other suppliers will be no better.

THE SUPPLIER FAMILY

This consists of an interconnected range of suppliers who are required to collaborate in transforming ideas into delivered products and services on a timely basis with relevant and high-quality products produced and delivered in a cost-effective manner. The building blocks of successful Supply Chains are numerous and their interactions complex. SCM today focuses on Business Processes: product design, planning, order management, stock management, instead of business *functions* such as sales, purchasing and production.

The key objective will be to transform the company's Supply Chain into an optimally efficient, customer-satisfying process where the effectiveness of the whole Supply Chain is more important than the effectiveness of each individual element.

KPIs OF SUPPLY CHAIN PERFORMANCE

*   Outsourcing trend;
*   actual customer demand – think about Takt Time (Reference: Chapter 14, Lean Manufacturing); speed;
*   flexibility;
*   pricing;
*   new software – Enterprise Resource Planning (ERP) systems, sophisticated application software, transparency of order/delivery, and so on;
*   reduced number of suppliers;
*   long-term relationships with suppliers;
*   suppliers located close by for improved access;
*   integrated information structure: EDI, electronic catalogues;
*   suppliers considered to be an essential part of the business;
*   suppliers involved in future product development programmes;
*   supply chain measures: the right products, the right quantity, the right moment, at minimal cost, flexibility, delivery reliability, delivery lead time, inventory levels.

Scoring methods used by Toyota:

*   Grade 1 supplier – high Risk of total shutdown, can only operate with very high level of assistance.
*   Grade 2 supplier – problem supplier – Risk of causing assembly plant shut down.
*   Grade 3 supplier – making progress but needs careful attention.
*   Grade 4 supplier – good but not yet world class.
*   Grade 5 supplier – exemplary performance and ability – long-term contracts.

Some Japanese companies, notably Toyota, have a concept they call 'SIC' which means 'sick suppliers' club'. The object is not to castigate them but to provide technical assistance in order to help them out of their sickness and achieve higher levels of performance.

SUMMARY

These points can also be turned into KPIs:

*   Maintain internal competency even in the components that are outsourced.
*   Know your core competencies and do not become supplier dependent.
*   Improve your own organisation first then show your suppliers how to do it.
*   Make sure that your suppliers are as capable as you in building and delivering high-quality components Just In Time.
*   Set up a mutual support centre with your key suppliers in which all must participate.

- Use your own people who understand your system to manage the Supply Chain. Do not assign it to outsiders and do not depend upon third-party certification – it does not work.
- Be flexible, different rules may apply to different types of supply. Some things will be required in small lots everyday, others will need to be delivered in larger quantities infrequently.
- Maintain control of logistics or you may end up sub-optimising on these costs.

SURVEILLANCE METHODS OF SUPPLIER CONTROL

There are many variants on the principle methods of supplier control. The Toyota example showed how this company managed its suppliers. The preferred supplier approach is one of the most powerful but there are also a number of methods available to ensure that supplier performance is maintained and improved.

First of all, a potential new supplier will require an audit. It would make sense that if our organisation is using Hoshin Kanri successfully then we would also want our key suppliers to do the same or similar.

Therefore the audit should be against this requirement and Chapter 18 gives guidance on this. However, it is unlikely that a new supplier will have such a system and an audit is likely to show many variances against this approach. Provided that the attitude of the supplier was satisfactory, the Toyota way of dealing with this would be to give the supplier the opportunity to prove themselves provided that they agree to allow Toyota to help them achieve their standards.

At first, Toyota's confidence would be low. Therefore there would be a high level of surveillance of the delivered product. This level of surveillance would then progressively decrease with the continued delivery of good work until they arrived at the optimum levels of performance.

This is not by any means unique to Toyota and there are many schemes which can be used.

Many of these include statistical sampling methods. These are useful when the quality levels are not high and are in the scope of sampling plans which are sensitive at levels of parts per hundred defectives or per cent defective per batch. British Standard 6001 is such a scheme. Initially a new supplier would expect all lots or batches to be inspected to the schemes covered in this standard. If this is to be used by the reader it is recommended that the sequential methods are considered. They appear more complicated but are far more economical when dealing with large quantities of product. Unfortunately, there is a degree of arbitrariness in the standard when attempting to select a suitable Acceptable Quality Level (AQL) in order to set the rules. The choice of AQL does not relate to the economics of the sampling and it is recommended that Barry Wetherill's book on economic sampling[1] be consulted. However, the sampling can become more economic if the suggestions for 'skip lot' inspection are followed. In this case, the sampling plans suggest that if more than 'X' lots are presented without defects, then only one batch in so many will be checked. If the supplier continues to perform at this level then there will be fewer batches checked and the supplier is promoted to preferred status. If however, a defective batch is found then the level of inspection returns to 100 per cent and of course the supplier is informed.

The value of this approach is that all companies like to be regarded as preferred and will attempt to protect this achievement by ensuring the supply of good product.

SUMMARY

It can be seen from this chapter that SCM is an area which lends itself to considerable creativity. The Toyota system is impressive but so are many others. What is important is to move away from

1   G. Barrie Wetherill, *Sampling Inspection and Quality Control* (2nd Edition), Science Paperbacks.

multiple sourcing and the related adversarial relationships approaches that are still very common and to develop partnering relationships both down and also, to encourage them, across the chain as well.

Try to encourage suppliers to operate Hoshin Kanri and if they do not know how then help them on the basis that it is in your interest that they do so. Reward the best with preferred supplier status. It will make them feel good and it will help them to pass the benefits back to you through better service.

13 *Six Sigma*

Hoshin Kanri – from Strategy to Action!

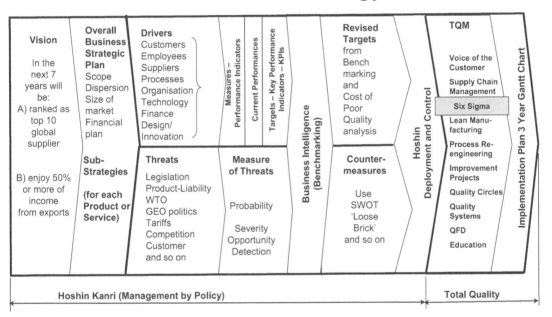

Figure 13.1   Six Sigma

S trictly speaking Six Sigma is not included in traditional Hoshin Kanri because the Japanese approach to continuous improvement embraces not only Six Sigma but also Lean Manufacturing. However, it is included in this book, as is Lean Manufacturing, because it has now become so well known that it can be covered as an overview here knowing that the reader will have access to a considerable library on the topic. In this chapter we will merely skim the surface of the subject. The reason being that in the development of Hoshin Kanri KPIs, the organisation will have identified a large number of KPIs where the gaps between Current Performance and Target performance are significant and to close them will require techniques which go beyond the basic problem-solving tools that are well known.

The challenge now is to find some way to close the gap. The means required will vary depending on the nature and the extent of the problem. Simple problems may only require simple treatment and may not need any sophisticated techniques or organisation to resolve them. Simply putting people into a state of knowledge may be all that is required. At the other extreme, some other problems will require quite complex diagnostic statistical tools requiring the skills of Six Sigma Black Belt training.

It has been claimed here that the term Six Sigma is not generally used in Japan. The reason is that the Japanese believe that their approach to project-by-project continuous performance improvement contains all of the tools and techniques that can be found in most Six Sigma programmes and probably many more. Also, they will include very many more than the 20-days training that Six Sigma Black Belt training will provide and this training will be ongoing and aspire to degree-level work In contrast Black Belt training is usually one off and seen as a definitive qualification even though it is only 20 days of classroom experience, admittedly with the addition of one or more live projects to support the work. Having said all of that, Six Sigma is a powerful approach and before it arrived there was nothing in the West that remotely covered the same ground. Most Continuous Improvement training programmes were excellent on the language data tools but statistical methods were virtually non-existent.

Six Sigma is a marketing term that was taken from Statistical Quality Control and used as the label by Motorola to distinguish their approach to project-by-project improvement which was heavily biased towards using factual data rather than opinion data to solve work-related problems. They claimed that those teams that used statistical methods regularly outclassed other teams that relied mainly on opinion data by an order of magnitude in terms of the value of their projects. The term was a clever way to encourage their people to challenge all variation no matter how rare, the reason being that in a pure and theoretical mathematical sense, Variable Data which is six standard deviations from the mean (Six Sigma) will only occur 0.14 times in a million trials provided that the data is centrally located and normally distributed. Since most processes are operating at somewhere between 2 and 3 Sigma, this means that error data of some sort will occur several times in only 100 trials.

It was Dr Taguchi, the famous Japanese engineer/statistician, who in the late 1950s first demonstrated, using his famous 'Quality Related Costs are a Quadratic function' argument, that Quality-Related Costs go up as variation increases, independently of any arbitrary limits set by designers. This means that variation is always a cost.

He argued the logic this way: almost all product components have an allowed tolerance on each of the dimensions to guide manufacturers as to what is acceptable. This allowable variation is given because some variation is unavoidable. It is impossible to make anything perfect. The allowance given depended upon the function of the product. For example, a dustbin lid would have quite a large allowance given on the diameter because provided that it went over the bin itself it did not matter much if it was a sloppy fit.

On the other hand, a precision component in a pressure valve on a space vehicle on a mission to Saturn or somewhere would need to be as near perfect as it was possible to be. For this reason, all dimensions were given tolerances. In many cases the designer was not sure of the effects of large tolerances but knew that small tolerances were safer from a function point of view. For this reason the designer would err on the safe side and many tolerances were probably tighter than necessary. Of course, those in manufacture did not know this. They assumed that the limits had been carefully calculated and made every attempt to keep to them. This applied to the inspector also. Any component found to be outside the stated tolerance was either rejected if it was too small or possibly reworked if it was oversize.

Not only did these rejections and the rework cost money and cause delays if the batch could not be completed, there was a further and sometimes much larger cost if the tolerance meant that higher precision and more expensive equipment would be required.

Taguchi challenged this thinking on the basis that because these limits or tolerances were to some extent arbitrary, there might be two successive components, one of which was a hair's breadth inside the tolerance and deemed therefore to be good whilst the other, which was fractionally over the limit, was deemed to be bad and yet for all intents and purposes, from a functional point of view, it was unlikely that there would be any difference.

Prior to Taguchi, traditional thinking was that Quality-Related Costs were a step function around the tolerances. Inside the tolerance, since there was no scrap or rework, then there was no Quality-Related Cost. Then there was a step jump when product variation reached those limits. Taguchi challenged this thinking by considering the fact that in most cases, the variation in component dimensions are frequently mutually dependent. For example, a number of gears on a shaft will each have their individual variation. When they are assembled together, their combined variation if fitted at random will either, at one extreme, cancel each other out or, at the other, possibly produce a result that is cumulatively unacceptable even though each individual may have been within its prescribed limits. In addition to this there was the situation where it was known that one particular machine, whilst producing good parts, was producing them near to the limit. This machine would demand a lot of attention and there would be a lot of time spent on inspecting the parts to ensure that they were satisfactory. On the other hand, another might be extremely precise and the components that it produced might be almost dead size. This machine would require very little attention and the parts would not require much inspection.

Taguchi then realised that Quality Costs were not a step function about the tolerance limits but were in fact a quadratic function about the Target dimension. As the variation increased away from the Target, the cost increased according to the quadratic function irrespective of any arbitrary tolerances. It was entirely related to the consequences of the variation. This increase is therefore parabolic. The quadratic function has a constant 'k'. In this case 'k' is derived from a calculation of the cost of inspection divided by the consequential cost of not discovering a bad part. For a low value of 'k', the parabola would be shallow as it would in the case of the dustbin lid. In the case of the space craft component the parabola would exhibit a very steep upward curve either side of the Target dimension as shown in Figure 13.2.

From this it can be seen that irrespective of whether the operation is making dustbin lids or aerospace parts, all variation is a cost. Therefore, it is important to identify the most expensive variables whether they are in manufacture, accounts (late payments for example) or any other

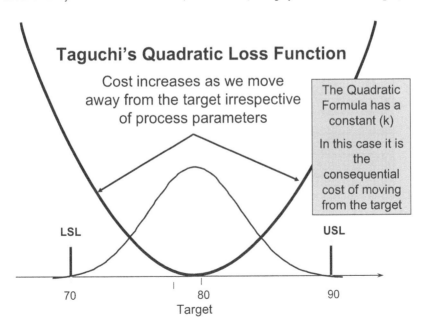

Figure 13.2   Dr Taguchi's Quadratic Loss Function

function of the business and to attempt to reduce them to the minimum. In order to do this effectively requires the use of statistical methods. Taguchi made his discovery in 1958 and it was several years later when Japanese business people considered this seriously. Even if this knowledge was available in the West it is unlikely that anything would have happened.

Statistical methods had been introduced into industry on several occasions but had failed to survive. The main reason was that the only resource available was the managers and engineers. They were too busy with their other duties to find time to use the statistical methods that they did not believe in anyway. In contrast, the Japanese had all those Quality Circles (see Chapter 17). They were trained in problem solving and the introduction of basic statistical methods enabled more effective diagnosis of the causes of problems and began to drive out variability. Eventually, many of them progressed to more sophisticated statistical tools right through to the use of Design of Experiments techniques. This reduction in variation led to a reduction in unpredictability which in turn led to smoother production performance, lower levels of inventory, Just In Time and all the methods of Lean Manufacturing. All of this happened in the early 1970s.

It is not surprising therefore that when Motorola began experiments using statistical methods added to the basic tools of Continuous Improvement they would have a similar experience.

Motorola later claimed that those departments that used Six Sigma had significantly fewer customer returns than those that did not.

Coining this name and conducting extensive training in the use of the statistical methods for the diagnosis and remedy of problems enabled Motorola to become one of the first winners of the prestigious 'Baldrige Award for Quality' and they are claimed to be responsible for very impressive improvements in all aspects of business performance.

The results were perceived to be so impressive that Six Sigma soon attracted the attention of other serious organisations in the USA and later on Jack Walsh, the high profile Chief Executive of GE. There, the concept was introduced company-wide with equally impressive results. Business performance at GE is now so impressive that the company has become the Benchmark for the rest of industry. Other star performers such as Allied Signal, Navistar, Polaroid, Bombardier and so on, also developed Six Sigma programmes and soon became disciples of the concept and advocated its use down through their Supply Chains.

Reduction in variation through the use of diagnostic statistical tools

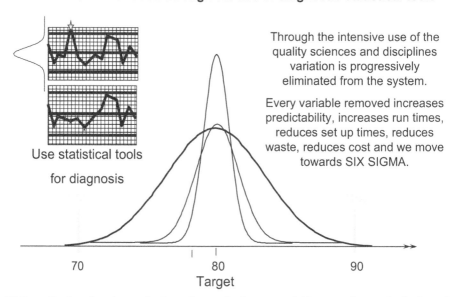

Use statistical tools

for diagnosis

Through the intensive use of the quality sciences and disciplines variation is progressively eliminated from the system.

Every variable removed increases predictability, increases run times, reduces set up times, reduces waste, reduces cost and we move towards SIX SIGMA.

70   80   90

Target

Figure 13.3   Reduction in variation through the use of diagnostic statistical tools

With such a success record, and backed by these influential names, it was bound to be only a matter of time before Six Sigma began to appear in the UK. During 1998, a number of British subsidiaries and suppliers to these large companies found themselves being introduced to the concept by their US customers with the result that Six Sigma is becoming an important new approach to business performance improvement.

HOW DOES SIX SIGMA RELATE TO OTHER PERFORMANCE IMPROVEMENT INITIATIVES?

Six Sigma is, therefore, one of a family of concepts within the general umbrella of Total Quality. Fundamental to the Six Sigma approach is the belief that all variation, no matter how rare, incurs a cost as discovered by Taguchi. Ultimately, the Goal is to completely eliminate all sources of error no matter how small. The concept is applied to all functions of the business both in operations, support functions, accounts and so forth.

There are two processes used in Six Sigma, as illustrated in Figure 13.4. The first is for the improvement of existing processes and uses the acronym DMAIC, which means Define, Measure, Analyse, Install, Control. These use all of the problem-solving tools in other disciplines and have further elaboration in Chapter 16 (Continuous Improvement).

The second is for the creation of new processes and products and uses the acronym DMADV, which means Define, Measure, Analyse, Design, Verify. This is the sequence of QFD and is covered in Chapter 19.

In the early stages, the tools which people are trained to use are relatively simple. They include techniques to collect and analyse data, diagnostic tools for cause analysis and the means to implement solutions and to hold the gains. Using terms borrowed from the martial arts, teams that have demonstrated the ability to use these tools effectively for the solution of real work-related problems are said to have achieved Green Belt status. However, as progress is made, new techniques are introduced to enable the maturing teams and individuals to tackle more complex problems. When this level is reached, the teams are regarded as being Black Belt. Achievement of this status is a strong motivator for the teams.

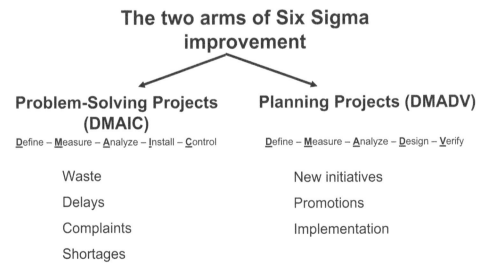

The two arms of Six Sigma improvement

Problem-Solving Projects (DMAIC)
Define – Measure – Analyze – Install – Control

Waste

Delays

Complaints

Shortages

Planning Projects (DMADV)
Define – Measure – Analyze – Design – Verify

New initiatives

Promotions

Implementation

Figure 13.4   The two arms of Six Sigma improvement

All of this is set in a structured approach using Hoshin Kanri Goals deployment, establishing the KPIs using tangible metrics to conduct Gap Analysis and to set stretched Goals.

The ultimate aim is the creation, implementation and development of an organisation in which everyone is involved in working towards their company being the best in its field.

One of the attractions of Six Sigma is the fact that the most important, practical and usable techniques are mostly quite simple even for those who are not mathematically inclined. This is true even at the Black Belt level. Only the most sophisticated of the techniques employed require a degree in mathematics to obtain their benefits. The need for these is relatively rare and in such cases outside assistance may be sought if these are required. Experience indicates that even the crudest application of the simplest concepts can produce stunning results.

The development of the Six Sigma concept by Motorola was the result of an observation that their leading competitors in Japan operating Total Quality-style management were able to conceive, develop and manufacture new products with lead times only a fraction of those achieved by Motorola and completely defect-free from the point of launch. It was clear to Motorola that if they allowed this situation to continue, it would not be long before they would be in severe economic trouble.

They learned that the concepts used so effectively by their Japanese rivals were based on the actions that they had taken as a consequence of Dr Taguchi's work.

Motorola recognised that terms such as Quality Circles, Kaizen, Just In Time, Total Quality and so on had all been badly represented in the past, therefore it was important to start with something fresh. The use of the term Six Sigma was inspirational. It enabled Motorola to avoid all of the discredited terms. It also enabled Motorola to focus everyone on the ultimate Goal of driving out variation whilst at the same time avoiding the use of another much maligned term, Statistical Process Control.

To the statistician, the term Six Sigma is immediately recognised as a measure of the probability of finding a variable which happens so rarely as to occur only around once in a million chances. This assumes that the data is more or less normally distributed about the average. Using the term with regard to programmes such as we are discussing here, the use is not intended to be so precise. The object is to convey the idea that all variation should be regarded as being tolerable. Always, we should seek better and better ways of doing things. After all, the competition will so really there is little choice.

Before illustrating the concept with case examples, for the benefit of those readers who are unfamiliar with statistically-based techniques, it is necessary to introduce a few fundamentals and to display the basic simplicity of statistical concepts normally involved. This applies to office operations as well and the attraction of Six Sigma is that all functions and activities in an organisation can use the tools employed.

For all practical purposes there are basically only two kinds of data, Variable and Attribute (or Countable) Data

Variable Data

Variable Data is exactly what it says it is. It embraces everything which varies, getting larger or smaller, heavier or lighter, faster or slower, and so on, either in discrete, incremental steps such as shown on a digital display or in analogue form (for example, the hands on a clock or a pointer on a measuring instrument). Such data include characteristics like dimension, weight, speed, time, voltage, current, capacitance, viscosity, moisture content, lead times, credit period and so on.

Attribute Data

Attribute Data includes all right/wrong, good/bad, is/isn't, did/didn't, error/no error, missing/not missing and so on, type situations.

There is a sub-group to this type of data called Subjective Data because it is subjective to the senses, and includes activities such as wine tasting, tea tasting, loudness when measured by the ear instead of an instrument, feel, smell and so on.

In Japan, long before taking the student on journeys into mathematics, they would provide the student with simple practical tools which work and produce results. The Japanese have also found that over 80 per cent of the problems which can be solved in industry require nothing more than this simple basic knowledge. Of the two types of data, probably 80 per cent of all applications relate to Attribute rather than Variable Data. All Attribute Data behaves in much the same way regardless of whether we are studying such diverse matters as 'errors in invoices', 'broken gear teeth', 'missing files', 'absenteeism' and so on.

Attribute Data always begins from zero possible occurrences. For example, a roll of cloth may have zero, one, two, three or more oil stains, marks or tears. In theory it could have an infinite number. A batch of invoices might contain zero, one, two, three or more errors.

If Attribute Data is plotted in chart form, it will always produce predictable patterns which will vary depending upon the average number occurrences of the feature being observed. For example, supposing a sample of 50 cans was taken at random from production, and the number which were found to be defective was recorded in chart form. If the average number of defectives in the sample was about 7 per cent, the result of a series of samples would appear as shown in Figure 13.5

Note that the spread of the data leans very slightly to the left but is more or less evenly distributed about the mean. Now supposing an improvement had been made to the process, and data again plotted to see the effect of the changes. The result might be as shown in Figure 13.6. Here we can see that not only has the average number decreased to 3.5 per cent, the shape of the distribution has changed as well with a definite skew leaning to the left.

Figure 13.6 shows clearly that the process has been improved. Notice that the Attribute Data begins to skew to the left as the mean approaches zero for this type of data. Now let us take the situation one stage further, and suppose that further improvements had been made. The result might well look like Figure 13.7.

Again, there can be no question that improvements have been achieved. Even though the improvement is only from 3.5 per cent to 1 per cent, the shape of the distribution of the data is

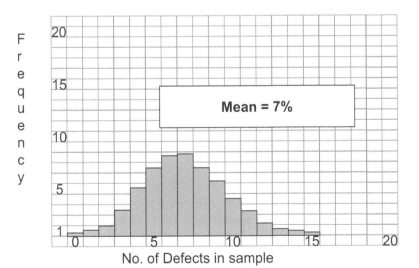

Figure 13.5   **Attribute Data with mean of 7 per cent**

Variation of Distribution

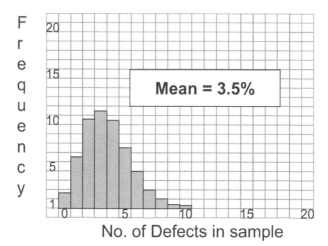

Figure 13.6   Attribute Data with a mean of 3.5 per cent

Variation of Distribution

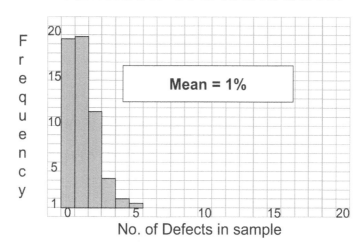

Figure 13.7   Attribute Data with a mean of 1 per cent

very different. This is a hypothetical example just to demonstrate the simplicity of using frequency diagrams for Attribute Data. Now let us consider an example of the use of this method.

Case 1 – the leaky catheter bag!

Having to wear a catheter bag may be bad news. To wear a leaky catheter bag is even worse, so it is hardly surprising that the company which makes this product conducts leak tests on 100 per cent of its output. The test requires that the product is immersed in a tank of water to a depth of approximately 5.5 inches. Air is then pumped into the bag at a pressure of 7 psi. Bubbles indicate any leaks.

A project team concerned with the problem of leaks collected a large sample of batch cards and then plotted the number of leaky bags per shift. The result looked like the graph shown in Figure 13.8.

Stratification case example – leaks in catheter bags

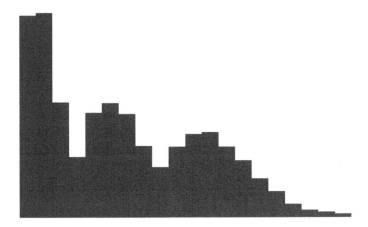

Figure 13.8   Attribute Data charted for leaks in catheter bags

It was nothing like the curves shown in previous figures.

One of the team members then suggested the possibility that the chart might be concealing three separate sets of data. The question then arose, what might cause the difference? One member remarked that there were three different welding heads: one in the store, one on the machine and the other being cleaned. Perhaps there was a head to head difference. When the data was re-plotted for each head separately, this was found to be the case (see Figure 13.9).

The challenge for the team was then to find out why one of the heads was better than the other two. When they found the answer, they were able to bring these up to the level of the best. The total time spent on the Data Collection and analysis was 3 hours. The cost of the improvements negligible. The benefit saved the company thousands of pounds per annum in defect costs, not to mention the improved reputation with its customer, the Department of Health and Social Security. The technique was extremely simple and the problem solved by a team of process workers!

Stratification case example – leaks in catheter bags

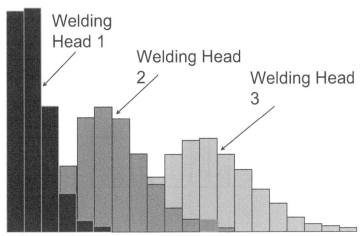

Figure 13.9   The data from Figure 13.8 stratified by welding head

Variable Data

Mathematically, the treatment of Variable Data is quite different from Attribute Data. But again, for practical purposes, in project work and for very simple control purposes, the means of plotting the data is very similar to the plotting of Attribute Data with the only minor difficulty being the selection of scales on the graph (see Figure 13.10).

For practical use, the resulting charts of Variable Data are usually very revealing. Here are a few examples.

Case 1 – service time – counter staff

When the average service time spent dealing with customers in a bank, shop, check-in at a hotel, or other similar data is plotted, the information revealed can determine the number of staff required to meet a given level of demands. It can also indicate the dispersion transactions for different types of service and point to possible means for improvement. For example, it is possible that the dispersion may be due to differences in types of customer demands. By segregating these different customers, the service time for some may be greatly reduced.

It can be seen from the aforementioned example that much can be revealed from the simplest of techniques; techniques which can be used by anyone, without any need for mathematics or deep statistical theory.

Techniques such as those described above are taught in simple but effective educational programmes aimed to empower the workforce. Through training in these basic skills, Japanese workers have managed to solve literally millions of problems of the level described in this text. Before moving on, let us take a look at a further example of the power of these simple techniques.

Case 2 – bandage weaving

The previous example of the catheter bags was recorded during a real-life example obtained from the first day of a 3-day course in basic Data Collection and analysis for line managers and supervisors.

Histograms

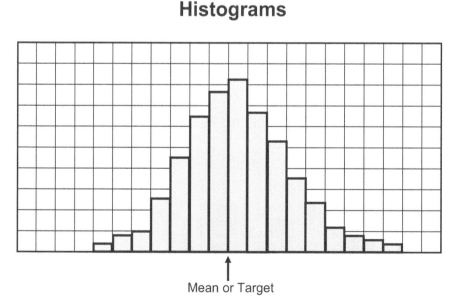

Mean or Target

Figure 13.10   A typical well-centred histogram

None had any previous educational background and in just a short time thousands of pounds of real savings had been made using the tools described.

On the second day, the participants were introduced to Data Collection using Variable Data. One group decided to check the lengths of bandages ready for shipment in the finished goods stores. Printed on the boxes, the length was specified as being 10 metres. About 50 boxes were selected at random and lengths measured. The results were as shown in Figure 13.11.

The chart shows that on average, the company was giving away over 1 metre of bandage per box. It was estimated that this had probably been going on for some 30 years, and cost the company £35 000 for each separate size of bandage. For a small company, this was a great deal of money. The worst aspect was the fact that the customer was probably totally unaware of the gift. How many people measure bandages? Certainly no one other than a Trading Standards Officer would even bother.

Case 3 – plant maintenance

Using exactly the same technique as described above, an engineering company obtained the cooperation of its workers to collect data on plant breakdowns.

Variable Data was plotted for time to failure on certain components which were known to have relatively short lives.

If failures occurred during the shift, disruption was high and cost around 2 hours of downtime for each occurrence. It was found that on average this occurred about every 260 hours of operation. This did not seem to be a big problem but in fact the real cost was much higher than was realised, not in the direct cost of lost time, but in the accumulation of work-in-progress (most of it is not progressing). There was also the question of reduced predictability of production output, which in turn led to stock outages and to keeping excessive stocks in finished goods warehouses to safeguard against this.

These costs appear on the balance sheet as stocks and inventory and also suffer depreciation and incur interest charges. Worse still, these unscheduled breakdowns result in lower levels of plant utilisation. The usual counter to this would be to obtain additional plant and of course appropriate manning levels. These will appear as direct costs on the profit and loss account, fixed but depreciating assets on the balance sheet and will tie up precious working capital.

When the failure pattern was revealed, it was agreed that the feed fingers be replaced every 200 hours even though they were still functional. These changes were made outside shift time, therefore

Histograms – Average Bandage Length

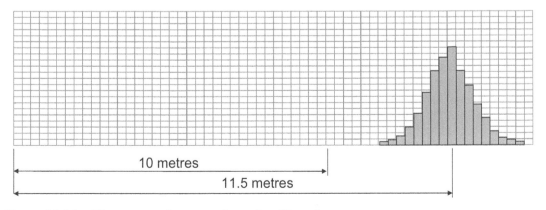

Figure 13.11　Histogram of average lengths of bandage

causing no disruption of workflow, and resulted in better predictability of scheduling times, no log jams in production and lower work-in-progress.

When collected by the workforce, this data is almost free and the workers enjoy being involved. Breakdowns are probably as much a frustration for them as they are to the scheduling department and to the managing director when they are forced to analyse their factory costs. In Japan, it is estimated that over 80 per cent of all problem solving requires nothing more than the application of these simple tools.

Case 4 – the cracked bed!

A medium-sized company employing around 400 people in the automotive components industry experimented with the implementation of Xbar/R control charts in the manufacture of high-precision automotive components. These are required to work in an exacting environment involving high levels of stress and change of temperature and the need for stable physical properties. Nevertheless, whilst these demands required the very highest levels of machine capability at the final stages of production, surprisingly wide latitudes of dimensional accuracy were tolerated in the early production processes.

These inaccuracies were thought to be unimportant prior to the heat-treatment process as it was thought that at this stage, scale and other surface problems were such that considerable grinding would be necessary afterwards at which time the variations could be removed.

The first experiment was conducted on an automatic lathe. In order to set up the parameters on the control chart, ten consecutive samples of 4 items were selected from the process. Care was taken at this stage to ensure that none of the settings on the machine were altered and that operations were continuous with homogeneous raw material. With an automatic machine, this meant ensuring that the supply of raw material was uninterrupted and did not require replacement during the sample period. This is important when setting up the basic control parameters.

Measurements were taken on the items selected and the action and warning limits plotted on the chart.

It was found that several of the readings were outside the lines which had been calculated from the data and this did not seem to make sense. If the lines were constructed from the data, how could the data be outside the lines themselves? At first it was thought that some error had been made in the calculations and it was checked several times, as was the theory and the measurements of the components.

Then it was then realised that the formula used to construct the diagram was based on the assumption that the data was distributed according to the laws of the normal distribution for process variables. When the averages of the samples of four were arranged in histogram form it was found that this was not the case. The data did not appear to conform to any distributions.

The engineer consulted the setters of the machines, and also the operators. Many possible theories were suggested as to why this should be the case.

The suggestion by one setter – 'cracked bed' proved correct. The machine had been purchased second-hand and apparently it was known to the setters that the machine bed was cracked from the time of purchase. When asked why they hadn't volunteered this before the reply was, 'No one ever asked!'

The bed of the machine was repaired by the tool room. Again samples were taken and still the results behaved in an abnormal way. However, whilst the engineer was in attendance at the machine, they noticed that one of the operators checked a component and decided to adjust the size, which they did with the aid of a mallet!.

The tool was held in the tool holder by a simple screw. The operator slackened the screw, tapped the tool lightly with a mallet, measured the next component, then attended to another machine.

At the same time, it was noticed that the surface finish on the components produced was very irregular. When the tool was inspected, it was noted that it had been reground to extremely peculiar dimensions. It was also noted that the shape of the cutting tool varied considerably depending upon which setter did the regrinding. It was obvious that somehow tool replacement must be standardised in accordance with best practice. Both problems were solved simultaneously.

A new tool holder was purchased with a micrometer adjustment, eliminating the need for the mallet. The tools themselves, which were made of hardened steel, were replaced by a new design which used replaceable, pre-ground carbide tips. This ensured the use of correct tool-cutting angles and foolproofed against unauthorised experimentation. They also required fewer adjustments. When these changes were introduced there was a remarkable change in the results. Not only did the machine behave precisely according to the rules of statistical theory, the variation had been reduced to such an extent that it was debatable whether it was necessary to do any form of in-process inspection, let alone use of Xbar/R charts.

The concept was subsequently applied to the entire machine shop. The setters and operators who had originally viewed the whole exercise with great amusement changed their attitude to one of interest, and then finally asked to be able to use the techniques themselves.

It was not long before frequency diagram curves were appearing for all sorts of measures. One setter used the technique to prove that one brand of drill lasted 20 per cent longer than its competitors and required fewer regrinds. This also made a significant reduction to both lead times and machine downtime.

Eventually, either Xbar/R charts, attribute charts, or the simplified charts were established on all key operations in the plant. In some cases, the reduction in variation eliminated the need for a number of subsequent operations. In the case of the 3" lathe, the accuracy produced eliminated the need for two grinding operations before heat treatment and an expensive grinding operation afterwards.

In addition to this, prior to and during the period of implementation of these methods, the company had purchased a variety of plant but on an ad hoc basis without much control and from vague specifications. Virtually none of the machines purchased lived up to the claims of the manufacturers and all resulted in the excessive use of production-engineering time to obtain the results required.

The engineer who had been responsible for the introduction of Statistical Process Control decided to use this method to develop a new product acceptance sampling procedure. Statistical Process Capability was established in the new plant at the suppliers' premises prior to shipment. The tests were then repeated after satisfactory installation at the plant. Stage payments were made to the suppliers following satisfactory results from the sampling. The final payment followed 6 months later when the product proved that it was capable of maintaining its contracted performance to the satisfaction of the specification. All plants which were purchased using this approach performed significantly more accurately with fewer breakdowns and for several years longer than those which had been purchased using traditional methods.

It is clear that the use of Six Sigma as a management concept provides considerable potential opportunities for industry.

In the words of Bob Galvin, the now retired CEO of Motorola and Six Sigma champion:

We did it because it was necessary if we were to confront Japanese competition, but now we do it because it represents a better way to manage our business and to involve all of our people. If the Japanese did not exist, we would have had to have invented them!

SIX SIGMA CASE STUDY

This case study, based on a paper given jointly by David Hutchins and Mobarakeh Steel at a conference held in Tokyo, illustrates how Six Sigma can produce incredible results but only when integrated with Hoshin Kanri and introduced into the right environment at the right time. Six Sigma concepts, as part of a Hoshin Kanri programme, were introduced in the late 1990s to Mobarakeh Steel Company in Iran (see Figure 13.12). Initially, they invited an explanation of the potential benefits of a TPM programme. It was their aim to become more competitive in order to reduce the tendency of their customers to buy foreign steel and to improve their own penetration of international markets. They were told that if they committed themselves fully to a Hoshin Kanri programme (they used the term TQM to avoid the potential confusion of strange terms being introduced) which included the principles of Six Sigma, they could improve quality and reduce cost to such an extent that they could cause problems for their competitors and even be accused of dumping. They might not have believed this, but last year that is exactly what happened. The company is growing with a full order book when, in contrast, some more local to home parts of the steel industry are in serious decline.

At the commencement of the project, Mobarakeh Steel Company produced 3 million tonnes of liquid steel per year and is located near Esfahan, which is an historical city and the second biggest city of Iran after Tehran.

Mobarakeh Steel Company produces hot- and cold-rolled steel strips in the form of coil and sheet. The nominal capacity of the plant was 3 million tonnes per year, but an expansion project; completed in 2005, extended the capacity to 4 million tonnes per year!

The main customers for these products are structural and constructional end users, gas and oil pipelines, car industry, house appliances, ship manufacturing, and so on. In addition to the main customers there are approximately 4000 indirect customers. The number of employees that are working in this complex are 6700; the number of direct suppliers is 800, but there are many indirect suppliers, totaling around 2000.

The history of management development dates back to the first year of operations in the plant in 1991. This began with the development of their management information system. This was mainly for operational activities from order entry to product delivery.

Figure 13.12   Montage of steel works

They introduced ISO 9000 in 1995 and were also certificated ISO 14001 in 1998. A suggestion system was introduced in 1995 which apparently had a significant impact on the work environment. Following this, Quality Circles were introduced in 1996 to help improve the teamwork culture in the company. Research and development is another system they began in 1995 and it continues to be developed to this day. Innovation in this respect includes not only product but also processes and management systems.

For the improvement of housekeeping, maintenance management, reduction of losses and cycle time and set-up time reduction, they have incorporated Total Productive Maintenance (TPM) as part of the Total Quality programme.

In fact all of these initiatives are now included under that umbrella. The main and core Objectives developed for Total Quality-based management were Policy Development and Deployment, Benchmarking activities, Supply Chain Management, Customer Focus activities and project-by-project improvement.

The main source of Total Quality projects in Mobarakeh Steel Company is the Strategy planning process – this includes the setting the Vision, Objectives and Targets – problem identification and defining Cost of Poor Quality projects. These were mainly identified by brainstorming sessions throughout the company. Using Pareto Analysis, approximately 100 projects were selected under this heading. Involvement at all levels was an important feature of this part of the development and 18 committees were established to manage project selection across all functions of the organisation.

For the Vision and Strategic Directions, they defined eight elements. The categories were: customers, suppliers, employees, processes, organisation, technology, finance, and design and innovation. These elements are more detailed than the four categories suggested in the Kaplen and Norden Balanced Scorecard approach and lead to a much better definition of improvement opportunities. The reason for choice is that these are actually the main matters that are important for the improvement of the total business.

The Mobarakeh Steel Company vision

To enjoy constant presence in a global and domestic markets as a leading organisation pioneer in quality, technology, production and sustainable development.

Supporting this are the eight strategic elements included with their respective Mission Statements.

An example of these elements is:

Employees: to maintain employees' healthcare and welfare levels, together with the promotion of self-interest and motivation among employees.

Benchmarking activities were also found to be an important subject that helped the Mobarakeh Steel Company to compare themselves not only with competitors but also with non-competitors who used similar processes.

Defining the KPIs was a major task for defining the business-critical projects for corporate-level mandated improvement activities.

Improvements in supplier relationships, and also Customer Focus activities using advanced Six Sigma quality planning tools such as the Affinity Diagram, QFD, the Kano Model, and Design FMEA, together with the more traditional problem-solving techniques, such as Brainstorming, Pareto and Statistical Process Control, proved extremely powerful and effective. Even during the training some significant improvements were made.

Summary of the development activities

Total training activity up to September 2002 was 80 000 man-hours. Of this an average of 35-days training was given by me to over 175 managers. This training spanned 3 years. During that time, I trained an engineer from Tehran University and several selected internal personnel to conduct further training at the lower levels. Top team meetings are very important, the presence of management and the top team has a big role on the successful outcome of the project; 3200 man-hours had so far been spent in top team meetings. Middle management meetings were 36 000 man-hours. From the total 6700 people employed, 4000 were actually engaged on improvement projects. The number of meetings with the customers was 10 300 man-hours and with the suppliers, 2700 man-hours. Figure 13.13 is typical of the training aids that were used to convey the statistical tools.

12 000 man hours was also spent on management meetings with employees. This is vitally important so that the people should see management involvement first-hand. It was also agreed that management should be involved in the projects and the matters that it wants to manage. Management meetings with employees was a 'catchball' approach so that the people felt genuinely involved. The net benefit that they obtained from these projects directly to date has been an accounted US$40 million! However, Mobarakeh stresses that this is only the direct effect. The indirect influence (not easily accounted in tangible terms) on the business is claimed to be several times this benefit. Figure 13.14 illustrates an exhibition that is held annually, partly to give recognition to the teams involved in making the improvements and also to demonstrate to other employees, customers and suppliers what is being achieved. These exhibitions have become extremely popular and have given the company a considerable and enviable reputation throughout the country.

Mobarakeh is now in the process of developing long-term relationships with their suppliers; before this initiative, supplier contracts were for 1 year, but the aim now is to increase the average term of contracts to 3–5 years. They also aim to achieve a situation where 50 per cent of their services are carried out by only 20 main suppliers. This way, the company can work very closely with them, help improve the suppliers' performance and also to develop closer relationships with them.

Suppliers are now considered to be an essential part of the company so they are now working with suppliers in the same way as for their own direct employees. As a consequence of this, a culture is being created in which people in the company consider the suppliers as their own partners. Also,

Some equipment used for teaching statistical tools

Figure 13.13   Statistics training kit

Total Quality Fair where ISO completed projects are presented

Figure 13.14   Exhibition by project teams

they involve suppliers in projects of mutual concern, for example, for safety and quality improvement projects. The results of these projects have a common benefit for both. I also conducted training for senior management of some of the suppliers who are now developing similar programmes with the help of Mobarakeh senior staff.

For the Customer Focus activities, every year they now have 800 direct meetings with customers. Also, they have several common quality improvement projects with most of the main customers. These include the car industry, house appliance manufacturers, pipe industry, motor manufacturing and others. Figure 13.15 shows one of the popular tools used in the improvement process.

One of the main features in the Customer Focus activities is the measure of satisfaction. Mobarakeh set up a big project on this to gather direct information on the opinion of the customers of their products and services.

Relationship chart completed on one of the training sessions

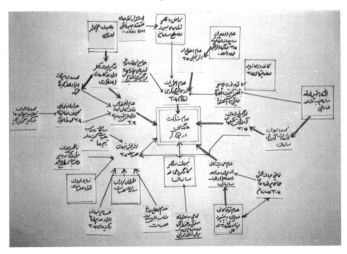

Figure 13.15   Relationships diagraph

In addition to the improvements in Supply Chain Management and Customer Focus, Mobarakeh have made huge improvements to production levels, cost reductions, reduction of plant stoppages, reducing defects, reducing the raw material consumption of the factories, reducing the electrical and energy consumption and reducing the melting time, amongst others. There are also many other types of project such as improving the relationship with the local community and production of coils for car body applications as a common project with their customers.

In total, the number of projects carried out during these 3 years, by Quality Circles retrained in the improvement methods, was 89. For these projects, the section heads were often also involved. They also carried out 134 research and development projects using Six Sigma tools, which were mainly with the technical experts of their company, universities and also customers and suppliers. Under the subject title of Direct Total Quality they carried out 376 projects, making a grand total of 559 projects.

The Suggestion Scheme also resulted in a significant improvement. As a consequence of the active involvement of the managers with the workforce, they gathered more than 30 000 suggestions from the people. Whilst the data does not exist on the performance of the scheme before the start of Total Quality, it is claimed that this is a huge increase. As a consequence, they executed 8564 small improvement activities. The benefit of these projects is not only improving the operational activities, but it also has a good influence on the relationship between management and the people. It also creates a very good feeling for the people who feel that they are effective in the company for getting the Objectives and doing that.

In summary, from the 6700 people employed, 4000 were actually involved in this project, which is 60 per cent of the total population, and the percentages of the people who are working under different titles, but still as a coordinated part of the whole programme, for example, research and development, suggestion system, Quality Circles and Total Quality, are: 9 per cent in research and development projects, 51 per cent in suggestion system, 16 per cent Quality Circles and 55 per cent Total Quality (includes projects using Six Sigma tools). There are some people who are working in projects spanning several aspects. Figure 13.16 shows the chief executive taking an interest in the improvement projects.

The reasons for the success of the Mobarakeh programme are almost entirely due to the incredible commitment of the chief executive and the top management team from the very beginning.

Project presentation: Chief Executive in centre and David Hutchins on left

Figure 13.16   The chief executive taking an interest

Presentations of awards for completed projects

Figure 13.17   Recognition awards ceremony for completed projects

Following the initial presentation to them in late 1997, the programme began in May 1998 with 2x2 days modules for the top team led by the chief executive officer. In these modules the umbrella programme for the whole company roll-out was developed. During the workshop, they agreed to follow the principle of not deploying to lower levels until the programme was secure and operative at the level above. Figure 13.17 shows the chief executive giving recognition awards to successful participants in the improvement activities.

Because of the complex nature of a large steel works with its production processes ranging from iron making, steel making, continuous casting, hot rolling through to cold rolling and finishing, and Support Processes including laboratories, instrumentation, maintenance, transportation, quality control, training, personnel, research and development, accounts, purchasing, customer support and sales and so on, similar modules were conducted for each. In all this resulted in 18 committees, all of which created their own Vision, Strategic Directions and KPIs. These were submitted to the top team to achieve compatibility both with each other and with the aspirations of the business executive. Following this, training was given in all of the concepts mentioned previously in this chapter.

In September 2002, an executive of the company presented all of the above information at the World Quality Congress in Harrogate.

It can be seen that to introduce Six Sigma successfully into an organisation takes more than simply sending a few selected people on a few courses. Even in a small organisation, the culture change necessary is likely to go far beyond the abilities of most people unless they have been specially trained in this and have the total support of top management.

The public course approach can work but usually it requires the existence of a change programme already sufficiently well developed to be able to absorb Six Sigma without suffering internal resistance. This is quite a rare occurrence.

14 *Lean Manufacturing*

Hoshin Kanri – from Strategy to Action!

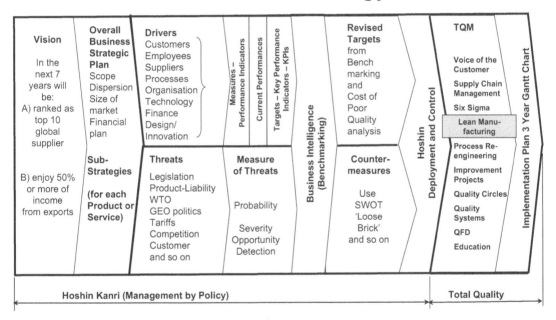

Figure 14.1   Lean Manufacturing

Lean Manufacturing is also one of the key concepts that might be used to close the gaps between where we are now and where we want to be for some KPIs. Unlike Six Sigma which tends to be a management-based approach for dealing with cross-functional problems, Lean Manufacturing makes extensive use of the workforce and it would be as well to read Chapter 17 on Quality Circles in conjunction with this one before making too many plans.

WHAT IS LEAN MANUFACTURING?

Lean Manufacturing is part of a business-wide Strategy which aims to improve flexibility, sharpen market responsiveness, improve output and simultaneously reduce overall costs. Lean Manufacturing is one of the key, but not only, means by which this is being achieved.

Lean Manufacturing is thought by many to have been the brainchild of American Academics. It is, in fact, a term coined by the authors of *The Machine that Changed the World* published by MIT to describe one aspect of the Toyota production system. We say one aspect because in companies such as Toyota, what in the West is known as 'lean' is in fact only one of the integral parts of Hoshin Kanri and, under that umbrella, part of what might be called Japanese Total Quality Management (JTQM) – to distinguish it from the Western perceptions of TQM which are grossly inferior. Initially as a consequence of the stunning success of *The Machine that Changed the World*, companies all over the world have been and are attempting to implement Lean Manufacturing with some success. However, as we have said repeatedly throughout this book, the full potential cannot be achieved without first having established a culture of JTQM and with it Quality Circles.

At the core of this Strategy is a series of related processes aimed to continuously and perhaps relentlessly minimise the consumption of resources that add no value to a product.

Lean Manufacturing may be defined as:

The name used for a collection of business-performance improvement tools and concepts that focus on enhancing Quality, cost, delivery and people's contributions through the application of world-class manufacturing principles, the elimination of waste and continual improvements in workplace safety.

A BRIEF HISTORY OF LEAN MANUFACTURING (AND A WORD OF CAUTION)

The concepts on which Lean Manufacturing are founded have their roots in the scientific management era of the first half of the 20th Century, the work of Fredrick W Taylor and Frank and Lillian Gilbreth being fundamental to its development. By the 1950s, through concepts developed directly from their work, the USA had become the most productive country on earth. However, the management systems which had evolved from these concepts were powerful technically but the way in which they treated employees was fundamentally flawed (see Chapter 16 – The Principles of Continuous Improvement). The method as it was in those days relied upon breaking all work-related tasks down to their basic elements and devolving all problem solving upwards to management.

A further problem not appreciated at the time was that management generally had far too little experience of shop floor activities and was not sufficiently familiar with the tasks in the daily operations. This resulted in huge inefficiencies which quickly began to develop in the organisations. These manifested themselves as excessive downtime due to long and poor set-up procedures, unexpected plant breakdowns due to poor maintenance, excess inventory resulting from the difficulties of managing large complex plant and Supply Chains with fluctuating customer demands.

During the 1950s, the emerging post-war Japanese industrialists began to challenge some of the precepts of this management approach and amongst the foremost of the pioneers were Toyota, Honda and a number of other high-volume-producing organisations.

First of all they challenged the social system of scientific management. Management managing with the employees being treated as robots was not working for them.

Realising that they could not go back to the Craftsmanship approach because it was not economical, they tried to bring it back to groups or teams under the Leadership of their own foremen or supervisors. They called these teams Quality Circles at Toyota and Gemba Kaizen activities in Nissan. This concept was formally launched at the Nippon Wireless and Telegraph Company in early 1962 and before the end of the year 35 other companies had followed suit, including the Toyota Corporation.

Despite the fact that Dr Juran, the American management guru, pointed this out to the Americans and indeed Europeans alike as far back as the early 1960s when he said, 'The Quality Circles movement in Japan is a powerful one which no country has been able to imitate. Through this concept, the Japanese will become world leaders in Quality,' nobody took any notice. At that time Japan had the reputation of being junk merchants to the world, making cheap imitations of Western products and the likelihood of them becoming world leaders in little more than a decade stretched credulity to the limit.

The Quality Circles concept was incredibly successful and proved to eliminate all of the disadvantages of so-called scientific management whilst retaining all of its advantages. In fact it enabled the concept of self-management in the workplace. Quality Circles developed at least a decade before the appearance of Lean Manufacturing. This is important because it was the Quality Circles which provided a base from which Lean Manufacturing was able to develop.

Once Quality Circles were established, they enabled management to begin building and developing not only the supervisor but also the management skills of the workforce. This all took place in the mid to late 1960s, by which time workers were skilled in process control using simple but effective statistical methods known as Statistical Process Control.

The development of Statistical Process Control was also an essential precursor to the Lean concept. In Chapter 13 (Six Sigma) Dr Taguchi's discovery that all variation results in increasing Quality-Related costs was described. As a consequence of this, Statistical Process Control was introduced into the training of the Quality Circles. This meant that Japanese industry had many thousands of people trained in problem diagnostics and scientific problem solving. In contrast, in the West, the only problem solvers were the managers and engineers. The number of problems to be tackled was hopelessly beyond the resources of these specialists and therefore the problems were not solved.

However in Japan, the Quality Circles combined with the use of statistical methods began systematically to reduce variation in business processes. As the variation was reduced, process predictability increased. This in turn made scheduling easier and this reduced inventory. By the early 1970s this had impacted significantly on inventory, waste and set-up times. It was at this point that perceptive people in the Japanese plant maintenance field recognised that this form of improvement could be regarded as a science in its own right. From that point, in around 1972, Targets such as Single Minute Exchange of Dies (SMED), stockless production (Just In Time) and so on began to emerge. Also run times were longer with fewer breakdowns, this in turn made set-up times shorter and created less waste in the production process. This then enabled the advent of the Pull system – never making anything until there was a customer – and the use of the so called Kanban (two card) system.

At that point in 1972 the Japanese Plant Maintenance Institute postulated that perhaps the workers could also carry out local plant maintenance, in effect, manage the operating efficiency of their plant and equipment. This included responsibility for the general management of the housekeeping in their work areas. This concept became known as the 5Ss, which is explained later.

In parallel to all of this, the development of local quality control through the use of statistical methods had produced an unexpected by-product. When process-related problems had been identified and eliminated, not only did quality improve but also the process itself became more predictable.

During the late 1970s to the early 1980s, what is known today as Lean Manufacturing was in operation in all leading Japanese organisations. However, whilst some specific elements of it had been identified by Western observers, this was only on a piecemeal basis.

Other US observers saw Just in Time and thought it to be a panacea, others saw 5S/5C, still others picked up on SMED, single part manufacture (including Kanban and Theory of Constraints, and so on), Jidoka and Andon set ups and Takt Time.

A detailed explanation of the Japanese term 5S is given later but refers to the following Japanese terms: Seiri, Seiton, Seiso, Seiketsu, Shitsuke. Because these do not translate perfectly into English there are two substitutes that are generally used, however, there are variants on these where some companies have customised them for their own purposes. 5S therefore may be translated into either five words beginning with 'S': Sort, Straighten, Sweep, Standardise, Systemise; or alternatively five words beginning with 'C': Clear out, Configure, Clean and Check, Conformity, Custom and Practice. Since both have approximately the same meaning they are popularly referred to as 5S/5C.

The various observers quickly wrote books on each of these and made a lot of money in the process. The fact is, and this is very important, none of these concepts stands on its own. Many Western companies attempted each of these with some modest success but the fact remains that the full power can only be released when they are all part of a consolidated company-wide programme under the umbrella of Hoshin Kanri.

The Western perception reminds one of the famous poem, 'The blind men and the elephant'. Each of them touched a different part of the elephant, the trunk, tail, leg, tusk, side and ear, and from their experience described the elephant that way – one thought it to be like a snake, the next a rope, a tree, a sword, a wall and so on. All of them were partly right but all of them were wrong!

Whilst each element of what is today called Lean Manufacturing might produce some return individually, the real power comes through the integration of not only the tools but everything included in integrated management systems. The full benefit can only be achieved through the vigorous support of Quality Circles activities throughout the organisation. This is why both Toyota and Honda have policies of 100 per cent global membership of these teams.

Curiously, none of the Western approaches to Lean Manufacturing appear to recognise the fundamental importance of Quality Circles or to use a more generic name, Self-Managing Workgroups. This is strange given the emphasis put on it by Toyota and Honda. Concepts such as 5S/5C, SMED and TPM cannot work efficiently or effectively without them.

In a truly Lean Manufacturing organisation today under the Hoshin Kanri umbrella, everyone is recognised as being the expert in their own job and everyone is working together for mutual success.

SOME TERMS USED IN LEAN MANUFACTURING

Many of these terms are also common to Six Sigma and other business improvement concepts.

Voice of the customer

Customers can be both internal and external and include everyone who is upstream from any given point in a process through to the eventual end user. In its ideal state, nobody makes anything until it is required by the immediate customer. In practice, stocks must be kept at some points for practical reasons but these should be continually challenged and where possible eliminated without Risk to the organisation or to create unnecessary delays further up stream or to the ultimate user. To be effective, it is paramount that the specific needs of these customers is understood and satisfied.

Value Stream Mapping

Most processes include activities that are either unnecessary or inefficient. Value Stream Mapping is a process-mapping tool that enables a searching analysis of all processes in order to eliminate all forms of waste.

The six big losses

1. *Equipment failure* – this causes production downtime. Equipment failure requires maintenance assistance and can be prevented with the use of appropriate preventive maintenance actions and especially TPM.
2. *Set up and adjustments* – this is the loss of productive time between different product types, and includes the warm-up after the actual changeover. Changeover time should be included in this loss possibility and should not be part of the planned downtime.
3. *Small stops* – typically less than 5–10 minutes and minor in-process adjustments or simple tasks such as cleaning and lubrication.
4. *Speed losses* – caused when the equipment runs slower than its optimal or designed maximum speed. Examples include machine wear, substandard materials, operator inefficiency, equipment design not appropriate to the application and so on.
5. *Losses during production* – includes all losses caused by less than acceptable quality after the warm-up period.
6. *Losses during warm up* – all losses caused by less than acceptable quality during the warm-up period.

Jidoka (autonomation)

A system to ensure quality, whereby if an abnormal situation occurs in production any worker can stop the entire line.

Just in time

Parts are made to the customer's order, one at a time as immediately required, not in batches.

Gemba Kaizen

Continuous workshop improvement: meaning eliminating waste and non-value-added work. 'There is always a simpler way' (Quality Circles are identical).

Kanban (meaning 2 card system)

A visual Pull System. For example, a storage location will contain one part. When that part is taken from the location for the next operation, the operator makes another part to replace it but only when the location is empty.

Push System

This is also known as 'making for stock' or 'making to forecast'. Demand is predicted but frequently inaccurately with the consequence of either 'out of stock' or 'excess stock' situations.

Pull System

Products are not made until there is a customer order.

Takt Time

This is the average rate of customer demand and the allowable time to produce one product at that rate. Each workstation in a production line should perform its operation within this time. For example, if customer demand is 160 units of product in an 8-hour day then the Takt Time would be 8x60/160 = 3 minutes. In other words one unit must be produced every 3 minutes which is Takt Time. If this is achieved exactly there would be zero inventory at that point.

Poke Yoke or Foolproofing/Mistake Proofing

There are two kinds of solution to problems, Reversible and Irreversible:

- *Reversible* means that the problem can return if the situation is not regularly monitored. This can involve a Process Audit.
- *Irreversible* solutions are those where the methods have been changed in some way making it impossible for the problem to return. This is known as Mistake Proofing or in Japan 'Poke-Yoke' (pronounced *poka yokee*).

THE SEVEN FORMS OF WASTE

A few years before the *The Machine that Changed the World* was published, Taiichi Ohno had published a book called *Toyota Production System*. In it he had explained the main foundations of Lean Manufacturing. These principles guided the Japanese companies that were found to be 'world class'. Taiichi Ohno devised seven categories which cover virtually all of the means by which manufacturing organisations waste or lose money; these have become known as 'the Seven Wastes'.

Waste is the use of resources over and above what is actually required to produce the product as defined by the customer. If the customer does not need it or will not pay for it then it is waste. This includes material, machines and labour. The Japanese word for waste is 'muda' and is often used in books, training courses and by Lean consultants to mean waste.

The seven wastes described by Ohno are:

1. Over-production
   - Producing more than the customer requires.
2. Waiting
   - Waiting for upstream products or advice, information or assistance.
   - Excessive machine time/downtime.
3. Transportation
   - Work-in-progress.
   - Bad organisation.
   - Double handling, poor handling.
   - Moving items over long distances.
4. Over-processing
   - Making more than the customer requirement.
   - Doing more than necessary.
5. Inventory
   - Stocks of parts or materials not being worked upon and stored between operations.
6. Motion
   - Excessive walking.
   - Searching for tools/parts.
7. Scrap/re-work
   - Making defective parts.
   - Re-work.

Others have included additional categories which include:

- untapped human potential;
- inappropriate systems;
- energy and water;
- pollution.

Ohno's Seven Wastes are a convenient way to classify the problems within a company which are causing the waste in first place, they play a valuable role in tackling inefficiency and reducing operating costs.

TOTAL PRODUCTIVE MAINTENANCE

TPM challenges the view that maintenance is no more than a function that operates in the background and only appears when needed. The objective of TPM is to engender a sense of joint responsibility between supervision, operators and maintenance workers, not simply to keep machines running smoothly, but also to extend and optimise their performance overall. The results are proving to be remarkable.

The Goals of TPM are measured using an Overall Equipment Effectiveness (OEE) ratio:

$$OEE = availability \times performance \times Quality\ rate.$$

$$availability = \frac{available\ time - downtime \times 100}{available\ time}$$

Downtime can be calculated by adding together the amounts of time lost due to equipment failures, set-up and adjustment, and idling and minor stoppages.

$$performance\ rate = \frac{ideal\ cycle\ time \times processed\ quantity \times 100}{operating\ time}$$

Speed losses are calculated by combining time lost due to idling and minor stoppages and time lost due to reductions in speed.

$$Quality\ rate = \frac{processed\ quantity - defective\ quantity \times 100}{processed\ quantity}$$

Defective quantity is calculated by combining defects in process start-up and reduced yield.

Typical calculations for OEE prior to the implementation of Just In Time-related strategies usually range between 40 per cent and 50 per cent with the former being the more normal. Experience indicates that it is possible to raise this to between 80 per cent and 90 per cent in a period of some 2 to 3 years from start up. However, the improvement will usually follow an almost exponential upward curve with the bulk of the gains being in the latter part of the period.

TPM was developed in Japan in 1971 by the Japanese Institute of Plant Maintenance (JIPM). TPM involves everyone in the company. The JIPM also identified what they refer to as the Six Big Losses mentioned earlier.

The JIPM states that:

Both operations and maintenance departments should accept the responsibility of keeping equipment in good condition. To eliminate the waste and losses hidden in a typical factory environment, we must acknowledge the central role of workers in managing the production process. No matter how thoroughly plants are automated or how many robots are installed, people are ultimately responsible for equipment operation and maintenance. Every aspect of a machines' performance, whether good or bad, can be traced back to a human act or omission. Therefore, no matter how advanced the technology is, people play a key role in maintaining the optimum performance of the equipment.

Whilst in the early stages, the workforce involvement will usually be limited to membership of multi-layer teams. In the longer term, usually in around 2 to 3 years, the operator involvement will have developed into fully autonomous self-managing maintenance group activities.

Typically, in the early stages, a pioneer team of managers, technical specialists (including maintenance department personnel and operators) work on one problem production line. Using the project–by-project disciplines, the team select specific problems from amongst the so-called Six Big Losses that they believe can be solved quickly and easily but which produce tangible and measurable improvements.

At this stage, the programme is then given a high profile and extended to include everyone in the plant. The initial teams of workers will be trained in the problem-solving tools and taught how to select process-related problems as projects. Managers and specialists will act as consultants to the newly-formed teams and guide them in the best use of problem-solving methods.

At this point the workers will be encouraged to carry out simple plant cleaning activities using the 5S housekeeping concept.

Whilst the exact translation of each of the 5Ss does not transfer directly into a convenient set of 'S' words in English, the following can safely be regarded as being very near equivalents.

SEIRI – Systemising and Standardisation (utilisation of equipment)

Classification, tool selection, material and suitable equipment for each task or activity, information selection and recording of that required to perform the task.

SEITON – Sorting (tidying up)

Finding the right place to keep objects and general organisation of the workplace.

SEISOU – Sweeping (cleaning)

Keeping the work area clean. Retain only the information and items needed to work on the specific tasks.

SEIKETSU – Sanitising (health, hygiene)

Creating good conditions of hygiene; checking illumination, atmospheric pollution, sound, temperature, and so on. Keeping visible records for easy evaluation and comprehension.

SHITSUKE – Self-discipline

Developing the habit of looking at procedures and rules. Self-control and self-direction.

WESTERNISATION OF THE 5S CONCEPT – 5S/5C OR CANDO

The Ss of 5S are originally Japanese words but have been translated to five English language 'S's – Sort, Straighten, Sweep/Shine, Standardise, Systemise/Sustain are some of the words which have been commonly adopted to use five meaningful English words beginning with S and which users find more easily adopted into a Western environment. Being precise here is a bit of a nightmare because just about everybody who uses the concept has their own preferences for terms and also sequence of the 'S's and there are several alternative 'S' words that have a similar if not near identical meaning. However, there are others which have a very similar meaning and these are often used as a matter of personal preference. The use of these alternatives does not materially change the use of the concept.

CANDO refers to Cleanup, Arranging, Neatness, Discipline and Ongoing Improvement but is fundamentally the same.

Sort/Cleanup

The first step of 5S involves the removal of rubbish, clutter and unnecessary objects. It also includes cleaning, sweeping, getting rid of dust and oil and so on. In a machine shop it would include the removal of broken equipment or tools and materials that have not been used in a significant length of time and are not likely to be used in the near future. Red Tagging is a technique often used at this stage where everything that might be removed is first of all tagged with a red label before the decision is made to remove it.

5S can also be applied to office work and would include removing old files, magazines, old software, clutter in drawers and papers that are not being used and are unlikely to be used in the future. This will free up space (sometimes a significant amount), make old box files available for current work once the old contents have been thrown out, make the work area more open, making it easier to walk around and find other more important items needed on a daily basis much more quickly.

Straighten/Arranging

Tools are put where they are needed, often utilising shadowboards thereby making sure they are to hand and labeled as they should be. Commonly-used items are stored within easy reach, reducing the need for bending, stretching and excessive walking. Wheels are put on items that have to be moved, perhaps tool boxes and portable workbenches or storage chests and drawers where tools can be kept in correct locations and are easy to find in the future.

Shine/Neatness

Once the rubbish and unwanted items have been eliminated and everything has been assigned an agreed location, this phase of 5S is concerned with maintaining the newly-agreed practices. Daily 5–10 minute cleaning routines are established to maintain a clean and tidy working environment. Operators accept responsibility for their own working area and for keeping equipment clean and in good order and making sure tools are kept where they should be.

Systemise/Discipline

Audits of the work areas are often used to help maintain standards. These can be carried out by the workers themselves as an extension of the system of 'self-management'. Trophies and other staff incentives, including making the additional annual management Hoshin Kanri audit results a part of staff appraisals, are widespread practices in most Japanese companies.

Sustain/Ongoing improvement

The cleaning activities encouraged at the commencement of a TPM programme can produce some quite unexpected results and even at this early stage it is not unusual to achieve a reduction of stoppages in the order of some 50 per cent. However, it takes from 2 to 3 years to achieve the really impressive benefits.

In parallel with this, the team leaders and supervisors will be trained in simple plant maintenance and the relevant technology. This will free up the time of the maintenance engineers to do more complex work and to develop their own skills. Later, this training will be extended to the operators themselves.

As the teams begin to mature, they will soon be able to look after the machines themselves. As they become more confident there is a marked change in attitude and a will to take wider responsibility for the performance of their operations.

INITIAL 5S/5C PROJECTS

These should be selected using the following criteria:

- Those which have a positive impact on the work environment, for example housekeeping.
- Those which are relatively simple but have a tangible payback.
- If possible, choose projects in which the advice of members of the workforce can be of value. (The man who knows that work area best is the person who lives there).
- Make sure that the projects selected can predictably be completed and the results implemented in around 3 months from the beginning or less. People will lose interest if the projects go on for too long. This is often referred to as 'quick wins' or 'picking the low-hanging fruit'.
- Be very careful not to take on anything too challenging in the early days. A failure at this stage would be a major upset in the implementation process and people will become demoralised if they feel that they are walking deeper and deeper into a swamp.
- Projects selected should be either measurable or countable and stated in a negative form. For example, 'loss of yield from process X' would be measurable and stated in its negative form. 'Too many breakdowns on line X' is countable and also in the negative form. The reason for the use of the negative is that the next question will be, 'What causes...? Usually there will be many theories offered by the team members.
- Before attempting to find the possible causes, it is also important to record the current state of the problem. Collect and organise data to show its severity, use graphical techniques such as the Pareto Diagram in order to dramatise the situation. Frequently, with housekeeping-related cases or cases where there may be severe wear or catastrophic breakdown, photographs or video can be ideal methods for recording the current state. They will also be useful historical evidence years later. At Short Bros. Ltd, the Belfast-based Aerospace Company, they have an exhibition showing the internal condition of all of the departments before they began the improvement process and then subsequently, the various stages of progress over the following years. It makes an impressive display.
- When the possible causes have been identified, before going on to the next stage it would be wise to seek the opinions of the relevant members of the workforce and anyone else who may have valid opinions. In one such situation in the early days at Short Bros. Ltd, a worker was asked why they thought leakages occurred around the small rivets which joined adjacent parts of an aircraft wing. The worker explained that they believed the shape of the tool fixture was incorrect and suggested an improvement. Their idea was implemented and proved successful. One of the more cynical of the managers asked, 'Why did you not tell us before?' The response was, 'You never asked!' The more the opinions of the workforce are solicited, the more enthusiastic they will become and the easier it will be to gain volunteers for autonomous workgroup activities when these first management-level projects have been completed.

- Typical problems and possible causes include:

Loss	Possible Cause
Breakdown losses	Checking and cleaning
Equipment failure losses	ditto
Set-up losses	Waiting instructions
Jig and tool losses	ditto
Start-up losses	Waiting materials
Other downtime losses	Waiting personnel
Minor stoppage and idling losses	ditto
Reduced speed losses	Quality instructions, Measurement and Calibration
Defect and re-work losses	ditto
Waiting instructions	Management planning
Waiting materials	ditto
Equipment downtime	Management organisation
Equipment performance	ditto
Methods and procedures	ditto
Skills and loss of morale	Management environment
Line organisation losses	Management training
Measurement and setting losses	Resource planning

- Finding the true causes from amongst the many theoretical causes requires the collection and analysis of data. Usually the data for the type of projects selected for TPM activities is easily recovered and does not normally demand the use of sophisticated techniques such as Designed Experiments and so on.
- In almost all cases the data will provide convincing evidence as to the true causes. When these have been determined, the team will then turn their attention to the selection of appropriate remedies. Wherever possible, the most popular remedies will be from amongst those which are irreversible, in other words, which are foolproof (Poke-Yoke). If non-foolproof solutions are to be implemented they will need to be included in periodic audits to ensure that the improvement is continuing to be applied.

Following the completion of these early projects, a full awareness programme can be implemented. The initial projects should be used to demonstrate management commitment and the methodology used.

Only start as many teams as can be safely supported through their early learning experience. As the teams develop their capabilities, it then becomes possible to increase both the number of teams and their range of problem-solving skills. They can also be encouraged to tackle more difficult problems and to introduce a degree of self-management. This can best be achieved by encouraging the teams to set themselves annual Targets for process performance improvements. This becomes possible if the organisation practices Hoshin Planning and Policy Deployment. Initially the teams should be taught to collect data to determine the overall operating efficiency of their unit of operations. This information can then be used to set Targets and enable the selection of appropriate projects.

RECOGNITION AND REWARD

In all organisations where success is known to have been achieved, considerable efforts have been made to give recognition to successful teams and to enable all of them to display their work.

Typically, TPM storyboards are erected at convenient locations near to the work areas to enable the teams to post their charts and other examples of their work. This is partly for recognition purposes but also to encourage others to offer suggestions to the teams.

Displays of completed projects are posted including photographs of the teams and any awards that they may have received. All of this activity is in order to demonstrate commitment and to ensure that the TPM concept has the highest possible profile in order to maintain the highest possible level of consciousness as to the importance attached to these activities.

Examples of success (Internet source)

Nissan, Tochigi Plant – results after 3 years:

- manufacturing cars, 7000 employees;
- number of cars passing Quality Control first time, no re-work increased by 70 per cent;
- number of breakdowns reduced by 80 per cent;
- overall equipment efficiency increased by 30 per cent.

Comment from company: 'We cannot management our plant without TPM'.

Nippon Lever, Utsunomiya Plant (manufacturing Lux soap, household cleaners) – results after 2 years:

- reduction in operating costs – £2.8 million;
- cost of introducing TPM – £90 000!;
- production efficiency:
  - domestic filling line – up from 76 per cent to 95per cent;
  - high-speed soap line – up from 54 per cent to 85 per cent.

Comment from company: 'The ideal status of a machine is to have no defects, no breakdowns. You may think that's impossible. But when you see the Nippon Lever plant, you realise it is possible.'

FUTHER TERMS

SMED (Single Minute Exchange of Dies)

Since it became evident in the late 1970s that Toyota, Nissan and so on were able to change the huge metal pressing dies used for the manufacture of chassis parts on their automobiles in less than 2 minutes and with virtually no interruption of the production process, set-up or changeover reduction has been an important element of Lean thinking for many organisations around the world. SMED is just one of many such techniques, but a very important one, used to help reduce changeover time.

Set-up time includes the time taken to physically make the changes to the process in order to produce the new product. Start-up time is the time taken to reach optimum operating conditions in terms of quality of product. SMED/changeover reduction simply refers to attempts to reduce the time taken to carry out the changeover process. Total elapsed changeover time is the time taken from the end of production of Product A through to full production of Product B.

Reductions to this time will improve OEE, make it possible to use the Pull system economically, reduce inventory and work-in-progress, develop flexible production and increase product mix which in turn will smooth production output (variations in relative demand for products produced on the same line can easily be accommodated). Leading to:

- increased efficiency;
- reduced stock requirement;

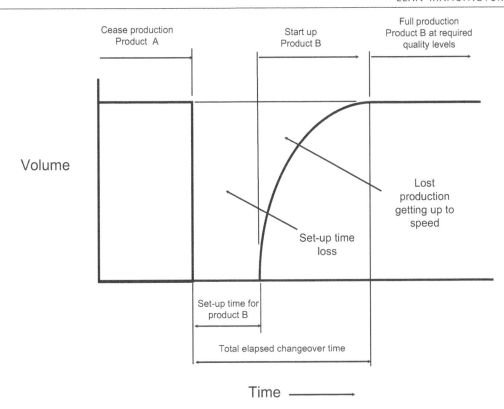

Figure 14.2   Single Minute Exchange of Dies (SMED)

- increased capacity;
- reduced work-in-progress;
- increased flexibility.

Kanban

KanBan stands for Kan (card), Ban (signal) and was originated at the time of the evolution of Just In Time manufacturing techniques.

Toyota Production System (TPS)

The production system developed by Toyota Motor Corporation has been designed to provide best quality, lowest cost and shortest lead time through the elimination of waste.

TPS comprises two pillars, Just in Time and Jidoka, and is often illustrated with the 'house' shown in Figure 14.3. The TPS is maintained and improved through iterations of standardised work and Kaizen, following PDCA, or the scientific method.

Development of TPS is credited to Taiichi Ohno, Toyota's Chief of Production in the post-World War II period.

Beginning in machining operation and spreading from there, Ohno led the development of TPS at Toyota throughout the 1950s and 1960s following a visit to Ford Motor Company in Detroit in 1950. Later it was disseminated to the supply base during the 1960s and 1970s.

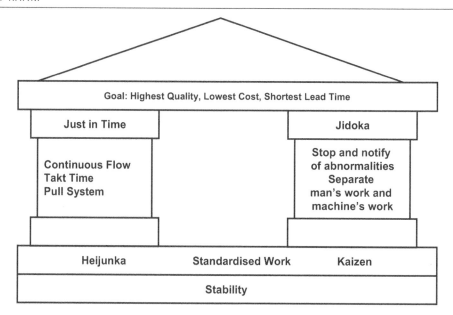

Figure 14.3   The Toyota 'house'

Heijunka

(This explanation of Heijunka was taken from wikipedia reference http://en.wikipedia.org/wiki/Heijunka).

'Heijunka' is a Japanese term that refers to a system of production smoothing designed to achieve a more even and consistent flow of work. Heijunka as a concept is closely related to Lean Production and Just In Time manufacturing. Heijunka means two different, but related, things. One is the leveling of production by volume. The other is leveling production by product type or mix.

Leveling by volume

If there is a demand for a family of products that use the same production process that varies between 800 and 1200 units then it might seem a good idea to produce the amount ordered. Toyota's view is that production systems that vary the required throughput suffer from mura and muri with capacity being 'forced' in some periods. So their approach is to manufacture at the long-term average demand and carry an inventory proportional to the variability of demand, stability of the production process and the frequency of shipments. So for our case of 800–1200 units, if the production process were 100 per cent reliable and the shipments once a week, then the production would be 1000 with minimum standard inventory of 200 at the start of the week and 1200 at the point of shipment. The advantage of carrying this inventory is that it can smooth production throughout the plant and therefore reduce process inventories and simplify operations which reduces costs.

Leveling by product

Most value streams produce a mix of products and therefore face a choice of production mix and sequence. It is here that the discussions on economic order quantities take place and have been dominated by changeover times and the inventory this requires. Toyota's approach resulted in a different discussion where it reduced the time and cost of changeovers so that the costs of smaller and smaller batches were not prohibitive and lost production time and Quality Costs were not significant. This meant that the demand for components could be leveled for the upstream sub-processes and therefore lead time and total inventories reduced along the entire value stream. In order to simplify leveling of products with different demand levels a related visual scheduling board, known as a Heijunka box, is often used in achieving these Heijunka-style efficiencies. Other production-leveling techniques based on this thinking have also been developed. Once leveling by product is achieved then there is one more leveling phase, that of 'just in sequence' where leveling occurs at the lowest level of product production.

The use of Heijunka as well as broader Lean Production techniques helped Toyota massively reduce vehicle production times as well as inventory levels during the 1980s.

Jidoka (autonomation)

This is a concept that is believed to have been first developed by a Quality Circle in one of the Honda Motor Cycle factories in the late 1960s/early 1970s.

Their claim was that if Total Production was stopped every time there was an interruption to the process anywhere on the line, the impact would be a reduction in work-in-progress and an increase in total production of some 7 per cent.

The story is that it took management some 6 months to think about this and agree to an experiment. The result was a stunning success. Output rose not by 7 per cent but by an incredible 15 per cent!

Most high-volume manufacturers would be understandably very wary of a technique which stopped total production every time something went wrong but it is very logical and here is an explanation.

Figure 14.4 shows a simple but typical production line with three streams of components coming together to make a final assembly.

Figure 14.5 shows a stoppage occuring at operation 'C'. Notice the build-up of inventory after 'B', 'F' and 'Q'. Operations 'G', 'H', 'J' and 'K' will run out of work and will then stop for the

Theory of AUTONOMATION (Jidoka)

Typical non-Jidoka system. If there are stoppages at one operation, the others continue to operate using buffers or on-line storage and 'push' – 'make to forecast' system

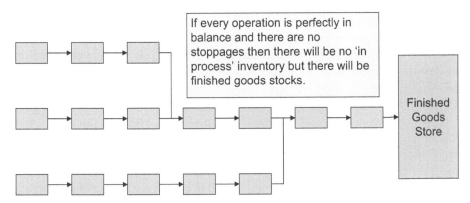

If every operation is perfectly in balance and there are no stoppages then there will be no 'in process' inventory but there will be finished goods stocks.

Finished Goods Store

In practice, this will never be the case because there will always be unscheduled stoppages – Figure 14.5 shows what happens when there are unscheduled stoppages.

Figure 14.4   A non-Jidoka system

Theory of AUTONOMATION (Jidoka)

Units of product

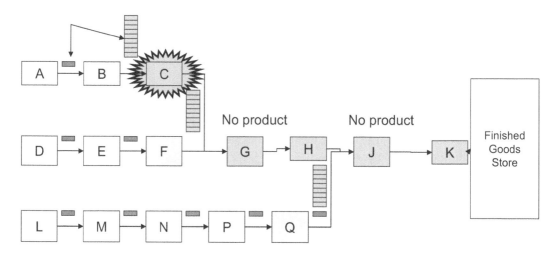

Figure 14.5   Stoppage at operation 'C'

same time as 'C'. When the cause of the stoppage at 'C' has been cleared, 'G', 'H', 'J' and 'K' will progressively also run but the inventory that has built up after 'B', 'F' and 'Q' will remain in the system if these activities run at their normal speed. They will only be eliminated by overtime at 'C', 'G', 'H', 'J' and 'K'. Of course, in a normal complex operation with tens or hundreds of activities, there will multiple random stoppages at many of the operations. Each of these will also create log jams of built-up inventory and a nightmare for production control. Also, it is unlikely that each of these minor stoppages will be recorded and only 'quick fix' remedies sought in order to get the line running again as soon as possible. Of course, the same problems will happen again because they have not been properly closed out. Now consider the Jidoka method.

The Jidoka system (as shown in Figure 14.6) – if 'C' stops then everything is stopped. There is no build-up of inventory in the system and the quantity of finished product reaching the store is the same. There will be no need to put in overtime or to speed up processes and scheduling becomes simple. However, the most important point is that each of these stoppages is recorded. At the end of the shift, each of them will become a project for the Quality Circles to work on. Consequently, the next day these will have been eliminated from the process which will of course run more smoothly with fewer unexpected interruptions. Eventually, in the ultimate state it will be perfect. As an example of this, one Japanese company, ASMO, which produces electric motors for automobiles, claims 97 per cent total plant 'uptime' in production. Most companies are lucky if they can claim 50 per cent!

In the full Jidoka system, illuminated screens are used above the production lines so that the actual state of production can be seen by everyone all of the time. Figure 14.7 shows such a display in one Japanese refrigerator manufacturing plant.

This is an accumulative record of the total stoppages since the start of the shift. Behind those figures accessible on a computer monitor in the work area will be a breakdown of that 13 minutes in the form of a Pareto Diagram. This will influence the choice of topics to be tackled in the Quality Circles meeting.

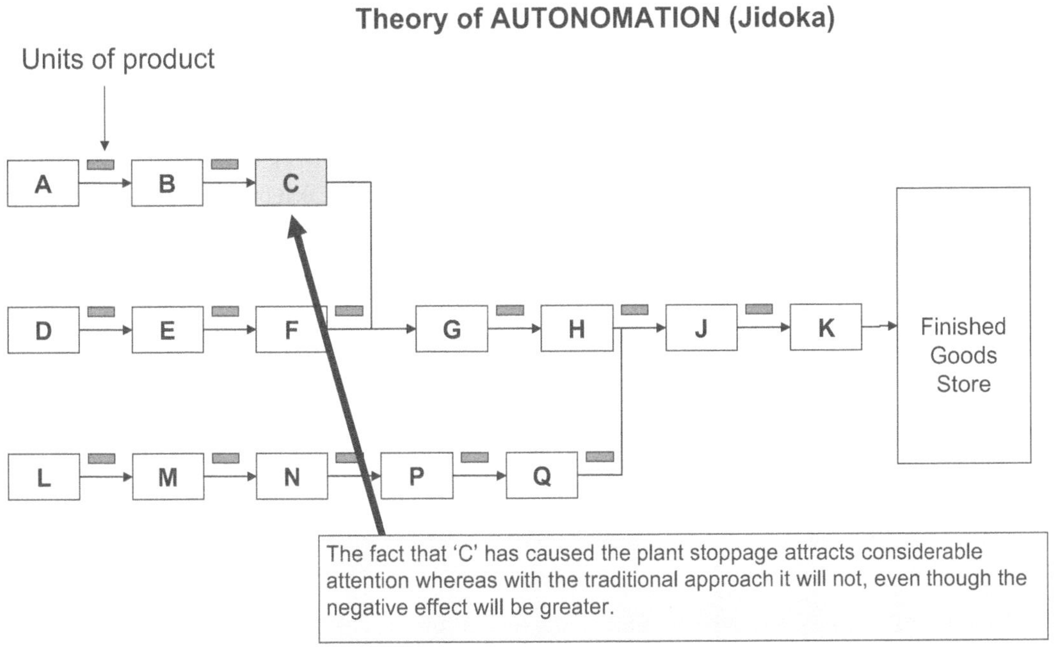

Theory of AUTONOMATION (Jidoka)

Units of product

A → B → C

D → E → F → G → H → J → K → Finished Goods Store

L → M → N → P → Q

The fact that 'C' has caused the plant stoppage attracts considerable attention whereas with the traditional approach it will not, even though the negative effect will be greater.

Figure 14.6   Use of Jidoka

AUTONOMATION

Example of use of overhead displays

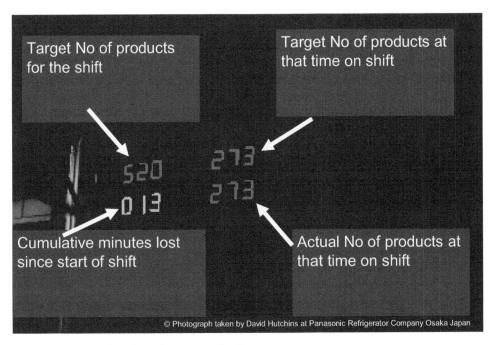

Target No of products for the shift

Target No of products at that time on shift

520

273

013

273

Cumulative minutes lost since start of shift

Actual No of products at that time on shift

© Photograph taken by David Hutchins at Panasonic Refrigerator Company Osaka Japan

Figure 14.7   Example of Andon-type display system

Takt Time

Takt Time is a German term and is calculated as being the pace of production needed to meet customer demand. If Takt Time is achieved exactly and there are no bottlenecks in the process then there will be zero work-in-progress in the operation.

It is the available weekly work time, taking into account the shifts worked and making allowances for planned stoppages (for planned maintenance, team briefings, breaks) divided by the anticipated average weekly sales rate (including spare parts) plus any extras such as test parts and anticipated scrap:

$$\frac{\text{AVAILABLE TIME}}{\text{CUSTOMER DEMAND}}$$

Example: If the customer requires 140 units in a 7-hour effective working time day, the Takt Time will be:

$$\frac{7 \times 60 \text{ (MINUTES)}}{140}$$

$$= 3 \text{ MINUTES}$$

This means a unit needs to be completed every 3 minutes. Therefore every operational step needs to be completed and delivered every 3 minutes (or multiples of it). To smooth out variations in process time within the operation Kanbans, multiple machines, cell production techniques and multi-tasking can be used.

CONCLUSIONS

Hopefully it is clear from the above that Lean Manufacturing is not simply a 'bolt-on' addition to the usual management process but is part of a radical change in management style and approach.

The full benefit of Lean Manufacturing can only be achieved with the company-wide implementation of both Quality Circles and the methodology of the project-by-project improvement process at all levels from the top down.

Of course, since most organisations tend to outsource more than 50 per cent of their operations, both service and manufacture, then Lean Manufacturing must also be taken through the entire Supply Management Process as well.

15 *Process Analysis and Process Re-Engineering*

Hoshin Kanri – from Strategy to Action!

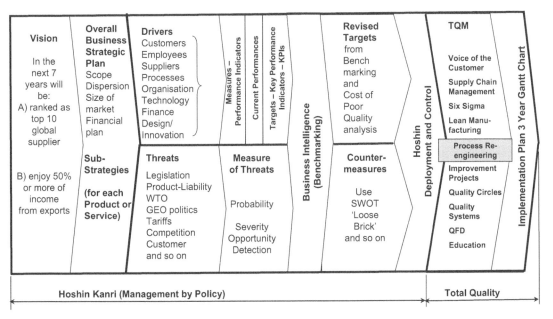

Figure 15.1   Process Re-engineering

The concept of Process Re-engineering is the fifth of the series of concepts which are available for closing the gaps defined by the KPIs. Whilst the concept stands alone as a management tool, it is also an integral part of Continuous Improvement (Chapter 16) and these two chapters should be read in conjunction with each other.

Process Re-engineering is a sub-element of Process Analysis and was re-popularised in the early 1990s. We say re-popularised because in fact it was one of the earliest techniques to be developed in the early days of Work Study back in the 1920s. Whilst it was a very popular concept in the 1950s and 1960s, somehow it went out of fashion until it was resurrected in the early 1990s.

Figure 15.2 illustrates the fact that organisations consist of multiple interacting processes, sub-processes and sub-sub-processes, each comprising people, methods, materials, equipment, environmental variation and measurements, making for a complex system of interacting activities. It is not surprising that in a growing organisation many, if not most, of these have never been

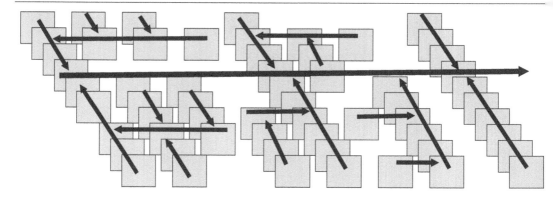

Figure 15.2   The complexity of processes

mapped or analysed, mainly because everybody was too busy doing other things. When we do analyse them, it is likely that there are many improvements that can be made.

Basically there are three types of process:

1.   The overall management process for the organisation as a whole. This is described in Chapter 10, Hoshin Policy Deployment and Control.
2.   Key Business Processes – whose outputs are the products and services which are the business of the organisation.
3.   Support Processes – these include finance, maintenance, training, and so on.

The SIPOC acronym is a useful way to think about processes at a high level and how they may be improved. However, in order to understand a process in detail it is usually necessary to go down one or more levels from this high-level view and also in many cases to include the Supply Chain right back to its origins. It is not unusual to find that the true causes of some problems are built in from long before the process reaches the point where it is in our control. If we do not map it back far enough this might not become apparent.

SIPOC stands for:

SUPPLIER > INPUT > PROCESS > OUTPUT > CUSTOMER

We can improve a process by:

• improving the quality of the inputs;
• improving the performance of the equipment;
• improving the procedures;
• improving the behaviour of the workers;
• improving the flow of information;
• improving the behaviour of the managers;
• improving the overall organisation;
• improving the inputs from service processes.

It is important to remember that optimising all of the sub-processes will *not* optimise the macro-process. This can lead to sub-optimisation and can result in a worse overall performance than before. An example might be a demand from the IT department that all other departments complete some particular documentation. This might be important from their point of view in order to speed up some work that they are doing. However, this might cause serious problems elsewhere which ultimately result in delays and other negative outcomes.

The danger of sub-optimisation is reduced if people understand how their process fits into the larger process and what the overall Objectives are. Of course, with a well-publicised Hoshin Kanri programme this should be an unlikely problem.

It is dangerous to give people only the minimum information you think they need to do their jobs (see Chapter 20, Education).

In general, straightforward Process Analysis as a tool for Continuous Improvement will produce multiple incremental improvements ranging from small to large depending on the situation. This technique can be used on any process in any type of organisation and it has always led to some significant improvements when used properly.

Process Re-engineering, on the other hand, will have far fewer opportunities but where they do occur, the benefits are likely to be dramatic step changes.

An example of the latter was Kodak. Some few years ago, Fuji launched the single use camera. Kodak were already concerned about the market share that Fuji had taken in the roll film market and this development was alarming. When they studied how Fuji had developed the camera they became even more alarmed.

At that time, Kodak's product development process took 2 years from the initial acceptance of a new idea through to it being launched in the market. Imagine their horror when they discovered that not only did Fuji take just 10 weeks, the product was almost perfect when it reached the retail outlets. Kodak admitted to themselves that even after taking 2 years, the likelihood would have been that when the product reached the market in bulk, there would be teething problems: shutters sticking, light getting in, jammed film and so on.

Kodak realised that they could not get down to 10 weeks by tweaking their existing product development process, they had to start with a clean sheet of paper and rethink the whole process.

They had to challenge the old thinking. Instead of a sequential process of Conceptual Design leading to Functional Design through to Design for Manufacture, with all the interim and iterative 'design reviews', they could collapse the total time if they performed all of these activities simultaneously. Apart from its impact on total time, they discovered other advantages. By commencing Design for Manufacture more or less at the same time as Conceptual Design and Functional Design, they discovered that these activities interacted with each other. As a consequence there were far fewer engineering change requests resulting in fewer design changes and delays to production. The savings were huge. This was a classic example of Process Re-engineering. Of course, such opportunities are reasonably rare so the concept does not present a magic bullet as some would have us believe, but it does mean that we should always be on the lookout for them in the hopes that we might have our own Kodak-style case study.

Of course, the process just described is now known as Concurrent Design and is practised by many organisations, especially the high-volume manufacturers who compete fiercely in being able to be the first to bring a new product to market. As a consequence, product development times have been slashed in recent years. For example, just a decade or so ago it took more than 5 years to develop a new vehicle, now it takes less than 1 year. Survival in the highly-competitive mobile phone market is almost totally dependent on being able to convert an idea into reality in the shortest time possible. All of this comes as a result of Re-engineering the design process.

PROCESS MAPPING FOR PROCESS IMPROVEMENT

Process Mapping and Process Analysis are best carried out by a team of people who are very familiar with that process and work on it (preferably at different stages). It is normally used when the KPIs in question consistently show a significant difference between desired performance and actual results. As a consequence, a team will have been formed with the task of finding the reasons for the gap and what needs to be done to make a substantial improvement. On the parts of the process with which they are not personally familiar it is important to consult those who are. Never take chances and never attempt to guess or use assumptions no matter how convinced you may be that you know the answers. Invariably you will have some big surprises in Process Mapping and Process Analysis so expect them and you will not be disappointed. Ignore this advice and your work will be low grade and this is a fact.

Requirements:

- several sheets of flip chart paper (it can be done on a computer with a data projector but most people find it more convenient to use paper and pen and then transfer it to the computer afterwards);
- Blu Tak or equivalent (kinder to the wall than adhesive tape);
- felt tip pens (that do not penetrate the paper and mark the wall);
- flip chart and easel.

Process Mapping as a precursor to either Process Re-engineering or Process Improvement is quite a different technique to that used for the production of Process Flow Charts.

In the case of Process Flow Charts, the charting normally begins at the first activity in the process from which everything else flows. In the case of Process Mapping for Improvement, it is usual and recommended that the mapping begins with the last activity in the process. Then it is mapped backwards to the beginning. The first time someone attempts this, it will probably feel like trying to write with the other hand or drive on the wrong side of the road but it will quickly become familiar with practice.

Step 1: voice of the customer

It is almost certain that many if not most of the KPIs will be the outputs of processes. A process in this sense is a series of connected activities that result in an output. Ideally that output will be a perfectly desirable result. Whoever is on the receiving end of that output we can refer to as the 'customer'. However, there are other terms that might be used such as 'end user', but before the end user there may be a series of people beyond the last of the activities that physically change the product or service, for example, stockist, distributor, shop or store and so on. Whilst they may not be directly concerned with the efficiency of its end use, they will be concerned with a variety of features that impact on them. For example, a shop will be concerned with the attractiveness of the packaging, ease of handling and so on. A stockist will also be interested in ease of handling but also delivery promises, picking errors, ease of stacking, invoicing and so on. These people can be referred to as 'interested parties' and they are directly on the process line through to the end user. Then there are others who might not be directly on that process line but who are nevertheless impacted by its performance. This can include the local community, share or stakeholders and the public at large. For example, a plan to build a new aircraft terminal might be attractive to the potential customers but will also impact on environmental groups such as those concerned with wildlife, noise, pollution, the local community, and so on. In fact the process will impact everyone upstream from any particular activity along a process that we choose to study.

Before commencing Process Mapping it is advisable to study the KPI very carefully and identify all that are linked directly to the process.List these KPIs on a sheet of flip chart paper.

Step 2: roughing out the process

Eventually it is recommended that the charting be done on flip chart paper stuck to the wall as shown in Figure 15.3, but at this stage we do not know for sure how many operations there are along the process and it will usually be many more than you think. Therefore it is good idea to rough out the process on a sheet of paper before transferring it to sheets which have been stuck to the wall.

Using the flip chart easel, at the top-right hand side of the paper draw a box about 15 – 20cm square and in it write the name of the very last activity in the process. Ideally this should be the end user.

Then to the left of it draw another box the same size and do the same again for the immediately preceding activity and connect the two boxes with a line with an arrow head at the right-hand end indicating the direction of the flow. Repeat this for each successive operation backwards through the process until you cannot go any further. Continue this as far as it is possible even when the activities are outside the scope of the project. The reason is that until the next step, which is Process Analysis, is taken we do not know how important these operations or activities are with regard to the problems we hope to solve. It may be, and it often is, the case that some of the causes of the problems may already be built in before the process reaches the point where we can influence what happens. Until we have done the analysis we may suspect this sometimes but we will not know for sure. Often we will have some real surprises.

The main advantage of starting the mapping process at the end rather than the beginning is that we will end up with the sequence of events that we are interested in. This is not a flow chart as such which if well produced will cover all eventualities. In our case we will only include those activities that are directly relevant to the problems that we wish to solve. A second advantage of doing it this way is that whilst the end of the process may be both clear and obvious, this will not usually be the case with the other end. Often this is obscure and is rather like the tributaries of a river. Deciding which are relevant is not easy but by working back to the end, the charters will intuitively include the relevant activities or operations.

At this stage the initial work will look something like Figure 15.3.

Step 3: preparation for process analysis

Now that we have scoped the project and have defined the beginning and end points, it will be necessary to transfer the chart onto the flip chart sheets on the wall. It is not recommended to

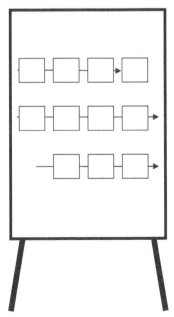

Figure 15.3   Process Mapping

attempt to do this work on the flip chart itself because if it is done properly, it will not be possible to get all of the subsequent detail on there and nobody will be able to read it.

At this point we need to find a convenient long wall without windows, masterpiece paintings or other obstructions so that we can stick the flip chart sheets along the wall end to end allowing approximately two of the boxes that we identified on the flip chart per sheet as shown in Figure 15.4.

Actually it is advisable to use sticky notelets rather than draw the boxes onto the flip chart paper at this stage. This is because it is very common to find that either something has been left out of the process or maybe the sequence is wrong. This happens more often than most people would think. At this stage it is advisable to ask those who work along each stage of the process whether they agree that it is correct. More often than not, it will be revealed that the sequence is wrong or that an activity has been left out. In many cases this will be the first time that the process has ever been mapped and it will evoke considerable interest especially if it is complicated or spans considerable physical distance from the first activity to the last. In many cases people will only know what they do and possibly the activities before and after their own but nothing beyond that. It has been found on many occasions that simply mapping the process can lead to some quite dramatic improvements.

Step 4: study the activities

Before going into the detail of what in the process might be the cause of the gaps between desired final output of the process and actual output, it is necessary to consider first of all whether the overall process is ideal. For this purpose the technique of Critical Examination can be very effective. It uses what are known as the 5Ws and a H technique: What, Why, When, Where, Who, How.

By asking what is being done, what should be done, what could be done, and so on, then asking the When questions, many useful ideas may emerge that will enable the process to be radically redesigned, which in many cases will revolutionise the response times and eliminate many unnecessary activities.

The form shown in Figure 15.5 can be used for this purpose.

Step 5: Process Analysis

Step 4 above may result in nothing being changed, the process is fine as it is. At the other extreme, it may be that it is changed completely or even eliminated. If any of the original remains, and usually

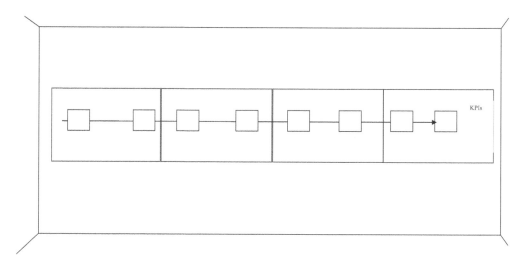

Figure 15.4   Posting to the wall

Process Re-engineering Critical Examination					Form 2.2

Process step: _____
Analysis date :_____

	Present Method	Reason	Choices	Preferred Method	Improvement
Aim	What to do?	Why doing it?	Can we do something else?	What should be done?	
Place	Where are we doing it?	Why there?	Can we do it somewhere else?	Where should it be done?	
Step	When are we doing it?	Why at that time?	Can we do it at another time?	When should it be done?	
Person	Who does it?	Why them?	Could someone else do it?	Who should do it?	
Process	How is it done?	Why is it done that way?	Is there another method?	What should be done?	

Figure 15.5   Critical Examination

it does, then the following process should be carried out separately for every KPI that has been identified prior to the Process Mapping stage. Each activity along the process should be considered separately from each other and each KPI selected should be considered separately, the reason for this being that each KPI will have its own distinct causes and their own distinct remedies. Therefore each KPI should be considered as a separate sub-project.

Now that the sequence and activities of the process have been identified and agreed, the Process Analysis phase can be commenced. To do this effectively it is absolutely critical that it is done exactly as the following advice suggests. Any variation in method at this stage will result in an inferior analysis and quite likely miss all of the important features that we are looking for.

In the Process Mapping stage we began with the last activity/operation and worked backwards. In the Process Analysis stage, we work the other way so we start at the beginning and work to the end.

At the first box on the left, the leader asks of the group, 'In what way could the problem be caused at this operation?' Anybody can answer and the idea is written down above or below the box. Some people cluster the answers around the box and other prefer to list them. It is purely a matter of personal preference. The leader repeats the question over and over until all the ideas have stopped flowing. Typical 'causes' will include: poor training, poor communications, no clear procedure, handling damage, contamination, sickness, holidays, low priority and so on. However, these are not simply vague meaningless statements because they are specific to that particular activity.

When, and only when, the ideas for that box have been exhausted the teams move on to consider the next box. Remember, this is not a race and the more exhaustively each activity is interrogated the more likely real improvement will be. A word of warning here: anyone who is facilitating this activity will need to make sure that the team do analyse each element exhaustively before moving on. It will seem tedious to the team at first but they will soon realise why this is necessary. Not all the real causes emerge in the first few moments. Sometimes it is a while before something quite important emerges. The danger is that if the team move on too quickly, they may miss some important detail and it is unlikely that it will come up later.

Eventually the team will reach the box representing the end of the process. At this stage it is important to consult as many people who work on the process as possible and solicit their opinions. Quite often they will identify some things that have been left out and will have opinions about the importance of some of the ideas mentioned. When ideas are obtained from others it is critically important that they get recognition for their help otherwise it is unlikely that either they or others will be so willing in the future.

At that point the Process Analysis is likely to look something like Figure 15.6.

In reality, the number of ideas against each box is likely to vary and some boxes will only have one or two or even no ideas against them. At the other extreme some will have many. Until we carry out the analysis we will have no idea.

Step 6: locating the root causes

If the Process Analysis has been carried out thoroughly, the true causes will be on the diagram. Unfortunately so will a large number of possible causes which may have a minor effect. If we were to test every one of these it would probably take forever so we will need to see if we can find any short cuts.

Fortunately there are a number of possible clues.

First of all, do any of the ideas repeat themselves at other operations? If they do the possibility is that there is an endemic deficiency in the process which could be a major cause. For example perhaps 'unclear instructions' happens at four places; 'lack of training' occurs five times. Further investigation of each of these may prove positive and is therefore likely to be important.

Another clue is where there is a cluster of possible causes at one or possibly two operations. It is worth looking at these more closely because they may be inter-related. For example, bad handwriting at one operation where forms are filled in might be linked to misread instructions at a later operation where the information on the forms is keyed into a computer. The solution to this might be to redesign the forms to eliminate handwriting and use tick boxes which will have the effect of making the forms easier and quicker to interpret and less vulnerable to mistakes.

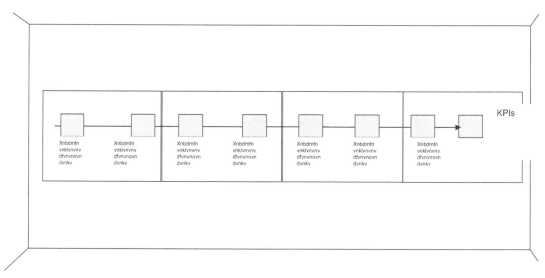

Figure 15.6   Identification of possible causes

Outside of these two possibilities, it remains to search the remainder and look for favourites. Each member of the team will undoubtedly have their own. These can be highlighted and a ranking method such as Paired Rankings used to help decide the order that they are to be checked. Sometimes it is possible to check all of them simultaneously with a check sheet but the circumstances will dictate the method.

Finally continue to look for ways to shorten the process. Do all of the activities add value? Is it possible to combine operations? Are there any iterative activities that occur following 'design review' in the design process? If so, ask why they are iterative. Is there any way that the number of iterations can be reduced? Are there any bottlenecks? If so how can they be eliminated? It may be possible to speed them up or it might be an idea to increase the resource. Bottlenecks always cause upstream holdups and increases in inventory. This is the Theory of Constraints which was well described in Ezra Goldratt's book *The Goal*.

DRILLING DEEPER

On many occasions it will be necessary to break some of the possible causes down into more detail if they are still too general in the way they are described. In this case the Ishikawa or Fishbone Diagram can be used effectively. This technique is described in Chapter 16 (The Principles of Continuous Improvement).

16 The Principles of Continuous Improvement

Hoshin Kanri – from Strategy to Action!

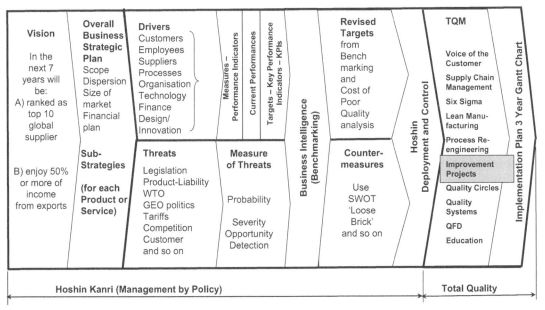

Figure 16.1   Continuous Improvement

The process of Continuous or project-by-project Improvement is at the core of all successful business improvement programmes. The tools included here are fundamental to all problem-solving and improvement activities whether it be Six Sigma, Quality Circles or any other disciplined approach. When combined with Process Analysis and Process Re-engineering and the higher-level tools such as Designed Experiments in Six Sigma Black Belt training there are very few problems that cannot be tackled and solved.

Quality Improvement is a never-ending process. Man has always been able to find better ways of doing things and the likelihood is that this will always be the case. The simple truth is that if we do not continue to improve our competitors certainly will and we will be left behind.

Improvement, of course, happens to some extent whether it is planned or not. In many cases it happens because a supplier has improved their products and forced improvement on us. For example, a new computer will have the latest operating system. This is not the sort of improvement that is considered here. This is evolutionary improvement and happens to all organisations alike.

This chapter is concerned with revolutionary improvement that has been deliberately introduced and encouraged throughout the organisation as a discipline for all to use as a means of continually improving the position of the organisation in its marketplace in comparison with its competitors. The fact that the organisation is improving at all is important, but it is the comparative rate of improvement which matters. Otherwise competitors may improve at a faster rate. If they are behind now it is fortunate but there is no guarantee that they will not catch up. On the other hand, the pressure may be to make up lost ground on others who are currently ahead.

This chapter is designed to show how Continuous Improvement can become a structured part of the organisation and the principle means by which the gaps between Current Performance and desired Goals from the KPIs can be closed.

IMPROVEMENT CAN OCCUR IN TWO POSSIBLE WAYS: EVOLUTIONARY AND REVOLUTIONARY

The fastest rates of improvement will demand the best methods and disciplines. Even the methods themselves are subject to improvement so inevitably the methods will change as new and better tools, techniques and number crunching software are found and applied. There was a step jump in our ability to effect change when we began to use sophisticated computer software to do some of the more complex Data Analysis for techniques such as Design of Experiments, correlation analysis and other techniques which require massive data processing. However, what does not seem to change is the sequence of events that is necessary in order to go from 'problem, effect or symptoms' (these three words have more or less the same meaning in problem solving) to 'solution' or 'remedy' and then through to 'foolproofing' or 'control'.

The first disciplined roadmap for methods improvement came from the Work Study discipline in the early part of the 20th Century. This was referred to as SREDIM:

Select – Record – Examine – Develop – Install – Maintain.

Dr Juran later simplified this to Symptom – Cause – Remedy which is nice and easy to follow and which is still my preference.

Today, as is shown in the Six Sigma Chapter, the fashionable acronym in popular use is DMAIC: Define – Measure – Analyse – Install – Control. Essentially all of these have the same general meaning and all follow the same sequence. Their use is merely a matter of personal preference.

There is another, which is still in popular use especially in the motor industry, which is known as 8D TOPS.

The 8Ds are described below:

- D1: assemble a cross-functional team of experts;
- D2: define the problem;
- D3: implement and verify Interim Containment Actions (ICAs) as needed. These are also known as 'temporary fixes';
- D4: identify and verify root cause;
- D5: choose and verify Permanent Corrective Actions (PCAs);
- D6: implement and validate PCAs;
- D7: prevent recurrence of the problem/root cause;
- D8: recognise the efforts of the team.

The US Government first standardised the 8D process during World War II, referring to it as Military Standard 1520, 'Corrective action and disposition system for non-conforming material.'

It was later popularised by the Ford Motor Company in the 1960s and 1970s. Today, 8D has become a standard in the auto assembly and other industries that require a thorough structured problem-solving process

The one attractive difference between 8D TOPS and the other approaches is D3, which demands a temporary fix to be put in place. This can be especially important where a random or unpredicted problem suddenly occurred and has resulted in a serious hazard. Clearly such a situation needs to be attended to as quickly as possible. None of the other acronyms deal with this because they are designed to focus on the problems that are endemic in the process and not the sudden unexpected critical events. However, with the inclusion of 3D, the choice of terminology is personal preference. Some organisations even invent their own acronyms but the sequence will be the same.

I prefer Sympton – Cause – Remedy even though it is less detailed because in my opinion it shows the connections between problem and cause and cause and remedy far more clearly than any of the others and it is easier to explain when training people to be able to conduct problem solving. Usually I do this and then superimpose the other acronyms afterwards as a form of reinforcement.

SYMPTOM – CAUSE – REMEDY

It was mentioned earlier that the words 'problem', 'symptom' and 'effect' have the same meaning in problem solving. However, we tend to use each of them in different contexts. If the car will not start or it uses excessive petrol we might say that we have a problem with the car. If we wake up covered in spots or swollen glands the doctor will refer to these as symptoms – but they are still a 'problem' as far as we are concerned! If we put bread in an electric toaster and the thermostat or timer is temperamental, the 'effect' may be burnt toast but again we would say that we have a 'problem' with the toaster.

Equally the words 'remedy' and 'solution' are also interchangeable. We tend to use the word 'solution' when we have used the word 'problem' and the word 'remedy' when we have used the word 'symptom'. In all other respects they may be regarded as being the same.

WHAT IS A PROBLEM?

Basically there are two kinds of problem. There are those that occur suddenly and usually unexpectedly such as a pipe rupture, measles, an explosion, a power cut and so on. These usually require 'firefighting' of some sort. We will refer to these as 'random' failures even if some of them occur fairly frequently. Then there are those that are endemic or 'residual' problems and are 'built in' to the process, they are more or less constant and are the main contributors to the underlying average deficiency in output from the Target. They will have been present from the initial design of the process and result in a less than perfect output. Because they are residual the likelihood is that we accept them as a fate and rarely give them any thought. As a consequence we ignore them and build them into standard costing as 'waste', 'set-up times', 'absenteeism', 'sickness' and absorb them as being a part of the operation. Because we allow for them in the Standard Costing Process we do not notice them unless they suddenly get significantly worse.

For example, in the printing industry there is a chart which is used by the scheduling department to calculate 'overs'. These are an excess quantity of materials which are allowed at the commencement of a print run to allow for in-process losses. For example, if a batch of printed product requires 100 000 units, then depending upon the number of colours and the number of operations, the chart might suggest that 120 000 are printed. If the run achieves the 100 000 with exactly the 20 000 losses allowed for, there will not be a negative cost variance and no inquest into the causes of the 20 000 unit waste. However, all of that waste had to be produced, taking up machine time and contributing to labour costs. The factory will have purchased machinery to process the waste which takes up floor space, add to depreciation costs and there will be the raw material. If these costs were to be challenged, it might be possible to bring the 20 000 down to 10 000 or 5000 in which case this would present a big saving especially if this saving were to be spread over the whole of production and accrued year on year.

It is because we have no sensitivity to these endemic residual problems that the firefighting problems which are more sensational and dramatic get all of the attention. They raise the adrenaline and are memorable. Also, the people who solve them are regarded as heroes and the most successful ones are in line for promotion. For this reason most organisations employ people who are good at tackling these problems. Some Department of Trade and Industry research a few years ago estimated that some 70 per cent of a manager's time is spent on firefighting, but the average level will stay the same because the firefighting process does not address these issues!

Figure 16.2 shows a typical performance chart for any process. Notice that the performance varies with time, which is to be expected. Most of the readings are fairly close to the average but note those marked '1'. They are way above the average and represent the intermittent random problems we have discussed. These have been tackled by firefighting and the level has returned to near the average. Note also the dip marked '2'. This indicates that for some inexplicable reason the process showed a dramatic improvement. The probability is that this went unnoticed but in reality it is just as important as those marked '1'. Had we studied the events that took place at around that time we may have found the cause of this unexpected improvement and if we had implemented a change then we may have made happen on purpose an event that happened initially by luck. Notice that the actual output performance of the process varies with time, which is to be expected. Rarely are these opportunities seized.

SOLVING THE RANDOM PROBLEMS

What is most important is the average level. We would prefer this to be at the level of perfection but this requires a radically different approach than that used to deal with the random problems that we have discussed.

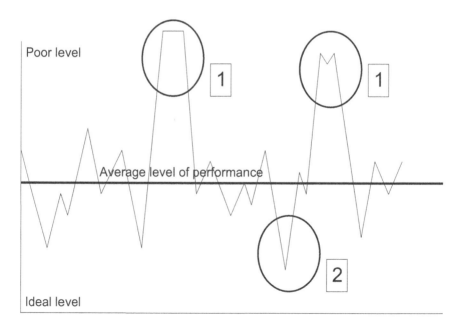

Figure 16.2   Random and residual failures

Solving the random problems requires a type of detective work to find out what changed. Everything was going well then there was a change. What caused it? Investigations might show a number of typical causes – a different person did the job and they were not so skillful (in the case of '2' maybe they were more skillful!), there may have been a change of materials supplier, the machine was in poor condition and so on. When the cause has been located it is often easy to find and apply a remedy. If the remedy solves the problem it will be necessary to 'foolproof' the situation. Some people do not like the term 'foolproof' and prefer 'mistake proof'. However this is not a good alternative because there may not have been a mistake, the change may have been deliberate. Sometimes the individuals concerned may not have accepted the change because they were not properly involved in the study.

RESIDUAL (ENDEMIC) PROBLEMS

In the case of the endemic problems which keep the average at an undesirable level, we cannot use the same approach as for the random problems by looking for a change because by definition nothing has changed. This is the way it has always been and how the process was designed. The average figure represents a level of ignorance. If we knew why it was running at this level we would have done something about it before. Therefore solving these problems requires a voyage of discovery. We need to establish a better understanding of the relationship between process variables and product results. We have no mechanism to do this without a structured and systematic approach. In Japan and throughout the Far East they do have such an approach and they also have the resources to do it. They have all those Quality Circles who have been thoroughly trained in problem solving. In addition the managers have been trained so problems can be tackled at all levels. Sometimes an improvement project requires a multifunction team, in other cases it requires a team from a single department, which is the case for most Quality Circles projects, and sometimes the project can be tackled by an individual.

The improved overall level of performance shown in Figure 16.3 is achieved largely through the use of the project-by-project improvement process described below, but the methods described can also be applied to the random problems as well.

As these random problems are eliminated and if the foolproofing process is applied, they will also help in reducing the average as will holding the gains of the random surprise improvements. As this

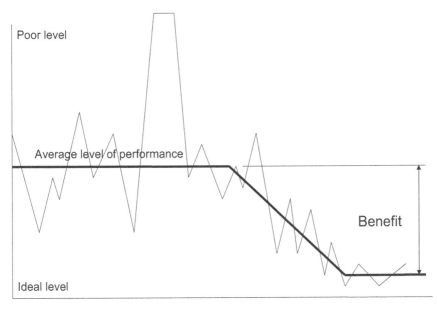

Figure 16.3   Continuous Improvement of residual performance

happens the variation around the mean is also reduced and the whole process becomes progressively more predictable. In turn this makes scheduling easier which will have a cumulative impact on work-in-progress, set-up times, waste of all descriptions and finished goods stocks. In fact it is the structured project-by-project process that brought about the Lean Manufacturing revolution in the first place.

THE PROBLEM SOLVING PROCESS FOR RESIDUAL (ENDEMIC) PROBLEMS

The problem to be tackled must be formally agreed as an improvement project. Improvements rarely happen simply by chance. When they appear to, the process is just as likely to drift back to its earlier state because nothing will have been put in place to hold the gains.

Formal project selection

An improvement project may be selected in several ways:

- it may result from a gap between where we would like to be and our Current Performance as identified when prioritising the corporate level KPIs;
- it may be the result of a customer complaint;
- a competitor may have be taking market share;
- it might be forced by a customer who demands an improvement;
- it may be selected by managers to close the gaps in some local-level KPIs;
- it might be chosen by a Quality Circle as a result of Brainstorming (see Chapter 17).

There are other possibilities but these are the main ones.

Once identified the project must be defined. The form shown in Figure 16.4 is a useful way of doing this.

FILLING IN THE FORM

The Project Name can be a code name or descriptive, but the purpose of the project, which will be a subtitle, must be clear.

The Boundaries (or scope) define the beginning and end points of the project. These should be as wide as possible using the SIPOC acronym – Supplier – Input – Process – Output – Customer concept. Experience indicates that a large number of problem causes are built in very early on in the process and therefore it makes sense to go back as far as is practically possible.

The Current Situation describes the process as it is before any changes are made and is a 'snapshot' of what is happening right now. It is very important not to change anything until the current method has been mapped and the current output measured. If not, when the finished project is presented, it might be difficult to convince the audience what has been and is being achieved. Some may argue that the old situation was not as bad as is being claimed or that the process was not very different from what is being presented. Once the process has been changed it will be difficult to describe the original situation if it has not been mapped. Sometimes it is a good idea to video or photograph the old situation to contrast it with the improvement.

Expectations are something of a guess at this stage because until the current situation has been thoroughly analysed it is difficult to guess what improvement is achievable, but there must be a Goal to strive for. Sometimes it might not be achievable and on other occasions the improvement team may surpass all expectations.

Improvement Project Team Charter		Form Proj. 1.1
PROJECT NAME:		
Purpose:		
Boundaries:	Start Point: End Point:	
Current situation:		
Expectations:		
Target cost/benefit:		
Sponsor:	*Choose Process Owner* *Help Process Owner develop team charter* *Attend first meeting*	*Monitor team progress at agreed milestones* *Provide Process Owner with resources* *Develop support for improvement effort with other senior managers*
Team Leader:	*Lead team, ensuring targets are met, follow the improvement process and update process sponsor* *Support team members' participation, communication and co-ordinate team's work* *Improve own leadership skills in working with team* *Call upon outside skills and resources as needed*	
Team Members:		
Facilitator:		
Authorised:	*Plan meetings with the process owner, attend all meetings, provide consultation on use of Process Improvement process and tools* *Facilitate meetings as needed (as agreed with process owner)*	

Figure 16.4   Keeping a record

Target Cost/Benefit links with Expectations and will provide a reference for the success of the project.

Not all projects have or need a Sponsor or Champion. It may be necessary to appoint them when a high-level project requires a multifunction team. In this case it is necessary to have someone at a high level to authorise the meetings and other details and also to sanction expenditure when required. The Sponsor is usually someone from higher management who has a strong interest in the outcome of the project.

The choice of Team Leader can be critical to success. Their Leadership skills are more important than their knowledge of the problem. However, if they have both Leadership skill and a real interest in the outcome of the project together with knowledge of the process, it is ideal. It is important that the leader encourages the team and does not impose their ideas on the group. They should always seek consensus otherwise the team will disintegrate and the results will be poor.

Team Members should be those who have a good knowledge of the process to be investigated. For management-level projects they will usually be multifunctional. At the Quality Circle-level they will usually be a team doing similar work.

All teams should have a Facilitator and this role is discussed in Chapter 17. The Facilitator is not part of the team but on the outside making sure that they have everything that they need to succeed with their project.

All projects, even the smallest ones, need to have the authority to hold meetings and to take time out from their normal line duties. The authority should come from a level high enough to ensure continuity with their work. Frequently this authority comes from the Sponsor.

There may be considerable work involved in establishing all of the above criteria but it will be well worth the effort.

ROOT CAUSE ANALYSIS

This discipline is theoretically quite simple but in practice it proves quite a difficult one to apply by those who are only accustomed to firefighting. For a firefighting project, usually we need to get results quickly. If there is an explosion, a pipe has ruptured, the scrap levels in a process have jumped alarmingly, the cost haemorrhage will be such that there is no time to lose. In such cases, the firefighter will go straight from 'symptom' to 'remedy' by making a guess at the causes. In many cases, the cause may only be too obvious.

A simple but relevant example might be someone walking into the doctor's surgery covered in spots at a time when chickenpox is an epidemic. It can reasonably be assumed to be another such case and will be treated accordingly.

However, maybe it happens not to be chickenpox! Perhaps the symptoms continue to get worse and the patient again sees the doctor. It is possible that they may again make assumptions and offer another type of medication. In some cases this may continue for some time on a hit and miss basis until either the patient gets better or seriously worse! On the other hand the doctor may be more of a diagnostician than this and instead attempts to find the cause before guessing at remedies.

To do this they will follow the Root Cause Analysis process which follows this sequence of events:

1. Question the patient about where they have been, what contacts they have had, what unusual activities have they been involved in and so on. In an industrial situation this will involve mapping the process from the point where the symptoms are observed backwards as far as possible.

2. Analyse the operations along the process one-by-one from the first through to the last, attempting to identify possible causes. This is known as Process Analysis and is covered extensively in Chapter 15, Process Analysis and Process Re-Engineering.

3. Identify the most likely major causes. This may involve the technique known as Paired Rankings also covered in Chapter 15.

4. Collect and analyse data to verify or reject the potential causes identified in '3' above.

5. Those causes found to be relevant may sometimes be taken directly to seeking a remedy or solution. In many cases they will require further breakdown. Here the technique known as the Fishbone Diagram may be used. This technique enables the possible causes to be broken down into the finest detail at which point the relevant ones can lead to solutions. The technique is really a more sophisticated form of brainstorming and enables related causes to be clustered as they are identified, which assists analysis later on.

6. Data may be collected on the main possible causes identified by the use of the Fishbone Diagram in order to find those which make the most impact.

7. Possible solutions are identified and evaluated for both cost and effectiveness. Some of these may be classified as 'reversible' and others 'irreversible'. A 'reversible' solution is one where it is possible for those who control the relevant operation to revert back to their previous methods. An 'irreversible' solution is one where it is impossible to revert back because the method has been changed in such a way that it this cannot happen. This type of solution is automatically foolproofed. An example where both types of solution are possible is an office operation where it is found that mistakes are being made in filling in the forms. A 'reversible' solution might be to provide training for those who fill in the forms or perhaps to give more clear instructions as to how they should be completed. An 'irreversible' solution might be to redesign the forms using 'tick boxes' to force us to use the right terminology and eliminate the possibility of bad handwriting.

8. Implement the new method avoiding 'resistance to change'. Resistance to change is one of the most common reasons why improved methods fail. Care should be taken to involve those who will have to change their habits, to listen to their possible objections (which may be valid) and accommodate their suggestions. Also it is important not to assume that the new proposals have automatically been adopted just because they are being followed whilst you are present. If you leave too quickly, there may be some resentment which may lead to an unwillingness to persevere with the new methods.

9. Maintain surveillance and continue to collect data for a realistic period to make sure that the changes made really do produce the hoped for results. It is possible that the improvement may be due to some other factor and it is not unusual for processes to improve as if by magic for no other reason than it is known that someone is taking an interest. In this case, the remedy might not be as good as was thought and once attention has moved elsewhere the problem might reappear. This is demoralising for all concerned. Do not take it as a negative if this happens. It may be frustrating but what it proves is that the process is capable of performing at a better level even though we may have been misled. We need to look at it again to find out what it is that might be known to others that, when care is taken, can produce the better results.

10. Present the results to upper management and formally close the project. Regular presentations to management are a must if there is to be a continuation of the improvement process. It enables upper management to see what is being achieved and by whom. It gives people much-needed recognition. It provides an opportunity to give recognition to anyone who might have contributed to the success and, in some cases, the opportunity to use the occasion to 'sell' the improvement process to suppliers and to staff from other departments and also to impress customers.

In summary, the process for multi-function teams and other management-led teams such as Six Sigma Black Belt-led teams looks like Figure 16.5.

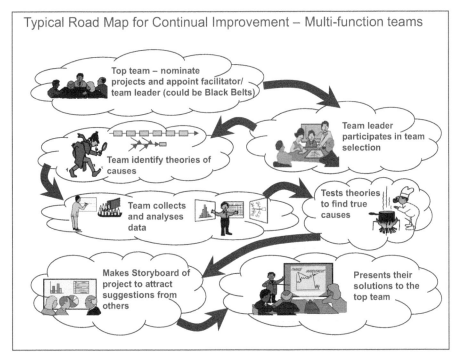

Figure 16.5   Road map for project-by-project Continuous Improvement

In the case of Quality Circles the sequence is only slightly different and looks like Figure 16.6.

TOOLS FOR CONTINUOUS IMPROVEMENT

There are literally hundreds of tools that can be used in project-by-project improvement. Some are more universally useful than others. Some are more popular and others may be very useful, but only in specialist applications.

Fortunately, it has been shown convincingly that over 80 per cent of problems may be solved by only the simplest of the tools available. These have become known as the Basic Tools. Some people are wary of these because they have grown to believe that difficult or high-cost or highly disruptive problems must require the use of sophisticated techniques. This is especially true for those who have been fortunate enough to have acquired a good degree involving the use of sophisticated statistical tools. Naturally they are always looking for opportunities to use their skills and will not give much credibility to the simple techniques. They should re-examine their premises because they will be very wrong. In normal everyday business life there are very few opportunities for the use of these tools other than on a few complex problems. There, they can indulge themselves in Design of Experiments, Regression Analysis, non-Parametric methods to their heart's content, but if they do and they are the only problem solvers, then sadly the overall business performance will remain squarely on dead centre.

The Fishbone Diagram include:

- brainstorming
- Pareto Analysis
- Check or data sheets
- histograms
- Fishbone Diagram
- Paired Rankings.

Typical Road Map for Continual Improvement – Quality Circles

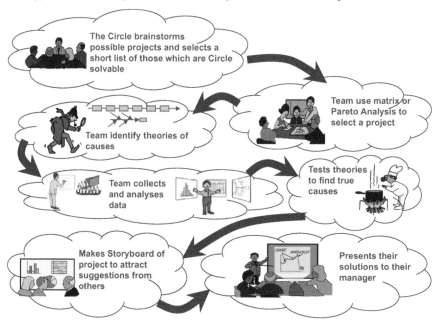

Figure 16.6   Quality Circles problem-solving road map

- Process Analysis
- Scatter Diagrams
- spot charts
- stratification
- checklists.

Each of these tools appears deceptively simple and it is this apparent simplicity that causes suspicion. More often than not, they are not used properly and people are not disciplined in their use. This is particularly true in the case of the language data tools – brainstorming, Fishbone Diagram and Process Analysis.

The power of these tools does not lie in each tool independently but in their use collectively and in the right sequence. This involves training and if the training is given whilst the participants work on a live project they will invariably save very considerable amounts of money, many times more than the cost of the course itself.

Other tools which have more specialist application are mentioned in the chapters on Six Sigma, Lean Manufacturing, QFD and Voice of the Customer.

THE PROBLEM-SOLVING PROCESS

The following series of figures shows typical situations for improvement.

We think of KPIs as if they behaved like this

Output target 5 tonnes per shift
Output actual 4.6 tonnes per shift

In-Process KPIs = (Target – Actual)
(Actual performance is usually stated by calculating the mean figure over a period)

Figure 16.7   KPI perceived behaviour

Study variation

Output target 5 tonnes per shift

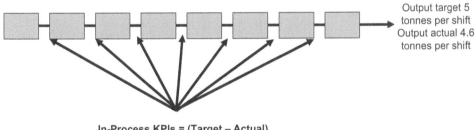

The 'In-Process' KPIs are often very numerous and frequently interact with each other.
In many cases it is only by studying the nature of the variation and locating the interactions that we are able to identify the root causes and find the optimum performance.

This requires the uses of more sophisticated statistical tools than are usually found practised in general TQ programmes.

Figure 16.8   KPI actual behaviour

Study variation

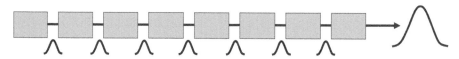

Output target 5
tonnes per shift

The 'In-Process' KPIs are often very numerous and frequently interact
with each other.
In many cases it is only by studying the nature of the variation and
locating the interactions that we are able to identify the root causes and
find the optimum performance.

This requires the uses of more sophisticated statistical tools than are
usually found practised in general TQ programmes.

Figure 16.9   KPI variation

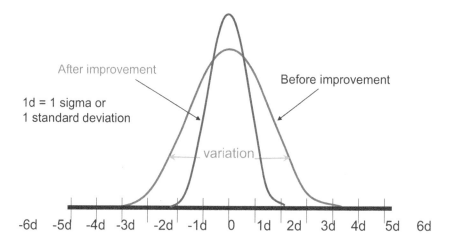

Objective: reduce the variation about the mean.
Typical projects – temperature, weight, mains voltage, diameter, line balance.

Figure 16.10   Variation about a mean value

In this case the project is intended to reduce excessive variation around a Target value. The task
will be to attempt to isolate the special causes of that variation and to eliminate them from the
process. Tools such as Statistical Process charts together with the Fishbone Diagram, check or data
sheets will be the main tools that will be useful here.

Figure 16.11 is typical of bottling and packaging where minimum weights must be stated on the
container. By reducing variation which will produce savings, an even bigger saving becomes possible
by being able also to reduce the mean value. In some instances, this can result in some very large
savings especially in high-volume manufacture.

Figure 16.12 is typical of projects where there are cost or time overruns. The object will be to
get as close to zero as possible both in terms of variation and the mean. Projects of this type could
potentially use all of the core tools of problem solving depending upon the complexity of the
situation.

Figure 16.13 in many ways is not dissimilar to the previous example except that it involves
Attribute Data – right/wrong, good/bad, is/is not – rather than Variable Data which is usually

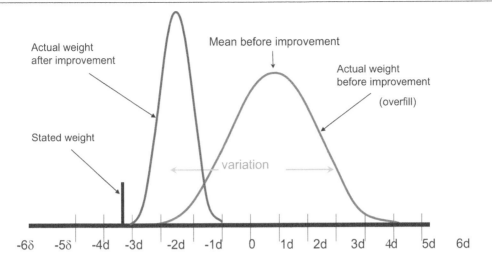

Objective: reduce both the mean and variation about the mean.
Typical projects – Package weights.

Figure 16.11   A situation where variation has been reduced and the mean lowered

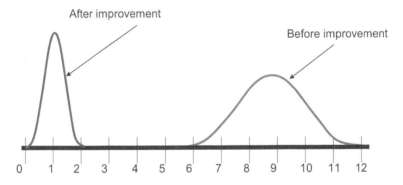

Objective: significantly reduce the mean and variability about the mean.
Typical projects – late deliveries, set-up times, lead times, cost overruns and so on.

Figure 16.12   Reduction of the mean and reduction in variation

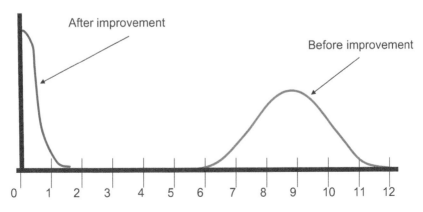

Objective: significantly reduce the number of occurrences of an undesirable event.
Typical projects – errors on invoices, number of breakdowns, number of accidents.

Figure 16.13   This is typical of Attribute Data situations

continuous. The object will be to achieve zero occurrences. Interestingly, whilst Attribute Data-related potential projects are considerably more numerous than those involving Variable Data, the majority of the more popular statistical textbooks give little or no treatment to this aspect of the subject. There are two examples in the Six Sigma chapter that illustrate the potential savings that can be achieved from projects involving Attribute Data.

17 Quality Circles

(Small group improvement activities such as Quality Circles, Kaizen, Autonomous Work Groups, Self Managing Work Groups)

Hoshin Kanri – from Strategy to Action!

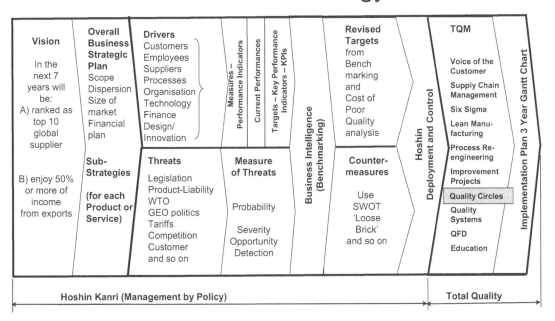

Figure 17.1   Quality Circles

For those of us fortunate enough to have a job, work takes up 30 per cent of our lives and whilst we are not working we are often thinking about it either positively or negatively. Our job (if we are happy) gives us our self-esteem. One of the first things that a stranger wants to find out about us is 'what do we do'. It determines our contribution to the welfare of our families and our role in the community. Work should be one of the most satisfying and rewarding parts of our lives. It is for some but for many, sadly it is the opposite.

It is a terrible indictment on our management approach that so many people get that sick feeling on a Sunday night (Friday night in Muslim countries), it's Monday again tomorrow. In some cases this can spoil the whole of Sunday counting down the hours of freedom. I once knew a Quality Manager who confided in me that he was physically sick in the mornings when he got out of bed just at the thought of going to work. He could not leave the company because his pension was tied to the job. Eventually he suffered a full nervous breakdown. I knew the company well and I can say that there were many other companies far worse than that.

Depression is for some a medical condition. For many it is the consequence of their jobs. People unfortunate enough to work where nobody asks them anything, does not involve them in anything and shows no interest in them other than to see that they have done what is required, can find that depression is not a medical condition, it is the fault of the management style of the organisation. Most companies keep statistics on sickness and absenteeism. In many cases people are just sick of coming to work!

It does not have to be this way, not for anybody. It is not efficient; the company does not get more output this way or make more money. In this situation everyone is a loser and autocratic management styles are a killer.

How much better it would be if instead it was possible to create a management approach wherein people thought, 'Oh good it is Monday tomorrow!' on a Sunday, to be able to look forward to the weekend but be more than happy to come back on the Monday because they are interested in what they are doing, where they feel appreciated and they are interested in the success of the business because they feel involved. They have the opportunity for self-development, there is teamwork, healthy enjoyable competition for some Goals and an opportunity to network with others. Is this impossible? No, in fact if the will is there it is no more difficult than reading the rest of this chapter.

If what is said above is true for the workforce, the same also applies to management. In an autocratic environment, each department is a fiefdom and is isolated from the others. Managers survive by keeping information to themselves, being judgmental and passing the buck at every opportunity. The term 'blame culture' is often an understatement.

Promotion comes to those who can deal with this and never appear to be in the wrong even though they are probably no better than anyone else. They just seem to have Teflon-like exteriors and the mud never sticks. They eventually get promoted but this is how everyone before them was promoted so they end up with a better class of enemy. Moving upwards gets tougher and tougher. To survive, one of the techniques used is intimidation. It comes in the form of larger office, huge pot plants, names on their doors, special restaurants, car park slots and so forth. These are called perks but they are really a means of intimidation. The tragedy is that those who eventually reach the top do so because they are skillful at this game. As a consequence, they have large cars, big houses and all the trimmings. They believe that this is the way to manage because it worked for them, but is it the best way?

Well, there was a time from the 1930s through to the mid-1970s when it would appear so because nobody had come up with an alternative. This was the way that the automotive industry operated and to some extent still does in the West.

It was responsible for breeding Communism, conflict and the misery of factory life as it was at that time. Karl Max commented on the *Division of Labour* by saying that the stomachs of the bosses get fatter whilst the arms of the workers get thinner. He postulated conflict as being the only way in which the workforce could redress the balance and communism was born. This was true until Professor Ishikawa and his colleagues, horrified at the way in which post-war Japan was following down this path, came up with an alternative.

Professor Ishikawa said, 'We cannot bring back Craftsmanship as it was in previous centuries because it cannot compete economically with the Division of Labour approach. Perhaps though it is possible to combine the advantages of the Division of Labour with the advantages of the Craftsmanship approach and avoid all of the disadvantages.'

His solution was to recommend that Craftsmanship be introduced to groups of people rather than to individuals. The main difference between a craftsman and a production line worker is that the craftsman has the opportunity for Continuous Improvement. They are trained to identify, analyse and solve work-related problems. They are respected by both management and colleagues alike. They know that the reputation of the company and its products depends upon them.

Ishikawa therefore suggested that small teams of workers be trained in problem solving and spend approximately 1 hour per week under the Leadership of their supervisor tackling problems and presenting their solutions to their manager. He suggested that the teams be called Quality Control Circles. The first company to experiment with the concept was the Nippon Wireless and Telegraph Company who initially set up nine teams. They proved incredibly successful and the concept then spread across Japan. By the end of the first year there were 36 companies and by 1979 there were a recorded 1 million Circles involving an estimated 10 million workers. The concept continued to grow not just in Japan but throughout the Far East and South East Asia. Today there are estimated to be more than 20 million Quality Circles in China and similar proportions per capita throughout that part of the world. The USA and many European countries did experiment with the concept in the early 1980s and some of the early ventures were extremely successful just as they had been in the East. Unfortunately, for a variety of reasons the process was usurped and today it is nothing more than a memory. However, there is the saying that what goes around comes around and if the West is going to have any chance of competing with the growing industrial might of China and India then Quality Circles are essential. They are also essential if we are to make work an enjoyable part of our daily lives. It might even help to reduce the crime rate.

Quite apart from these considerations, Hoshin Kanri cannot operate successfully in an authoritarian environment. Not only must the culture be participative throughout the organisation, it must continue down through the Supply Chain as well (Chapter 12, Supply Chain Management). This fact is well illustrated in the book *The Toyota Way* and is regarded as essential additional reading for anybody seriously interested in the establishment of a Hoshin Kanri culture.

Not only are the above points important, it necessarily follows that if an organisation concentrates solely on the 'management solvable' problems and ignores workforce involvement then by definition they will underachieve by 20 per cent which will prove fatal in the marketplace.

The Hoshin Kanri approach requires that we galvanise the resources of all our people to work towards making our organisation the best in its particular field. 'Our' people must project an image both at work and in their private lives of pride in the organisation of which they are a part. This can only be achieved if 'our' people think that their organisation is better for their being there, and that they are recognised for their contribution.

This recognition comes in the form of being listened to and being given an opportunity to participate. It is impossible to achieve these Objectives under the system of management operating in our society at present, however participative we may think that it is. To achieve even partial success it is necessary to change fundamentally the system of management operating currently across all sectors of industry. The quality of working life is at least equal in importance to the quality of the product or service. Ultimately, quality must be the basis of everything we do and the level of quality achieved will be the sum of all of our activities.

During the Policy Deployment process in Hoshin Kanri, problems become more and more specific as they cascade through to the workforce. For example, the term 'poor yields' which might be used to describe a form of poor performance at top management level will breakdown and breakdown as it is analysed at each lower level. Part of that problem might relate to the warehouse and be solvable by a Quality Circle. The forklift truck drivers may not understand 'yield' but they do understand broken pallets, picking errors, shrink wrap damage, flat battery and so on, which is what it would have broken down to after it had cascaded through the organisation.

If the problem were to be tackled at the 'poor yield' level, it would almost certainly require a Six Sigma Black Belt-led team to investigate the complex array of interactions between the various elements of the process.

If we do not involve the workforce in this way then either we must put up with these problems, in which case we must also accept that we will underachieve by an average of 20 per cent, or we must use expensive resources to use their valuable time trying to solve those other people's problems in which case they cannot attend to the more complex problems that they are trained to deal with.

MATURING BEYOND PROBLEM SOLVING

By organising the workforce into Quality Circle-type teams, not only can the Circles tackle and solve work-related problems, there follows a transformation in job design. Managers begin to increase their trust of their staff, in turn the staff increases their respect for their managers and this continues progressively until a full state of self-management is reached. At some stage in this process the teams progress beyond solving problems and move towards the phase of making Continuous Process Improvements. In those countries where this has been allowed to happen, there has been no limit to this development process.

For example, in Chapter 14 (Lean Manufacturing), the concept of Jidoka is described. It is a complex idea that results in significant reductions in 'work-in-progress' and stoppage time. This concept was conceived by a Quality Circle at one of the Honda plants back in the 1970s and is today a fundamental part of Lean Manufacturing. Another Lean concept, 5S/5C also mentioned in that chapter, could not have evolved if it had not been for the prior existence of Quality Circles in Japan.

In Nissan, what Toyota refer to as Quality Circles, they label as Gemba Kaizen activities. This has led to some confusion in the West where many believe they are different activities. In the West the term Kaizen is still popular in some organisations and thought to be different from Quality Circles

A QUALITY CIRCLE IS

A small group of between three and 12 people who do the same or similar work, voluntarily meeting together regularly for about an hour per week in paid time, usually under the leadership of their own supervisor, and trained to identify, analyse and solve some of the problems in their work, presenting solutions to management, and where possible, implementing the solutions themselves.

'A small group of three to 12 people'

The Circle should be seen as a team and not as a committee. The workgroup in which the members are employed must also see it as 'their section's Circle' and not as an elite group in their work area. Although some members of the workgroup may not wish to participate in the weekly meetings, Circle members should actively encourage them to make suggestions and solicit their ideas on Circle projects. Of course they should also make sure that they give them credit for their ideas and not claim them as their own.

If the work area contains more enthusiasts than can be included in one Circle, additional Circles may be formed progressively once the earlier Circles have become established. Those as yet unfamiliar with Quality Circles specifically may fear that such a development can lead to conflict and rivalry between groups, but this is extremely rare. It is far more likely that they will cooperate with each other, even helping to collect data for each other's projects and occasionally, if need arises, form cross-Circle sub-groups for the solution of specific problems. Such developments are a sign of maturity in Circle activities and are to be encouraged wherever possible. In cases where there are only one, two or three people in the work area, it may not be possible to form them into a Circle, but usually they will have considerable interaction with other more heavily-populated sections. Not only will there be plenty of opportunity for them to become involved in the projects of Circles in these areas, but it may frequently happen that the Circle will repay the help that they give by working on some projects of their choice. Again this is a sign of maturity and cannot be expected in the early stages of development.

'Voluntarily meeting together'

The meaning of the word 'voluntarily' is hard to define, but basically, in the context of Quality Circles, it means that no one has to join a Circle. People are free to join and free to leave. If someone joins a Circle and subsequently chooses to leave it, there should be no pressure, inquests or recriminations. Obviously, if someone drops out of a Circle it should be regarded as a danger signal that all might not be well in the group, and the Circle leaver should be discreetly asked the reason for leaving. If there is a problem, and it can be overcome, then that individual may, if they choose to do so, return to the group if the opportunity exists.

The fact that people join a Circle because they want to rather than because they have to means that they are prepared to work and have accepted the basic rules which have been laid down.

The reality of this was very quickly learned by the Japanese when they first began Circles in 1962. Those companies which recognised the value of voluntariness soon developed strikingly more effective programmes than those in which membership was compulsory.

Whilst the number of volunteers may be quite small in the early stages, when people may possibly be suspicious of management motives, the number should begin to increase dramatically as soon as the achievements of the earlier Circles become known and confidence is gained.

If a pilot scheme of say five Circles is successful, then in a matter of days, weeks or months, depending upon the circumstances, people should be saying. 'Why can't we have a Circle in our section?' or 'Why are all the Circles on the day shift? Why can't we have a Circle on nights?' and so on.

When managers from other departments realise that the areas with Circles are improving their performance, they will soon begin to request an equal opportunity.

The fact that membership is voluntary does not mean that the organisation has to wait until people knock on the door and request a Circle to be formed.

In the early stages most of the initial members of Circles have been invited to join but not compelled. They should be free to drop out at any time if they wish, even in the middle of training. In a sense, they are actually only volunteering to attend the next meeting, although dropping out is fortunately relatively rare.

'Meeting regularly for about an hour per week'

Whilst some variation in timing exists, it is generally agreed that when circumstances permit, the regular weekly meeting is preferred to once fortnightly or to irregular times on a weekly basis.

A regular meeting time is habit-forming, and the day of the meeting will soon be associated in the minds of the members as 'Circle day' and in such cases, members are much less likely to forget to attend or inadvertently commit themselves to other tasks which conflict with the meeting time. This sometimes happens in other cases.

Two diametrically opposite attitudes are frequently taken to the idea of Circles meeting for an hour per week. Some people cannot imagine that much can be achieved in such a short time; others are more concerned that they might be losing 8 hours per week production from a group of 8 people. In the latter case, the facts show otherwise, for two important reasons.

1. Circles will usually agree to hold their meetings at a time which causes least interference with work schedules. For example, in process work, they may hold their meetings during a maintenance period, job changeover, or after completion of the weekly work schedule. When this is impossible, they may agree to hold the meeting at the beginning or end of the shift, or during the lunch break. Of course, in these cases agreement as to payment will have to be reached.

2.   One of the most striking benefits of Quality Circles is typically an increase in productivity which will more than compensate for the lost time. This is because Circle members are usually extremely conscious of the factors that interrupt their work, and these problems are likely to become early Targets for a Quality Circle.

In the case of those concerned about the short length of Circle meetings, it must be recognised that Circles do not work in the same way as committees. Normally Circles do not keep minutes as such, or spend half the meeting time discussing minutes of the last meeting; they just get down to work straight away. The techniques used by the Circles and described in the next section are extremely effective when used in this type of small-group activity, and both members and others are usually amazed how much they achieve in only 1 hour per week.

'In paid time'

We say in 'paid time' rather than normal working hours because there are some cases, such as those described above, when it becomes difficult or impossible to hold the meeting during scheduled work periods.

This may be particularly relevant in shift work operations, when Circles may sometimes span shifts. If the Circle comprises members from each of three or more shifts, it may be possible to hold the meeting during an overlap between two shifts, but the members from other shifts will either miss the meeting, or have to attend outside shift time. The pay arrangements for this will have to be worked out between all concerned, not, of course, overlooking the views or the arrangements of non-Circle members. Contrary to popular belief, Circle members in Japan are also paid for their time when these situations arise.

'Under the leadership of their own supervisor'

Some people ask why the supervisor should be the Circle Leader. They may say, 'Why can't the Leader be selected or elected from the members of the group?' Whilst there may be circumstances where this arrangement may be desirable or necessary, they are very few and far between. Even when this is the best alternative, it is rarely ever better than using the appointed supervisor.

Some managers who are unfamiliar with the working of Quality Circles sometimes fear that they will lose control and that the Quality Circle is a way of bypassing them. Supervisors might certainly fear this if they did not have the opportunity of being Circle Leaders. Additionally, they would fear that their work people might use the Circle as a means of highlighting the supervisor's shortcomings and therefore regard the Circle as a threat.

Nothing could be further from the truth. Management's motives in setting up Quality Circles are to make better use of the existing structure, not to create alternatives. Circles are concerned with work-related problems and not with grievances, wages, salaries or conditions of employment. If these items are contentious then the group must take them up through the appropriate channels in the usual way. Circles are not part of the bargaining, negotiating or grievance machinery; neither do they impinge upon the activities of those who are responsible for these aspects of a company's affairs.

Because the Circle is purely concerned with work-related problems, and because the supervisor is the appointed Leader of the group, it follows that direct supervisors should at least have the first option to be the Circle Leader.

However, once the group has been formed, the members, and others in the work area, will quickly realise that it doesn't matter who the Leader is because Circle decision making is a totally democratic process. When the Circle members are in the meeting room together, everyone has one vote and no one's opinion is any more or less important than anyone else's.

The smart Circle Leader will soon learn that it is not easy to be both the Leader and to think up ideas at the same time, and so may, after a short time, offer to rotate the Leadership of each meeting around the group. Not only will this enable the official Circle Leader to contribute their own ideas, but it is also a very effective part of the people-building process and gives confidence to the members of the group. A Leader who develops in this way will usually gain considerable respect from the members as a result.

From the Leader's and the organisational point of view, this development may lead to further advantages. If the work area is large and there are others wishing to form a Circle, the Leader may allow the original Circle to become self-propelled while they form a new Circle in the section.

When this Circle has developed, the supervisor may then keep an eye on both groups. Should there be any reason why the supervisor cannot be, or does not want to be, the Circle Leader, then assuming the desire is there amongst the members of the work group, an alternative must be found.

First of all, the supervisor must be given confidence that the Circle, if formed, will not constitute a threat to their authority, and the group should be made very much aware of this. The group must be encouraged to discuss its work with the supervisor and where possible solicit their ideas. When it comes to the management presentation, the supervisor should always be invited to attend.

In situations where the supervisor neither wishes to participate in the Circle nor is prepared to allow a Circle to be formed in the work area, it is up to management to make a decision whether one of its appointees should be allowed to continue in a position which obstructs both the wishes of management and work people alike, and the action taken in such circumstances is beyond the scope of this book. It is, however, encouraging to note that such situations are extremely rare.

'To identify, analyse and solve problems in their work'

The key point about this part of the definition is the fact that the Circles identify their own problems in their own work area. That is not to say that other people may not make suggestions. Indeed, the essence of Quality Circles ultimately should be that the Circles really become managers at their own level.

People can only manage if they are fed with information, and the more information which is fed to the Quality Circle from management, management specialists, people in other departments and so on, the more effective the group will be. 'Self-control' is the foundation of Circle activities.

When people arrive for their very first Circle meeting, they may have been attracted by the possibility of using the Circle as a means of highlighting the faults of others. For example, they may complain about the quality of the products they receive from the previous section, poor quality materials, tools and equipment, inadequate service from specialist departments, and so on. However, when they join the group they realise that this is not at all the purpose of the Circle. They are told that, 'Whilst we can complain about those other people, we cannot do anything about them.' In almost all cases, there are plenty of problems in their own work area, which can be under their control, and where they can apply their own knowledge and experience to get results.

It is this aspect of Quality Circle activities which gives the members the greatest satisfaction. Because they are not meeting to criticise the work of others, they find that they can make real progress with their projects. When asked what they like most about Quality Circles, one of the most frequent answers comes back, 'We find we can get things done', 'These problems have been around for years, and now we are making progress.'

'Presenting solutions to management'

This is the focal point or highlight of all Circle activities around the world: the presentation to management. Sometimes after weeks of collecting data, trying out new ideas, having discussions with all kinds of people, when the members of the Circle have installed their proposal, or are convinced of the value of their improvement, it is necessary to present their ideas to their manager.

The group is usually proud of its achievement and the teamwork involved. It will probably have worked very hard, may have spent lunchtimes, evenings or even weekends working on its ideas if its members have been enthusiastic enough, and frequently they are. Consequently, the presentations of their ideas to management are the culmination of all this activity.

It would be unfortunate if they were unable to convince their manager of the benefits of their ideas simply because they were badly presented or because the members were forced to present their ideas in the form of a report which might not be read. Therefore, training newly-formed Circles in presentation techniques is extremely important. They may use two or even three meetings to plan and prepare their presentation.

It would also be unfortunate, if an unthinking manager, given the enthusiasm and hard work of a Circle, was 'too busy to listen'. It would probably mean the end of the Circle. Therefore, management has an obligation to allow the group to make a formal presentation of its proposal, and to make constructive comments afterwards.

It is important that all members of the Circle participate in the presentation as members of a team. Whilst there is no obligation on management to accept the ideas of a Circle, they must be given serious consideration. If management decides to turn down a proposal, it really owes it to the Circle to give a good explanation for its rejection. Fortunately, Circle projects are usually so carefully thought through that outright rejection by management is quite rare.

'Implementing the solutions themselves'

Because Circles are usually concerned with problems in their own work rather than with those over the fence in the next department, they can often implement the solutions themselves. This is particularly true of housekeeping problems, reduction in waste material, energy saving and so on. They also frequently find better ways of doing their own jobs. For example, employees in the credit control department of a division of a fairly large company formed a Quality Circle. For their first project the members decided to analyse one of their work routines that they found to be particularly tedious. The result was that they reduced the work content by 16 hours per month. In the process of this work they highlighted another problem which, when solved, saved a further 17 hours a month, making a total monthly saving of 33 hours. For their third project, they decided to brainstorm all the possible ways they could make use of the time saved. Someone suggested that they might follow up the invoices with a telephone call. The effect of this idea was to reduce the average credit period by nearly 2 weeks, thereby making available to that company a considerable sum of money.

This concept demonstrates how people can effectively become involved in the success of an organisation through the development of self-control in 'small-group'-type activities. These activities can be organised in several different ways and can include task force operations, value analysis teams, value engineering, project groups, action centred groups, 5S Housekeeping activities, TPM and so on. Each plays a different but important part in participative activities. True 'self-control' can only be introduced through Quality Circle-type activities.

The Quality Circle is a specific form of small-group activity and serves a distinctly different purpose from other kinds of group, team or committee activities.

THE PRINCIPLE OF 'SELF-CONTROL'

Quality Circles represent a sophisticated form of 'self-control' or group self-management. This ultimately goes far beyond simple problem solving, although problem solving is usually the point where they start. Some managers are wary of this, fearing that it could lead to anarchy, but the opposite is true. From all of our experiences throughout the world, Quality Circles have been proven to act responsibly and to interact with management in ways otherwise not thought to be possible. All our experience indicates that it makes a manager's life easier not more difficult.

The size of the group that comprises a Quality Circle is important. Too large a group makes it difficult for everyone to participate. If there are more people in the work area than can be accommodated in one Circle, there is no reason why others should not be formed to involve the remaining employees. They are unlikely to conflict with each other. Most Circles have between six and ten people, and the concept works well with groups of this size. Sometimes there are Circles of only three to five people simply because there is only that number of people in the section.

CIRCLE DEVELOPMENT

Once a Circle has been formed, all being well, it will pass through three distinct phases of development to the fourth ultimate stage. Whether or not it ever reaches this final stage is entirely dependent upon the Objectives and support of management.

Phase 1: initial phase – the problem-solving phase

During this phase, the Circle will have been trained in simple techniques which will enable its members to identify, analyse and solve some of the more pressing problems in their own work area. These problems will include:

- wastage of materials;
- housekeeping problems;
- delays, hold-ups, and so on;
- inadequate job instructions;
- Quality;
- productivity problems;
- energy consumption;
- environmental problems;
- handling;
- safety;
- Quality of work life generally.

These will usually be the problems that are uppermost in the minds of most employees.

Phase 2: monitoring and problem solving

After a short time, when several of the simpler problems have been resolved and many others have just 'disappeared' as a result of other improvements in the work environment, the Circle will begin to develop a 'monitoring' mentality. The members will have been trained in simple control techniques and will use these to maintain the improvements already made.

Phase 3: innovation – self-improvement and problem solving

There is almost a natural progression to the self-improvement phase from phase 2. As the Circle begins to mature, and most of the techniques taught have been well practised and understood, the confidence of the group will have grown considerably. The members will also have gained a wider acceptance by their colleagues in their own and other departments and also by management. In other words, they will be treated with greater respect.

It is about this time that the Circle will progress from 'just solving problems' to the mentality of seeking ways of making improvements. Obviously, this will take longer in some cases than others.

Phase 4: self-control

Apart from Japanese-owned organisations in the West, it is unlikely that any have reached this stage of development, the reason being that this stage of Quality Circles development is simply not understood by Western managers. Whether it is reached at all is as much dependent on managers and others outside the Circle as it is on the Circle members themselves.

Having passed through phases 1, 2 and 3, the Circle will be very mature, and trusted by management. The organisation will have realised much of the background, speak the same work language and no one member should be inhibited in any way by the presence of another. Whilst in exceptional circumstances some variation of this important rule may be necessary, generally speaking, such variations should be avoided.

Circles comprising members from different disciplines or with different work experience will find that the more fragmented they are the more difficult it will be for them to select a project which is of interest to all members. Those least directly affected by the potential achievement will show less interest than the other members and, if some of the work-related jargon is unfamiliar, boredom may be induced, with a resulting loss of morale and possibly the loss of some members.

Another problem may arise if some members have a higher educational background than others. In such cases there is a tendency for the more educated members of the Circle to 'take over' the problem and solve it on behalf of the group. Whilst in most cases this may not be evident to those outside the Circle, a very important confidence-building aspect of Quality Circles will be lost.

That is not to say that the Circle cannot utilise the services of specialists or others if it so wishes. For example, the members may invite such people into the Circle for a specific project if they feel it will help produce a more soundly thought-out solution. In such cases, these guests are really acting as consultants to the Circle, and a supportive management should actively encourage this process.

This arrangement fits in well with the concept of 'self-control' which should be the ultimate aim of corporate management in developing Circles in the first place.

SYSTEMS ARE IMPORTANT BUT SYSTEMS DO NOT MOTIVATE PEOPLE!

In earlier chapters it has been seen that at the corporate level, Goals and Objectives will be established for the organisation as a whole through the Hoshin Kanri process. To achieve these Goals, it is necessary to establish systems and procedures for each department or function throughout the organisation: a system for quality control, production control, inventory control, budgetary control and so on. Many UK and Western companies have been particularly good at this, probably as good as anyone in the world. But systems do not motivate people and it is the management of people which has presented the most problems.

The reason why Quality Circles emerged in Japan was largely due to the fact that during the early stages of their post-war reconstruction, the Japanese found themselves confronted with precisely the same industrial problems that the rest of the world is still faced with today: labour alienation, worker indifference, strikes, absenteeism, excessive sick leave and grievances. It was largely a result of the way they addressed themselves to these problems that led them eventually to Quality Circles, and Western organisations should do the same.

SUMMARY OF PEOPLE MANAGEMENT NEEDS

- Success in business depends upon being at least as good as the competitor in all facets of the organisation's activities, generating confidence and creating a good image.
- To achieve this, it is necessary to establish corporate Objectives for the whole organisation in every function and at every level, which is a key aspect of Hoshin Kanri.
- It is necessary to design a system for the organisation and deal with Quality Control, budgetary control and all activities.
- Systems do not motivate people, and if people do not really care, no amount of system will make any difference. People need to be involved.
- To involve people successfully it is necessary to modify the Divison of Labour method to be able to incorporate the principles of Craftsmanship. In other words, it is necessary to introduce the concept of 'self-control' to reintroduce Craftsmanship to groups or teams of people.
- People need Leadership. Therefore, it is necessary to identify and train group leaders or supervisors. This training should be a continuous development process. Each supervisor should be trained in such a way that they have the desire to make each employee the manager at their own level.
- Quality Circles are a special type of small-group activity which form a vehicle for people development and lead to complete self-control within the constraints of corporate policy.
- Management gets results through people – to be competitive it is necessary to galvanise the resources of the entire workforce.

HOW QUALITY CIRCLES WORK

The basic tools

The most common activity of newly-formed Quality Circles is problem solving. Sometimes problems can be solved through discussion and consensus but more generally they are solved by using problem-solving tools.

These are tools to identify problems, collect and analyse data, examine causes, suggest solutions, evaluate the solutions and implement them. There is also a discipline. All too often people involved in problem solving jump to conclusions and make decisions based on opinions, not facts. Even when facts are used, the results may not match the prediction because the data were inadequate. Many people, who have had years of training and experience in problem solving, frequently make these types of error and so great care must be taken to ensure that anyone involved in these activities has been made keenly aware of the pitfalls and the limitations of both the techniques and their own knowledge.

One of the main fears of managers, who are as yet unacquainted with the mode of operation of Quality Circles, is that Circles made up of groups of people who have experienced very little education, and who are performing unskilled and semi-skilled tasks, may not be able to achieve very creditable results. This is because they do not realise the power of the simple techniques that Circles use to solve problems at their own level.

These basic tools, usually seven in all, were not invented for Circles specifically; they gravitated into Circles during the formative years in Japan through a process of trial and error. They are referred to as the Seven Basic Tools, because they have proved to be particularly effective when used in this type of small-group activity. They are only the Fishbone Diagram – a sort of 'get-you-started' kit. Later on when the Circles mature, their members will want to use the tools in more and more sophisticated ways and will add further skills to their list when they are found to be relevant to their work.

The tools include:

- Brainstorming (explained below);
- Data Collection (brief explanation below);
- Data Analysis (see Chapter 13);
- Pareto Analysis (explained below);
- Cause and Effect Analysis (which includes both the Fishbone Diagram and Process Analysis explained in Chapter 13);
- Histograms (see Chapter 13);
- Control techniques (see Chapter 13).

If presentation techniques are included, the list becomes the eight basic elements of Quality Circles.

Brainstorming

The idea of brainstorming is to use the collective thinking power of a group of people to come up with the ideas they would not think of by themselves. It is particularly effective when used in Quality Circle activities.

Brainstorming is the basis of much of the work carried out by Quality Circles and is used in one form or another at two, sometimes three, stages in a Circle's project. It is used:

- to identify problems;
- to analyse causes; and occasionally
- to highlight possible solutions.

Some problems, once evaluated, have only certain obvious solutions, and brainstorming would not be used in those cases, but in others there may be an almost unlimited number of possible alternatives and brainstorming is particularly effective.

During the brainstorming session all ideas are written down. No idea should be thought of as stupid or ridiculous, and no discussion is allowed at this stage. In this way, the Circle will usually highlight a large number of problems.

These ideas will be wide-ranging and cover almost all aspects of the Circle's work. To this list may be added the suggestions of others. Their manager, the specialists and others in their section may all contribute their ideas to those of the Circle members. When the Circle members feel the list is adequate or complete and is representative of the problems they are confronted with, they will then commence their evaluation.

Their Goal is to highlight just one problem out of the many they have identified which will form the basis of their project.

One quality manager, when looking at such a list commented, 'Although I recognise every problem on that list, I have never seen them written on one sheet of paper before and I did not realise that there were so many!' And that was for one single work area!

Because the Circles only tackle one problem at a time, it may seem timewasting to carry out such an exhaustive classification of problems, but this process is really quite important. It is only through it that the Circle can be sure that the problems identified by each member of the group are given equal consideration. Once the ideas have been listed they are then evaluated.

Basically, they fall into three general categories:

- non-Circle controllable;
- partially Circle controllable;
- totally Circle controllable.

Whilst it may not always be possible to separate the second and third categories, it is necessary first of all to remove those which the Circle believes are totally outside its control.

It does this by systematically going down the list one by one, and asking the question, 'Can we do anything about this problem?' If the answer is 'no', that item is scratched from the list. For example, a Circle which conducted a brainstorming session may have decided that some of the problems outside their control were:

- insufficient labour;
- poor-quality drawings;
- too much waiting time;
- lack of bench space;
- wrong working-height of benches;
- poor coffee;
- standard of supervision;
- job satisfaction;
- safety shoes;
- morale;
- weight of components, and so on.

The members decided that these were matters that they could complain about but could not do anything about. Because there were other avenues through which they could voice their opinions about these problems, they felt that they were outside the scope of the Circle.

Of the remaining problems, a new Quality Circle would normally sort them in order of easiness to solve, taking the easiest first. Sometimes there may be a problem which frustrates the group so much that it decides to tackle it regardless of its complexity, and there is nothing wrong with that. It would be as well, however, to warn it not to tackle anything which it feels will be too complex or time-consuming in the early stages, since failure can lead to a loss of confidence at this sensitive stage and the Circle may even disintegrate under such circumstances. A quick success, however small, is very important to a newly-formed Circle. Not only do the members acquire a sense of achievement, but others outside the group will notice that the Circle is getting things done.

Data Collection (check sheets)

Following brainstorming and selection of a project, the Circle will collect data to identify the seriousness of the problem and also to find the possible causes.

Whilst Data Collection itself may be easy there are many pitfalls:

- Where to collect data?
- When to collect?
- How much to collect?
- Who is to collect?
- What data?
- And so on.

In the early stages, it is not important to spend the time and effort giving Circles 'in depth' training in sophisticated Data Collection and analysis techniques; this can come later. Initially they will only need simple methods so it is important to make sure that Circle members are made aware of the limitations of the techniques they are using and if they need to be more certain about the accuracy of their data, they should enlist the services of a trained statistics specialist to work with them.

The most frequently-used data gathering technique used by Circles is the check sheet. The time period for Data Collection is determined and listed in columns across the sheet. The tally check method is normally used as the data is obtained.

Pareto Analysis

Pareto was an American-Italian scholar who discovered that about 80 per cent of the wealth was in the hands of about 20 per cent of the population. About the same time another academic named Lorenz found that this relationship seemed to hold good in a wide variety of situations, for example, an analysis of the value of items held in a store is likely to reveal that about 80 per cent of the value is contained in about 20 per cent of the items. The same is frequently true of quality failure costs, such as scrap, re-work, customer complaints, machine or equipment breakdown time, delays, telephone usage and so on.

When this relationship exists, a column graph with each column representing a separate feature will usually result in one or two bars being considerably longer than the others, as shown in the Figure 17.2.

This figure shows far more dramatically than a list of numbers that the biggest problem or the most frequently-occurring event is item D. There are several advantages in using this approach:

- The Circle members themselves will be more impressed by the length of the first one or two bars.
- It is a useful way of communicating the results of the Data Collection to non-Circle members, particularly those who may have assisted in the collection of the data.
- It makes a big impact in a management presentation, and shows the thoroughness with which the Circle has carried out its work.
- Once the data have been illustrated in this way, the Circle can really see whether it has made improvements as it can compare similar data which may be obtained after implementing its ideas.
- It is a Goal-setting mechanism which tends to concentrate the attention of members and non-members alike on the few important problems, rather than spread across the many trivial ones.

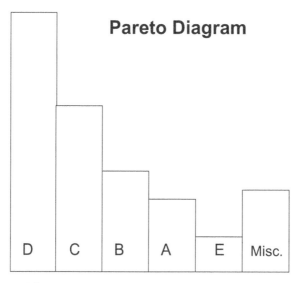

Figure 17.2   Pareto Diagram

Cause and Effect Analysis

When the principal problem has been selected by Pareto Analysis, the Circle will want to classify the most probable causes. To do this they will construct a cause classification diagram (also known as a Fishbone or Ishikawa Diagram as shown below). This diagram is constructed by using the brainstorming process described earlier, but this time, instead of simply listing the ideas, it is helpful if similar or related ideas can be grouped together. The cause classification diagram enables this to be achieved.

The problem or effect is written in a box on the right-hand side of a large sheet of paper, fixed to the wall or on a flip chart where it can be seen by everyone as before in brainstorming. An arrow is then drawn pointing towards the box on the right-hand of the diagram as shown in Figure 17.3. The Circle must then decide the most appropriate headings under which the probable causes can be listed. In most cases there are four, and these are:

1.   manpower – the people doing the work;
2.   machines – equipment or tooling used to do the work;
3.   methods – specifications or job instructions;
4.   materials – supplied or required to do the work.

Occasionally others such as vendor, supplier, environment, office and so on may be more applicable, or included in addition to those mentioned above.

These headings form the ends of further arrows pointing towards the main arrow already drawn on the sheet of paper

Once the diagram has been prepared the Circle is ready to commence the brainstorming process of identifying what it thinks are likely to be the most probable causes. Someone is selected to act as Leader and to write the ideas on the diagram as they are suggested.

As a general rule, it will usually take a Quality Circle one meeting to complete a diagram similar to the one shown above, and frequently this will take place during the same meeting in which the Pareto Diagram was roughly drawn and the problem selected.

Cause and Effect Analysis – Ishikawa or Fishbone Diagram

Purpose: To identify 'ALL' potential causes of the problem by key criteria.

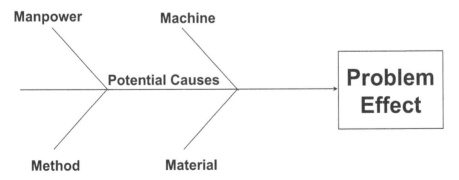

Figure 17.3   Cause and Effect Diagram

Cause analysis and Process Analysis

Some problems require a deeper analysis than that which is afforded by the cause classification diagram. In this case, three possible alternatives exist:

1. *Conduct a further cause classification* but this time on the cause that has been highlighted as the prime suspect.
2. *Carry out cause analysis.* This only varies slightly from cause classification but involves the Leader in asking questions of the group as a whole.
3. *Process Analysis. So* far, we have discussed problems that occur at only one stage or point in an operation, but sometimes they may occur over several stages. In this case, the Circle may decide to carry out Process Analysis – see Chapter 15 for details.

Such a diagram is an extremely useful way of highlighting common elements. Factors such as lack of job instructions, contamination, or lack of training may be evident at each stage, indicating that there may be serious widespread problems.

Project presentations

When the Circle members have completed their analysis and verified their solutions, they will feel proud of themselves. They will have enjoyed working together as a team and will be looking forward to presenting their ideas to their manager, and sometimes to others who may be relevant to the specific problem they have tackled.

This presentation should be the highlight of their activities. All through their project they will have been mindful of this, and so the presentation will be the climax. It is therefore extremely important that management does not in any way underestimate the importance of this occasion.

Management presentations fulfill the following Goals:

- give recognition of the Circle's achievements;
- allow management to judge for itself the value of Quality Circles;
- enable others, possibly less committed, to see how Circles work, in order to gain wider acceptance.

It must be emphasised that management is under no obligation to accept a Circle proposal if it does not wish to do so. It is the responsibility of the Circle members to 'sell their idea in such a way that it appears attractive to management'. They should be trained to speak the manager's language, in other words to present their ideas in the context of measures which are uppermost in the minds of most managers, namely: cost improvements, Quality improvements, scheduling or inventory improvements and so on.

Rejection of Circle proposals by management is fortunately extremely rare. This is mainly because there are usually few secrets in Circle activities, and if it becomes obvious that a Circle is heading towards a totally unacceptable conclusion, there are usually many opportunities to warn it of this. If the members still insist on pursuing the idea that is up to them, but the Circle will be encouraged to offer alternative ideas to give management a choice when it comes to the presentation.

Following the presentation, and hopefully the acceptance of the proposal, the Circle will begin thinking about its next project. At this stage the members may wish to brainstorm all over again, or in many cases, take the next problem on the list. It can be seen therefore that the brainstorming sheet is a worksheet. They will only conduct a further brainstorming when they begin to feel that the list needs topping up, or that many new problems have surfaced, or when they have noted problems relating to them on other Quality Circles' brainstorming lists. They may also add items retrieved from Quality Control defects analysis, customer complaints, suggestions from non-Circle members and of course the deployed KPIs from the Hoshin Kanri process.

THE TECHNIQUES IN PERSPECTIVE

To conclude this section let us look at the way in which these techniques would normally be applied:

- A new Circle, or one which has exhausted its previous list, or one which feels that new and important problems have arisen in its area will conduct a brainstorming session.
- When the list is complete the Circle will segregate the ideas into
    - not Circle controllable;
    - partially Circle controllable;
    - totally Circle controllable.
- Several smaller problems easily dealt with will be given priority.
- The Circle will vote on a theme. Possible themes include
    - Waste materials
    - Lost time
    - Safety
    - Energy
    - Customer complaints
    - Materials handling
    - Housekeeping
    - and so on.
- Having selected a theme, the Circle will list the problems relating to it that were highlighted during brainstorming.
- Next the members will produce a check sheet in order to determine the relative importance of each item.
- From the check sheet they will produce a Pareto Diagram. This will highlight the few important ones and separate them from the many trivial.
- The problem thus selected will be analysed using cause classification.
- The cause classifications will be evaluated by using the job knowledge of the members to identify what they believe to be the most likely key causes.
- The first potential key cause will be evaluated to determine whether or not it is the true cause.
- This evaluation may involve the use of further cause classification relating to the cause now highlighted.
- Alternatively it may call for cause analysis, Process Analysis, Histograms, drawings showing defect locations, check sheets and Pareto Analysis depending upon the circumstances.
- When the true cause has been established the Circle must seek a solution. This may involve either brainstorming or experimentation or both.
- Alternative solutions may be evaluated in order to establish the best solution, or to offer management a choice. Some of the possible solutions may be 'irreversible', in other words once they have been implemented it is impossible for the problem to return. For example, a form used for conveying some information may have been redesigned so as to eliminate the need for handwriting and instead require ticked boxes. Such a solution is often referred to as 'fool proofing' or 'mistake proofing'. In Japan the name is 'Poke Yoke'.
- In other cases the solution may be 'reversible'. This includes solutions which require a change in method but it is possible for the old method to be used. These solutions require periodic monitoring to ensure the continued use of the more appropriate alternative.
- Following the establishment of the 'best' solution, the Circle will prepare a management presentation.

- The management presentation will involve all of the members of the Circle and sometimes two or three meetings will be required to prepare their materials and the method of presentation.
- The management presentation will be made to the manager of the section together with others who may be affected by the suggestions.
- When relevant, management will make a decision whether to accept, partially accept, or reject a Circle proposal.
- In the event of partial acceptance or rejection, it is important that management give the Circle clear reasons for its decision, which, if carried out tactfully, will normally be accepted, albeit reluctantly, by the Circle. Rejection can usually be avoided when it is expected by presenting management with a choice of two or more alternative solutions. These should, of course, be evaluated prior to the presentation.
- Finally, the Circle will monitor the results for a period to ensure that the solution is working and to make any necessary adjustments to the process in order to maintain the improved performance.

QUALITY CIRCLE ORGANISATIONAL DEVELOPMENT

For Circle programmes to be successful it is necessary to be very careful in the preparations. Failure to do this is almost certain to lead to disappointing results. If Circles are going to alter the culture of an organisation for the better, people must be made aware of and prepared for such changes.

Quality Circles still operate in companies such as Wedgwood at Barlaston in Staffordshire, UK and have been doing so since 1981. When asked recently how much the Quality Circles had saved the company over the years, the Quality Manager responded, 'I have no idea, it must be many millions but more important than that, we would not be here now if we had not done it.' The Chief Executive of Wedgwood was also asked why it is that Quality Circles have survived for so long and he responded, 'It is because I am still here and we have stuck to the knitting. So many companies keep searching for some magic bullet but there isn't one, there is only good management and the support of Quality Circles is one aspect of good management.'

We are not aware of any cases where Quality Circles have failed because the workers have lost interest or have run out of ideas. In almost every case it is because of management's failure to continue to support the programmes. Why should they fail to support something that clearly works? There are many reasons. The most common is the change of chief executive. The new one is often unsupportive of initiatives started by their predecessor. Another common reason is that the programme was not properly introduced in the first place, with unrealistic expectations, poor-quality training and little commitment right from the start. Unfortunately it is these failures that have convinced others that Quality Circles are a flawed concept. The media has encouraged this view with the consequence that the West has probably lost some 25–30 years of Leadership in the development of professional management systems.

Even the most genuinely expert advice available in the world need not be expensive, and a properly introduced programme will pay for itself over and over again. In fact, some companies go so far as to claim that they would not have survived the recessions of the 1990s if it were not for Quality Circles. The disillusionment that can follow a failed Circle programme may mean that it is better not to start than to start and fail.

MANAGEMENT GETS RESULTS THROUGH PEOPLE!

Prior to the implementation of Circles it is necessary for top management to educate and persuade the middle managers into believing that managers get results through people and to convince middle management that Circles are not a threat to their authority. Top management must give confidence to both middle management and to direct supervision that it recognises that of course there are problems in its work area; there are problems in everybody's area, there are problems right across the whole organisation. 'We know that, we accept it, and believe that Quality Circles can help get them solved.' If Circles are successful in a given work area, then that work area manager should be congratulated, because it is obvious that they support the Circles' activities.

The role of top management

The visible and real support of plant or corporation top management is essential to the success of Quality Circles. Circles are only part of a corporate policy which goes far beyond the Circles themselves. Top management's role in Quality Circles has seven vital aspects:

1. establishment of corporate policy and corporate plan (through Hoshin Kanri);
2. setting corporate Goals and Objectives (through Hoshin Kanri);
3. management commitment;
4. allocation of resources;
5. monitoring;
6. auditing;
7. support.

The role of middle management

The attitude of middle or line management towards Quality Circles is quite critical. The vitality of individual Circles will frequently be a direct reflection on the relationship between the manager and the Quality Circles in their section or department.

Initially, because Circles are normally only started in a small way with three to five Circles, it is unlikely that every manager will be affected. When managers have been briefed on Quality Circles, different attitudes will become evident. Some managers will say, 'It's all been tried before', 'I don't think it will last' or 'It is OK in other companies but it won't work here' and so on. In reality they are expressing a fear that they themselves may not be able to make it work, or that they will feel that they may be exposed in some way. Fortunately, such feelings rarely, if ever, present a major problem. Usually, if the initial briefings are carried out successfully, there will be a number of other managers who see things differently. These managers are likely to respond by making such comments as, 'I think it's a great idea, pity we didn't think of it 20 years ago' and so on. It is highly recommended that the initial Circles are formed in departments led by such managers.

'Start where the grass is greenest' is a good maxim. Supportive departmental managers are essential to the success of a Circle programme. Once the early Circles have been established, all being well there should be notable achievements which will not go unnoticed by other managers. Eventually, some of the initially more negative managers will request Circles to be started in their work areas. Of course, there may be some who will never wish to start. Such hardened attitudes will require management decisions beyond the scope of this book.

The supervisor as Circle Leader

Recognition of the importance of the supervisor's role in management in Japan preceded the development of Quality Circles by at least 10 years. During that period, the Japanese developed an extremely sophisticated approach to supervisory development which has no equivalent anywhere in the world.

By the time Quality Circles emerged, Japanese supervisors were highly trained and were better trained managers than many people two or three levels higher in non-Japanese societies. Consequently, Quality Circles were almost a natural extension of this development. Obviously, it would be unrealistic to expect non-Japanese organisations to spend 10 years reproducing this same development before commencing Circle activities. Fortunately that is not necessary. It has been found that Circles can be formed successfully even in cases where the supervisor or group Leader has received no formal management training whatsoever prior to the decision to commence Circle activities, provided that training and development are conducted in parallel to Circle activities. These must never be overlooked. If supervisory development does not take place, it is fairly certain that the Circle programme will suffer, if not fail completely, and some form of supervisory development will always prove to be an extremely worthwhile investment provided it is done properly.

Selection of supervisors as Circle Leaders

Because the introduction of Circles is not usually preceded by years of specialised supervisory development, the selection of the initial Circle Leaders is critical. Normally, it would be unwise to consider the creation of more than five or six initial Circles at a given location. There are several reasons for this, the most important being:

- First impressions are extremely important, and because the organisation is unlikely to have any previous first-hand experience with Circles, it is necessary to be able to give the new Circles all the support they need. A large-scale development is likely to frighten those who are as yet uncommitted into a defensive position. People feel less threatened by a pilot programme, which can easily be terminated if necessary.
- There will be a wide range of management styles, relationships and attitudes within the organisation, some of which may be adverse to the Circle concept. These cannot be changed overnight. Only a small proportion of managers and supervisors have attitudes conducive to Circles in the early stages.

If they do not want to lead a Circle, and both management and direct employees want to form a Circle, then management is faced with two options:

1. Ask the supervisor if it is acceptable to them for a Circle to be formed with the group electing their own Leader. If the answer to (1) is negative, management will be faced with the choice of either abandoning the idea of a Circle in the area initially, or of moving the supervisor to another area.
2. If (1) is accepted, it is imperative that the supervisor is kept in touch with the activities of the group, and that they should always be given the opportunity to attend Circle presentations. They should never be bypassed.

The above advice will enable most organisations to make a start. Some will find the general attitudes of managers, supervisors and workpeople more favourable initially than others, but it is highly unlikely that the positive factors will be totally absent and a pilot scheme will almost always be possible. This pilot scheme should be seen as being rather like a newborn baby. It will need nursing and caring for until it is strong enough to stand on its own feet.

If the first Leaders are carefully selected, the first Quality Circles are likely to be successful. Success breeds success, and all being well others will be impressed with the results and will soon want Quality Circles in their own area. The rate at which this demand will increase cannot be forecast and varies from one company to another. At one extreme, a company may commence five Circles and only progress to seven or eight a year later. At the other extreme, some companies, such as Wedgwood, created an incredible 180 Circles in just over 2 years. Paradoxically, whilst the success of the early Circles may greatly influence other supervisors to start Circles, the converse may also happen amongst a minority.

Some supervisors, perhaps those who have the least self-confidence, will be reluctant to start Circles because they are worried that they may not equal the achievements of the earlier groups. Such supervisors may need additional training designed to increase their self-confidence before they are given the opportunity to lead a Circle.

Circle Leaders should be trained to train their own Circles as part of their own development. Of course, there are few Circle Leaders who would be able to do this entirely unaided, but the initial Circle Leader training should be designed to achieve this with the help of the Facilitator.

After Leader training, which normally takes three or four days, the Leader and the Facilitator together should train the Circle. The Facilitator's role in this training is supportive. At the first meeting of the group, in most cases the Facilitator will probably do most of the work. However, if an informal atmosphere is created, even the most nervous new Circle Leader will break in to explain some of the points. As the Leader's confidence grows, they will take over more and more of the training. The Facilitator will gradually recede into the background when it is judged that the Leader has effectively assumed control. The rate at which this withdrawal of the Facilitator takes place will vary from one Circle to another. In some instances it will happen quite quickly. The Leader may already have experience as an instructor, or have been a football or netball coach, and will therefore quickly take over. Others without such experience may require more initial support.

Ideally, supervisory development should precede the development of Circles in the same way that it did in Japan. Because this is not essential, it does not mean that it can be overlooked entirely.

Whilst a Circle Leader training programme for supervisors will be sufficient to commence Quality Circle activities, it must be regarded as only basic training. Supervisor/Leader training should be a continuous development process which may carry on indefinitely within the company's corporate plan.

The training should be designed to be 'people building' and not simply be concerned with the acquisition of knowledge for its own sake. For example, Etsuro Tani of the Nippon Steel Corporation writes in a paper:

Indispensable for the promotion to the foreman (kocho) rank is to finish the formal special course and the assistant foreman study course, and the foreman cannot be promoted to the general foreman (sagyocho) unless he completes the latter special course and the general foreman education course. In this way education is inseparably related to promotion.

Formal courses of importance to supervisory development are summarised in the following:

Introductory Course, full-day course – 10 days.
General introductory lessons about company life are given to all operators newly employed. Inculcated into their mind are the importance of the iron and steel industry, the outline of Nippon Steel Corporation and the pride and consciousness newcomers shall have as Nippon steel men. This is similar to induction training courses conducted by some Western companies, but has considerable depth.

Foreman's Special Course, 3 hours, twice per week for 40 weeks, totalling 240 hours.
Employees of middle standing with over 3 years experience are to be trained in this course on Quality Control with daily standard work operations as the basis for the training. The aim is to give practical

and special knowledge essential for jobs assigned to foremen and equivalent in problem solving and Leadership.

Assistant Foreman Study Course, full-day course of 6 weeks duration.
This course is aimed at building up the capabilities of assistant foremen practically to carry out Leadership in the capacity of foreman and at teaching the basic techniques to accept Leadership in the workshop.

Latter Special Course, full-day course of 5 months duration.
Trainees are foremen and their equivalent who are expected to become general foremen, to teach them the technical knowledge they will require to perform the general foreman's duties.

General Foreman Education Course, full-day course of 2 months duration.
The trainees are candidates for the general foreman rank, to build up their abilities for management control work and the actions essential for good management.

In addition to these courses, supervisors and foremen are encouraged to study in correspondence courses, described as self-improvement programmes, and are given the opportunity to attend seminars, give papers, take journals and operate Quality Circle activities as a part of their normal work activity.

This intensive process of training in management skills does not just apply to Nippon Steel; it is common to the whole of Japanese industry. If other countries really want to achieve the same level of progress in their industries as is currently happening in Japan, it is necessary for them to develop a similar level of intensity of training. The courses should not be designed by colleges which cannot be responsive to individual needs but by the companies themselves as part of their own development programme, and based on their own specific requirements identified in the corporate plan. At the beginning of each year, the education and training programme for each division or section should be determined from the overall policy and Goals of the enterprise. Preferably, this should be worked out by a special committee comprising the heads of each division or section.

The techniques selected to be introduced through the training should be those which will enhance the skills already acquired, so that the individuals may do their work more effectively rather than for purely academic purposes. Basically the Objectives should be to:

- create the sense of corporate identity/corporate loyalty and corporate pride;
- give a greater awareness of corporate Goals;
- improve decision-making ability;
- improve problem-solving skills;
- improve Leadership skills;
- improve communication and presentation skills;
- develop training skills;
- increase self-confidence;
- improve relationships with managers and with workpeople.

QUALITY CIRCLES, THE SPECIALISTS AND NON-CIRCLE MEMBERS

The specialists

This group will include such specialists as Work Study personnel, Quality Control, production engineering, operation and maintenance and so on. If they are not properly informed about what

Quality Circles are and how Circle development will affect them, they are quite likely to see Quality Circles as a threat. Typically, they will think, 'My job is solving problems, why should you teach others to do my job?' Of course, during times of recession, this observation may be especially pertinent. It would be a pity not to dispel such fears before Quality Circles are established because, far from being a threat, Quality Circles, if anything, put more demands on the specialist not less.

Subsequent follow-up visits have shown that the specialists rank amongst the greatest enthusiasts of Quality Circles. This is for two main reasons:

- The type of problems usually dealt with by Circles are rarely the same problems that are attractive to the specialist. Consequently there is little conflict of interest.
- The Circle quickly discovers that specialists have access to information and knowledge outside the scope of the Circle, and so they often invite them to join the Circle as consultants, usually for the duration of that project.

Non-Circle members

Almost every organisation will find that most departments will contain one or more employees who are not members of the Circle. This will either be due to a lack of interest, or because the department is too large for everyone to be able to join. In such a case it is hoped that it may be possible at some stage to form another Circle. There is no reason why two or more Circles should not be formed in a section.

However, it must be clearly understood by everyone, particularly the Circle members, that they belong to 'their section's Circle' and they are not an elite group. Failure to recognise this is one of the problems that frequently plague organisations in the early stages of development. It can lead to considerable alienation between the two groups and cause the break up of the Circle.

Causes of alienation between Circle and non-Circle members include:

- management pressure;
- overzealous Facilitator Leader;
- showing favouritism;
- Circle not involving others;
- rival factions in the department.

Let us now take each in turn:

Management pressure

Sometimes management does not fully appreciate the importance of the rule that Circles pick their own problems, and that the 1 hour per week is the 'Circles hour'.

Interestingly, the Circle is less sensitive to this problem than non-Circle members of the department. They will detect quite quickly that management is 'steering or manipulating' the Circle and will accuse its members of being 'management favourites'. Generally speaking, it will annoy one person more than others. This person then attempts to 'pick off' a Circle member whom they think is sensitive and tease that member about Circle activities. The first indication of this to an outsider will be one of the Circle members dropping out of the group, followed by another. Usually, the defectors will be reluctant to give reasons for leaving because that would leave them open to further problems with their colleagues.

If the Circle is genuinely left to choose its own problems and is continually made aware of the importance of involving non-Circle colleagues, the problem is unlikely to arise. The problems it selects will be those that everyone would like to see tackled and, all being well, the Circle members should become popular with their non-Circle colleagues as a result.

Overzealous Facilitator

The pressure on a newly-appointed Facilitator must never be underestimated. Those selected will usually be well advanced in their own career and in all probability will have exercised some considerable courage in accepting the appointment. They will be very sensitive to their interpretation of senior management expectations from the Circle's programme.

The worst situation may occur when they think that top management is looking for a quick payback. This will lead to the same type of problem outlined above under 'management pressure', only this time it will be the Facilitator who is manipulating the Circle. Frequently the Facilitator does this quite unconsciously. The most likely time for such interference occurs after the brainstorming session, when the Circle members are attempting to select their problem.

After the problem classification stage, it would be easy for the Facilitator, particularly with a new Circle, to 'guide' it towards an 'easy' first problem. Unwittingly they may guide it towards a problem that looks as if it has a good payback, or one which has been bugging management. As before, the non-Circle members will be sensitive to such manipulation. It is not a bad idea to allow them to participate in problem selection.

Leader showing favouritism

Following the initial introduction of Circles, some non-Circle members may become hypersensitive to the relationship between the supervisor and Circle members. In a few cases, individuals may attempt to evaluate every action of the supervisor to see if favouritism exists. The Circle Leader therefore must be extremely careful to avoid the likelihood of such problems and must treat everybody in the department equally, regardless of their attitude towards Circle activities.

Circle not involving others

This is usually a training problem and indicates that the Facilitator and Circle Leader have not taken enough care to ensure that everyone can participate. Many Circles involve non-members by circulating questionnaires to solicit ideas. Publicising Circle activities by displaying worksheets in the department is an excellent way of encouraging outside interest provided that there is little Risk of graffiti.

In a number of companies, the Circles make their first presentation to the section before their management presentation. Apart from ensuring that non-members are familiar with the Circle's method of working, it enables them to offer suggestions as to how the presentation might be improved and gives them a sense of involvement.

Rival factions in the department

This is a problem outside the scope of Circles directly and does occasionally, but thankfully rarely, occur. The problem usually boils down to there being two conflicting personalities in the section, each with their own loyal supporters. If all the supporters of one person are in the Circle, the others may be alienated. If it is possible, the problem may be avoided by attempting to involve members of each group. Occasionally, fortunately rarely, however, it has prevented a group from being successfully formed.

THE STEERING COMMITTEE

Because of the deep-rooted implications of Quality Circles, it would be impossible to commence a successful programme before all people affected have been given an opportunity to decide for themselves whether they want to become involved. To ensure a positive response at all levels, it would be necessary to give awareness presentations to top management, middle management, trade union representatives, specialists and supervisors.

Assuming that the general reaction is favourable and that there are no major objections, it is then possible to draw up an action plan for the development of a Quality Circle programme. First of all it will be necessary to determine who will be responsible for this development. Of course, up to this stage responsibility must have already been assumed by someone or some small group. Usually the chief executive, a director or high-level manager will have to make the decision to invite an expert to talk to top management. After this presentation, one or two other directors or senior managers may have taken an active interest, and so a small team will have been formed. They will plan the next steps.

These steps will normally be the awareness presentations to the other groups mentioned above. In some small companies all of these groups may attend a single session together. In other cases several sessions may be necessary. However, following these sessions, all being well, a number of people from different levels and functions are likely to express a keen interest in the subject and to want to play an active part in the subsequent development. These people, together with those already involved, may form what is usually referred to as a 'steering committee'.

Some organisations prefer to use the term 'support group', as this term does have certain advantages, although the former term is more common. Membership of the steering committee therefore, is, like that of Quality Circles themselves, a voluntary involvement. Not all the volunteers will necessarily have put themselves forward, they may have been invited, but as in the case of Circles no one should be forced to join. Perhaps the first point to consider about committees is why it should be preferable to have just one person in charge of the entire programme. For example, some people may think that the Facilitator should take all this responsibility. There are several arguments against this.

Firstly, many of the decisions and plans will frequently be made before the Facilitator is appointed or the importance of the Facilitator's role appreciated. A more important reason, however, is that it is extremely unlikely that there would be any one person who has such intimate knowledge of and familiarity with each department and level of people that they could successfully cover all the tasks and work that are to be carried out by the steering committee.

A further consideration is continuity. If the steering committee's responsibilities are vested in one person, it becomes very much a case of putting all the eggs into one basket. That individual, in the execution of their duties, would accumulate such a store of knowledge as to become eventually irreplaceable. In other words, the Circle programme would be dependent upon one person and could even become a personality cult. If that person were to leave the company, or suffer some misfortune, the programme might very easily collapse, or at least suffer a major setback. The formation of a good steering committee will prevent all of these Risks.

Once these negative reasons for the existence of a steering committee are accepted, there are also some very positive reasons. The steering committee can, if properly constructed, very effectively create the necessary consensus style characteristics essential for the development of a healthy Circle programme and these can be linked to the down flow of ideas from the Hoshin Kanri process.

Who should belong?

If the steering committee is reasonably representative of all interests, it will be 'in touch' or 'wired in' to the feelings of all members of staff. It will also induce confidence.

For example, shop floor workers in a factory who are worried about some aspect of Quality Circles may find it difficult to talk to a senior manager or someone from another section or department. However, if there is someone on the steering committee at their own level, or who they find accessible, then they will have no worries about approaching that person with their observations. Not only is this important from that individual's point of view, it is also valuable to the steering committee itself, because now they will be more sensitive to the general mood and to peoples' perspective of the Quality Circle programme.

Supervision

In some companies the role of the supervisor, group Leader or foreman is more clearly defined than in others. It is just as important that someone from this level should find a place on the steering committee as any other. Some supervisors may be nervous about how Circles will affect their role, and it would be dangerous if the steering committee was not sensitive to these feelings and neglected to have them represented.

Middle management and specialists

This level or group is usually the linchpin of a Circle programme. The attitudes of middle managers both individually and collectively will determine to a large extent the 'flavour' of that company's Quality Circle activities. Middle managers, particularly those who lack confidence, are likely to feel the most exposed by the developing programme. If care is not taken to develop middle managers at the same time as the Circles, some managers may become afraid of the growing confidence of their people. Also, through the acquisition of skills in using the Circles techniques, some managers may become nervous if their people are speaking a language that they themselves do not understand. Key middle managers therefore – those who are more closely associated with other middle managers – can play a vital role in the steering committee activities.

Top management

A steering committee will be largely ineffectual if it does not contain as a member one of the ultimate decision makers at site level. Someone who can sign cheques is usually a reasonable guide. Otherwise the steering committee will lack authority, and all the important decisions will be made by a third party, that is, top management. It also means that the committee will be required to make representations to top management for decisions to be made and, in all probability, top managers may not appreciate the importance of requests made, simply because they have been less involved.

It is a tremendous boost to everybody's confidence to see the active membership of the steering committee by the chief executive. This is the most impressive manifestation of 'management commitment'.

Summary

The steering committee should span all functions and all levels and be directly linked to the Hoshin Kanri process. It gives continuity, and shows commitment. It gives confidence to others through accessibility to members.

THE TASKS OF THE STEERING COMMITTEE

The basic responsibilities of a steering committee can be listed under 16 separate categories:

1. link to corporate planning and corporate policy evaluation;
2. Quality Circle-programmes policy making;
3. policy review;
4. constraints;
5. Facilitator support;
6. guidance;
7. continuity;
8. monitoring;

9. presentations;
10. publicity;
11. recognition;
12. reward;
13. assessment;
14. appreciation;
15. liaison;
16. development.

Corporate planning and corporate policy

Quality Circles will be a key feature of the 'people' Driver determined in Chapter 4. It is suggested that the definition of Japanese 'company-eide Quality Control' stated earlier in this Chapter might be used as the basis of such a policy.

Quality Circle-programmes policy making

Establishing the policy and guidelines for Circle activities will be the most intensive activity of the newly-formed steering committee.

Such questions as 'resource allocation' both at plant level and Circle level, 'constraints', 'when Circles hold their meetings', 'where the meetings will take place', are just a few of the items which will require resolution. We recommend that the steering committee should commence its activities in the same way as the Driver policies were created in Chapter 4. The result will be a Quality Circles policy statement, covering all aspects of the programme.

Policy review

It is unlikely that any initial policy will be absolutely perfect and issues are bound to arise. These may stem from the steering committee members themselves or from other employees. Periodic reviews of the policies should be carried out by the Steering Committee

Constraints

It should be made very clear that Circles must never take on as projects issues relating directly to wages, or terms or conditions of employment. It is quite important that any such constraints are clearly understood by potential Circle members *before* they are invited to join a Circle. People are likely to become quite resentful if they are informed afterwards.

Facilitator support

The Facilitator should always be a member of the steering committee and will usually be the main source of information. In a larger company with several Facilitators, it would be unreasonable for all of them to be represented. Usually, one of them, who in this case could be termed a coordinator, will probably be more senior than the others. The coordinator would be their steering committee representative and would report back to the other Facilitators at a Facilitators' meeting.

The steering committee will be the Facilitators' main source of support. In companies which have a participative, consensus style of management, this support will not be so important, but in others, particularly those which suffer from strong inter-departmental rivalries, the support of the steering committee may be the difference between success and failure. This is further evidence of the value of having a broadly-based steering committee.

Guidance

Occasionally, hopefully not too often, the pattern of workflow might threaten the activities o: a Circle. For example, a meeting might be suspended in order to meet a shipping requirement Individual managers will be uncertain when this would be acceptable and the steering committee will find many instances where it is required to give guidance on such matters. Additionally, the Facilitator will also require frequent confirmation on specific points of policy.

When this book was being written, several of the case study contributors sought the guidance of their steering committee before agreeing to submit a paper. In some cases, it was necessary for the steering committee to vet the paper in order to give clearance for publication.

Continuity

Whilst the majority of companies with successful Quality Circles programmes have very active and involved steering committees, there is nevertheless an awareness, or fear, that in a number of companies the steering committee only pays lip service to the Facilitator. Whilst this might appear to be satisfactory in the short term, particularly if the Facilitator happens to be a charismatic figure, the committee will suffer ultimately if that Facilitator is suddenly lost. A personality cult around the Facilitator should never be allowed to develop and can only be avoided by a visible and active steering committee.

Monitoring

In the early stages of Circles development in an organisation, the character of each Circle will vary widely. At one extreme the Circles might exceed all expectations, the bulk of the remainder might need some support but would be basically self-sufficient. However, there might also be one or two Circles that were like cold porridge – if we stopped stirring them, they would settle down.

If some Circles do appear better than others, there may be lessons that can be learned from the more impressive Circles and transferred to others. The same logic applies to Circles in different companies. Monitoring, therefore, can include cross-fertilisation. Steering committee members should be prepared to visit other companies and compare their approaches. In this way, everybody can benefit from everybody else's experience.

Presentations

The management presentation is the culmination of all of the work carried out by the Circle on its project. If the members have been successful, they will be proud of their achievement and will want to show what they have done.

For the majority of projects, these presentations will be made to the members' own manager, and perhaps to others who are directly affected by their recommendations. Sometimes, however, it is a good idea to allow certain projects to be presented to the steering committee. This has several advantages:

- The Circle members will be confronted with a number of people they do not normally meet and the meeting will demonstrate to them the breadth of support that exists in the company.
- Some steering committee members may not be closely and directly involved in Circle activities and it gives them an opportunity of seeing for themselves what the Circles are achieving and the enthusiasm generated.
- It is worth while allowing the early Circle projects to be presented to the steering committee as a whole so that it can see how the programme is developing. Many steering committees have not really 'jelled' until after they have had such an experience.

In one company, the steering committee, which was heavily represented by the personnel department and trade union activists, was seen by several members as an extension of the industrial relations negotiating committees. Instead of being constructive, the members were adopting defensive postures. This resulted in a Quality Circle policy statement which read like a productivity agreement. Fortunately, however, one of the first Circles managed to reach the presentation stage with their first project and this was presented to the steering committee.

This presentation had a profound effect on both management and union members of the steering committee alike. Several of them admitted astonishment that Quality Circles really did operate in the way that they had been told. This resulted in a dramatic change of attitude amongst steering committee members, who subsequently adopted a totally different approach to Circles, with the result that the steering committee has become the focal point of that company's Circle activities. The company concerned is part of a large group of companies and this steering committee has subsequently been a major influence in the establishment of Circles at other sites.

Publicity

This topic can be considered under two headings – internal, and external. Internally, the steering committee will consider the importance of publicity both as a means of giving further stimulation to existing Circles by publicising their achievements and as a means of encouraging others to participate. Externally, the steering committee may see a value in advertising the company's support for Quality Circles as a means of enhancing the Committee's own reputation in the marketplace.

- *Internal publicity* – the internal forms of publicity may include use of noticeboards, newsletters and paraphernalia.
- *Noticeboards* – these may be used to keep employees informed of the activities of Circles in their area. The photographs of Circle members may be posted and a description of the Circle projects included. In some companies, a separate position on noticeboards has been devoted entirely to Circle news and members are encouraged to contribute material.
- *News sheets* – there are now a great many companies who publish their own internal news sheets, and these are discussed in a later chapter. The production of a news sheet is hard work, but generally news sheets are regarded as worth while. Of course, some larger companies have a regular newspaper anyway, but generally it is not possible to give Circles more than occasional exposure through this medium. Publishing a special newsletter for Circle members gives every Circle a regular opportunity to publicise its own activities and to learn about the achievements of others.
- *External publicity* – external publicity for Circle activities should develop in the West if more and more companies become confident of the permanence of their programmes. In Japan, many organisations see this as an extremely valuable way of demonstrating the care they take to produce good products and reliable service.

Recognition

Steering committee members themselves should make every effort possible to take an active interest in Circle activities. This means that in addition to attending the regular steering committee meetings, the members should ask if they can sit in on occasional Circle meetings and presentations. Not only does this give the steering committee members a better insight into the health and vitality of the programme, but also, and most importantly, it demonstrates to the Circles the extent of the committee's interest in their activities.

This personal level of interest is one of the most important forms of recognition for the Circles. It must be emphasised of course that steering committee membership does not imply any extra powers than would otherwise be held, and that all such contacts with Circles should be made through the usual channels. This would usually be via the section head, but it would be as well for such impromptu visits to be made also in cooperation with the Facilitator.

Reward

No topic has evoked so much discussion of Circle achievements as the subject of reward. Quality Circles can be rewarded for their achievements in many ways, but direct financial rewards should never be given. If this rule is ever violated, the Quality Circle programme will have entered the bargaining arena and Quality Circles of the kind described in this book will cease to exist. In its place, there may remain a money-swapping trade-off structure which will only survive until it has been submerged by jealousy, envy and disagreement.

Part of management's attraction to Quality Circles is the opportunity it affords to create a sense of corporate identity and corporate loyalty, and for people to feel that their organisation is better for their being there. This cannot be achieved if direct financial rewards are given, but there are many other forms of reward discussed later, which contribute positively to this objective and are extremely attractive to Circle members.

Assessment

Just as individual Circles vary, so do Circle programmes. Of the 100 or so locations initially trained by the author, whilst all have been successful as far as the Circle programmes are concerned, there are nevertheless extreme differences in the vitality of the programmes. The reasons for these differences are many and complex. Undoubtedly the biggest factor is that in periods of recession some Circle programmes may fail simply because the companies themselves cease to exist. However, apart from such dramatic situations, well-designed Circle programmes have proved to be extremely hardy even during times of redundancy.

The factors which most obviously affect the success of a programme include:

- lack of pre-preparation;
- low key Steering Committee;
- wrong choice of Facilitator;
- industrial relations tensions;
- lack of management support;
- trade union suspicions;
- inadequate Leader/member training;
- underestimating the importance of all of the techniques;
- insularity – lack of contact with other organisations.

These are just a few of the possible causes of disappointment.

It is of enormous benefit for a steering committee to establish contact with the steering committees of other companies. Unfortunately, at the time of writing no such organisation exists in the West but it is hoped that further attempts will be made if Quality Circles again begin to flourish and grow.

Appreciation

The steering committee should always be alive to the importance of ensuring that all Circles receive adequate recognition for their achievements. Various departmental managers will differ in their personal recognition of this. Consequently, some Circles will feel more appreciated than others. The steering committee should be aware of this and can help overcome any difficulties by giving some Circles more exposure in news sheets and so on. The aim should always be to keep the whole programme at the same healthy level.

Liaison

The Circle programme does not exist in isolation from other company activities, some of which may overlap the work of Circles. In the context of organisational development, it may be necessary for the Quality Circle steering committee to interface with other groups concerned with other concepts such as task force and project group activities in order to produce an integrated programme.

Development

As the programme develops, it will eventually make more and more impact on other activities. The ultimate power of Quality Circles may be realised when Circles become an integral part of company activities – in other words, when everybody can be a member of a Circle. The ultimate aim should be 100 per cent membership, and Quality Circles are simply the way a company manages its people. Before this stage is reached, it will be necessary to establish a formal relationship between functions such as Quality Control and Quality Assurance and Quality Circles. All being well, the people in charge of such functions should have realised the importance of Quality Circles in the achievement of their own objectives, and they will be feeding information to the groups. This information will include customer complaints data, articles from Quality journals and anything else which Quality Control thinks will enhance Circle activities.

This also applies to other functions such as production engineering, Work Study, accounts and so on. The steering committee can play an extremely important role in the encouragement of such developments.

SUMMARY

It may be seen from the foregoing that the composition and constitution of a steering committee is vital to the success of Quality Circles. It may also appear that such activities may be time-consuming. This is not true. The first few meetings may be lengthy and frequent, but once the policy has been established and the Circle programme commenced, the meetings will become shorter and less frequent. In an ongoing programme, the meetings would normally last for about 2 hours, and occur monthly or bi-monthly.

Those organisations that have already begun Circle programmes but have not yet established steering committees would do well to start such committees immediately. One well-known American company did not do this, and the programme collapsed when the Facilitator left. Fortunately, it has since been re-established, but they now have an active steering committee.

- Quality Circles are intended to strengthen the existing organisation – not create bypasses or alternatives.
- Quality Circles will help to create a more cooperative work environment and build bridges between all institutionalised activities.
- Quality Circles represent no threat to any part of the organisation including the trade unions.
- Top management must be totally committed to every aspect of the concept if success is to be ensured.
- Middle or departmental and functional management are the key factors in determining the success of circles within that segment of the operation.

- The supervisor is usually the Circle Leader. Others may lead Circles later when the programme is well established.
- The support of trade union representatives is extremely valuable and is consistent with the objective of achieving greater involvement for their members and helping to create a better work environment. Quality Circle programmes should not cut across any legitimate union interest
- The specialists in an organisation are vital to Quality Circle projects, particularly when their special skills and knowledge are required.
- Non-Circle members should be given the opportunity to become involved wherever possible.
- The steering committee provides a cross-functional supportive framework for circle programme development.
- The Facilitator is the focal point of the programme and in most cases should be a full-time appointment.

18 Business Management Systems (Auditing Hoshin Kanri)

Hoshin Kanri – from Strategy to Action!

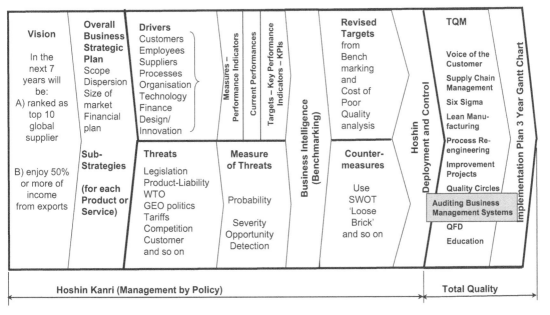

Figure 18.1   Auditing Hoshin Kanri

Hoshin Kanri and its associated TQM process are Business Management Systems in themselves and in order to complete the PDCA Cycle described in Chapter 10 they will require regular and systematic auditing for which a procedure will be necessary. Also, it will be necessary to have an effective auditing process for the evaluation of the supply chain. Fortunately we can make use of the auditing procedure which supports ISO 9001:2000 thanks to its eight management principles and the fact that the standard clearly states that the audit must be against the system operated by the organisation.

This is convenient because it means that it is possible to use these auditing principles as a means of auditing a Hoshin Kanri organisation, provided that the Hoshin Kanri Business Model and the Deployment process as explained in Chapter 10 on Policy Deployment have been clearly defined.

Fortunately the way in which the principles of the ISO 9001:2000 auditing process is designed, means it can be used to audit any management system whether it is specifically designed with ISO

9000 in mind or not. The reason for this is that the auditing process should be carried out against the management system that has been adopted by the organisation and not against some preconceived idea as to what it should be like in the mind of the auditor.

Theoretically, the auditor should, if they have been properly trained, begin the audit with an open mind. At the commencement of the audit, they must be prepared for the possibility that the management system they are about to audit might be totally unlike any that they have ever seen before. The question they should be asking themselves at every stage must be, 'Does it work?' If it does the job which it is required to do and that this is clearly stated then it will be totally satisfactory even if it is entirely unique.

It is for this reason that we are able to 'hitchhike' on the ISO 9001:2000 auditing process and adapt it to our needs.

However, it must be clearly understood that we strongly warn against the use of third-party auditors to carry out this activity. Those who conduct the Hoshin Kanri audits must fully understand the Hoshin Kanri system and be part of the organisation that designed it. ISO 9000 itself and more especially the perceptions of ISO 9001:2000 auditors in general (with exceptions) do fall significantly short of the requirements of Hoshin Kanri in practice.

Regular and competent internal and Supply Chain auditing are essential features of successful Hoshin Kanri programmes. This requires the training of those who will be involved in this task. The principles of Business System Auditing are similar to those used in auditing financial systems, but there are differences.

Apart from these reasons, auditing a Hoshin Kanri-structured business would require the most intimate knowledge of business Strategy some of which would almost certainly be classified to the extent that even a confidentiality agreement will not suffice. Therefore, the employment of any third-party auditing should never be contemplated. To do so would immediately threaten the integrity of the concept and it would also require a more intimate knowledge of the organisation, its policies and its Supply Chain arteries and capillaries than it would be prudent to share with outsiders irrespective of any contractual agreements regarding confidential information.

Of course, if it is necessary for commercial reasons to have third-party certification to ISO 9001:2000 or some other standards, these should not be seen as a substitute for first-party auditing of Hoshin Kanri.

AUDITOR TRAINING

Auditors should be fully qualified in auditing technique. The training and experience in auditing required by the accountancy professional bodies is recommended because such people have credibility in the eyes of upper management whereas others who lack this level of understanding of the fiscal structures and how they are supposed to work may not. It is also recommended that such personnel are made aware of the special auditing requirements laid down in ISO 19011 which deals with auditing technique for QMS. This combined with the accountancy-level training should equip the auditor with everything necessary for effective Hoshin Kanri audits, review and report writing.

THE EIGHT MANAGEMENT PRINCIPLES

Principle 1: Customer focus

ISO 9000:2000 is compatible with Hoshin Kanri in that it states, 'Organisations depend on their customers and therefore should understand current and future customer needs, should meet customer requirements and strive to exceed customer expectations.' This is consistent with the first of the eight Drivers in our Hoshin Kanri Model and with the content of Chapter 21 which provides a checklist of a large number of the possible Performance Indicators related to this topic.

Principle 2: Leadership

The content is very vague here and it is necessary to go to ISO 9004:2000 for a better idea as to what is meant. We would recommend that the Hoshin Kanri organisation interprets this as the means by which the executive team worked from the Vision through the Deployment Process and back through the feedback loop.

The Standard states: 'Leaders establish unity of purpose and direction of the organisation. They should create and maintain the internal environment in which people can become fully involved in achieving the organisation's objectives.' It can readily be seen that this would not present a problem for any company which practices Hoshin Kanri.

Principle 3: Involvement of people

People at all levels are the essence of an organisation and their full involvement enables their abilities to be used for the organisation's benefit.

The standard provides a list of potential benefits all of which are possible. Unfortunately, this principle more than most is virtually useless without any suggestion of 'how to'. Interpreting this principle for the Hoshin Kanri organisation, the support for participative approaches such as Quality Circles and the participative aspects of Lean Manufacture should be clearly stated.

Principle 4: Process approach

A desired result is achieved more efficiently when activities and related resources are managed as a process.

This begs the question, 'Is there any other way of managing activities that have inputs and outputs?' Again, the lack of any 'how to' is a problem that needs to be addressed. Consideration should be given to the possible use of the SIPOC approach to Process Management (Supplier, Input, Process, Output, Customer) and evidence of the use of the PDCA concept both within the processes and for the process overall.

Principle 5: System approach to management

Identifying, understanding and managing inter-related processes as a system contributes to the organisation's effectiveness and efficiency in achieving its objectives.

The Hoshin Approach more than covers this principle in Chapter 10, Policy Deployment and to some extent so does this chapter.

However, the key benefits listed for this principle in the standard include: 'Continually improving the system through measurement and evaluation.' It is hard to see how 'measuring and evaluating' something will by itself actually improve it. All inspection can do by detecting a bad product is to remove it from the process. Since inspectors are only human the likelihood is that they will miss many of the bad products (in most cases a minimum of 10 per cent and generally many more) and quite frequently reject some of the good ones. All inspection can do to a good product is to add cost to it. Better to make it good in the first place and reduce the need for inspection. We recommend that there must be tangible evidence of Continuous Improvement activities for closing the gaps identified by the KPIs.

Principle 6: Continuous Improvement

Continuous Improvement of the organisation's overall performance should be a permanent objective of the organisation.

Yes but this applies to all of the eight principles. Unfortunately Continuous Improvement featured much more prominently in some of the earlier versions of the draft standard than in the final version. There is no indication anywhere as to how improvement projects can be selected, tackled and solved. This makes it impossible to audit properly especially if many of the auditors do not understand the topic. To date, the author has never seen Continuous Improvement being practised anywhere near what he would regard as being satisfactory in any organisation which only has ISO 9001:2000 and which has not also incorporated some other Quality Initiative. For the Hoshin Kanri organisation, we recommend that an internal support structure be created for the promotion of the overall Improvement process in the form of a steering committee or business improvement council. This might also include a sub-group for the support of the Quality Circles and participative Lean Manufacturing activities. These should have structure and terms of reference in order to give them formal credibility and this should be auditable under this clause.

Principle 7: Factual approach to decision making

Effective decisions are based on the analysis of data and information.

Since decision making based on facts is the essence of Hoshin Kanri, auditing on this topic should be straightforward. It is fundamental to the process of conversion of Drivers into specific Performance Indicators and then to KPIs.

Principle 8: Mutually beneficial supplier relationships

An organisation and its suppliers are interdependent and a mutually beneficial relationship enhances the ability of both to create value.

It should also say that a healthy organisation cannot abdicate its responsibility for the quality of its products or services to a supplier. The supplier should be seen as an extension of its own processes and control should always be in the hands of the outsourcing company. In too many cases, organisations allow the supplier to dictate what can be and will be achieved. For example, an automobile company may rely entirely on the sophisticated skills of a gearbox manufacturing specialist and not retain any such expertise. In this situation the gearbox manufacturer will dictate Price, quality performance levels and delivery schedules. This is totally unacceptable in a Hoshin Kanri organisation. We very much recommend that Process Mapping includes mapping the key processes right through the Supply Chain with all the inputs and outputs clearly defined. There should be a seamless join at all the interfaces between the end user and each element in the Supply Chain and at key points also across the Supply Chain. In an age of sophisticated production control software such as SAPS and so on, this is getting easier. Transparency in both directions should be a key Goal.

AUDITING AGAINST THE REQUIREMENTS OF ISO 9001:2000

Terms used to identify different classes of audit:

- first-party auditing – auditing oneself;
- second-party auditing – auditing of suppliers;
- third-party auditing – auditing by an accredited auditing authority (for example, BIS, Lloyds, and so on).

Note that the term Business Management System has been used throughout this chapter but in terms of ISO 9001:2000 specifically, it would be referred to as QMS. The change has been made because the term Quality has different meanings for different people. Some refer to the big Q and the small q. The former term refers to the reputation of the organisation as a whole and the small q means 'product quality'. Since we are talking generally about the organisation as a whole we have used the word 'business' in an attempt to avoid the confusion.

BUSINESS MANAGEMENT SYSTEMS

General requirements

Objective

This sub-clause identifies the generic systemic requirements for an organisation to establish and maintain an effective Business Management System as an integral part of the organisation for the operation of its activities.

Auditor's approach

Some of the requirements of this clause are likely to exist in whole or in part in most organisations. Identification of these elements will be the starting point for auditing the Business Management System. This means identifying the essential process controls required for managing, performing and verifying the achievement of product quality.

The auditor should consider whether the current arrangements are sufficiently managed as processes. The auditor should consider the appropriate inputs needed to achieve the desired outputs for all the processes, whether new or current.

The auditor should follow the process approach (refer to Chapter 15) to provide a more objective means of evaluating the requirements of the standard in terms of expected results. This means looking along the path of a process and its intermediate interactions rather than by just determining the method of process operation.

It will usually be easier for the auditor to start with the overall management process, that is, management, resource, product realisation, and measurement, analysis and improvement as they apply to the main activities of the organisation as a whole, then consider each key Business Process; these are those which result in a product or service being delivered to a customer or user. Then consider the relevant Support Processes such as training, maintenance, production control, personnel selection and so on.

Possible activities

- Check that the processes which are needed for the overall Business Management System have been clearly mapped.

- Has the sequence of process operations, for example, by use of flow charts and Process Mapping techniques, been clearly defined and verified?
- Have the key interactions and Performance Indicators between processes been identified?
- Are the performance requirements for the Key Business Processes and the relevant Support Processes identified, documented and communicated?
- Is there adequate monitoring, measuring and analytical methods in use to ensure the availability of resources and information necessary to support the operation and control of these processes?
- Is there adequate control of outsourcing requirements included in the Business Management System?

Documentation requirements

Objective
ISO 9001:2000 does not require documentation to be in any particular format or style, neither does Hoshin Kanri. However it must be designed and maintained in such a way as to ensure that all aspects of the Business Management System can be properly understood by all concerned and effectively implemented. It must be kept up-to-date at all times and be readily accessible.

Auditor's approach
The auditor should consider the balance between the extent of the documentation needed and the competence of personnel required for achieving process, performance and product conformity. The ISO 9000 system has been strongly and rightly criticised in the past (and to some extent is still today) for encouraging an excessive build up of bureaucratic and totally unnecessary documented procedures.

The auditor should review the documentation against the requirements of both Hoshin Kanri and ISO 9001:2000. If the organisation already has an established, documented, Business Management System, it could be appropriate and effective to develop, for example, an overview document describing the inter-relation between its existing procedures and the requirements of Hoshin Kanri.

Possible activities
The auditor should review the documentation needs for the Business Management System for supporting the organisation's processes. Effective documentation should be brief, and charted data such as flow diagrams, relationship charts, Fishbone Diagrams and so on are encouraged provided that they convey the intended information clearly. The principle 'one picture is worth one thousand words' has considerable merit!

When auditing the format of the documentation, the auditor must consider how, if and under what conditions the documentation is used. This applies equally to physical, verbal and electronic forms of data and information.

Business System manual

Objective
ISO 9000:2000 requires that an organisation establish a quality manual to provide information on its Business Management System and this has considerable merit in all management systems although we would prefer to refer to it as a 'Business Management System manual'.

Auditor's approach

The requirement for a Business Management System manual should be central to the documentation of a Business Management System and the majority of organisations will have such a document. However, it is likely that in the event of a complete makeover of the organisation towards Hoshin Kanri, it might be as well to completely revamp whatever might already exist and start afresh.

The auditor must review the Business Management System manual to ensure that it is up-to-date and that it is a true representation of current practice.

Possible activities

The Business Management System manual should include a description of the content of the Business Management System, details of the documented procedures for the Business Management System and a description of the interaction between its processes. The detail needs to be sufficient to be used by the organisation or external parties to check that the processes exist, that they are operational and that they are fit for their purpose. The interaction between its processes can be represented by the use of organograms, algorithms, flow charts, Process Mapping or descriptions.

Control of documents

Objective

ISO 9001:2000 requires that all documents containing information critical to the operation of the Business Management System must be identified, available and controlled. This also includes relevant documents of external origin. This is just good husbandry and important.

Auditor's approach

The auditor must conduct a review of the document controls being used, and a review of the status of current documents.

Possible activities

Documented procedures should be established to define controls for the identification, approval, issue and removal of Business Management System documentation. The procedures should clearly define the categories of documentation to which they apply. Documentation should be available and accessible when required.

Control of records

Objective

ISO 9001:2000 requires that an organisation shall keep records to demonstrate that its Business Management System operates effectively. Again this is good husbandry, especially in an age of increasing litigation. Quite apart from any other reason, good and accurate records may be critical in the defence against claims. Records that document the Business Management System and conformity to the requirements should be prepared, maintained, legibly and adequately identified, indexed, readily retrievable, stored in a manner to prevent deterioration, damage or loss, and retained for an appropriate period.

Auditor's approach

The auditor should review Record Control activities to ensure that the organisation has addressed all the requirements for records.

Possible activities

The records kept depends on and should be designed to demonstrate the fulfillment of requirements: complete, legible and adequately identified and accessible to relevant personnel and stored in a safe place. Protection from possible theft, fire and water damage should always be considered.

Management responsibility

Objective

In an organisation which is practicing Hoshin Kanri, this section is essential if the concept is to be fully effective. It has always been popular to blame top management for a lack of commitment when a management initiative fails.

The potential benefits of a Business Management System are highly dependent on management at the highest level in an organisation (that is, top management) being committed to its establishment and use as part of the everyday management of the business. For a Business Management System to be really effective, top management need to lead in promoting involvement at all levels of an organisation in achieving its objectives.

Accordingly, top management commitment to the Business Management System should be demonstrable and visible in:

- focusing on the importance of customers;
- setting and communicating the direction of an organisation;
- initiating actions and making the resources available to achieve the quality policy; and
- ongoing involvement with the Business Management System and its improvement.

It would be advisable to check the Vision Statement and the subsequent Driver Policy Statements to ensure that these points are covered.

Auditor's approach

The auditor needs to confirm that there is objective evidence of top management commitment to, and involvement in, the business management system, such as:

- Top management visibility and involvement in promoting improvement through Quality Initiatives and undertaking reviews of the Business Management System. This should be evident from the cascade from Vision Statement through to the KPIs and then through the Deployment process.
- Top management involvement in establishing the quality policy and business Objectives and communicating these within an organisation.
- Top management involvement in ensuring the provision of adequate resources.

Possible activities

Top management could show that they are committed to business performance improvement through:

- personally developing and communicating the Hoshin Kanri Vision through to KPIs and the participative programme (Americans might say 'walking the talk');
- directly participating in the review of Business Management System resource needs and availability: this would be the closed loop feedback of Management Review;
- together with all of the top management, championing and funding improvement initiatives;
- playing a direct role in the Management Review and other key processes, for example, Business Management System planning;

- regularly attending business improvement meetings;
- initiating and being involved in communications concerning business improvement:
- any other activity that demonstrates Leadership with respect to the Business Management System.

There should be a high level of visibility of these activities by all of the management team.

Customer focus

Objective

To ensure its ability to satisfy its customers, top management are responsible for ensuring that all levels of organisation are aware of the needs of the marketplace in which it operates and that they are able to determine current, new and potential customer requirements.

Hoshin Kanri-based programmes usually adopt the principle that everyone is a customer, supplier and processor simultaneously, the next upstream person or activity being the customer. This continues through to the eventual end user. The needs of these customers usually consist of both stated and unstated needs. It is the responsibility of top management to identify the unstated needs of the external customers and for daily management to identify the internal customer's needs and their relative importance to all levels of customer. Perceived importance of these needs is likely to fluctuate constantly due to the performance of competitors, the media and other influences.

Auditor's approach

It is important to find objective evidence of the satisfaction of this requirement. There may be considerable 'opinion data' but little in the way of facts because this is a new requirement. In the previous version of the standard, this area was covered by Contract Review. This has been greatly expanded to require objective evidence of customer satisfaction. It is important for both the auditor and the organisation to be aware that customer satisfaction cannot be determined by the absence of customer dissatisfaction. Simply meeting the requirements of a specification may not create customer satisfaction. For example, a competitor may perform some non-stated requirements not subject to contractual review to a higher level than the organisation and this may lead to a relative degree of dissatisfaction.

Greater visibility will need to be given to the way in which top management ensure the gathering and processing of information on customers and the marketplace. It may also be used as an input into the Management Review process and as data for Continuous Improvement activities.

Possible activities

Check how top management decide where, how and when an organisation should use its resources to ensure that it:

- obtains information relating to customer requirements; and
- works towards satisfying its customers by meeting those requirements.

Does it do this effectively and what objective evidence is there to indicate that this is satisfactory?

This objective evidence should include the consideration of options for gathering information relating to customer needs and expectations, such as:

- conducting and analysing customer and market research;
- communication and review activities involving
  - account managers

      —   contract or project managers
      —   customer service personnel
      —   individual top management contacts (managing director to managing director meetings);

- enquiry and order handling processes;
- customer second-party audit personnel;
- customer helpdesks;
- interactive Internet websites.

Is there objective evidence to demonstrate that top management ensures that the information obtained is analysed and used as input for:

- the development of business policy;
- the establishment of meaningful Drivers and objectives;
- identification of KPIs;
- Business Management System planning?

Business policy

Objective

The business policy as developed in the Strategy and Policy element demonstrates the formal commitment of an organisation towards effective business management and its plan for the future. The business policy developed by top management must create an overall sense of direction and, through the synthesis approach through to the establishment of the KPIs, set and show the principles of action. Through the Policy Deployment process it should enable the setting of business Objectives throughout the organisation.

Auditor's approach

A Policy statement should not be a bland document of objective, without linkage to any specific tangible measures such as the KPIs. For example, they frequently contain some very lofty Objectives such as 'foster the creativity of our staff'. This sounds attractive as few would disagree, but what does it actually mean? Without some more tangible measures, no one could substantiate claims as to whether or not this is being achieved. As a statement it is fine but the auditor must look behind the words and discover how this is to be measured, what the judgment criteria are and what mechanisms are in place to close the gaps between Target and actual performance.

Does the policy review ensure that the business policy:

- Includes clear commitment to meeting all of the stated requirements for the product or service and to the Continuous Improvement of the Business Management System?
- Facilitate the establishment and review of Quality Objectives?
- Is realistic and achievable bearing in mind the need to set stretched Goals?

Possible activities

The business policy should be achievable, but the word 'achievable' is subjective and there will be different opinions as to what might be regarded as 'achievable'. In our opinion, we think that it should be the collective opinion of the business team and not the auditor as to what is to be regarded as 'achievable'. The auditor should check with all who will have been responsible for the creation of the policy as to whether it has their full agreement. Are all personnel aware of the business policy and the obligations it places upon them?

Is the business policy documented and periodically reviewed for continuing relevance and adequacy? Is it amended or revised as needed? When changes are introduced, are these communicated to all levels as soon as practicable?

Planning

Objective

It is necessary to ensure that, throughout an organisation, measurable business Objectives and KPIs are established to enable the Vision Statement and the associated KPIs to be achieved. These should address:

- the Business Management System as a whole;
- the Business Management System's processes;
- the output of the Business Management System (the product or service).

The Objectives set should translate the business policy into actions to be attained. These should be established at relevant functions and at levels that can influence the achievement of the objectives.

Auditor's approach

The auditor will need to determine:

- How much involvement is there by top management?
- Are the Objectives cascaded down to the relevant functions and levels of the organisation?
- Do the Objectives relate to the processes of the Business Management System and, as appropriate, also to product and services?
- Are all the Objectives measurable?

Possible activities

Do the business Objectives address both the broad corporate business issues, and also the issues that are specific to individual functions and levels within the organisation?

For each business objective, are there suitable indicators defined which allow for the monitoring of the achievement of these objectives? Is there an achievable timescale defined for their realisation?

Is there a check to ensure that the Quality Objectives:

- are consistent with each other and with the quality policy?
- are agreed to be realistic by those concerned?
- have the potential to add value?
- are agreed to be achievable by those concerned?
- are capable of being measured?

Are the Objectives communicated (for example, via training or briefing sessions) to relevant personnel, and deployed through internal communication?

Business Management System planning

Objective

It is top management's responsibility to:

- ensure the setting up of the Business Management System, in accordance with the requirements of Hoshin Kanri;

- ensure that there is a planned approach to undertaking changes and enhancements to the Business Management System;
- ensure that there is a structured approach to the achievement of the planned objectives; and
- enable the achievement of the planned Objectives by the identification, definition and realisation of the relevant processes and resources.

Auditor approach
Of concern to the auditor will be evidence of the input data, how and where it was obtained, whether it is sufficiently objective, how it has been used in the planning process and how the system was validated.

Possible activities
Determine how the necessary inputs were identified and evaluated. The methods used should ensure the completeness, accuracy and absence of conflict between the various inputs. Frequently, the tools of QFD and Process Mapping and Analysis might be used very effectively for this purpose.

Responsibility, authority and communication

Objective
To ensure effective business management by providing adequate means for avoiding conflict or gaps and confusion, it is necessary that roles, responsibilities and authorities are defined, documented and communicated.

Auditor's approach
The auditor must review the existing arrangements and check the adequacy of these to determine the effectiveness of communications.

Possible activities
Are the responsibilities and authorities of all personnel who perform duties that are part of the Business Management System well defined? Are there clear definitions of responsibilities at the interfaces between different functions?

Such definitions can be required for all levels and functions within the organisation and the interfaces with related organisations which include both customers and suppliers. Interfaces with Support Processes must also be considered.

Line management responsibilities should ideally include the management within their area of operations. Where prime responsibility for performance improvement rests with line management, the roles and responsibilities of any related specialist function within the organisation should be appropriately defined to avoid ambiguity with respect to responsibilities and authorities. This should include arrangements to resolve any conflict between quality issues and productivity considerations, for example, escalation to a higher level of management. Chapter 4 of Dr Feigenbaum's book *Total Quality Control* is probably still the best text available on this aspect of quality and it was first published in 1951!

Management representative

Objective
To provide a focal point for authority and feedback to upper management for the management of the Business Management System.

Auditor's approach

The auditor will need to confirm that arrangements for achieving this are in place but in all probability it will be this person who acts as being the main support role for the auditor. The auditor will need to establish whether the management representative actually does have the authority and responsibilities identified in their job description. Frequently this is not the case.

Possible activities

Does the management representative have well-defined responsibilities and authority to ensure that the Business Management System is implemented, operational and continually monitored?

The management representative may be supported by other personnel who have delegated responsibilities for monitoring the overall operation of the business improvement function. Top management should ensure that any other duties or functions assigned to these personnel do not conflict with the fulfilment of their delegated responsibilities when supporting the management representative. This can sometimes happen when the individuals report to different personnel for different activities. There will almost always be a time conflict when this is the case.

Is the management representative kept fully informed of the performance of the system, and do they have active involvement in periodic reviews and, ideally, are they actively involved in the setting of the objectives?

Internal communication

Objective

Top management should provide processes to facilitate effective communication within an organisation of information on, or affecting, the Business Management System and its performance.

Auditor's approach

Do the activities of Hoshin Kanri and especially the business-Process Improvement activities have a high level of visibility? Some organisations do not like to paper the walls with information, but visibility is important to ensure continued awareness of how the performance-improvement process is working and to give visible recognition for achievement.

Possible activities

Confirm how top management establishes effective arrangements for the internal communication of relevant performance-improvement information to and from its personnel.

Such information could include information on:

- customer, competitor and marketplace requirements;
- statutory and regulatory requirements;
- competitors and competitive products and market share data;
- customer, competitor and own advertising materials;
- supplier news;
- information from the media particularly trade magazines;
- product requirements, including any changes;
- quality policy;
- the performance of the Business Management System, for example, audit results, customer satisfaction results;
- responsibilities and authorities.

Ideally an organisation's personnel should be involved in:

* opportunities to input to the development and communication of the policy and Hoshin Kanri objectives;
* opportunities to input into changes affecting workplace quality such as the introduction of new, or modified, responsibilities and reporting structures, work patterns and practices, equipment, materials, technologies, processes, procedures, through Quality Circle activities, TPM, 5S/5C programmes and so on;
* determining how any changes are best communicated.

Management review

Objective

Management Review is the completion of the closed feedback loop of Management Control (Macro-level PDCA Cycle) for ensuring that the Business Management System continues to:

* be relevant, to both existing and anticipated customer needs and requirements and marketplace trends;
* achieve what it sets out to achieve;
* be implemented in the correct manner;
* be visibly and practically active in all parts of the organisation at all levels.

It will take several years in medium to large organisations to fully implement Hoshin Kanri and its associated concepts to the level of maturity. It is advisable to start small and, after some quick wins, gradually spread it throughout the organisation. It will spread more rapidly in some parts of the organisation than others. This is normal. However, at the annual Management Review, the rate of uptake should be an issue for debate and decision making as to how best to involve all functions.

It is top management's responsibility to identify the decisions and actions relating to opportunities for improvement, and to verify that previous outputs have been actioned. Management Review is intended to help an organisation maximise its rate of improvement, react to changes in the business environment and identify and authorise the necessary changes to the Business Management System, policy and objectives.

Auditor's approach

This review could be seen by the auditor to be at the core of the management system and represents the Check and Act part of the macro organisation-wide PDCA Cycle. The Business Management System is the Plan, the Do is represented by the response to the Quality Objectives, and the output from the Do is the input to the Check or Management Review. The output from the Review then becomes the input to the Action which will include specific actions by individuals and the Continuous Improvement activities.

The auditor will need to establish: is there a review process, how does it work, what are the inputs and how are they obtained, what are the outputs and are they effectively actioned?

Records should be fairly comprehensive and include:

* details of tangible inputs and outputs;
* how subjective opinion data is treated;
* the substantiated justification for decisions.

Possible activities

Whilst ISO 9001:2000 advocates Management Reviews it does not specify the frequency at which they should occur. Typically a Hoshin Kanri organisation will have a top Management Review of the entire organisation annually, site reviews half-yearly and local departmental reviews on a monthly basis. Management Reviews at departmental level are held formally and on a regular basis. (An informal meeting once per month in the local pub is definitely not a substitute!) The review should be a regular part of the management process. Ideally, there should be a monthly review of day-to-day issues; these reviews can be conducted at middle management level. This may be followed by a quarterly review at a higher level with a more in-depth review half-yearly followed by a top Management Review on an annual basis. This should include an internal audit of the entire management system at two levels: how well the system is working throughout the organisation and how well the Objectives have been met in each part of the organisation. Some will have progressed better than others and then reasons for the differences will provide valuable information to create the plan for the next 12 months. A Management Review may be a stand-alone activity but could also be integrated with other activities such as quality meetings or board meetings. Stand alone is better otherwise it will compete for time with other 'crisis business issues'.

The planning for a Management Review, should include:

- who should attend;
- an annual review, which may be conducted by a horizontal slice across the top of the organisation with inputs from managers, quality specialist advisers, other personnel, supplier/outsource representatives;
- lower-level reviews, which may be conducted by a team comprising a diagonal slice through the organisation including all key personnel in the quality system plus representation form customers and suppliers where relevant;
- the responsibilities of individual participants involved in the reviews, and information to be reviewed.

The reviews could address:

- the suitability and appropriateness of the current quality policy, and progress towards it achievement;
- updating current or creating new quality Objectives and KPIs for Continuous Improvement;
- the adequacy and effectiveness of current processes;
- the adequacy of resources (personnel, equipment, material);
- recorded instances where processes and procedures have been ineffective, this could also include analysis of success;
- the adequacy of current products and services including product support;
- the results of internal and external Business Management System audits carried out since the previous review and the effectiveness of response to non-conformances and observations;
- improvements to the Business Management System;
- Risk analysis of the effects of foreseeable changes to statutory and regulatory requirements and international economics and politics;
- actual and potential impact of new product development.

The review process must be interactive with Business Management System planning in order to realise improvement opportunities and actions required to meet the future aims of the organisation.

Resource management

Objective

To ensure that the necessary resources of personnel, materials, plant, machinery, equipment, apparatus, facilities and methods are available and adequate to provide the means of customer satisfaction.

Auditor's approach

In many organisations much of what is required in this clause probably exist piecemeal but are likely to be disassociated from each other. This will be as a consequence of a heritage of functionally-based management rather than process-based. The task of the auditor will be to first of all determine what actions have been taken to make sure that everything is in the right place at the right time. Normally the 5S/5C approach is the best way to achieve this and it would be advisable for the auditor to be aware of the methods used in this concept, especially the Red Tagging technique.

Possible activities

Determine whether the organisation has determined its resource needs from the Business Management System and product-realisation planning. How well has it determined how and when these resources are to be acquired and deployed and what still needs to be done?

Check whether resource provision is regularly reviewed for continuing adequacy, using data from previous Management Reviews and audits and also analysis of monitoring and measuring results.

Human resources

Objective

ISO 9001:2000 states that an organisation must be able to demonstrate that all personnel whose jobs affect product quality are educated, trained and competent and contribute to the achievement of the Quality Objectives. We would extend that to include all relevant business Objectives. We would also add that not only must they be trained but they should actively be encouraged to be involved through both Quality Circle and Lean Manufacturing activities.

Auditor's approach

The auditor should check if the emphasis has been placed on how the organisation determines 'competence' rather than simply training given. For example, a person may learn all there is to know about swimming from lectures in a classroom but it does not follow that they can actually swim! In this clause, it is important to find out how the organisation determines competence to perform and how personnel are given the opportunity to demonstrate their use of the training given.

The auditor needs to discover how the organisation defines the competence requirements for personnel performing work that affects business performance. They therefore need to obtain whatever evidence there may be of how:

- performance and/or skills against determined competence requirements are reviewed;
- individual awareness of relevant business objectives;
- the need to ensure awareness could be addressed by a quality awareness and training programme that explains the organisation's Business Management System and the specific role of the individual in that programme. This can be particularly effective when included in induction education and training programmes;
- education and training is provided for everyone in the value chain. This should include suppliers and other forms of outsourcing. It may also include customers.

Where training or other actions are taken as part of the resolution of a Quality-related problem, the effectiveness of the remedy must be verified and action taken to hold the gains. This may be done by including the training in the induction programme for future performers of the relevant task.

Possible activities

Check if there is a structured approach for the continual and systematic evaluation and review of job/task competence requirements to ensure the availability of competent personnel. Determine whether the activities address key issues such as:

- evidence of competency;
- understanding of the importance of their jobs and tasks to the Objectives of the organisation;
- an understanding of the needs of their own internal customers and suppliers;
- induction training;
- evidence of the use of these skills and knowledge in performance improvement activities.

A variety of tools may be evident such as:

- skills matrices, QFD tools, training-needs analysis and performance appraisals and employee survey data.

Infrastructure

Objective

An organisation must provide the infrastructure necessary to conduct its operations and realise product conformity and continuous improvement of the facilities.

Auditor's approach

The auditor should be aware that people are more likely to do good work and adopt positive attitudes if the work environment is conducive to this. Also, there are product needs considerations such as 'clean room' environment, problems related to the ingress of dust and dirt, the build up of static electricity, contaminants and vibration from surrounding operations, transportation and storage and so on.

One leading department chainstore regards this as being the number one most important consideration when auditing a potential new supplier for the first time. If the toilets are not clean or adequate, or the facilities for the employees to keep their outdoor clothes and the canteen facilities below standard, they will fail the supplier irrespective of other considerations.

Possible activities

The auditor might ask themself: is this a good place to work and is it conducive to doing good quality work? This question will relate to the provision of buildings, workspace and associated facilities needed to perform the processes of the Business Management System and achieve the realisation and delivery of the required product. This will involve:

- production and service delivery facilities;
- communication and transport facilities;
- office space;
- computer hardware and software and filing facilities;
- monitoring and measurement equipment;
- laboratory and test buildings;
- inspection areas;
- storage areas;
- handling facilities.

Work environment

Objective
The 'infrastructure' clause is concerned with the provision of the appropriate facilities. This clause is concerned with the control and operation of those facilities with respect to its impact on the business Objectives and quality of life at work.

Whilst it must be acknowledged that people cannot be expected to do quality work in an environmentally hazardous environment, these considerations are well covered in ISO 14000.

Auditor's approach
For this concern, one very effective approach would be to use empathy. How would I like to do that job in this environment day after day and is it conducive to doing good work? It is a good idea to begin this aspect of the audit by checking the restroom facilities, where food is served and eaten before going on to check the other features. If any of the work is out of doors do people have facilities to change their clothes, take a shower etc.? The conditions might be satisfactory on the day of the audit but how about the extremes of winter and summer? Is the heating adequate? Is there air conditioning? Do people have to look at Computer screens in direct sunlight? Is it draughty? It is a good idea to ask the workers but the responses need to be carefully evaluated and checked against any evidence that might be available.

Possible activities
The auditor must consider all of the critical work environment requirements such as control of:

- temperature variation;
- humidity;
- light and noise;
- air cleanliness and dust;
- electrostatic build up;
- vibration;
- working garments;
- hygiene and contamination control.

Product realisation

Objective
Planning for product realisation includes everything that is necessary to produce the desired product. This sub-clause sets out the generic requirements for the planning and development of product realisation processes.

Auditor's approach
Some form of planning is almost bound to exist. The key question for the auditor must be, 'Does it work and does it cover all of the requirements?' It will be necessary to study the content of the standard very carefully in this respect because any failure here could lead to possibly catastrophic results later.

The auditor should also take account of market pressures on the organisation to make promises to its customers that it has difficulty in keeping. Frequently, the time taken to plan properly is grossly underestimated with the consequence that the organisation is tempted to take shortcuts. This is particularly common when the planning process has to be iterative.

Particular attention will have to be given to ensuring that the needs for process monitoring and measurement and product verification/validation are a clearly established as part of product realisation planning.

Possible activities

Product planning usually requires tools which will enable the distillation of large quantities of sometimes conflicting information into a coherent plan. It may contain many compromises. For example, the customer requirement may be the drainage of a large area of land to reduce the likelihood of flooding. However, there will certainly be conflicting requirements from a variety of interested parties, for example, local farmers, the Royal Society for the Protection of Birds, the Ramblers Association on the one hand, while on the other may be the local community, parent groups and property developers.

Frequently in such situations the process will be iterative with many revisions until some acceptable compromise or a legal decision is made.

The requirement for records is critical, as they will provide objective evidence of the extent of product and process conformity and constraints and the achievement of Quality Objectives.

Tools may include Affinity Diagrams, Relationship Diagraphs, Tree Diagrams, House of Quality, Hazard Analysis, FMEA, and Process Decision and Programme Charts (PDPC).

Customer-related processes

Objective

To clarify the specific stated and non-stated product-related needs of customers and other impacted people and organisations, to ensure that these needs can be met with regard to statutory and regulatory requirements and to review capability against historical performance where relevant prior to acceptance. This includes the ability to satisfy post-delivery requirements which may include subsequent product support.

Auditor's approach

Most, if not all, organisations will have some existing arrangements for enquiry and order handling and Contract Review, and it is the task of the auditor to determine whether these are adequate for the work concerned. It is worth reviewing past performance if the data are available and if the process has not been changed significantly.

Possible activities

Check what information is collected and how it is used for analysis of customer and market research data related both to the product itself, relevant supporting services and statutory and regulatory information. Is this information adequate?

Compare this information with that obtained for previous designs and product performance.

Customer communications

Objective

Communication with the customer is essential if customer satisfaction is to be achieved. This may be easy in some situations such as project engineering, where there will be considerable interaction, but at the other extreme, where the customer may be buying from a catalogue on the Internet, it will be extremely difficult.

Auditor's approach

Whilst some market-leading organisations have recognised the importance of this, generally speaking, the probability is that the auditor will find many opportunities for improvement under this requirement. Many organisations are quite vulnerable to aggressive attack by competitors who have not only taken the trouble to improve their knowledge of customer requirements but have also been better at communicating their capabilities and concerns for the satisfaction of the customer. Inevitably the more active organisations will find the small differences that there may be between their performance and their competitor which they can then exploit to advantage. It might be advisable to first of all establish what is being done before identifying the gaps and possible blind spots.

Possible activities

It will be necessary to determine what it has to output to the customer and what information it needs to obtain from the customer.

Some communication may be channeled through customers' supplier auditors, technical interfaces (for example, the two organisations' design departments), helpdesks, product servicing and repair, sales and purchasing, high-level communications at top management level, the finance department (particularly accounts receivable) and the legal department.

Customer Focus groups are also a very effective form of communication. Some organisations also promote open days for customers to mingle with the people who produce the products.

Design and development

Objective

Innovation and design are frequently the main activities that determine market success. Many organisations are so obsessed with being the first into the market with a new product that they take high-Risk shortcuts with the inevitable consequences. Frequently in such cases, the competitor who arrives a little later but with a good product eventually wins the market. The objective here is to create a design and development organisation that is responsive to customer needs and can produce designs that will satisfy those needs on time and at cost, and meeting the Quality Objectives.

Auditor's approach

Even where the design process appears to comply with the requirements of the standard on paper, there are many pressures on the design process to take shortcuts. If this has been the practice in the past it will not be easy for the organisation to adopt a more disciplined approach. Interviews with people at different points in the product development process will frequently reveal the truth of what is happening. The repair shop is a good place to check. They see the products coming back for repair and know the reasons for the defectives. Check engineering change requests and the modifications columns on drawings. If there have been serious shortcuts taken in the design process these are the places where they will visually show up. Also check warranty claims and free replacements.

The organisation cannot avoid its responsibilities for control over the design function through outsourcing.

Purchasing

Objective

To ensure that outsourced products and services are consistent with the quality Objectives defined in the Business Management System. It is worth noting that outsourced processes are really the organisation's processes that it has chosen to allow others to manage. The organisation is still responsible for ensuring that purchased products and services are conducted in a suitable manner, as these will have a direct influence on customer satisfaction.

Auditor's approach

Wherever possible a number of key suppliers should be selected for interview. Care should be taken that there is a degree of randomness in the choice. This is to avoid the possibility of being sent to some who have a special relationship. Travel might be a problem here and this might restrict access. In some cases telephone interviews or mailed questionnaires may be used. These are not at all ideal but are better than nothing. Check also the methods used for supplier rating, preferred supplier status, methods of incoming goods control, evidence of supplier training and participation in joint continuous improvement activities.

Possible activities

There are six main categories of activity:

- analysis of a supplier's performance history;
- use of preferred supplier status, skip lot inspection if the method is used and other forms of motivation to comply with contract requirements;
- references from other customers and credit rating;
- second-party audit data;
- certification and membership of trade associations;
- trial orders.

Production and service provision

Objective

This is to ensure that all of the resources identified as being necessary for production and service are provided under controlled conditions and that where necessary these are validated to demonstrate the ability to achieve planned results.

Auditor's approach

This clause is particularly important from the auditing point of view because it requires a study of a great many interactions at all stages of the production process. All of the principles of the standard apply to all of the interactions.

Possible activities

It includes all the operations necessary to realise the agreed product, whether they are conducted at an organisation's site, a customer's site or elsewhere. As such, it can be applied to activities such as delivery, installation, commissioning and post-delivery product servicing and maintenance.

An organisation has to undertake the planned activities and implement any additional actions to establish controlled conditions.

Validation of processes for production and service provision

Objective

When the output of a process cannot be readily or economically verified by subsequent measurement, an organisation must implement suitable controls to ensure that the process performance can be relied upon to achieve planned results. This is referred to as Process Validation. Typical examples of such processes include pasteurisation of dairy products, specialised heat-treatment processes and sterilisation of canned foods.

Auditor's approach

Processes should be mapped in one form or another. The auditor will check to ensure that this has been carried out and that stated processes comply with current practice, and also that the outputs of these processes are measured, evaluated and monitored against KPI requirements.

Possible activities

The auditor needs to:

- identify production and service provision processes, the output of which cannot be readily or economically verified;
- identify what additional controls need to put in place to have confidence in the conformity of its output;
- confirm that these controls are effective in ensuring that the process achieves the required results.

These activities need to be planned and implemented to ensure that the necessary controls are put in place as part of the introduction of such processes, and that they are addressed as part of the management of any subsequent changes.

Provision should also be made for the periodic review of these arrangements to determine the need for any process revalidation.

Identification and traceability

Objective

This sub-clause requires that where appropriate, an organisation should ensure that, throughout production and service provision, it can establish the means to be able to identify the product and its measurement and test status throughout the product-realisation process.

The degree of traceability required will sometimes be determined by contract and sometimes by the needs of the Business Management System.

Auditor's approach

There is no specific procedure required for this activity and the means used will depend upon the circumstances. The auditor must judge for themself whether the methods used work and if they are foolproof. Frequently traceability is important as part of good housekeeping and to be able to trace suppliers. For example, identical plastic-moulded products may be supplied from several different sources but they may use the same mould tool which is passed from one to the other. If one or the other had used an inferior mix of plastic it would be necessary to be able to trace the source. In this case traceability could easily be achieved by inserting an indexable serial number in the mould cavity. In this case no other form of identification would be required.

Possible activities

A management record and control system which may include such features as:

- batch and other forms of travel documents which include the history of the items;
- product identification, which may include bar coding and computer-based tracking systems or other forms of labeling and marking;
- quarantine and bonded areas which require authorised documentation for storage and retrieval.

Customer property

Objective

Frequently an organisation may require customer-supplied materials, equipment or products for use in its product.

Auditor's approach

Because this requirement extends beyond products to include information, equipment and facilities, the auditor should attempt to discover what property is involved and how it is being protected, particularly with regard to deterioration and loss. In the case of intellectual property, how is it protected from theft or replication? One effective way to think about this aspect it to use empathy. If it were my property what would I want and expect from those to whom it has been entrusted?

Possible activities

Where such circumstances exist, the organisation must take care to protect and maintain customer-supplied property whilst under the organisation's control or use. If it is lost, damaged or otherwise found to be unsuitable, this must be reported to the customer, records kept and agreement reached with the customer as to how the situation might be rectified.

Preservation of product

Objective

To ensure that products are protected at all stages during processing, handling, storage and transportation though to its intended destination and beyond if necessary. For example, bathroom furniture is often coated with protective materials to reduce the Risk of damage or spoiling during the installation process. It also includes warnings against improper use or handling.

Auditor's approach

It will be necessary to study the process from the start to the finish, asking the question, 'In what way might this activity affect the preservation of the product? What actions are taken to prevent occurrence and what actions have been taken to prevent re-occurrence? What records are there? How are they maintained and how do they link to the Quality Objectives? What training and awareness is given to those who impact on the product and is it adequate for the level of protection necessary?'

Possible activities

Process Mapping followed by Process Analysis can be used to reveal the likely points where product degradation, damage or spoilage may occur. For example, swarf or metal filings may enter a valve during subsequent operations. The remedy would be to put plastic plugs in the holes after machining. Corrective and preventive action can be taken and recorded. Data should be obtained from downstream activities to feedback Risks that may exist in earlier operations.

Control of monitoring and measuring devices

Objective

The control and maintenance of monitoring and measuring devices is fundamental to the achievement of consistent quality and to ensure that all equipment is fit and appropriate for its intended use. For example, a steel rule may be in good condition and well calibrated but it could not be regarded as a precision instrument and would not be considered satisfactory for precise repeated measurements.

Auditor's approach

The key point for the auditor is 'fit and appropriate for the intended use'. The auditor must be satisfied that the means used for monitoring and measuring are appropriate for the results required and the level of accuracy necessary. It would be uneconomic for an organisation to specify unnecessarily high levels of accuracy. Generally speaking, for each lower decimal place of precision given, the cost in terms of training and skill, maintenance of equipment required increases by more than an order of magnitude and there is no point in over-gilding the lily. Calibration and re-calibration and the frequency of these activities is vital to the maintenance of a good measuring and monitoring system. It is also important that the customer uses the same criteria. There have been numerous examples of a customer returning perfectly good product to the supplier only to find that that their measuring equipment that was faulty.

Possible activities

The monitoring and measuring equipment used must be judged according to need. Whilst a steel rule may not be adequate to measure the thickness of a car component, at the same time no one would expect to be required to use a micrometer to measure the width of a photograph to put in a frame.

Activities include: maintenance of equipment conformity, through appropriate calibration, records of wear, adjustment, repair, protection, labeling and so on; maintenance and control of reference standards; maintenance and control of standards room and clean room environments; training and re-training and competence assessment in the use of relevant equipment.

Measurement, analysis and improvement

Objective

To demonstrate conformity of product to agreed customer requirements.

To ensure conformity of the Business Management System and to continually improve the effectiveness of the Business Management System such that the organisation's ability to meet customer requirements is constantly improved.

Auditor's approach

The auditor should attempt to determine the overall level of consciousness of personnel towards the Quality Objectives. It is not by any means unusual for both the quality manager and the chief executive to give an extremely convincing account of the importance attached to the Business Management System throughout the organisation, how it is at the core of business activities and so on. However, this may be in stark contrast to other people's perception which in the extreme may include complete ignorance by some personnel whose jobs are fundamental to success. Of course, the auditor must not be misled by the hardened cynic. Where there is significant difference of perception within the organisation the auditor must seek objective evidence before making an observation.

Possible activities

A regular review of all of the Objectives identified in the business management system and the means by which they are monitored and measured. The results might be used in a Gap Analysis of Current Performance against Target performance and how action is to be taken on the difference.

Monitoring and measurement

Objective

It may seem obvious that without customer satisfaction an organisation might be in trouble, therefore most would be doing everything possible for its achievement. Surprisingly even in highly competitive markets this is often not the case and the objective here is to encourage an organisation to focus its quality management Strategy towards customer satisfaction as a means to improve its business performance.

Auditor's approach

Because the means by which this requirement are so many and varied and because it is also a major part of Strategic Planning, the auditor must be very open-minded as to how this is being achieved. Again, the important considerations must be 'Does this approach work? Does the organisation really know what its customers think of them or are they fooling themselves? Have they any idea of the difference between customer satisfaction and customer dissatisfaction and where they might be in between particularly with reference to the position of their competitors? Are they using the information obtained to really improve business performance in terms of marketshare, customer retention, and prompt payments?' The result of the auditor's analysis is likely to produce more observations than non-conformances.

Possible activities

The collection and analysis of customer-related data, its presentation at Management Review meetings, dissemination to employees and other relevant personnel or groups, trade associations and the media.

Internal audit

Objective

To determine whether the organisation is working in accordance with the Business Management System and conforms to the requirements of the Hoshin Kanri Management system.

Auditor's approach

The auditor should be concerned with the competency of those selected to conduct audits, the degree of impartiality and objectiveness and whether the frequency of audit and action taken on observations and non-conformances are adequately addressed.

Possible activities

Personnel selected should be chosen to ensure impartiality and objectivity, should be competent with the necessary audit skills but should not audit their own work. People skills should include the ability to work on their own and as part of a team and to be able to share their observations with relevant personnel and their personality and experience should enable their opinions to be respected.

The frequency of audits will be determined by the relative importance of the various processes and functions to be audited, the stability of the processes and their management and changes to work practices including the impact of Continuous Improvement activities.

Follow-up actions should include the verification of the actions taken and the reporting of verification results.

Monitoring and measurement of processes

Objective

To demonstrate the ability of processes to produce the required results it is necessary to monitor and measure the process to ensure that the Objectives are being achieved according to planned arrangements.

Auditor's approach

The key questions again for the auditor are, 'Is this system appropriate for the purpose intended and does it work?' The history of the operation is important. If it is a long-established process, has worked well in the past, the controls have been sufficient to enable in-process corrections and the data used for Process Improvement and there is no good reason to believe that this has just been good fortune, then it would be reasonable to assume that it will continue to work into the future. However, just because nothing has gone wrong does not mean that it cannot and the auditor must still conduct a thorough check to ensure that success has not simply been the result of chance.

For new processes, the measures and monitors must be considered more carefully. There will be little historical data and competency may not be guaranteed. The auditor will need to check carefully the basis on which the quality plan was established, its maturity and the degree to which it is under surveillance.

Possible activities

These will depend upon the nature of the work and may range from very sophisticated and complex three-dimensional operations involving large numbers of highly trained personnel at one extreme (for example, air traffic control), through to simple counting and physical checking at the other. The relevant data will therefore come in a variety of forms ranging from continuous streams of computer or process monitoring to basic paper-based systems.

Monitoring and measurement of product

Objective

There is an old adage that says, 'Look after the process and the product looks after itself!' Hopefully yes but it cannot be guaranteed and it is important to monitor and measure the product which, if deficiencies are detected, will enable improvements to be made to the process where necessary.

Auditor's approach

It is worth bearing in mind that the respected researchers Harris and Cheney discovered that 90 per cent of product inspection is visual and does not use any aids of any kind, to err is to be human and people, just because they are human beings, will miss at least 15 per cent of what they believe they have observed. Task and human-related factors reduce this further and it is not by any means unusual for competent, motivated and intelligent people to miss as many as 90 per cent of defects that are clearly visible when pointed out. The message is – do not believe that 100 per cent inspection produces anything like 100 per cent segregation.

The auditor should be concerned as to whether the means of monitoring and measuring are appropriate and effective – what is the evidence?

Activities

Identification of appropriate product monitoring and measuring methods; personnel selection-based task-related factors; human factors such as the effect of age, gender, eyesight; workplace design and ergonomics – lighting, heating and noise; use of product monitoring and measurement.

There should also be provisions for undertaking correction and corrective action in the event of non-conformities being detected during the monitoring and measurement of the product.

Control of non-conforming product

Objective

Clearly the objective here is to ensure that anything that is outside stated and agreed physical or performance-related parameters be identified and isolated until a decision is reached regarding its future.

Auditor's approach

Non-conforming product raises questions about other activities in the Business Management System. Not only is it important to identify what is done when non-conformities arise, it is also important to find out how they have arisen because frequently this will expose a variety of weaknesses in the Business Management System not easily discovered by traditional methods of auditing.

There is a wide range of possibilities, maybe the product was rushed through the design stages, maybe upstream controls were inadequate, or perhaps the supplier selection process is suspect and so on. The key question is, why?

Possible activities

The main concern is the identification, isolation and subsequent disposal of non-conforming product to prevent its intended use until a decision has been made to either re-work, scrap, obtain customer permission to use, but under concessionary controls. The control process continues until the product has been corrected, irretrievably disposed of or accepted under agreed conditions by the customer.

Analysis of data

Objective

In the late 1980s Motorola apparently found that engineers who used a factual approach to decision making and problem solving produced results that were over ten times more effective that those who relied on opinion data. Frequently we do not have the data and are pressed for decisions now, many managers resort to opinion data but despite frequently long-held beliefs, this is invariably either wrong or does not always lead to the best option.

Auditor's approach

During an audit the auditor will be overwhelmed with subjective opinion about most things. It would be easy to become pedantic and insist on objective factual evidence in each and every case but this would be impossible and unnecessary. The auditor must be realistic. Data comes at a Price and its collection must be worth the effort. The key question must be, 'Is this data essential for the effective achievement of the Objectives identified in the Business Management System?' The Objectives themselves may require more objectivity, for example, the quality policy statement may say something like, 'We will become the best producer of XXX by the year 20XX.' Sounds good but what does it mean? How do we intend to measure 'best'? Different people in the organisation may have quite different opinions about this, so the organisation will have to be more specific. At the level of the business policy document, this level of subjectivity is acceptable but behind it there must be a much more clear explanation supported by metrics. 'If you cannot measure it you cannot manage it' – Lord Kelvin.

Possible activities

Data Collection is the obvious activity but the questions arise, what data and in what form? It is easy to over-react and end up with paralysis by analysis so it is vitally important to be rational as to what data is required, what it is for and how it should be obtained. Many organisations are wary of the cost of collecting data but in many cases it can even be free provided the best means are used. There is much opportunity here for creative thinking.

Improvement

Objective
Quality in the marketplace is relative to the performance of whoever is perceived to be the best at any one time. Since competition means that the pole position is always changing then an organisation will soon be left behind if it cannot improve at a pace at least equal to its rivals.

Auditor's approach
Many organisations will claim to have a Continuous Improvement process but this is frequently informal and ineffective. It is crucial that the auditor has a good understanding of this aspect and is able to judge the difference between a really good improvement process and lip service.

An organisation that does Continuous Improvement well will be easily recognisable and it would be as well for the new auditor to become quickly acquainted with some of the better organisations in this respect. This will not be difficult as they usually win many awards!

Possible activities
Improvement activities will result either from gaps between desired performance and actual performance, which usually result in incremental improvement, or from the need to raise performance to new levels or achieve some completely new objective. These are referred to as planning projects. The former frequently use a number of tools known as the problem-solving tools, whereas the latter use a different set known as QFD.

Preventive action

Objective
The objective here is to prevent the occurrence of potential problems. If the problem has never occurred, it involves an estimation of the probability of occurrence and its possible effects.

Auditor's approach
The difficulty with this clause is the problem of deciding how far an organisation should go in the prevention of hitherto non-occurring problems. The decision must be based on a combination of the probability of occurrence against the consequences if the event did occur. For example, some may have considered that the events of 11th September should have been predicted and allowed for in the design of the Twin Towers. Until it happened the first time and given the likelihood having no statistical data, it would be hard to be too critical. However, now that it has happened, not only must this be taken into account for new designs but consideration must be given to the future protection of existing structures. It is no longer an unforeseeable event.

The auditor will have to use considerable judgment in deciding how far is sensible in this respect.

Possible activity
This may include reliability prediction techniques such as failure FMEA, Fault Tree analysis, Weibull Analysis, Bayesian statistical distributions, Duane modelling (for long-life products where life testing may take years, an item is put on test under simulated severe real-life conditions and will be kept well ahead of production items in order to detect wear or fatigue before it appears in actual products). This technique is used in the aircraft industry, environmental and life testing.

19 *Quality Function Deployment*

Hoshin Kanri – from Strategy to Action!

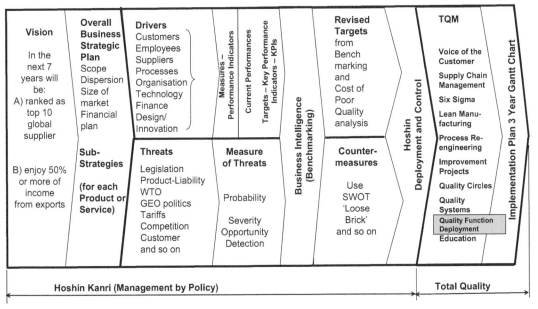

Figure 19.1   Quality Function Deployment

QFD differs from the tools of Continual Improvement in as much that the latter is concerned with the improvement of something that already exists whereas QFD is a collection of tools which can be used for planning something new. This can be a new product, a function, even the development of Hoshin Kanri. Indeed several of the tools of QFD have already been used in the earlier chapters to create the Vision Statement and conversion to KPIs. It is the seventh of the key means for achieving the Goals of Hoshin Kanri. It is a term used to describe the systematic application of techniques for ensuring Quality throughout each stage of the product or service development process, starting with market research and ending with feedback on customer satisfaction.

In other words it is a method for transforming market demands into design Objectives and measurable Quality Goals for each stage in the product/service development process.

QFD is a process which begins with attempting to identify the vague needs of the ultimate Target beneficiary of the intended product or activity, crystallising these into specific tangible and measurable Goals and, through a synthesising process, progressively organising these needs into specific and measurable actions and responsibilities and a plan for implementation.

STEP 1

First of all decide what we are intending to achieve and who is the intended customer. For example, to implement Hoshin Kanri; to organise a conference; to design and implement a totally new pay structure for the organisation; the development of a completely new product (we have used the development of a radio-controlled racing car as an example in the text below).

STEP 2

Attempt to determine customer's (or impacted party's) stated and likely unstated needs. At this stage we should consider the questions shown in Figure 19.2 to enable us to take a broad view of the situation.

We tend to think of the direct purchaser of our products or services when we use the word customer but we need to take a much broader approach and consider everyone who may be impacted since their needs or possible objections may put a number of constraints on what we plan to achieve.

These additional but important groups we may call 'stakeholders' and include our own workforce.

Other examples are Government regulations, non-exclusivity policies (they may multi-source), their own stakeholders' policies, local environmental groups, the local community (a proposal for a new airport terminal is a case in point!), the opinions of the market and our customers' own customers, and so on.

The company has customers but so do people at each stage in the operation. The next downstream operation is the customer of the one before it.

The same questions apply:

* Who are *our* customers?
* What are their needs?
* Do we satisfy their needs?
* How do we know?

Supply Chain Management

Do we involve key suppliers in our customer focus policy?
Which suppliers should be involved?
(suppliers of services and know-how, as well as products)

Do we know who our real competitors are?
Do key employees know who the competitors are?
Do we know competitors' strategies for increasing market share?
Do we know what they are doing to make our life difficult?

Do we know what our customer really wants?
Do key employees know what their customers and the ultimate customers really want?
Do we have a POLICY for employee involvement?

Figure 19.2   External key issues

- Have we ever asked?
- How much of the difference is determined by our suppliers?
- Do they know?

There is more on this topic in Chapter 11, The Voice of the Customer.

AFFINITY DIAGRAM METHOD

The first of the QFD tools is the Affinity Diagram method. This was first mentioned when discussing the definition of the Vision and the Mission elements but using a slightly adapted method for that purpose. Here it will be described in its classic or normal form.

Customer needs are many and varied and this is a complex issue. It can and usually does produce sometimes huge quantities of 'language data' that may appear seemingly impossible to deal with.

Fortunately, the Affinity Diagram is an excellent tool to help with this.

The Affinity Diagram has many slight variants with different names because since its origination in Japan by experts from JUSE, it has been adapted and renamed by several people.

For example – Professor Shiba from MIT in the USA calls it the KJ method and refers to the inputs as 'fuzzy data' from his work on concept engineering and the technique is widely known by that name for that reason. In Germany there is a variation known as MetaPlan which uses small hexagonal plastic-coated magnetic disks. There are several other variants. In the family of brainstorm-related tools it can be described as a clustering technique and can also be used following a brainstorming session as a means to cluster the ideas generated.

The Affinity Diagram method is used to clarify the nature of a problem, coordinate ideas, or obtain new concepts through the integration – on the basis of affinity, of language data taken from a chaotic event or uncertain conditions.

Step 3

Select a theme in order to clarify the nature of a problem, coordinate ideas, or obtain new concepts. For example, 'Customer needs for a specific new medical product' or 'Inspire the workforce to support our Hoshin Kanri programme'. At first glance, the Affinity Diagram method looks quite simple, but its apparent simplicity can be a trap. It can take many uses of the technique before a high level of skill is reached in using it so do not be dismissive or fooled by its apparent simplicity. When used properly and with respect it is an extremely powerful aid. Depending on the theme chosen, it can require a good deal of time to complete but it will have been worth every minute of the time spent so please be patient and persistent. From experience it is a fact that rarely is the first attempt at grouping the ideas necessarily the best one. After a gap when participants have been away from the session for a while, they will frequently return to find an altogether better structure for the ideas.

Step 4

Collect language data and make data cards ('Post-it'-type stickers can be used). Write simple, concise sentences to generate the language data. These data are written on small pieces of gum-backed paper. There can be only one idea for each card. Ideally there should be around 50 data cards, depending on the theme. The maximum is 100. More than that makes the process unwieldy and it is difficult to make sense of the results. If there are too many data cards, it is usually possible and advisable to split the theme into two or more sub-themes. Read each card, and put cards that have the same or a very similar idea together. Place any cards that are not relevant to the selected theme to one side, we will call these 'outliers'.

Step 5

Sort and cluster the Data Cards. Put a large sheet of brown paper or a number of clean flip chart sheets on the wall and stick on the data cards randomly. Begin reading the cards, and read each one several times. You will find cards that appear to be similar. Those cards are said to have 'affinity'. Data cards having affinity are collected and grouped together. On each of the cards, underline any key words that define the affinity with the others on the cluster or group.

Observe the following points in sorting the cards:

- Sort the cards by affinity.
- Sort the cards intuitively. Do not sort them by logic but by how they feel intuitively.
- Do not try to force the cards into any arbitrary categories.
- Do not make up a story and sort the cards to suit.
- Put cards that have absolutely no affinity with others to one side.

Step 6

Create affinity cards by creating a new card making a concise sentence, ideally containing each of the key words underlined on the data cards in each group or cluster. Be sure not to write more than what is implied by the sentences on the data cards. To do this it is a good idea to underline one word in the sentence from the key words on each of the relevant cards. Place each affinity card over the appropriate cluster of data cards. You now have groups of cards with an affinity card on top and the solitary data cards that have no affinity are kept to one side.

Step 7

The second round of sorting, which is iterative and can be repeated as many times as necessary, is done in the same way as the first round and called re-sorting. Study the cards again very carefully and see if they might be grouped differently and possibly in a manner in which some if not all of the 'outliers' found in Step 4 might be included. Write a new set of affinity cards and place them on the corresponding stacks of newly-grouped data cards.

Repeat this step until you have only a few groups of cards and a minimum number of 'outliers'. This completes the card sorting and preparation of the affinity cards.

Step 8

After completing the sorting of data cards and preparation of affinity cards, read the affinity cards at the top of each data card cluster carefully and rearrange the clusters on the paper, thinking about the overall layout.

Note that some clusters may have affinities with each other in which case they may be grouped next to each other and that higher level of affinity described with an overarching affinity card. For a large project there might be a hierarchy of such clusters and ultimately an affinity card which describes the complete set of data cards and the collective group of affinity cards.

Paste the cards more firmly on the sheet of paper if adhesive stickers have been used because these can quickly lose their adhesion and fall to the floor. Draw frames around the affinity groups to make it easy to understand and complete the Affinity Diagram so that it looks similar to example shown in Figure 19.3.

Notice that there are small clusters with affinity cards which are in turn grouped with higher order affinity cards. Each affinity card should include a short sentence which adequately describes the collective meaning of the content so that it is meaningful to those who did not participate in the activity.

These figures show how the Affinity Diagram method is a very effective way of bringing order out of chaos and to be able to take vague ideas and organise them in a coherent manner.

In Figure 19.4, the Affinity Diagram method has been used to identify the potential specification requirements for the design of a model racing car. However, note the use of the word 'potential'. It must be remembered that the Affinity Diagram has only ordered our thinking. Just because we think some of the content of the data cards *might* be important it does not mean that it *is* important. If

Affinity Diagrams – example

Radio control system for a model racing car

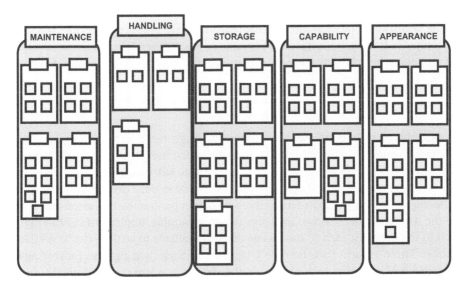

Figure 19.3   Affinity Diagram

Affinity Diagrams – example

Radio control system for a model racing car

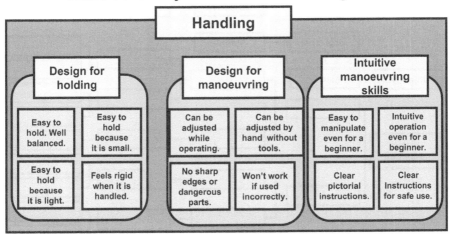

Figure 19.4   Affinity Diagram detail

we are to give equal attention to everything we have identified we do not know if we are attaching too much importance to something that the customer may consider trivial or not important at all and paying too little attention to something that could be absolutely essential. Later on these ideas will require prioritisation

In summary, it can be seen that the Affinity Diagram is a very effective method for first of all collecting the random thoughts of a group of people and then organising them in a coherent way in order to conduct further analysis. The Tree Diagram technique which follows enables us to structure and refine these ideas for further analysis.

TREE DIAGRAM

This technique normally follows the Affinity Diagram and works in exactly the same way as the filing system on a computer. It works by progressively breaking a broad general aim into successively more and more detail until it has become a number of specific activities that cannot be broken down further.

Figure 19.5 shows the method.

Step 1

If, as suggested, this technique follows the Affinity Diagram, the structured language data can be relocated using the same hierarchy. When the transposition has been completed, it will usually expose a number of deficiencies or gaps in the logic. These can be dealt with using this technique. The method is as follows: on a large piece of paper (experience indicates that in most cases it is better to use paper to rough out the diagram before later transferring it to a computer programme) write the primary objective in a box on the left-hand side as shown in Figure 19.5 (for example, implement Hoshin Kanri). In the next column to the right, list each of the means that are available to achieve that objective and link them as shown. These 'means' then become Objectives in their own right so moving again to the right, list the means of achieving each of these in the same way as before. Continue this process until it is not possible to break them down any further and this last column should now be very doable specific tasks or actions. The first step in using the Tree Diagram is now completed.

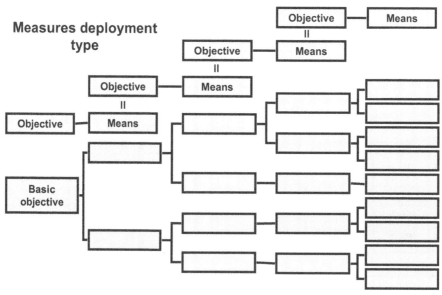

Figure 19.5   Tree Diagram

Step 2

Study the diagram carefully to see if there is anything that might have been overlooked. Do not rush this stage as it is important to include as much detail as possible.

Using Affinity Diagram data in the Tree Diagram – example

The first step is to write the objective in the box on the left. A partially-completed example of the Radio Controlled Car project would be as shown in Figure 19.6.

Usually when represented in this way, it becomes clear that the breakdown is not complete and the final column may need a further level of breakdown to go from the general to the specific. For example, one lower right-hand box in Figure 19.6 says 'clear pictorial instructions', this could breakdown further into 'digital photographs', 'artists sketches', 'video clips', 'DVD', 'PowerPoint slides' and so on.

At this level of detail it is possible then to move to the next stage and assign priorities to the individual 'means'.

This might involve a range of possible methods depending upon the situation such as voting, mailed questionnaires, interviews, Paired Rankings, and so on. However, when the object is to determine customer preferences, the Kano Model, named after its inventor Dr Noriaki Kano, which is described below, has been found to be a very powerful tool.

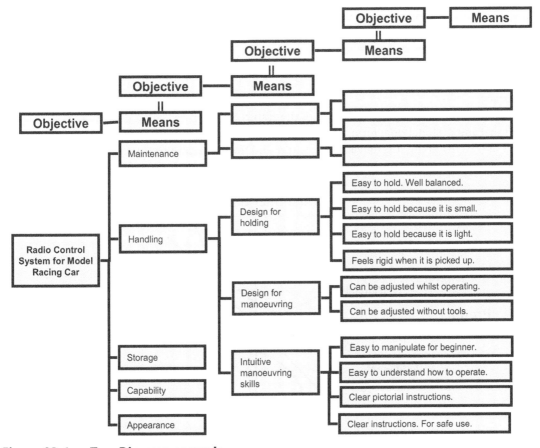

Figure 19.6   Tree Diagram example

THE KANO MODEL

So far the Affinity Diagram and the Tree Diagrams have enabled the identification of needs and how they are structured. Prioritising them is important in order to ensure that time and effort are devoted to those which make the most impact on the objectives. The methods available are questionnaires, interviews and so on. The method that we would recommend here as a means of clarifying the importance of some of the key features is the Kano Model.

It suggests that customer requirements can be grouped into five main categories:

1. attractive but not essential;
2. must be;
3. neutral – indifferent to it;
4. can live with it;
5. dislike.

Diagrammatically, the Kano Model is as shown in Figure 19.7.

In Figure 19.7, and using a popular family car as an illustration, fuel consumption would be an example of a 'one dimensional' feature. The lower the consumption the more it is liked. The braking system would be an example of a 'must be'. There is no positive 'customer satisfaction' from having efficient brakes but there would be considerable 'customer dissatisfaction' if it did not. A retractable radio aerial might be an example of an 'attractive' but non-essential feature. It is nice to have but is unlikely to be a factor in choosing the car unless everything else was identical to a competing model.

Finally there may be some possible features to which the customer is completely indifferent. This might be some extra button on the stereo system.

Using the Kano Questionnaire it is possible to group the various key features identified into their relevant categories using the Affinity Method which will enable them to be assigned their respective importance.

The questionnaire requires that each of the features to be investigated is considered in both its functional and dysfunctional form. Each interviewee must consider the items from both conflicting points of view. By doing this for each key feature and from a broad spectrum of potential customers of the product or service the data obtained can be analysed using the table shown in Figure 19.9.

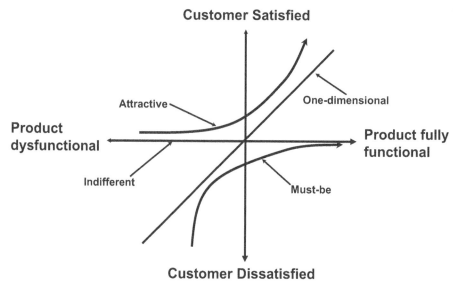

Figure 19.7   The Kano Model

A pair of questions in a Kano Questionnaire

Functional form *The speed of this computer is fast*	• I like it that way • It must be that way • I am neutral • I can live with it that way • I dislike it that way
Dysfunctional form *The speed of this computer is slow*	• I like it that way • It must be that way • I am neutral • I can live with it that way • I dislike it that way

Figure 19.8   The Kano Questionnaire

Kano Evaluation Table

Customer Requirements		Dysfunctional				
		1. Like	2. Must-be	3. Neutral	4. Live with	5. Dislike
Functional	1. Like	Q	A	A	A	O
	2. Must-be	R	I	I	I	M
	3. Neutral	R	I	I	I	M
	4. Live with	R	I	I	I	M
	5. Dislike	R	R	R	R	Q

A; Attractive	O: One-dimensional
M: Must-be	Q: Questionable result
R: Reverse	I: Indifferent

Figure 19.9   Kano Evaluation

By analysing each set of answers the table shown in Figure 19.10 can be created which will provide the QFD team with all the information they require to give the relevant weighting to each of the parameters identified.

Interestingly one Six Sigma Black Belt student being trained used this technique to find out from a line of production workers what the key issues that impacted on production performance were. This unusual application produced some very revealing results.

Customer requirement

Tabulation of responses

C.R.	A	M	O	R	Q	I	Total	Grade
1	1	1	**21**				23	O
2		**22**			1		23	M
3	**13**		5			5	23	A
4	6	1	4	1		**11**	23	I
5	1	**9**	6	1		6	23	M
6	7		2	3	1	**10**	23	I

Figure 19.10   Kano Analysis

COMPLETION OF THE TREE DIAGRAM

When the specifics have been analysed by whatever means the Tree Diagram can be completed by adding three extra columns: 'Feasibility', 'Effects' and 'Overall' as shown in Figure 19.11.

By using symbols the chart becomes easy to read and prepares us for the next step, which is to build the diagram into the left vertical axis of the House of Quality Matrix.

THE HOUSE OF QUALITY MATRIX

This matrix is the central component of QFD and it is where everything comes together to create the final plan of the project. Figure 19.12 shows a simple but typical construction of the House of Quality. Note that there is a central matrix with additional 'rooms' to the top, right and bottom of the diagram. More of these can be added as required and there is considerable room for creativity in the design of a House of Quality.

Note also that the Tree Diagram can be located on the left-hand side of the central matrix. When the House of Quality is used this way it can be a continual monitor of performance against KPIs. If the chart is made large enough to cover a complete wall, it can be regarded as being somewhat like the British Prime Minister Winston Churchill's World War II War Room. As changes occur in the marketplace priorities will change amongst the Performance Indicators. When these are highlighted on the House of Quality chart, attention can quickly be drawn to the new priorities and resources deployed. This will create an organisation which is capable of very rapid change.

Notice that in the core of the example shown in Figure 19.14, symbols are used to identify who is responsible for each activity. This is denoted by the small circles with a dot in the centre. Circles without a dot mean that this function is involved in the relevant activity. The triangle identifies who may not be directly involved but must nevertheless be kept informed. No symbol indicates those who are not at all involved.

One of the main attractions of the House of Quality is the fact that a very wide range of interacting variables can be seen on one diagram: in some organisations, all of the key functions with their respective responsibilities. In this example, the matrix was used to log the ongoing performance of the KPIs and to initiate improvement projects where performance was below that required.

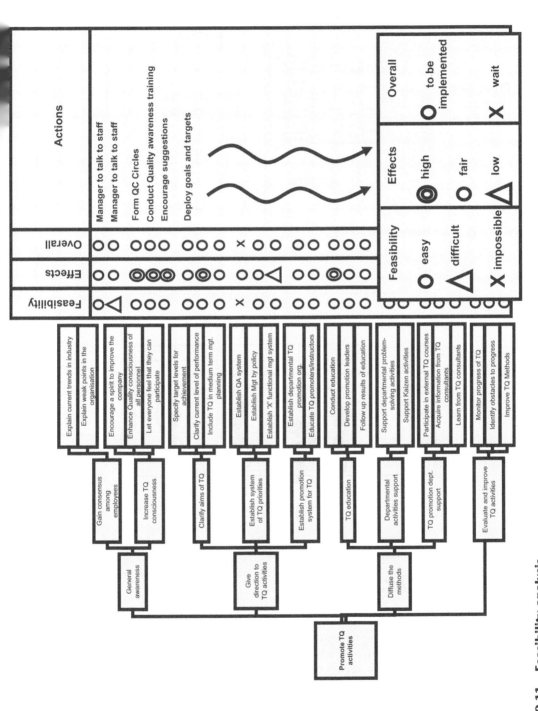

Figure 19.11 Feasibility analysis

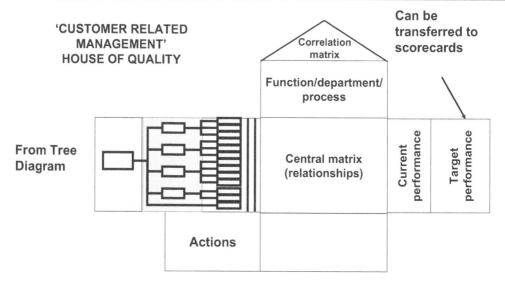

Figure 19.12   The House of Quality

Figure 19.13   'The War Room!'

THE ARROW DIAGRAM

QFD projects which result in the need to implement a large programme with multiple complex events which all interrelate with each other may benefit from this technique.

There are a number of variants which include PERT (Programme Evaluation and Review Technique), CPA (Critical Path Analysis), and so on, but they are essentially all very similar and we will use the more generic title Arrow Diagram.

There are many different brands of software that cover this topic. Perhaps the most popular is Microsoft Project which is easy to use and which produces excellent results.

The construction of an Arrow Diagram is simple if care is taken. Figure 19.15 shows the basic principles and terminology used in their construction.

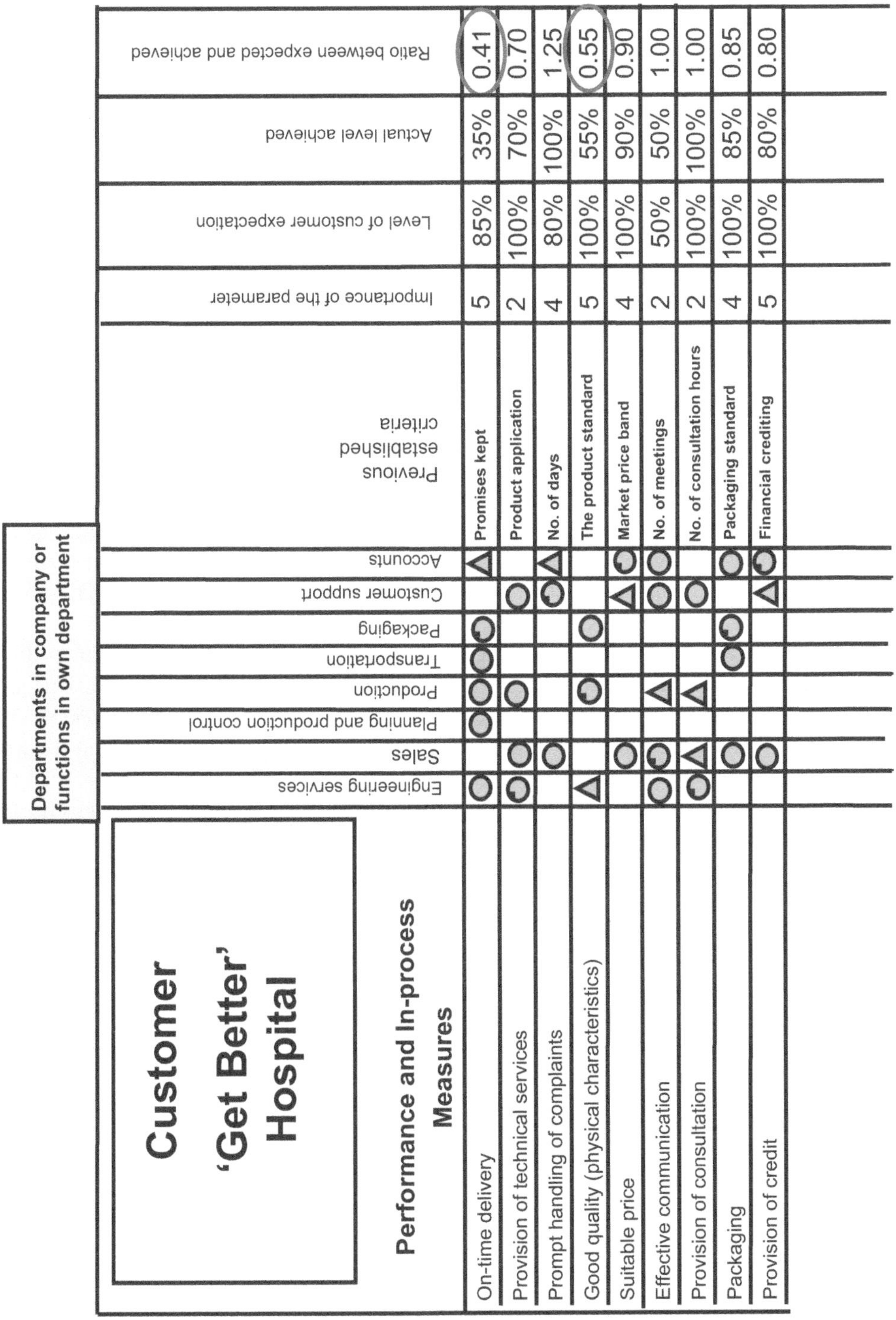

Customer 'Get Better' Hospital

Departments in company or functions in own department

Performance and In-process Measures

Previous established criteria	Importance of the parameter	Level of customer expectation	Actual level achieved	Ratio between expected and achieved
Promises kept	5	85%	35%	0.41
Product application	2	100%	70%	0.70
No. of days	4	80%	100%	1.25
The product standard	5	100%	55%	0.55
Market price band	4	100%	90%	0.90
No. of meetings	2	50%	50%	1.00
No. of consultation hours	2	100%	100%	1.00
Packaging standard	4	100%	85%	0.85
Financial crediting	5	100%	80%	0.80

Performance and In-process Measures (customer criteria):
- On-time delivery
- Provision of technical services
- Prompt handling of complaints
- Good quality (physical characteristics)
- Suitable price
- Effective communication
- Provision of consultation
- Packaging
- Provision of credit

Departments: Engineering services, Sales, Planning and production control, Production, Transportation, Packaging, Customer support, Accounts

Figure 19.14 Assigning responsibilities

Arrow Diagrams

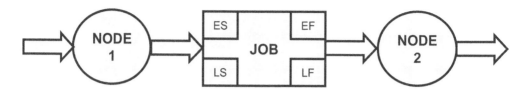

JOB - This is the activity that requires a length of time for completion.

NODE – This is the beginning and the end of a task and each is the connecting point to another job.

ES – Earliest start time possible.
EF – Earliest finish time possible.
LS – Latest start time possible.
LF – Latest finish time possible.

Figure 19.15   The Arrow Diagram

Figure 19.16 shows how the chart is constructed for a simple operation involving two parallel streams of 'jobs'. The connection between nodes 3 and 4 shows how two activities on the separate streams are depicted when they must be performed at the same time.

Just prior to each job, the numbers above the line indicate the Node connections, for example, 2 – 3 and the number below the line indicates the time that the job is expected to take which is usually but not always given in days.

The following diagram shows that jobs on the lower path must be completed in the time allowed whereas those on the top path have some 'float' whilst the others are being completed. This lower path therefore determines the overall time that it will take to complete the complete project. Whilst some delays can be tolerated in the jobs on the top line, any delay to any of the jobs on the lower line will increase the time for the whole project by that amount. This path therefore is called the 'critical path' and is emphasised by using a thicker line or, if possible, a red line. Conversely, if the time for the overall project is too long, it can only be reduced by reducing the time for jobs on that line. However, as this time is reduced, the float for each of the jobs on that line is also reduced. When this reaches zero then any further reduction in the overall time must also include a reduction in the time for jobs on that line as well.

In a simple example such as Figure 19.17 it would be easy to detect and deal with this. However, for a complex project it would be necessary to use a dedicated computer programme to make the calculations.

FOOLPROOFING (POKE YOKE)

Even with the power of the techniques of QFD there is no guarantee that every feature of the plan will necessarily work without a hitch of some kind. In fact, the more innovative the plan is the more vulnerable it will be to a failure of some sort.

Chapter 8 on Risk Management goes into this in some detail and the technique FMEA can be used to analyse the features where the Risks might be high or their realisation being severe to catastrophic. However there is another technique that is popular in QFD which is known as Process Decision Programme Chart (PDCP).

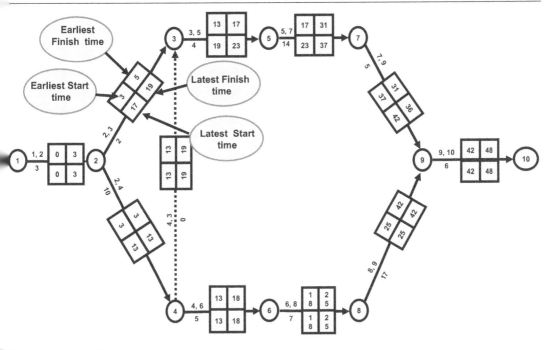

Figure 19.16   Chart data

Arrow Diagrams

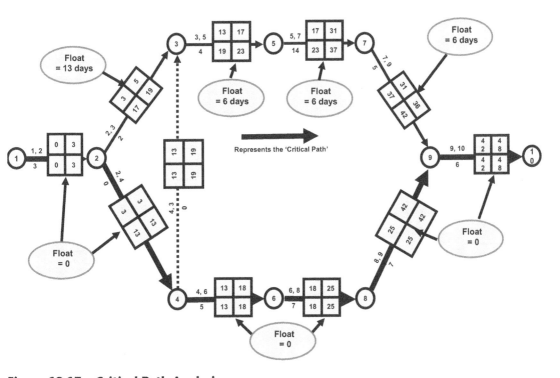

Figure 19.17   Critical Path Analysis

PROCESS DECISION PROGRAMME CHART

This technique is somewhat similar to Fault Tree Analysis which is itself a variant of the FMEA approach. Figure 19.18 is based on a similar example in Japanese Training materials and shows a simple PDPC chart for the delivery of a package by air to Heathrow Airport.

The chart has been designed to try to eliminate the Risk of a package being delivered 'upside down' due to the fragility of the contents. The process begins with the obvious decision to mark the box 'this side up'. This might seem a good idea but is it foolproof? It would appear not for two reasons: 1. the handler may not read the message or, 2. they read it but this leads to two more possibilities – firstly they may not be able to read English or secondly they can read it and observe the caution in which case no problem or alternatively they still turn the box upside down because it is easier to carry. By following the alternative routes and the precautionary measures that have been taken to deal with the possible outcomes, it can be seen that in the end the package was designed in such a way that it was impossible for the package to be delivered upside down. This is the essence of PDPC and also Poke Yoke.

Interestingly, this technique was introduced by the author to members of the accounts department of a large steel works. They were in the middle of designing a new pay scheme for the entire organisation which would eliminate direct payment by results. Normally the introduction of a company-wide scheme of such proportions would be fraught with problems and disputes. Amazingly, by using this technique to preempt and deal with the most likely problems, the scheme was introduced with virtually no issues from anyone.

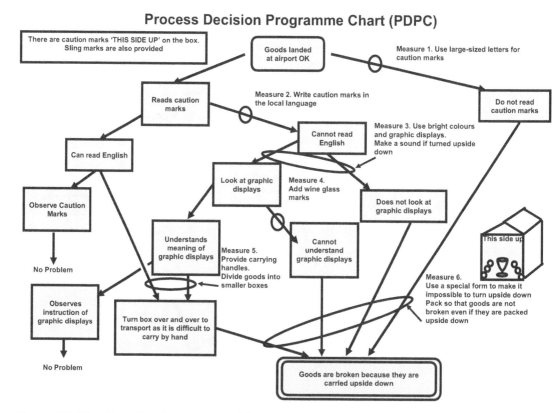

Figure 19.18   Completed process decision programme chart

SUMMARY

Just six of the techniques of QFD have been included in this chapter but there are many more. These include Gantt Charts, Design of Experiments, Cause Relationship Diagraphs, Dynamic Programming and Linear Programming, and many variants of those that have been included. It is recommended that the reader becomes familiar with all of these powerful techniques in order to get the best benefits from Hoshin Kanri.

Also note that the Affinity Diagram and the Tree Diagram were used in the early chapters of this book for the creation of the Hoshin Kanri programme itself. The hospital example of the House of Quality was modelled on a real-life matrix (not from a hospital) with the KPIs on one side and responsibilities across the top. That organisation from which it had been taken has now used Hoshin Kanri along the lines of the text in this book since 1998 and as a consequence has moved from an insignificant place in its market to being amongst the world leaders.

20 *Education*

Hoshin Kanri – from Strategy to Action!

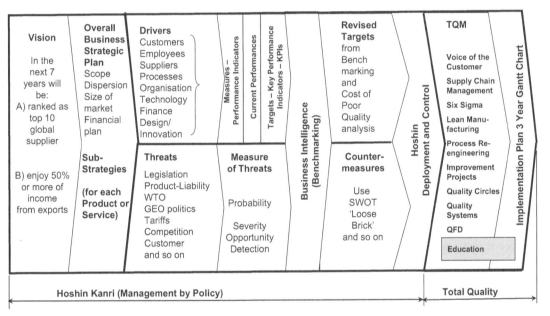

Vision	Overall Business Strategic Plan	Drivers	Measures – Performance Indicators	Current Performances	Targets – Key Performance Indicators – KPIs	Business Intelligence (Benchmarking)	Revised Targets	Hoshin Deployment and Control	TQM	Implementation Plan 3 Year Gantt Chart
In the next 7 years will be: A) ranked as top 10 global supplier	Scope Dispersion Size of market Financial plan	Customers Employees Suppliers Processes Organisation Technology Finance Design/ Innovation					from Bench marking and Cost of Poor Quality analysis		Voice of the Customer Supply Chain Management Six Sigma Lean Manu-facturing Process Re-engineering	
B) enjoy 50% or more of income from exports	Sub-Strategies (for each Product or Service)	Threats Legislation Product-Liability WTO GEO politics Tariffs Competition Customer and so on		Measure of Threats Probability Severity Opportunity Detection			Counter-measures Use SWOT 'Loose Brick' and so on		Improvement Projects Quality Circles Quality Systems QFD Education	

Hoshin Kanri (Management by Policy) ⟶ Total Quality

Figure 20.1   Education

This is the last but by no means the least of the 'how to' topics covered in this book that should be regarded as being the principle means to achieve the Goals of Hoshin Kanri.

It is a short chapter and is included partly because whilst the word 'training' is taken seriously by some in industry, the word 'education' is rarely if ever mentioned. This is probably because whilst the linkage between 'training' and work performance is reasonably clear in many instances, it is more difficult to establish a causal link between education and performance. Also, there is a tendency in Western society to think that education is something that happened to the individual whilst at school and remains static thereafter. In contrast, Japanese industrialists regard continuing education as a lifetime experience. Professor Ishikawa repeated many times that 'Quality begins and ends with education.'

Some have difficulty in understanding the difference between training and education. One way to think of it is to consider the old adage: I do not mind my children getting sex education but I am not so keen on them getting sex training! Education is required if we think it important to give our people the big picture. This is well illustrated in the story about a person who visited a stone quarry. He saw a number of workers with hammers and chisels cutting away at the rock face. There were heaps of rubble all around them and the place looked chaotic. The visitor asked them what they were doing. They just shrugged their shoulders and said, 'We have to break the rock into chunks of stone.' That was all they had been told. Further on in another part of the quarry the scene was very different. There was a worker cutting the stone carefully into blocks which they had stacked one on top of the other and the work area was very neat and tidy. The worker was asked what he was doing and they replied, 'I am cutting the stones for a beautiful cathedral, here is the architects drawing.'

What is the difference between the two scenarios? In one case the worker has been told what their work is for and in the other case they have not.

The example may be extreme but it is not so far removed from reality in many organisations. The reason for the blind spot regarding education is possibly due to the long time over which industrial society was in the grip of the so called 'scientific management' culture.

Possibly one barrier for Westerners to overcome is the belief that learning becomes more difficult as we become older. This depressing thought fortunately has no evidence to support it. In fact, research on healthy subjects indicates virtually no fall off in the ability to learn, only in the motivation supported of course by the belief which then becomes self-fulfilling.

A healthy elderly person can easily learn how to draw their pension, fill out a football pool coupon, or make a complicated bet on a horse with no trouble. Why? Because they are motivated. On the other hand, unless they have some specific reason for doing so, they will protest that they are 'too old to learn' if confronted with learning to use an email service on a computer. However, give them the motivation and they will learn it as quickly as anyone else. There was the case recently of someone known to me who was their mid-70s. They would not use a computer and protested that they could not understand them. Their son and family then moved to Australia. This person very soon purchased a computer and was sending emails and sending and printing digital photographs. Why? Because they were motivated.

Another factor is that people become progressively more cautious as they get older. This gives the impression that they are getting slower. The reason is that older people will want more information from which to make a decision than when they were younger. The reason probably is that they had got their fingers burned a few times by being too hasty and are less inclined to make the same mistakes again.

Eyesight is another consideration. It is a fact that a 60-year-old needs ten times as much light to see the same as a 20-year-old. This is a progressive condition and there is nothing that can be done to stop it. It happens to everybody. This is why an older person thinks that a youngster is damaging their eyes by appearing to read in what they think is near darkness whilst the youngster will notice that the older person always reads a newspaper by a window. Not only does the light not penetrate to the retina so well but also the contrast gets proportionally less.

One final point on the question of ageing is that in Western society, we are actually conditioned to believe that education is only for the young. It is built into the curriculum.

At primary school, a child is given a broad education covering almost all facets of life. They learn a little bit about everything. However, as they progress year by year into secondary education, the range of topics gets fewer. Then, when the children are approaching GCSEs, they are made to focus almost entirely on between three and ten selected subjects depending upon perceived ability. After this, they may leave school altogether and spend the rest of their lives believing that they are poor at learning, or continue onwards. In this case they specialise even more and just three subjects are selected for 'A' levels. Following this and being successful they go on to university and then just specialise in one subject. If for example they plan to become an engineer then everything else such as history, geography, languages, the classics and so on are dropped completely.

The effect of this on the individual is to condition them into believing that none of these things is important to them. Engineers learn more and more about engineering, doctors learn more and more about medicine, and everything else falls by the wayside.

In Japan it is different. Of course they specialise but people are still encouraged to take an interest in the broader subjects. Since learning is regarded as a lifetime experience they will continue to learn across a broad range of subjects long after their initial formal education has been completed. Some of this is encouraged in companies with particular emphasis on matters relevant to the company. All employees will see videos of foreign countries where their products are sold. They will learn about the cultures and habits, the scenery and a great deal about ecology and the importance of environmental protection.

This makes work more interesting and people appreciate the time and effort that the company has put in to broadening their lives and general knowledge and of course they are more motivated as a result.

ACTION LEARNING

This topic was originated by the late Professor 'Reg' Revans in the 1940s at the National Coal Board and popularised in the 1960s and 1970s especially in continental Europe, but it did not catch on in the UK to any extent until the mid-1980s and even then was slow to be accepted. This is unfortunate because it has been shown to be a powerful concept. Since its early days it has been adapted and today takes many forms. One of the main tenets of his work is the observation that people learn by questioning. One approach to enable this to happen is to rotate managers around different departments in the organisation. The object is for them to learn each other's best practices but at the same time to obtain a better understanding of the activities of these departments as both customers and suppliers to their own.

There are other examples to support this. In 1950, Toyota executives and senior managers were given the opportunity to visit the Ford Motor plants in Detroit, USA. At that time Ford's manufacturing methods were vastly superior to those used by Toyota. Ford, not seeing any threat from Toyota, allowed them to see everything they wanted. On returning to Japan, the Japanese commented that whilst Ford were superior, nevertheless they could see ways in which even that could be improved and then set about doing so.

Another valuable lesson that can be obtained from this approach is 'empathy'. This is very much part of the learning culture in Japan and begins right from the earliest days at school. In the UK, meals are provided by 'dinner ladies'. These are local people who come to the school each day to prepare and serve the meals to the children. In Japan, typically they do not do this. Instead, several children are selected each day to leave the class during the morning and are taught how to prepare the food. They make the meals for themselves and the other children. Other children are assigned to serve the food as waiters and waitresses. This changes from day to day on a rota basis. The object is for the children to learn to appreciate how it feels to be both the server and the served.

This same idea was used fairly recently by Pickford's, the furniture removal company. In this case there was a television documentary showing the managing director of the company acting as a removal operative. He did this for some days or possibly longer but each day in the evening he called back to the office on his mobile phone to give an account of his experience and how he thought that the company could improve the service and what it felt like to be a removal operative.

Empathy in this way is a prominent form of learning in Japanese industry and is probably one of the best ways to bring about Hoshin-style culture change in Western society.

If mangers just stopped and thought, 'How would I like to do that job all day, day in and day out?' or 'How would I like it if I were treated like that?' then perhaps we could make some breakthroughs.

SUMMARY

Education should not be something that ceases when people leave school or university. Work can only be interesting, rewarding and enjoyable if people know why they are doing it and the results of their actions.

People are more motivated if they feel that the organisation is showing an interest in them and that they are respected.

Learning can be a lifetime experience and there is no limit to the age at which people can learn. We just have to convince them why it is useful for them to learn.

Learning and appreciating other people's jobs is stimulating and everyone can learn from each other through Action Learning techniques.

Empathy is an excellent way to break down resistant cultures by fostering the feeling, 'How would I like to be treated this way?', 'How would I like to do that job the way it is designed?', 'Can I design it some other way to make it more interesting?'

21 *Suggestions for Performance Indicators*

It is definitely NOT a good idea to read this chapter before reading and doing the work required in Chapters 1 to 5. If this advice is ignored, the likelihood is that the Performance Indicators selected and prioritised will not be the best ones and will be influenced by this chapter. This chapter is included as a prompt to check whether anything of importance has been inadvertently overlooked.

Ideally the Performance Indicators should be the work of the top team at corporate level and subsequently, the work of middle managers at departmental level as part of the Policy Deployment process described in Chapter 10 before referring to this chapter in the book.

If it becomes apparent that a significant number of items have been left out in any one section, it is likely to indicate a blind spot on this topic and the team should consider further research and reading in this area before moving on. This is frequently the case with the customer topic for reasons that are mentioned in Chapter 11, Voice of the Customer.

Suggested Performance Indicators listed in this section are not exhaustive by any means but include many of the more common ones. They are not segregated as to whether they are at corporate or middle management level, nor are they prioritised in any way. There are many that may have been listed in one category that might also appear in others. They are there simply as a memory jog and that is all.

Experience shows that however well the Affinity Diagram is used, there will always be blind spots and some important items will generally be overlooked. This will not matter if Hoshin Kanri is a living part of the business because anything important that shows up later can and should be included immediately.

DRIVER 1 – CUSTOMER

The role of the customer

Checklist of some possible customer-related Performance Indicators:

Typical Questions	Potential Measures
Are we customer focused?	Customer satisfaction index – scores
	Number of customer suggestions implemented
	Regional customer's choice
	National customer's choice
	Foreign customer's choice
	Customer needs analysis

Customer exposure throughout the organisation
Build-to-order time and delivery time
Number of customer complaints
Complaints satisfactorily resolved
Complaints not satisfactorily resolved
Number of repeat complaint calls
Training of customer-facing employees
Customer praise
Customer loyalty and retention
Percentage customers increase purchase volume
Number/value of concessions and production
 permits
Customer expectations versus perceptions
Percentage calls transferred or passed up the
 organisation
Average weekly calls per service area
Rate of parts outage
Number of on-time deliveries
Number of returns
Price relative to competitive market price
Price deviation from budget
Cost variances
Customer willingness to pay for products
Customer collaboration on improvement
 projects
Customer-supported seminars
Extent products are more user-friendly
 compared to competition
On-time delivery
Positive press index
Negative press index
Dealer satisfaction index
Quality ratings
Warranty costs
Loss of sales
Goodwill gestures
Mail shots
Press release

DRIVER 2 – EMPLOYEES

From a descriptive point of view this topic has been covered in some detail in Chapters 17 (Quality Circles) and 20 (Education). Therefore we will only include the list of suggested possible Performance Indicators.

How well do we make use of the skills and capability of our employees to achieve the aims of the Vision?

- Hoshin Kanri-style management recognises that each person is the expert in their own job.

- Hoshin objective 1: to use the collective thinking power and job knowledge of all of our people to make our company the best in its business.
- Hoshin objective 2: to attract the highest-calibre labour from the local market. This is achieved by being seen as a caring employer.

People have:

- a sense of pride and self-esteem;
- loyalty to group and to organisation;
- a need to contribute;
- a need to be listened to.

Questions

	Job satisfaction index
	Employee surveys
	Multi-skilling
	Education courses
	Number of Quality Circles
	Training hours per employee
	Suggestion Scheme
	Number of useful suggestions per employee
	Number of suggestions accepted
	Labour turnover
	Absenteeism
	Response to job advertisements
	Sickness
	Average employment length
	Number of degrees per capita
	Number of high-level qualifications
	percentage of managers with degrees
	percentage of managers with people skill qualifications
	Number of multi-skilled employees
Are we making best use of our people?	Number of functions with shared process (that is, procurement, product development, finance)
	Number of internal best-practices captured and deployed company-wide
	Number of multi-skilled employees
	Number of 'out of process' adjustments
	Number of employee suggestions
	Number of cross-functional improvement teams
	Attendance balance at meetings
	5S/5C activities
	TPM
Do we develop our people?	Employee satisfaction index
	Bad-feelings index
	Communication of company Objectives to all levels of the organisation (frequency)

	Communication of company performance to all levels of the organisation
	Number of organisational layers
	Number of awards
	Training hours per employee
	Employee absenteeism (per cent)
	Average salary versus industry
Are we recognised as an attractive employer?	Number of company-sponsored community events
	Number of charities sponsored
	Charity dollars as a percent of sales
	Number of community pollution violations
	Lost time accidents
	Inter-company visits
	Recognition presentations
What is our employee satisfaction?	Rate of voluntarily labour turnover
	Providing resources, technology
	Quality of Leadership surveys
	Commitment of employees to Values, Goals and Objectives of company
	Employee satisfaction surveys
	Training investment
	Hours between recordable accidents
	Hours between lost-time accidents
	Percentage sickness time (sometimes people are only sick of coming to work)
	Competitive salaries and benefits
	Compensation plans – does it involve opportunities for employees to share in company's financial success?
	Number of internal promotions

SUPPLIER MANAGEMENT

Outsourced processes are really our processes that we have chosen to pass to others. However we are still responsible for them as if they were made by us. If we devolve that responsibility, then we have no control and we are at the mercy of others. For example, it had been our practice for a long time to leave the design of gearboxes to our supplier. As a consequence we have also allowed our technical skills for the development of these products to disappear. The supplier on the other hand has become an expert and we are ignorant.

Later, we need a gearbox with special features which the manufacturer does not want to make. He raises objections to our requirements on the grounds that it is too expensive, cannot be made in time, will be unreliable and so on. Because we have lost the expertise, we have no argument and in effect have lost control to him.

No Japanese producer would do this.

- Positive trends in purchasing and procurement include:
    - reduced number of suppliers;

- long-term relationships with suppliers;
- suppliers located close to customers for improved access;
- integrated information infrastructure: ERP;
- suppliers considered to be an essential part of the business;
- suppliers involved in future product development programmes.

Supplier evaluation and rating

In the early 1980s, from a Japanese workforce of approximately 40 000 people, Toyota had 110 supply quality engineers and 400 key suppliers. Most of the suppliers were geographically close to the assembly plants.

In contrast, Ford in the USA also had approximately 40 000 employees and just over 100 supply quality engineers but they had more than 4000 suppliers!

This means that the Toyota Engineers could spend ten times as much time with the suppliers than Ford. Actually it was more than that because the Ford Suppliers were located all over the USA so the engineers spent much of their time travelling.

How efficient is our procurement and manufacturing processes?

On-time receipt of materials and services from supplier

Supplier invoice accuracy

Total number of suppliers

Percentage of supplier base change

Percentage of suppliers certified

Transparency between us and between suppliers

Days of supply of inventory at suppliers

Length of relationship with supplier

Is supplier relationship one of cooperative continuous improvement?

Equipment uptime/downtime

Time WIP sits idle

Percentage of external suppliers from preferred external suppliers

Number of standardised parts

Cost per unit

Finished product first pass yield

Manufacturing cycle time for typical product

Percentage reduction of manufacturing cycle time within last 5 years

Number of defects per million parts

Plant utilisation rates

Pipeline capacity versus. average demand

How do we compare on Supply Chain Management?

Total materials cost

Number of suppliers

Supplier margins

Supplier satisfaction index

Supplier quality rating

Purchasing economies

PROCESSES

Take care of the process and the product looks after itself!

This topic is covered in both Chapters 15 and 16 in some detail so we will only include Performance Indicator suggestions here.

Over production	Producing more than the customer requires
	Takt Times
	Single part manufacture
	Doing more than necessary
	Bottlenecks
Waiting time	Waiting for process
	Excessive machine time/downtime
	Long setup times
Transportation	Work-in-progress
	Bad organisation
	Double handling
	Moving things long distances
Inventory	Obsolete stock
	Lost/misplaced stock
	Damaged stock
	Slow-moving items
	Stocks of parts or materials not being worked upon and stored between operations
Motion	Excessive walking
	Stretching and reaching
	Strains and fatigue
	Searching for tools/parts
Scrap/re-work	Making defective parts
	Re-work
Production flexibility	Supply Chain response time
	Extra handling
	Slow cycle times
Lead times	Average process time/ideal process time
	Part-assemblies
	Repair loops
	Incorrect rejections
	Avoidable destructive tests
	Wrong calibration
	Raising concessions
	Chasing corrective action
	Re-inspection
	Handling damage
	Re-packing
	Inaccurate counts

Damage
Mis-location
Slow moving
Product late and not accepted
Faulty workmanship
Poor workmanship

ORGANISATION

Mis-placed advertising
A low response
Loss of leading edge
Returns
Short deliveries
Late deliveries
Unidentified goods
Re-orders
Wrong products
Inaccurate figures
No access
Theft
Wrong materials
Wrong assembly
Strip downs
Wrong product
Avoidable variants
Over-specification
Unused space
Obsolete stock
Wrong location
Avoidable repeat journeys
Transit damage
Internal audit – non-conformances
No action
No management reviews
Actions on management reviews
Projects not completed
Lost documentation
Slow collecting rejects
Wrong site
Insufficient training
Wrong equipment
Amendments to instructions
Penalty clauses
No spares
Poor image
Lost/misplaced correspondence
Unanswered telephone calls

Misdirected telephone calls
Out of date telephone directory
Out of date internal directory
Loss of corporate secrets
Failure to patent
Undercutting
Better image
Disinformation

TECHNOLOGY

Do we develop and improve our technologies? Amount of investment in technology
Budget for new technology
Technology collaboration with Supply Chain
Technology promotion for suppliers
Number of patents
Collaboration with technical universities
Joint projects
Funding for new technology
Scholarships for technical post-graduate degrees
Collaboration in development of new technology
   with non-competitors
Papers presented at conferences
Papers published in technical press
Awards for technological development
Ranking in independent surveys for technical
   achievement.
Successful implementation of new technology
Instances of technology transfer
Number of breakthroughs (product or service)
Training investment
Rate of new technology introduction
Percentage of sales from technology introduced
   within the last 5 years
Gross profit from new technology
Time to develop new technology
Percentage total operating expenditures/
   expenditures on research and development
Technology portfolio compared with competition
Net present value of portfolio

FINANCE

How is our financial strength and profitability? Revenue growth index
Profit growth per annum
Inventory turnover per annum
Performance to budget

Operating income per employee
Product line profitability
WACC
Cash flow
Cost of sales: rate that it remains flat or decreases
Market share
Market share in key industries
Market share growth
Income as percentage of sales
Margin as percentage of sales
Industry profitability against Targets
Profitable volume growth versus GDP growth and
    market growth
Annual Inventory Turns
Annual WIP Inventory Turns
Contribution of the lowest contributing product/
    service
Expense accounts
Percentage estimate for cost of poor quality/sales
    revenue
Negative cost variances
Credit rating
ROI
Product liability

Are we a low-cost/Lean Manufacturer?

Inventory cost
Inventory turnover/days supply
Hours per product (company-wide/individual plant)
Labour cost per product (company/plant)
Capacity utilisation rate (company/plant)
Product line profitability
Sales/Employee
Unit cost compared to competitors
Gross profit from new products

DESIGN AND INNOVATION

Are we fit and fast?

Product development cycle time
Comparative product development cycle time
Days lost pending decision making/budget
    approval
Competitive response time index
Response to customer index
Model-year changeover downtime
Responsiveness to change compared to industry
Production flexibility
Percentage of research and development resources
    dedicated to up and coming technologies
Production flexibility

	Supply Chain response time
	Product build time
	Product strip down time
	Errors
	Low reliability
	Over-specified limits/tolerances
	No priority on changes
	Exhibition failures
	No market
	Too many variants
	Ridiculous timescales
	Inaccurate forecasts
	Trouble shooting
Modifications and change requests	Number of Modifications
	Parts not fitting
	Second operations
	No engineering change requests
	Cost of engineering change requests
Are we innovative?	Number of patents (trend versus industry average)
	Number of patents that are commercialised
	Number of new products
	Number of employee suggestions
	Research and development dollars versus industry average
	Number of breakthroughs (product or service)
	Percentage total operating expenditures/ expenditures on research and development
	Training investment
	Number of products in the pipeline
	Number of new designs/products per engineer
	Rate of new product introduction
	Percentage of sales from products introduced within the last 5 years
	Gross profit from new products
	Number of new product introductions compared to Target
	Time to develop innovations
	Time to market for innovations compared with competition
	Percentage total operating expenditure/ expenditure on research and development
	Percentage new designs/number of engineers
	Pipeline portfolio compared with competition
	Net present value of portfolio
	New market sales for existing products
	Papers presented at conferences
	Papers published
	Awards for innovation

22 *Implementation Plan*

Hoshin Kanri – from Strategy to Action!

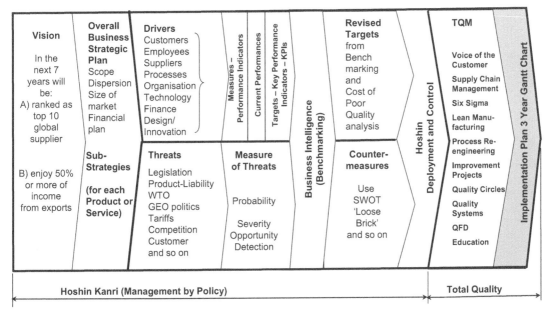

Figure 22.1   Implementation Plan

If the reader has been using this book as a means to implement Hoshin Kanri then it is probably about 3-years-old by now and it will be looking a bit dog-eared unless they followed the rule of reading everything before doing anything.

Three years is typically the time that it would take an average organisation to get their Hoshin Kanri programme to a level where it was widespread throughout the organisation and also down through the Supply Chain. However, even then there will still be much work to do in order to consolidate and really begin to give the competition something serious to be worried about.

The time that it will take will vary enormously from organisation to organisation as will the relevant importance of the material in each chapter. It is worth mentioning here that the chapters on the TQM topics, particularly those on Voice of the Customer, Supply Chain Management, Six Sigma, Lean Manufacturing and Continuous Improvement, are written at appreciation level. Further text material will be required on all of those topics when they are being introduced. In fact each would demand a full text on those subjects in their own right.

Most organisations find a bar chart to be the most helpful planning tool for the roll out programme and the book therefore concludes with a suggested layout, but it is by no means a definitive version.

TYPICAL BAR CHART

It should be stressed that the bar charts shown in Figures 22.2 to 22.4 are only typical and represent one organisation's plans for implementation and should be used as a guide not a template for any other programme.

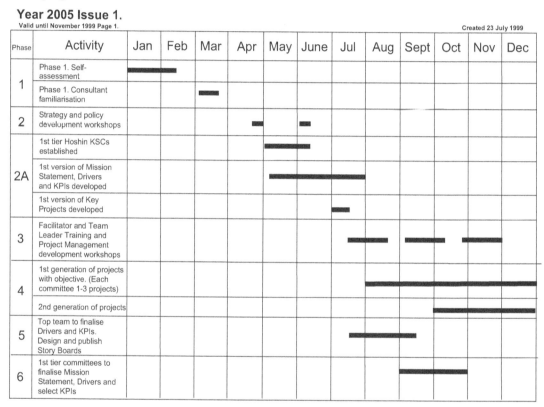

Figure 22.2a   Typical activities for year one in bar chart form

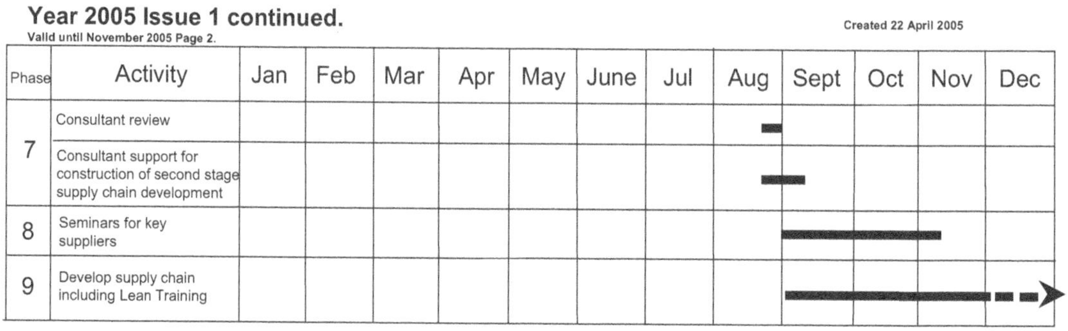

Figure 22.2b   Typical activities for year one in bar chart form

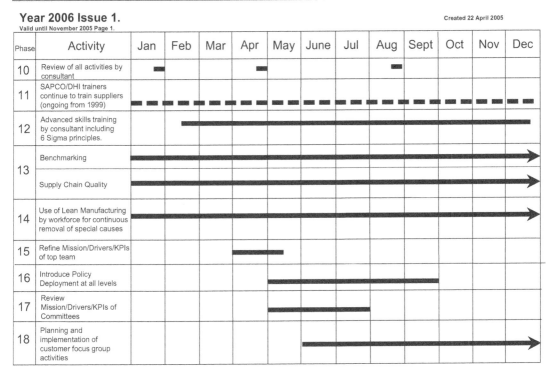

Figure 22.3   Typical activities for next 2 years successively

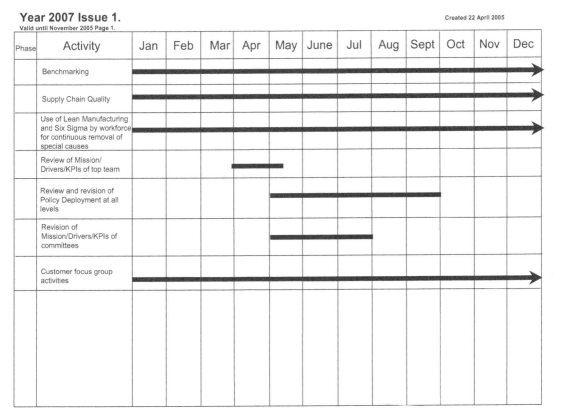

Figure 22.4   Typical activities for next 2 years successively

This concludes the content of this book. It is my sincere wish that it proves useful to a wide spectrum of organisations and if it results in any way as a means of making work more interesting, more enjoyable and a more important part of people's lives in the community today then it will have been worth the effort. So good luck and I hope that the book has proved useful.

Index